Each Mind a Kingdom

American Women, Sexual Purity, and the New Thought Movement, 1875–1920

BERYL SATTER

University of California Press

BERKELEY   LOS ANGELES   LONDON

University of California Press
Berkeley and Los Angeles, California

University of California Press, Ltd.
London, England

Library of Congress Cataloging-in-Publication Data

Satter, Beryl, 1959–
    Each mind a kingdom : American women, sexual purity, and the
New Thought movement, 1875–1920 / Beryl Satter.
        p.   cm.
    Includes bibliographical references and index.
    ISBN 0-520-21765-9 (alk. paper)
    1. New Thought—History.   2. Women—Religious life—
United States.   3. Eddy, Mary Baker, 1821–1910.   4. Christian
Science—United States—History.   5. Twelve-step programs—
History.   6. United States—Church history.   I. Title.
BF639.S124   1999
289.9'8'0973—dc21   98–38227
                                                              CIP

Manufactured in the United States of America

10   9   8   7   6   5   4   3   2   1

The paper used in this publication meets the minimum requirements
of ANSI/NISO z39.48-1992 (R 1997) (*Permanence of Paper*).♾

In Memory of My Parents

Mark J. Satter (1916–1965)
Ted Stone (1910–1978)
Clarice Satter Stone (1918–1983)

Each mind is a kingdom of thought. We have all power over the kingdom of our own thoughts.

Emma Curtis Hopkins, *Bible Interpretations*, 1891

Contents

Illustrations

Charts

Figures

Acknowledgments

This book had its origin on the day that I wandered the stacks of Harvard Divinity School and noticed a book by a woman named Frances Lord; it was pale green, had a white lily on its binding, and was entitled *Christian Science Healing*. The Women's Studies in Religion program at Harvard Divinity School provided the ideal setting for me to begin investigating that book, its author, and the broader issues that would ultimately form this book. I would like to thank Constance Buchanan, Margaret Miles, Phyllis Cole, and especially Amy Schrager Lang, who offered insight and encouragement at that very earliest stage of the project. T. J. Jackson Lears gave me the benefit of his learned advice at the work's second stage. Jon Butler and Nancy Cott advised the work as a Ph.D. dissertation in the American Studies Program at Yale University; they were unfailingly gracious and interested. I owe a particular debt to Nancy Cott, who was my dissertation director. She gave me stellar scholarly support throughout the dissertation process, and through many drafts of this work thereafter. I have tried hard to live up to the standard she has set in her own work for intellectual rigor, meticulous research, and compelling historical writing.

The dissertation upon which this book was based was thoroughly reconceptualized during a year off, courtesy of the Pew Program in Religion and American History Faculty Fellowship. An academic leave provided by the Rutgers University Faculty Academic Study Program enabled me to complete the work. The interlibrary loan librarians at Yale University and Rutgers University and the archivists at the Evanston Historical Society and the Chicago Historical Society made available to me the sources upon which this book is constructed. Most of all, I have relied upon the fine archives of the Institute for the Study of American Religion (ISAR) and the learning and generosity of the ISAR's founder and chief archivist, J. Gordon Melton.

Without Melton's extensive collection of early New Thought materials this book could never have been written. I also owe thanks to fellow scholars of New Thought, who have been unfailingly generous with their work, including Gary Ward, Gail Harley, and Alan Anderson.

Donald Meyer read the dissertation and offered insightful criticisms. Gail Bederman shared drafts of her book *Manliness and Civilization* with me before its publication; I am indebted to her analysis and her generosity.

Some of the friends and colleagues who spent long hours discussing the ideas contained in this book include Jerma Jackson, Mia Bay, Kathi Kern, Mary Poole, Scott Sandage, and Jacqueline Goldsby. I am indebted to people who read sections of the book, including Loretta Stec, Mia Bay, and Jan Lewis, and to Fran Bartkowksi and Amy Schrager Lang, who read later versions of the manuscript. My greatest thanks go to the following people who read early, bloated versions of the manuscript and offered sage advice on how to improve it: Norma Basch, Ann Braude, Nancy Cott, Richard Fox, and especially Sarah Schulman and Kirsten Swinth, who offered me detailed advice that I followed religiously.

My partner Kathryn Tanner read many versions of the manuscript and was always eager to discuss the book with me. For that, and for her love and support, I thank her. I am grateful to the people whose friendship sustained me throughout the writing of this book: Mary S. Blyth, Donna Bryan, Beth Rosenberg-Brewer, Sarah Schulman, Judith Berns, Ira Sheffey, Edie Lee, Kathryn Thomas, David Frankfurter, Faulkner Fox, Saul Olyan, Alfred Thomas, James Williams, and Margaret Shiffrar. My aunt Elsie Brown and my uncle Milton Brown did not live to see this book's completion; I acknowledge here their concern for and interest in the lives of others, and my gratitude for having had them in my life. My sisters Susan Satter and Julietta Satter and my brother David Satter encouraged me to persevere in my writing. I am especially grateful to my brother Paul Satter, who taught me to take risks and to care about history.

Chart 1. The Spread of New Thought, 1875–1920.*

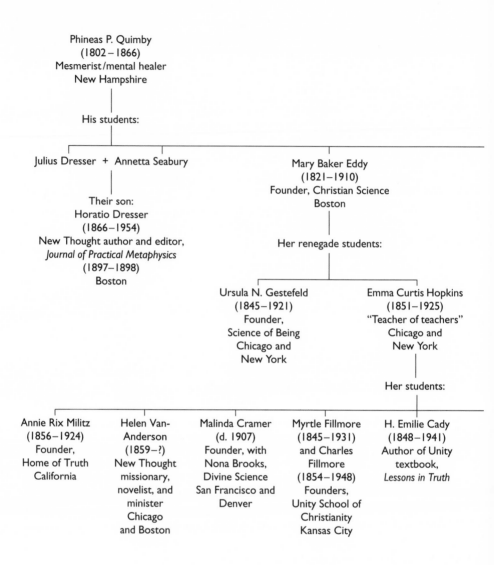

Phineas P. Quimby
(1802 – 1866)
Mesmerist/mental healer
New Hampshire

His students:

Julius Dresser + Annetta Seabury

Their son:
Horatio Dresser
(1866–1954)
New Thought author and editor,
Journal of Practical Metaphysics
(1897–1898)
Boston

Mary Baker Eddy
(1821–1910)
Founder, Christian Science
Boston

Her renegade students:

Ursula N. Gestefeld
(1845–1921)
Founder,
Science of Being
Chicago and
New York

Emma Curtis Hopkins
(1851–1925)
"Teacher of teachers"
Chicago and
New York

Her students:

Annie Rix Militz
(1856–1924)
Founder,
Home of Truth
California

Helen Van-
Anderson
(1859–?)
New Thought
missionary,
novelist, and
minister
Chicago
and Boston

Malinda Cramer
(d. 1907)
Founder, with
Nona Brooks,
Divine Science
San Francisco and
Denver

Myrtle Fillmore
(1845–1931)
and Charles
Fillmore
(1854–1948)
Founders,
Unity School of
Christianity
Kansas City

H. Emilie Cady
(1848–1941)
Author of Unity
textbook,
Lessons in Truth

*Figures to the left of Hopkins promote the denial of desire;
figures to the right of Hopkins promote the expression of desire.
Designed by Julie Zolot.

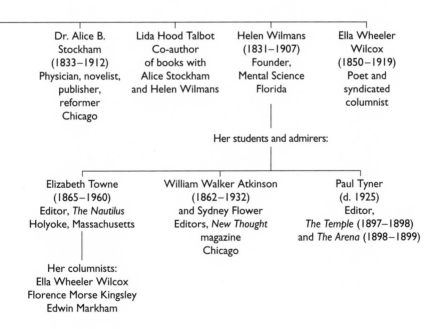

Warren Felt Evans
(1817–1889)
First New Thought Author
Boston

Praised by:
Alice Stockham
Helen Wilmans
H. Emilie Cady
Elizabeth Towne

Dr. Alice B.
Stockham
(1833–1912)
Physician, novelist,
publisher,
reformer
Chicago

Lida Hood Talbot
Co-author
of books with
Alice Stockham
and Helen Wilmans

Helen Wilmans
(1831–1907)
Founder,
Mental Science
Florida

Ella Wheeler
Wilcox
(1850–1919)
Poet and
syndicated
columnist

Her students and admirers:

Elizabeth Towne
(1865–1960)
Editor, *The Nautilus*
Holyoke, Massachusetts

William Walker Atkinson
(1862–1932)
and Sydney Flower
Editors, *New Thought*
magazine
Chicago

Paul Tyner
(d. 1925)
Editor,
The Temple (1897–1898)
and *The Arena* (1898–1899)

Her columnists:
Ella Wheeler Wilcox
Florence Morse Kingsley
Edwin Markham

Introduction

New Thought in Late-Victorian America

On the steamy morning of June 14, 1888, Chicago's Central Music Hall was packed, from the orchestra to its highest gallery seats, with well-dressed middle-aged women. Fanning themselves in the heat, they eagerly awaited the Reverend Mary Baker Eddy, about to deliver her first public talk outside of New England. Eddy soon appeared on the stage, a solemn, diminutive figure in a simple black-and-white silk dress. The audience of four thousand rose in respectful tribute and then listened intently to Eddy's speech, entitled "Science and the Senses." Eddy explained that sin, sickness, and death had no absolute reality, but were mere errors—that is, false conceptions created by our faulty senses. True Science, on the other hand, was a power so great that it could destroy all error, including sin, sickness, and death. Christian Science was merely the modern revival of the spiritual and healing Science that Jesus had practiced, Eddy claimed. If one wanted to be healed or to heal others, one had only to recognize this true Science; it was as simple as that.

When Eddy finished her talk, her audience rushed the platform and showered her with hugs and kisses. The newspaper accounts only fanned the flames of her triumph. Eddy had shown herself to be "a woman of impressive appearance and intellectual force," wrote the *Chicago Daily Tribune*. Her voice was "exceedingly penetrating" and had an oddly "electrical quality," wrote the *Daily Inter Ocean*, while the *Chicago Times* reported that Eddy "seemed to be conjuring her audience," so rapt was their attention.[1]

Eddy's Chicago triumph seemed to prove that her Christian Science had surpassed its nomenclature of the "Boston Craze" to become a national movement. This success was not the entire picture, however. As Eddy was en route to her first experience of adulation in the midwest, her organization was crumbling at home. That same spring of 1888 a Mrs. Abby H.

Corner of Medford, Massachusetts, had engaged in Christian Science heal-ing—that is, silent prayer—to help her daughter, who was having a diffi-cult childbirth. Both her daughter and the infant died, and Mrs. Corner was indicted for manslaughter. Anxiety over the trial fueled a mood of dissen-sion and fear among Eddy's Boston followers. Instead of finding Eddy to be a reassuring leader, they focused on her apparent lust for money, her de-mands for unquestioning loyalty, and her growing paranoia over the evil designs of former students. Three days before Eddy gave her acclaimed Chi-cago speech, a stormy session of the Boston Christian Science Association culminated with the defection of one third of Eddy's followers. She re-turned from her Chicago triumph to find in shambles the Boston Christian Science group she had laboriously constructed over the previous ten years. Nearly despairing over the future of her movement, Eddy considered aban-doning Boston altogether and simply starting over in Chicago.[2]

Eddy had reason to seriously consider such a relocation of her tottering movement. Chicago had had a thriving Christian Science scene since 1883.[3] The year Eddy visited the city, Frances Lord's *Christian Science Healing,* Ursula N. Gestefeld's *Statement of Christian Science,* and the *Christian Science* magazine were published there and Emma Curtis Hopkins' Christian Science Theological Seminary opened there. There was one problem, how-ever. The women leading the Christian Science movement in Chicago, for-merly students of Eddy's, had now become her rivals. Despite their sporadic protestations of loyalty to Eddy, Chicago women such as Hopkins, Lord, and Gestefeld were in fact promoting their own doctrines, variously known as Mind Cure, Mental Science, and Christian Science.

By 1888 Eddy was losing control of the movement she claimed to have originated, and not only in Chicago. While Eddy's followers in Boston aban-doned her in increasing numbers, Boston itself was the location of at least six similar schools of mental healing that viewed each other as allies and Eddy as an enemy. Eddy could not find words harsh enough for these apos-tates; "whining dogs," "Malicious Animal Magnetizers," and "mental as-sassins" were some of the phrases she used to describe them. But by the late 1880s, their followers far outnumbered her own. According to one es-timate, of five thousand people active in mind-healing in Boston in 1887, less than one thousand were loyal to Eddy. "There are twenty false lectur-ers and teachers to one that is true," Eddy mourned, and evidence from the period supports her admission that her followers comprised only a small proportion of the nation's mental healers.[4]

The following study focuses on these "false lecturers and teachers," the women, together with some men who, between 1885 and 1910, formed the majority of the metaphysical milieu of which Eddy was merely one wing, and who, after Eddy's death in 1910, continued to spread their faith to vast numbers of Americans.[5] Throughout the 1880s, these groups were often confused with Eddy's Christian Science. They called their beliefs Mental Science, Divine Science, Spiritual Science, Unity, Mind Cure, Science of Being, Home of Truth, and even, until Eddy definitively copyrighted the term in the 1890s, Christian Science. At that point the groups' leaders united their separate faiths in a loose national alliance and agreed upon "New Thought" as the umbrella term for their movement.[6] Yet from the 1880s on, there were so many influential New Thought teachers that it is historically more accurate to view Mary Baker Eddy as an important contributor to the turn-of-the-century New Thought movement than to view New Thought as the long-forgotten context for Eddy's Christian Science. Eddy will thus be treated as a contributor in this study. Eddy disliked New Thought healers, but she shared enough of their basic beliefs—and personally trained enough of their major leaders—to be seen as an intellectual contributor to the movement she abhorred.

Although Eddy strove to separate herself from the New Thought movement, it is easy to see why many turn-of-the-century Americans failed to see the distinction between Eddy's Christian Science and the broader New Thought milieu. There were significant overlaps between the theology and practice of both groups. Both believed that the mental or spiritual world was the true reality, while the material world of daily life, the world of "matter," was merely a secondary creation of the mind. Both also believed that human beings had god-like powers. As God created the universe through pure thought, so on a lesser scale did people create their own worlds through their thought. Since human thought had creative power, negative thoughts materialized into negative situations, while spiritual thoughts could form a positive reality. Both believed in thought transference, claiming that either intentionally or unintentionally, people "picked up" the thoughts of their neighbors.

New Thought and Christian Science proponents therefore attempted first to enlighten people about the creative powers of their minds, and then to teach them how to control their minds, and thus the world around them. The first step in controlling the mind, they believed, was to train it to ignore the information imparted by the senses. Science had proven that the senses provided false information. As Christian Science and New Thought manuals often pointed out, our eyes report that the sun travels around the earth, while in truth the earth revolves around the sun.[7] Clearly the mind needed a more reliable source of information. According to Eddy, this more reliable source was scripture. According to New Thought writers, it was either scripture, pure reason, or intuition—all three were in any case believed to agree. Both groups thus encouraged people to retrain their minds on the basis of a spiritual rather than a material reality, and to refute both the sense-information and the "mental errors" of those around them. The result of such mental discipline would be the creation of a perfect world.

Both groups achieved notoriety as a result of their claims to heal the sick through thought or prayer. Their healing practices were simple applications of their faith in the creative power of human thought. They believed that mental fears created both emotional and physical distress. One attained health and serenity by accepting that physical, material, or emotional conditions had no ultimate reality. The healer's job was to convince the patient that since Spirit or Mind was all, her problems or pains did not truly exist. Because of the power of thought transference, the healer could impart this information mentally and silently. The patient would mentally absorb the healer's thoughts and then be healed. In Eddy's own words:

> Argue at first mentally, not audibly, that the patient has no disease, and conform the argument so as to destroy the evidence of disease. Mentally insist that harmony is the fact, and that sickness is a temporal dream. Realize the presence of health and the fact of harmonious being, until the body corresponds with the normal conditions of health and harmony.[8]

And in the words of one of Eddy's rivals, Warren Felt Evans:

> We . . . affirm . . . that the deepest reality of the disease is not physical, but mental. . . . [in the case of a man who injured his arm] recognizing both the fall and the fracture, we would affirm that the immortal man is not injured, and that no sooner was the wound made than an everywhere-present Divine Life goes to work to heal the hurt. We would steadfastly believe this, and form in our mind the idea of the change to be effected, in order to . . . aid nature by accelerating the curative process.[9]

There were significant theological differences between Eddy's Christian Science and most New Thought groups. New Thought leaders embraced reason, intuition, or an amalgam of the world's scriptures and esoteric traditions as sources of spiritual truth. Eddy felt that truth could be found only in the Bible and in her own writings, both of which she believed to be divinely inspired. She also maintained the Christian understanding both of God as a transcendent being wholly distinct from humanity, and of humanity as needing to acknowledge complete dependence on this higher power. Thus although Eddy accepted New Thought claims about the creative power of human thought, she also feared it, since a reliance on the "mortal" mind's power detracted from one's reliance on God. This was in sharp contrast to the beliefs of the mental healers, who reveled in the mind's creative ability, which they equated with the "Divine Within." [10]

Eddy saw the proliferation of New Thought or Mind Cure groups in the 1880s as evidence of the distortion of her teachings, rather than of their spread. She finally abandoned the idea of starting over in Chicago, and instead, from 1890 until her death in 1910, set about restructuring her church so that power rested only in herself and in her hand-picked (and all-male) board of directors. She created elaborate application procedures for membership in an authorized Christian Science church. She also restructured the church service itself, replacing speakers or pastors, who might have offered personal interpretations of the Bible and Eddy's texts, with "Readers" who simply recited her preassigned weekly scriptural passages and Bible lessons without comment. [11] Eddy also worked relentlessly to clarify the distinction between her faith and that of the wider New Thought movement, regularly blasting New Thought leaders as malicious mesmerizers or worse.

New Thought leaders also attempted to organize. In the late 1890s the mental healers who did not follow Eddy united under the banner of the International Metaphysical League, which soon renamed itself the International New Thought Alliance. [12] Although many groups who had no affiliation with Eddy called their teachings "Christian Science" throughout the 1890s, the distinction between Eddy's "Christian Science" and "New Thought" has held to this day.

Today Mary Baker Eddy is seen by non-Christian Scientists as the most successful representative of an obscure late-nineteenth-century Mind Cure or New Thought religious milieu. Historians generally agree that Eddy's brilliant institutionalization of Christian Science enabled her faith to survive to the present in a way in which the eclectic New Thought movement could not. Evaluating this historical judgment requires a comparison of the respective fates of the two movements in American culture.

Eddy's bureaucratization of Christian Science enabled a movement that was in shambles in 1890 to rise phoenix-like from the ashes by 1900. Christian Science stunned and sometimes frightened contemporaries with its meteoric spread. From a single congregation of twenty-six members in 1879, it had expanded to 86,000 members by 1906, to 202,000 by 1926, and to 269,000 by 1936. The movement's growth tapered off, however, at that point. Currently, Christian Scientists make up only two-tenths of one percent of the U.S. population. [13]

Unlike Christian Science, New Thought remained an open, eclectic, and easily splintered movement. Beginning in the 1890s, numerous attempts were made to unite the diverse New Thought sects into a national organization. These umbrella groups never survived more than a few years without major defections. Yet the popularity of New Thought principles seemed only to increase as the remnants of its institutional identity crumbled. Unlike Christian Science with its rigid, authoritarian structure, the very looseness of New Thought's organizational structure allowed popular New Thought authors to adapt to and influence mainstream American ideas.[14]

Despite the familiarity of Christian Science and the obscurity of New Thought, it was New Thought principles about the creative power of thought that struck early twentieth-century Americans as the wave of the future, and which remain operative in American culture today. As early as 1901 William James could report that "mind-cure principles are beginning to so pervade the air that one catches their spirit at second hand." The movement seemed to grow more influential over the next two decades as inspirational and self-help bestsellers such as Ralph Waldo Trine's *In Tune With the Infinite* spread the New Thought message to literally millions of Americans. New Thought principles also reached Americans both through journals such as B. O. Flower's *Arena* and Orison Swett Marden's *Success* and through magazine articles by New Thought authors in mainstream publications such as the *Atlantic*, *McClures*, the *Ladies Home Journal*, and *Good Housekeeping*.[15]

Throughout the twentieth century, New Thought's central premise — the power of thought to alter circumstances — had a strong allure for millions of Americans. By the early 1920s there were three to four hundred active New Thought centers in the U.S. and Canada. The doctrines of the movement experienced upsurges of popularity in the 1930s and again in the 1950s. New Thought was promoted by organizations such as Kansas City–based Unity, one of the original New Thought churches, which in 1954 processed six hundred thousand prayer-requests yearly and published a magazine with a circulation of two hundred thousand. It also reached Americans through popular literature, from Emmet Fox's *Sermon on the Mount*, a 1930s bestseller that is still in print today, to Norman Vincent Peale's *The Power of Positive Thinking*, which in 1954 sold more than any nonfiction book except the Bible.[16]

In the 1970s and 1980s the principles of New Thought affected the lives of vast numbers of Americans, many through involvement in the various branches of Alcoholics Anonymous. AA's view that alcoholism can be healed through spiritual discipline and its references to God as one's "Higher

Power" owe a debt to New Thought healing practices. Other individuals affected by the principles of New Thought were members of "human potential" organizations, such as Werner Erhard's EST (now known as the Forum), Insight, Actualizations, Silva Mind Control, and Lifespring. These groups offered programs for corporate employees and attracted millions of dollars a year in revenues. According to a 1986 *New York Times* article, scholars believed this "new age" perspective was "working its way increasingly into the nation's cultural, religious, social, economic and political life." One researcher described it as the "most powerful social force in the country today."[17]

The popularity of thought-as-power continues to grow. Bookstores around the country are selling 1990s reprints of early-twentieth-century "Religious Science" and "Divine Science" bestsellers. Talk-show host Oprah Winfrey dispenses her New Thought philosophy daily on a show watched by millions. The success of evangelist minister Robert Schuller and his "possibility thinking" is enshrined in his $16.5-million-dollar "Crystal Cathedral." The Codependency Movement, an offshoot of Alcoholics Anonymous that claims to treat the disease of denying one's emotions and giving too much of oneself to others, is embraced by large numbers of Americans. The movement's practices could have been lifted straight out of a nineteenth-century New Thought manual. According to Lynne Namka, author of *The Doormat Syndrome*, "[c]hanting affirmations to yourself daily is an important recovery technique. 'Energy follows thought,' . . . You actually become what you think."[18]

New Thought has had a century-long presence in the United States. Yet most historians of American culture view New Thought as little more than a crude religion of success, a tone set by a 1934 article by A. Whitney Griswold entitled "New Thought: A Cult of Success." According to Griswold, "New Thought was a get-rich-quick religion, a something-for-nothing religion; that was the secret of its appeal." New Thought expressed the "voice of the poor clerk," he claimed, who believed that one could obtain success by simply wishing for the "correct endowment of virtues." Building on Griswold, a number of historians in the 1960s and 1970s argued that New Thought outgrew its roots as a nineteenth-century metaphysical movement to become the "single greatest conveyer of the success ideology in the twentieth century." As Horatio Alger narratives epitomized the success literature of late-Victorian producer culture, they argue, so were New Thought tracts the paradigmatic success literature of modern consumer capitalism.[19]

The most recent and sophisticated studies of New Thought are in this vein. Donald Meyer's 1965 classic, *The Positive Thinkers,* argues that New Thought encouraged believers to passively wait for the Divine Mind to fulfill their desires. New Thought encouraged Americans to demonstrate their trust in "Divine Supply" by spending rather than saving, thus serving the needs of an economy based on consumption. Gail Thain Parker's 1973 study *Mind Cure in New England* points out that New Thought authors typically urged their readers to both "float in harmony" with the cosmos and "hit hard and win" in the world. By encouraging Americans both to hold on to and let go of their egos, New Thought literature helped Americans manage the conflicting impulses that were roused by the transition from producer capitalism (with its calls for self-denial and strenuosity) to consumer capitalism (with its encouragement of spending and self-gratification).[20]

This picture of New Thought as the popular ideology of twentieth-century consumer capitalism does not take into account the first thirty years of the movement, from approximately 1875 until 1905. This early period, which forms the heart of the present study, has never been adequately explored by historians. Yet a look at its most prominent characteristics quickly undermines the dominant view of New Thought as a simple faith of accommodation to consumer capitalism. It was popular not only with struggling young businessmen, but with white middle-class women. Indeed, the majority of late-nineteenth-century New Thought authors, healers, teachers, patients, and congregants were white middle-class women.[21] While women were overrepresented in all Protestant denominations at this period, many New Thought followers understood themselves to be part of a women's religious movement that would herald a new "woman's era."

Late-nineteenth-century New Thought was embraced not by self-indulgent consumers, but by prominent middle-class reformers, both male and female. As the journal *Mind* reported in 1901, New Thought material was "read with avidity in economic societies and social clubs, in political and moral reform organizations, in liberal Christian associations, and by individuals interested in the rescue of science from the pitfalls of materialism."[22] These early progressives—liberal and radical Protestant ministers, women's suffrage activists, pioneering investigative journalists, social purity leaders, and proponents of Bellamyite Nationalism and Christian Socialism—believed that New Thought meditations would help to bring about a new era in the development of the "race."

Perhaps most significantly, a look at this era reminds us that early New Thought was notorious for being a stunningly effective method of *mental healing.* The apparent successes of New Thought healers made them the envy of physicians and neurologists, who were forced to appropriate their most effective ideas and techniques. These included not only practices of silent meditation, but also the beginnings of a reconceptualization of the nature of the mind and its relation to matter, heredity, "influence," self-hood, and desire.

For these were the issues that occupied early New Thought authors— and understandably so. Between the 1870s and the 1910s, New Thought could most accurately be defined as a religious healing movement that claimed that "spirit," "mind," or human thought had the power to shape matter, overcome heredity, and mold desire. The precise meanings and functions of *mind, matter, spirit,* and *desire* were of central concern to New Thought authors. Their journals were rife with debates over whether "mind" was masculine or feminine; whether "matter" was nonexistent, or infused with mind; and whether desire was an evil to be "denied" or the saving truth to be embraced. In short, whether the goal was health and spiritual development or wealth and personal power, New Thought authors believed that the most basic challenge confronting them was how to understand the meanings of *mind,* and its relation to matter, heredity, and desire.

Befitting a movement whose primary concern was the nature of mind, this study presents an intellectual and cultural history of New Thought. My focus is more on ideas than on institutions. This book does, however, identify major New Thought leaders, detail their missionary methods, and outline the means by which they turned their faith into lucrative careers. It indicates some of the organizations—from journals, metaphysical clubs, meditation circles, theological seminaries, and "colleges" to summer camps, lecture circuits, mail-order ministries, and national conventions—that early leaders created to promote their ideals.

Most interesting about New Thought, however, are the interconnections between New Thought and turn-of-the-century woman movement leaders, early progressives, and proto- and pioneering psychologists. New Thought will be analyzed, therefore, as a popular intellectual discourse that both drew upon and deeply influenced the ideas of woman movement leaders, early progressive reformers, and turn-of-the-century neurologists and physicians. What linked New Thought to the core intellectual concerns of these three contemporaneous groups was their shared involvement in a broad cultural debate over precisely which qualities constituted ideal manhood and womanhood, or the ideal gendered self. More specifically, these groups were united by their shared engagement in a pervasive but now-forgotten late-nineteenth-century contest over whether the key to progress, civilization, and race perfection was (Anglo-Saxon) male desire or female virtue.[23] Was the nation in need of male rationality or female spirituality?

Who offered the more complete paradigm of human mind or selfhood—
the desirous, competitive, and rational white man, or the desireless, spiritual, and altruistic white woman? Did man represent the rational mind that
must dominate feminine "matter" and physicality? Or did woman represent the moral spirit that must dominate unruly, masculine matter?

It is important to stress that although New Thought leaders participated
in this argument over the respective meaning and value of male desire and
female virtue, they did not create it. The debate, which engaged social theorists, woman movement leaders, reformers, and physicians, was the culmination of a century-long struggle between white middle-class men and
white middle-class women for cultural dominance. Although external to
New Thought, the debate nevertheless provides the most appropriate framework for understanding it. New Thought texts were immediately compre-
hensible to, popular among, and even healing for, many late-nineteenth-
century middle-class Americans because they wrestled with slippery
concepts that were at the core of that broader cultural battle for authority
between proponents of white middle-class manhood and those of white
middle-class womanhood. They discussed and ambiguously reworked the
meanings of gendered definitions of mind, matter, spirit, selfhood, and
desire.

REFORM VERSUS SOCIAL DARWINISM:
FEMALE VIRTUE VERSUS MALE DESIRE

The struggle over whether desirous men or virtuous women ought to be
leaders of civilization was essentially a debate over the sort of gendered behavior, and consequent economic and political behavior, that was most
likely to further the evolutionary development of "the (Anglo-Saxon)
race." Because the turn-of-the-century debate about gendered selfhood
that framed New Thought has both slipped from popular memory and been
overlooked by historians, I outline it briefly here.[24]

On one side were those who took what can loosely be called a social
Darwinist perspective. The major spokesmen for this outlook included British philosopher Herbert Spencer, American sociologist William Graham
Sumner, and many late-nineteenth-century British and American physicians. These men felt that (Anglo-Saxon) male desire, channeled through
male rationality and will, fueled the competitive drives that created economic prosperity and civilization itself. The free competition of driven, desirous men led to the "survival of the fittest," and hence to race improvement toward ultimate perfection. State intervention in the economy was

anathema, since it interfered with Darwinian laws that were equally applicable to nature and to society. Aid to the poor must be avoided, since it kept alive those who had proved themselves "unfit." Unions and other forms of political organization among the poor were similarly futile means of keeping afloat those whom nature had condemned to perish.

Many social Darwinists believed that "refined" women's higher education and political activism were racially devolutionary. Essentially, they viewed men as impassioned "mind" and women as passive "matter." Women did play a role in evolutionary development—as potential wives, they were the prize that compelled Anglo-Saxon men to compete for ever greater achievements. Once married, women were to "minister" to men's sexual "necessities." As mothers, they were to devote themselves to their children. But white women were not believed to have the intrinsic passion and desire that white men drew upon to fuel their intellectual, economic, and cultural achievements. The delicate minds and maternal instincts of women formed a closed energy system. Intellectual development of white women would therefore render them infertile and lead to race suicide. Women should also be barred from educational and political leadership because a defining feature of civilization was the difference between men and women. Intellect was male, emotion female. An intellectual woman was by definition manlike, and even atavistic, since she erased a key sign of advanced civilization—the development of selfless reproductive women and passionate but rational and productive men.[25]

This perspective was opposed by those who took what might be called a social purity or reform Darwinist perspective. Figures articulating aspects of this outlook included Lester Ward, Benjamin Flower, and most late-nineteenth-century woman movement leaders, including Elizabeth Cady Stanton and Frances Willard. As with the social Darwinists, the ultimate goal of the purity-oriented reform Darwinists was to spur the evolution and perfection of "the race." They also agreed that scientific law held the key to social and racial improvement. They defined the laws of science differently, however. Truly scientific laws were not the cutthroat, amoral laws of nature, but the unchanging, spiritual law that pure woman, not desirous man, best represented. Indeed, they argued that the competitive desires of (white) men had now become a destructive force. In the public sphere, these lustful, competitive desires led to unethical business practices and created massive economic inequalities that threatened to sabotage the American dream of a republican commonwealth. In the private sphere, unchecked male passions led to marital rape and forced maternity. The offspring produced by marital rapes would be passive and sickly, like their mothers, and mindlessly sensual, like their fathers. It was desirous men, not educated women, who led to devolution or race suicide, they argued.

Social purity activists and reform Darwinists felt that these threats to civilization could only be averted through the leadership or influence of "woman." They viewed (Anglo-Saxon) woman as rational spirit and man as lustful matter. While the mind of competitive man was warped by his raging desires, "advanced" woman lacked destructive desire. Instead, woman's "mental force" was fueled by her "heart force"—understood not as irrational emotion, but as high-minded love and spiritual morality.[26]

As a rational, pure, and deeply moral being, the New Woman could help redeem a race and a nation now threatened with moral dissolution.[27] Instead of representing laissez-faire practices that sanctioned selfishness and greed, she stood for social scientific or sociological efforts to rationally understand and altruistically improve society. She understood that aid to the poor was not a suicidal negation of the laws of natural selection, but the obvious response of a refined people motivated by the eternal laws of love, spirituality, and maternal self-sacrifice. Her higher education and growing political involvement in society would accelerate the nation's evolution toward a new era, one crowned by a new model of selfhood. No longer would humanity be bifurcated into desirous, impassioned, and rational men and spiritual, passive, and irrational women—into male "mind" and female "matter." Rather, both men and women would aspire to a pure, desireless, and rational character. Manly and womanly "spirit" would triumph over masculine "matter" or sensuality. The pure woman, not the desirous man, would be the model of selfhood in a dawning "era of woman."

Without the broader context of this racialized evolutionary discourse about gender, early New Thought texts are virtually incomprehensible. They are filled with seemingly arcane debates about mind, matter, desire, and selfhood. For example, Mary Baker Eddy insisted that matter was masculine and spirit feminine. New Thought author Warren Felt Evans insisted, to the contrary, that matter was feminine and spirit masculine. New Thought author Helen Van-Anderson claimed that the sick could be healed by meditating upon the following "denials":

> There is no life, substance or intelligence in matter; there is no sensation or causation in matter; there is no reality in matter . . .

Yet Mental Science founder Helen Wilmans believed that "affirming" matter was the key to health and happiness. "I cannot repeat too often the great fact that there is no dead matter. . . . It is on this mighty truth that man's salvation depends," she explained. Divine Science founder Malinda Cramer told her patients to "deny" desire. Others counseled the opposite. New Thought author H. Emilie Cady emphasized, "*[d]esire in the heart is always God tapping at the door of your consciousness with His infinite supply.*" New Thought author and social reformer Abby Morton Diaz called on women to renounce their "I-hood." In contrast, Wilmans stated her opposition to womanly self-denial in unmistakable terms.

> Next to the word God comes that limitless and unconquerable word "I" . . . We must refuse to believe that an assumption of humility is pleasing to God. . . . Let us begin at once to exalt ourselves.[28]

What was the meaning of these debates? Why would discussions of this sort dominate popular manuals ostensibly devoted to healing?

When New Thought is set in the context of the turn-of-the-century debate over whether masculine "mind" or womanly "spirit"—or male desire or womanly virtue—encouraged race progress, the meaning of New Thought texts and the reasons for contemporary interest in them become clear. Early New Thought authors offered competing versions of the proper relations among contested, explicitly gendered concepts of mind, matter, selfhood, and desire. They thereby created new models of womanhood and manhood that overlapped with, but were not always identical to, the competing paradigms of selfhood offered by social Darwinists and social purity leaders. In so doing, they not only engaged in what was arguably the primary cultural debate of their era, they also appeared to heal the nervous illnesses of late-Victorian women and men who were sickened by the contested yet rigid gender norms of their day.

This study thus goes beyond putting women back into the history of New Thought—it also recovers a New Thought discourse about gender, or about the constitution of the male and female self. It uses the concerns of New Thought authors to highlight a broader turn-of-the-century debate over manliness and womanliness. It demonstrates the continuity between the deeply ambiguous writings of New Thought authors and now-forgotten concerns about racialized, gendered selfhood that structured the intellectual and political debates of the early Progressive era.

NEW THOUGHT AS A DISCOURSE OF DESIRE

Early New Thought leaders offered diverse answers to the question of what constituted healthy womanhood and manhood. They can be broadly divided, however, into two competing schools. In the late nineteenth century, the dominant group insisted that health and spiritual development depended upon the "denial" of matter, selfhood, and desire. This "anti-desire" school of New Thought was popular among woman movement leaders, purity reformers, and Christian Socialists. The dissident, minority group heralded the interactivity of mind and matter, the importance of selfhood, and the divinity of desire—both sexual desire and the desire for wealth. This "pro-desire" school was popular among more economically marginal women and men.

The existence of these competing schools helps to explain the most puzzling aspect of late-nineteenth-century New Thought—its rapid transformation. Within a few short years at the turn of the century, most New Thought tracts shifted their focus from the attainment of health through denial of desire to the attainment of prosperity through the expression of desire. By the early twentieth century New Thought began to fit the image historians have presented us with—that of a cult of success or of accommodation to consumer capitalism. The internal debate between rival schools enables us to see that the movement's twentieth-century transformation was the result of an alteration in dominance between two competing perspectives within late-nineteenth-century New Thought. More important, it indicates that New Thought's sea change is not most accurately portrayed as a shift from a focus on health to a focus on wealth. Rather, the shift was from a rejection of desire to an acceptance of it.

The transformation of early-twentieth-century New Thought, however, involved more than the defeat of one school or generation and the rise of another. Instead, some of the same women leaders who had initially taught the importance of "denying" matter and desire suddenly, in mid-career, began to insist that desire was holy and that "matter" was alive. Indeed, some late-nineteenth-century New Thought women went on to write the earliest, and some say the crudest, manuals about how to meditate one's way to success. This seems a puzzle. Why would white middle-class women, supposedly barred from all economic concerns, help originate the twentieth century's most popular form of success literature? Why would a faith of Victorian womanhood, middle-class reform, and proto-psychology turn into a crass cult of success?

I answer this question by recasting it. Instead of asking why some supposedly pure and sheltered white middle-class women wrote books that praised the divine desire for wealth, I ask what it was about desire—the desire for wealth, as well as for personal and sexual expression—that had become so problematic for middle-class women. That "success" and "womanhood" were seen as antithetical—and, not coincidentally, that "selfhood" had become deeply troubling for middle-class white women—has a history that needs to be told; it should not be assumed to be natural. New Thought women authors, who debated the meaning of "woman" as well as of wealth, of "the self" as well as of "desire," help us uncover that history. Their texts illuminate more than late-Victorian white middle-class women's odd relation to ideals of economic success. They interrogate the deeper issue of how these women struggled with, and were damaged by, mainstream understandings of the relations between female selfhood and desire.

By analyzing New Thought in the context of the turn-of-the-century debate over competing paradigms of gendered selfhood, this study presents a new interpretation of the shift from Victorian ideals of male and female subjectivity to modern ones. It makes the complexities of white middle-class women's desire central to the story of the emergence of modern constructs of manhood and womanhood. It reinterprets not only New Thought, but also the white middle-class woman movement and early Progressivism in light of the battle over Victorian gender ideals and the emergence of modern paradigms of gendered subjectivity.

The New Thought debate on desire provides a remarkable record of a struggle, largely by marginally educated white women, to rework their era's definitions of womanliness and manliness. Yet the nineteenth-century fascination with desire cannot be reduced to gender tensions alone. Desire is a highly ambiguous concept that lay at the heart of nineteenth-century social thought.[29] Desire was lauded by Romantics, dissected by economists, explored by Transcendentalists, and spiritualized by theologians. New Thought was a popular outgrowth of Transcendentalism, German idealist philosophy, and liberal Protestantism, and a full intellectual history of New Thought as a discourse of desire would need to explore these roots. The aspect of desire that has been most neglected by intellectual historians, however, is the extent to which it was intertwined with Victorian ideals of manliness and womanliness. By focusing on New Thought as a gendered discourse of desire, we can see gender implications of the nineteenth-century fascination with desire that more traditional intellectual histories leave opaque. We also get a fuller sense of the specific meanings of desire for late-Victorian women. When female New Thought authors spoke of desire, they referred to material and sexual desires, but more broadly to their fundamental cravings for the right to think, feel, and act for themselves. They were talking, in short, about subjectivity. Their writings help us understand why New Thought discussions of selfhood, of love and sexuality, and of consumption and economic productivity were so inextricably connected. All were fundamentally about desire.

I also treat New Thought as a discourse about *white* ideals of womanhood and manhood. The New Thought network my research has uncovered appears to have been entirely white and Protestant. This does not mean that African Americans had no interest in New Thought. On the contrary, discussions of mesmerism, hypnotism, telepathy, and other phenomena related to New Thought were common in African-American race uplift manuals. Authors from Pauline Hopkins to W. E. B. Du Bois drew upon spiritualism, mesmerism, and hypnosis to explore, from an African-American perspective, the same sorts of issues that white New Thought authors explored—the components of the gendered and racialized self.[30] My analysis of New Thought as a discourse of gendered selfhood is limited to white authors not because New Thought was inherently off-putting to non-whites, but because the African Americans who practiced mental healing operated in separate networks that I have been unable to recover.

What do we find, then, in New Thought debates about desire? Some "anti-desire" New Thought authors explained with remarkable candor the ways in which an embrace of desirelessness could allow women to distance themselves from compulsory heterosexuality and compulsory motherhood. Other anti-desire New Thought leaders penned utopian novels depicting a world modeled on spiritual, desireless womanhood rather than on desirous, competitive manhood—predating by twenty years Charlotte Perkins Gilman's *Herland*, which explored similar themes. These authors claimed that if women and men learned to "deny" masculine desire and matter and "affirm" the pure, womanly mind and spirit, then marriage would be perfected and a new sort of race could be created. This new race would be modeled not on the desirous, greedy, competitive Anglo-Saxon man, but on the pure, moral, and cooperative Anglo-Saxon woman. The chains of heredity would be broken, and "the race" would achieve its full evolutionary potential.

"Pro-desire" New Thought women authors, meanwhile, claimed the opposite. They argued that the race was being sabotaged by the repression of healthy desire. Paralleling and sometimes anticipating the works of such theorists as James Mark Baldwin, George Herbert Mead, and John Dewey, they claimed that mind and matter must be accepted as mutually influencing, mutually positive forces within the human psyche. These women promised that New Thought affirmations of godly desire would both

strengthen the individual and liberate the race from its "bondage" to ener-
vating doctrines of sin and self-hatred. Some of these authors offered dev-
astating critiques of the ideal of desireless womanhood promoted by both
social Darwinism and social purity or reform Darwinism. They insisted
that desire was a critical component of a liberated self. They attempted to
create, with varying degrees of success, new paradigms of manhood and
womanhood within which (white) women could claim both "mind" and
"desire"—some of which have now been entirely forgotten.

Whether they were "pro-" or "anti-" desire, New Thought writings
pinpointed the weaknesses in late-Victorian paradigms of manliness and
womanliness. They help us understand why those paradigms crumbled so
quickly in the early twentieth century, and why the models of gendered
selfhood that replaced them took the forms they did. With a clarity unusual
for their time, New Thought authors understood that mind was a gendered
symbol. They wrestled with the gender implications of separating, spiritualizing, or merging "mind" and "matter," thus participating in the primary
philosophical debate of their time. They also participated in the primary
political debate of their time between laissez-faire capitalism and cooperative altruism. They highlighted the complex ways in which white middle-
class women's subjectivity, like that of white middle-class men, was en-
meshed in beliefs about evolutionary racial hierarchy. New Thought authors
helped pioneer modern discourses of gendered and racialized sexuality.
Ultimately, some New Thought authors helped to create and popularize the
subconscious-mind-as-reservoir-of-energy discourse that molded the direction of American understandings of selfhood.

In short, female New Thought authors and their male associates debated
and helped shape white Protestant Americans' beliefs about mind, body,
spirit, and will. They explored the ambiguous ways in which these foundational concepts were related on the one hand to spending, sex, and desire,
and on the other to newly emerging understandings of manhood and womanhood. Their ideas were not necessarily radical; the fact that these authors
were often female and generally not elite does not mean that they transcended the power relations of their day. But their texts, if not always sub-
versive, are still worthy of study.[31] They show how late-nineteenth-
century women struggled to create a new kind of white woman's self or ego
in the midst of a culture that was rapidly changing the ground rules of
gender. They reveal the origins of modern gender ideals that continue to
impede women's ability to claim a strong ego, to speak honestly about their
experiences, or to attain cultural legitimacy without the most carefully

crafted of ruses. New Thought women sought to reconfigure female identity to fit within a new economic order and a new order of subjectivity. Their lives and their writings help to illuminate the constrictions that still bind.

Chapter 1 outlines the late-nineteenth-century debate over the meanings of male desire and female virtue. This now-forgotten debate set the stage for the popularity of New Thought as a mental-healing movement. Chapter 2 analyzes the ideas of two foundational figures in New Thought: Mary Baker Eddy and Warren Felt Evans. It demonstrates that opposing views of the relations among mind, matter, selfhood, and desire—and of the implications that these relations had for the behavior of middle-class men and women—were at the heart of these authors' teachings in the 1870s and 1880s. Chapter 3 details the rise of Emma Curtis Hopkins, a renegade student of Eddy who embraced the ideas of Evans and went on to teach every major New Thought leader of the 1890s. It also describes the methods by which Hopkins's students—the majority of whom were women— created New Thought schools and churches throughout the country.

Chapter 4 interprets novels by three female New Thought authors. Because these authors feared women's animal-like inner selves, they defined women's "freedom" as desireless, selfless service to others. Yet because Victorians believed that wealth was the product of channeled male desire, the denial of desire meant a denial of wealth—which was the precondition for sheltered true womanhood. These novels demonstrate why the denial of desire was both an attractive and an ultimately unworkable strategy for late-nineteenth-century white middle-class women. Chapter 5 analyzes the life and thought of Helen Wilmans (1831–1907). Wilmans was a student of Emma Curtis Hopkins who wrote *The Conquest of Poverty* (1899), one of the earliest examples of New Thought as a "Religion of Success." Wilmans explored the connections between women's selfhood on the one hand and economic independence and entrepreneurial ambition on the other. Rejecting the anti-desire school's definition of women's freedom as loving service to others, Wilmans drew upon survival-of-the-fittest rhetoric to fashion an aggressive and desirous model of female selfhood.

Chapter 6 explains why some prominent turn-of-the-century political reformers were enthralled with New Thought. These reformers were convinced that the beliefs and practices of the anti-desire school of New Thought would help hasten the dawn of a new era—one in which womanly spirituality would finally triumph over manly desire. Chapter 7 describes the transformation of New Thought in the early twentieth century. As the Victorian norms that upheld the "woman's era" began to crumble, new discourses of popular psychology emerged to replace evolutionary doctrines. Now pro-desire New Thought authors, long fluent in discussions of the "inner mind" and the nature of desire, found an enormous new audience. They both incorporated the language of psychology and molded the ways in which Americans interpreted that vocabulary. The conclusion briefly traces the history of New Thought ideas to the present day. It suggests that current New Age and self-help manuals offer tantalizing clues about the forms of gendered selfhood now emerging at the turn of the twenty-first century.

1 The Era of Woman and the Problem of Desire

This is a time known pre-eminently in the history of the world as "woman's era."

Mrs. Theodore W. Birney, President,
National Congress of Mothers, 1897 [1]

One great law permeates the whole sentient world, that before there can be action, there must be desire.

Lester Ward, 1882 [2]

In a memoir written in 1899, the women's suffrage, social purity, and temperance activist Mary Livermore described the closing decades of the nineteenth century as a thrilling time for American women: "Great organizations of women for missionary work were formed, and managed solely by themselves. Women by the hundred thousand wheeled into line for temperance work. Women's clubs sprang into being,—clubs for social enjoyment and mutual inspiration and help. Woman Suffrage Leagues multiplied. Everywhere there was a call for women to be up and doing, with voice and pen, with hand and head and heart." [3]

By the end of the nineteenth century, white middle-class women had reason to feel supremely confident about the future of (white) American womanhood. In the decades following the Civil War, the numbers of middle-class and elite women in higher education had increased dramatically, from only 11,000 in 1870 to 56,000 in 1890. The number of women employed as teachers had quadrupled, from 84,000 in 1870 to 325,000 in 1900. White women were making progress in the professions as well; for the first time, they won positions in medicine, journalism, education, and government. [4]

Most exciting of all was the fact that growing numbers of women were involved in all aspects of social reform. Some middle-class women devoted themselves to aiding poor wage-earning women. They investigated the labor conditions of working women, established boarding houses, employment agencies, and referral services, and offered training, legal aid, and structured entertainment for wage-earning women. Small numbers of college-educated women formed the first settlement houses in the midst of urban slums. The women's suffrage campaign continued, receiving an added impetus when the nation's two major women's suffrage groups merged in 1890 to form the National American Woman's Suffrage Association.

Even larger numbers of women devoted themselves to uplifting the nation's moral character. Women across the nation joined the Woman's Christian Temperance Union. Founded in 1874, it experienced a fivefold increase in its membership in the 1880s under the dynamic leadership of Frances Willard. By the end of the 1890s, it was the largest women's organization in the nation. Women's missionary organizations were thriving. Middle-class women also organized mother's clubs, moral-education societies, and kindergartens. They joined social-purity leagues, which were devoted to holding men and women to a single, high standard of sexual morality. By the 1880s, the social-purity crusade had merged with moral-education societies and expanded to encompass campaigns to rescue prostitutes and raise the age of consent (of women for sexual intercourse), provide sex education for children and traveler's aid societies for women, and improve facilities for women in prison. By the 1890s, local social-purity groups had organized into the American Purity Alliance, while the moral-education and mothers' groups had formed the National Congress of Mothers. All of these groups received strong support from the General Federation of Women's Clubs, the structure organized in 1890 to unite the white women's clubs of the nation.[5]

Contemporaries referred to this new activism of women in the professions, higher education, and economic, political, and moral reform as the "woman movement."[6] More conservative social-purity–oriented woman-movement leaders often justified their political behavior not in terms of their rights as citizens, but in terms of the ways in which their high-minded service could benefit the nation. "Woman," they argued, was naturally pure and refined. Unlike man, who was motivated by selfish desire, woman was motivated by her altruistic "mother-heart." She entered the realms of politics and reform because her maternal self-sacrificing service was precisely what was needed to save a nation riven by class conflict, amoral wealth, and rampant political corruption. As suffrage and temperance activist Elizabeth Boynton Harbert argued in 1883, "Forever be silenced the selfish assertion, 'all the rights I want. . . .' [T]he time has come when the patriot men of America must . . . summon women to the glorious service of aiding to save our nation from the combinations of vice and selfishness. . . . [O]ur hour for self-sacrificing service is here."[7]

Many also believed that women had a unique weapon in their struggle to save the nation—the pure "moral force" of their almost mystical powers of "influence." The "irresistible" power of womanly influence was invoked repeatedly by a wide range of authors in the final decades of the nineteenth century. Womanly influence was institutionalized as a method of cross-class uplift. The Charity Organization movement, for example, was based on the premise that the urban poor had degenerated morally because they had been separated from the refining influences of their social superiors. Charity Organization administrators therefore sent a "friendly visitor," usually a middle-class woman, to call on slum dwellers. She was to spread her moral influence like "a tidal wave" over the slums, "flooding every part" with "sweetness and light." Charles Sheldon's 1896 bestseller *In His Steps* included accounts of how womanly influence transformed the idle rich and vicious poor alike. He described how the "dirty, drunken, impure, besotted" residents of an urban slum were "subdued and tamed" simply by hearing the prayerful song of a refined Christian woman: the slum "lay like some wild beast at her feet, and she sang it into harmlessness," Sheldon wrote in a typical passage. Womanly influence even had its own iconography. A pamphlet for the Salvation Army depicted an Army matron saving a prostitute through her "influence"—graphically depicted in the form of rays of light pouring from the outstretched hands of the matron onto the head and hands of the prostitute (see figure 1).[8]

Given woman's innate purity and powerful influence, there was no limit to what could be expected from the concentration and conscious focusing of her "moral power." The avowed goal of many late-nineteenth-century women's clubs and congresses was to enable just such a concentration to form. As Jane Cunningham Croly, the organizer of the first Woman's Parliament (in 1869), explained, "The function of the Parliament is to crystallize the intelligence and influence of women into a moral and reformatory power, which will act definitely upon all the varied interests of society."[9] Indeed, many white middle-class women activists did not hesitate to assert that if moral, loving, selfless women came together, their powerful influence would save the republic, elevate "the race," and inaugurate a new millennium—that is, a new era of spiritual peace and harmony. As one member described her expectations of the 1873 Woman's Congress, "We regard this association for the advancement of women as a step toward the coming millennium. God grant that woman with her refinement, her love, and her religion may be the means in the hands of God of helping the weak, ennobling humanity and converting the world."[10]

As proof that a new millennium, inaugurated by refined womanhood, was about to dawn, growing numbers of women pointed to an exciting new "science" that was spreading across the nation. The origins and even the

Figure 1.   Womanly influence. Womanly spirituality uplifts other women.

name of this science were obscure. Some said it was founded by a rural New Hampshire mesmerist named Phineas Quimby. Others spoke of the Boston leader Mary Baker Eddy or the Swedenborgian minister Warren Felt Evans. Some called it Divine Science, Christian Science, or Spiritual Science. Others referred to it as Mental Therapeutics, Mental Healing, or Mind Cure.

But whatever its name and origins, all agreed on the miraculous abilities of this new religious science. The mental healers, who often called themselves "teachers of science," were able to mentally or spiritually influence the minds of patients whom they did not speak with, touch, or, in some cases, even personally visit. Like other recent scientific breakthroughs, such as electricity and the telephone and telegraph, this mental science was immaterial and unbounded by constraints of time and space. Mental or Christian Scientists also taught their clients, frequently long-suffering nervous or neurasthenic patients whom doctors had pronounced incurable, to heal themselves. They did so, in the main, by training patients to deny the power of matter and desire, and to affirm the power of mind and spirit. By simply meditating upon "denials" (such as "There is no life, substance, or intelligence in matter") and "affirmations" (such as "Your desires are Spiritual, not carnal"), invalids were miraculously healed, and "unspeakable" lifelong vices were overcome. Newly healed women and men proclaimed the new Christian Science a revival of the healing ministry of Jesus, who also "healed with a word." [11]

Small but growing numbers of women believed that in the hands of today's high-minded and spiritual woman, Christian or Spiritual Science could be a tool that would speed the millennium—and inaugurate a new "woman's era." As Helen Wilmans, who had once been a reform journalist and who had become a mental healer, declared, "It is a noticeable fact that the Mental or Christian Science movement is a woman's movement. . . . [I]n this movement woman's *real* voice has been heard for the first time in the history of the race." Temperance and women's suffrage activist Louisa Southworth argued that the recent emergence of mental healing marked a "New Era" in which "women . . . [go] forth to do both moral and physical healing by the power of the Spirit." Southworth added, "Christian Science with a depreciatory air is frequently termed a woman's religion. We accept the gift, and glory in the fact that a richer inspiration . . . has come at last to give woman her proper status in the world." Elizabeth Boynton Harbert explained the full implications of the new mental-healing techniques: "when woman recognizes that she is free . . . she will give to the world a new race, and the golden age will dawn. It is dawning even now. . . . *Woman is at last free, because she . . . has discovered the spiritual laws through which her work is to be accomplished.*" These "mental and spiritual laws," Harbert explained, included the power to heal by thought, the "law of the spoken word" and "thought transference." [12]

The conviction of many leading woman movement activists that (white) women were pure and spiritual beings, that their influence could bring forth a new era in the history of "the race," and that Christian Science or Mind Cure techniques of healing by "thought transference" might be the "spiritual laws through which [their] work is to be accomplished" all require explanation. Why would the new "Mental or Christian Science" techniques of affirming "mind" and spirit, and of denying "matter" and desire, appear to have healing potency for nervous or neurasthenic Americans? Why would woman-movement leaders view these healings as the obvious harbingers of a "woman's era"? Why would some white middle-class women believe that they could use new "spiritual laws" to transform society and bring about a new era in the history of civilization? Why were they sure that they could heal a world sickened by lust, intemperance, and brute economic competition—"manly" qualities now grown out of control—simply by drawing upon "womanly" qualities of spirituality, self-sacrifice, and love?

The turn-of-the-century debate over "manly" values versus "womanly" ones had extremely broad ramifications. The two sides proposed starkly competing visions of how the nation's personal, political, and economic life ought to be organized. Yet their arguments often hinged on competing definitions of the seemingly abstract terms of "mind," "matter," "spirit," and "desire." These concepts were central to the issue at hand—first, because Victorians believed that they represented the essential components of male and female identity, and second, because Victorians used competing visions of manliness and womanliness to symbolize competing visions of the larger social order.

The terms of the debate were set earlier in the century, when intellectuals, religious leaders, and activists argued over whether "matter" was female, and its opposite the masculine mind, or whether matter was male, and its opposite the feminine spirit. Later in the century, the debate focused more sharply on whether manly "desire" was the fuel of competition and hence progress, or whether it was the poisonous threat to civilization that must be contained by womanly altruism and spirituality. Competing understandings of progress were thus debated in terms of mind, matter, spirit, and desire. They were tied to contrasting ideals of gendered selfhood—that is, contrasting views of what constituted ideal manhood and ideal womanhood.

The debate between manly and womanly values came to a head in the late nineteenth century, when prominent white male theorists drew upon medical, anthropological, and evolutionary discourses to demonstrate "scientifically" the ironclad linkages between male desire, female domesticity, industrial capitalist society, and the development of the Anglo-Saxon race. These theorists argued that competitive manhood and passionless, sheltered womanhood formed the basis of civilization itself. But an articulate group of white female activists quickly inverted these arguments. These women heralded themselves as the epitome of Anglo Saxon racial development, claimed science as a womanly spiritual discourse, promoted cooperation over capitalism, and strategized toward the final eradication of devolutionary male desire.

To understand fully the millennial claims of these late-nineteenth-century middle-class white women, and to understand why they interpreted what would soon be called "New Thought" meditation and healing as both a religious and a scientific sign of the coming woman's era, we must first survey the century-long struggle over the constitution and respective value of white middle-class male and female selfhood or subjectivity. Arguments about the nature and gender of mind, matter, spirit, will, science, and desire were in many ways a coded debate about the larger issue of whether middle-class white women should have expanded opportunities, or whether their activities should be limited to the physical reproduction of the middle class. It was a debate in which New Thought healers, whose meditations explicitly reworked their patients' understanding of mind, matter, spirit, and desire, were well qualified to intervene.

GENDERED HIERARCHIES OF MIND, MATTER, AND SPIRIT, 1820–1870

Middle-class white men of the antebellum North claimed to embody rationality, will power, and self-control. Political theorists had justified the gradual extension of suffrage to broader groups of white male citizens by arguing that since all had an inherent capacity to reason, all should be given both an equal opportunity to develop this reason and an equal say in political decision-making. At the same time, however, middle-class white men justified their social dominance by claiming that those excluded from power simply did not share the basic prerequisite for political independence—that is, a rational nature. Nineteenth-century doctors and scientists "discovered" that African Americans, American Indians, women of any race, and sometimes even the working class as a whole were biologically incapable of the abstract, rational thought that characterized the white middle-class male.[13]

If white middle-class men identified themselves with the rational mind, they increasingly linked women to emotions and the body. Nineteenth-century physicians made women's reproductive systems the explanatory center of women's existence. Statements such as "[i]t is only because of the ovary that woman is what she is" (from 1844) and "the Almighty, in creating the female sex," has "taken the uterus and built up a woman around it" (from 1877) typified the nineteenth-century medical view.[14] These theories of women's subordination to their reproductive functions nicely matched the long-standing Christian association of men with mind and reason and of women with the dangerous body.

Nineteenth-century medical theories were one strand of a complex of ideas that linked religious, economic, and political norms to an ideal of health and character that only white men were deemed capable of achieving. Regular medical theories were predicated upon a belief in the power of manly will and human intervention to control the body. This belief in will over matter aligned mainstream medicine with evangelical Christianity. Medical doctors insisted that although people physically suffered from the sins of their parents, this bodily inheritance could be overcome through will power under the guidance of doctors. Evangelical Christianity held that although all inherited a sinful nature, this flaw could be overcome through iron-willed struggle under the guidance of ministers.[15]

Doctors' emphasis on the role of the will in taming an unruly body intersected with and promoted the specific economic ideologies that were also supported by evangelical Christianity. The Christian desire for salvation impelled believers both to work incessantly (to demonstrate their devotion to God's will) and to abstain from enjoying the fruits of one's labors (since excessive pleasure was sinful). This perspective meshed with the laissez-faire view that any man could succeed as long as he was assertive and frugal rather than weak-willed and profligate. The closed-energy interpretation of human physiology encouraged a similar willed asceticism: like economic advancement or religious salvation, physical health was dependent upon mastering the body's wasteful impulses. Weakness, illness, madness, or even death would result if one allowed one's body to "spend" its vital energies on debilitating sensual pleasures.[16]

Willful self-control was also central to republicanism, one of the chief strains in antebellum political ideology. According to this ideology, the government of a republic was distinguished by its unique devotion to the public good. Such a government was dependent upon the morality of its citizens; they must be virtuous and concerned with the welfare of the whole. The virtue of the republic's male citizens was ensured by their economic independence, since men who were independent would not be easily corrupted. This is where male will came into play. Only the man whose will was powerful enough to control his disruptive desires could achieve the economic independence that was the cornerstone of political virtue.[17]

The links between physiology, religion, politics, and economy were particularly explicit in medical understandings of male sexuality. Ministers regarded excessive sexuality as sinful, while republican thinkers viewed it as a symbol of political corruption. Medical understanding of sexuality linked its abuse to moral and economic as well as physical ruin. The nineteenth-century slang for orgasm was "spending," and semen was identified with the "vital force" men needed to conserve if they were to have the necessary drive to compete socially and economically. The dreaded male diseases of the century were masturbation and "spermatorrhea," or nocturnal emissions—that is, the voluntary or involuntary loss of semen. These diseases were dreaded because they demonstrated "moral bankruptcy." They epitomized the power of body over mind, and so represented a dangerous reversal of the rule of mind over body upon which economic, political, and moral order depended.[18]

The healthy, moral, civic-minded, and financially stable individual—that is, the person of character—was depicted as controlled yet strong-willed and aggressive. That this paradigm of health excluded middle-class women by definition becomes clear when one contrasts medical ideas about menstruation with those about semen. Mainstream physicians viewed menstruation as an illness; adult women were therefore unhealthy by nature. They believed that obstructed or irregular menstruation, broadly defined, caused all illnesses suffered by women. Doctors argued that mental or emotional exertion was dangerous for women because it diverted blood from their reproductive region and so created a hysterical mind and a barren body. While male health depended upon will-power and self-control (necessary if men were to retain their vital spermatic fluids), women's health required that they dull their minds and remain placid (in order to allow their potentially dangerous menstrual fluids to be regularly released).[19]

The passive and retiring behavior deemed essential to middle-class women's health clearly disqualified them from active participation in the competitive economic world. There was nevertheless a fit between the behavior enjoined upon white women by doctors (and by ministers) and the actual economic contributions of middle-class women. Women's physiology demanded that women react to the needs of others rather than initiate activity. The woman who selflessly devoted herself to providing food, clothing, shelter, and education to her brother, husband, and son provided her family with critical though invisible economic support. Her unpaid and hidden labor gave the men who benefited from it the illusion of being "self-made" and made them feel more in control of their destiny.[20]

There was an incipient gender conflict built into this system, however.

Home production declined steadily, so that by mid-century middle-class women's economic role revolved more around the purchase of goods than it did around the production of them. Women were expected to be ignorant of economics, yet they were given the task of "spending"—the very trait men so feverishly battled, both economically and physiologically, within themselves. Some feared that unworldly wives would spend hard-working men into financial bankruptcy.[21]

The medical image of woman as little more than a placid, reproducing animal is contradicted by the popular image of the nineteenth-century woman as moral guardian. This contradiction is lessened by the fact that it was not all women, but only white women of the middle class, who were depicted as angels in the home. White middle-class women were members of the dominant social class, and their attributes symbolized not only the difference between all men and all women, but also the difference between men and women of the middle class and all others.[22]

White middle-class women were therefore understood as the opposites of working-class women and non-white women. If working-class and non-white women were animalistic, strong, and active, then white middle-class women were passionless, weak, and passive. White middle-class women could be both ruled by their uteruses and without sexual passion because their reproductive organs were believed to perform maternal rather than sexual functions. Any lingering fears that women's passions might exist were assuaged by the belief that women were naturally self-denying, and would therefore readily sacrifice the very longing for pleasure that men claimed did not exist in women.[23]

The idea that white middle-class women, like all women, were more animal than spiritual was supported by the fact that their adult lives often centered around childbearing, child-rearing, and the daily care of their families' bodies—all labors uncomfortably close to the animal side of existence. White middle-class women transformed the cultural significance of these labors, however. They presented their maternal role not as animalistic reproduction but as the epitome of spiritual, selfless service to others. Drawing on the Christian association of superior morality with self-sacrifice, they claimed their maternal self-sacrifice to be evidence of a superior spirituality, and thus an ambiguous model of power. As author Catharine Beecher explained, only the morally superior should have public power. The highest proof of morality was self-sacrifice. Self-sacrificing women were therefore the paradigms of morality, and should have public power. This argument, which drew upon the prevailing norms of its time, proved enduring. Middle-class women used the idea that their maternal natures were indicative of a superior, self-sacrificing spirituality to justify their engagement in religious, philanthropic, and reform activities before the Civil War.[24]

Middle-class women's claims to be moral, spiritual, and self-sacrificing also provided them with an important though indirect political role. They were to encourage the moral virtue upon which republican government depended. Though the virtue of male citizens was grounded in their economic independence, it could be further enhanced by the spiritual influence of their mothers and wives. In a young democratic culture obsessed with "self-government" and in which selfishness and sin were seen as equivalent terms, women were enjoined to impart to their sons and husbands the selflessness that would make them good citizens. Some of the earliest calls for advanced education for women were based upon the claim that in order to impart moral and political virtues to their children, women needed first to be trained in those virtues themselves.[25]

Middle-class women's claims to power based upon self-sacrifice and spiritual superiority were inherently problematic, however. They did not challenge the idea that women were naturally passive. Women were not, therefore, supposed to actively inculcate moral values through lessons or arguments. Instead, the mother was to "influence" her children by strictly controlling her own behavior. The mother was to be, not merely to speak about, the moral, peaceful, selfless person she wished her child to become. She could do this only by harshly suppressing any hint of "selfishness" in herself.[26]

Middle-class women's claims to spiritual power also reenforced the ultimately debilitating association of women with the "feminine heart." For nineteenth-century Americans, the heart symbolized love and self-sacrificing concern for others, and was gendered female.[27] A faith in the existence of the feminine heart within man played a critical role in the American ideology of competitive individualism. It allowed man to compete freely, since his worst excesses would be checked by both the feminine without (the influence of virtuous mothers and wives) and the feminine within (man's own gentle heart). Competitive individualism and sentimental selfhood were two sides of a coin.

The ideology of sentimental selfhood defined man as a whole, containing both an active, aggressive "outside" and a moral, intuitive "inside." It defined woman, however, as a half, though supposedly the "better half," since she contained only the internal virtues of intuition and morality, lacking the external virtues of endurance and drive. Claims that middle-class women embodied spirituality and intuition, therefore, crippled women (since a purely spiritual and intuitive person could not act independently), while they enabled men (who could pursue their dreams unimpeded, since any behavioral excesses were checked by their "feminine heart" within).[28]

Middle-class women's claims to an empowering spiritual nature also failed to challenge their exclusion from mainstream paradigms of health. Indeed, in some ways their claims to spiritual power only aggravated their situation. Because the spiritual was defined as the opposite of the physical, "spiritual" women went to great lengths to downplay their physicality. Their efforts to demonstrate their lack of physicality were encouraged by the dictates of both medicine and fashion. The results, however, only made their bodies more problematic. For example, nineteenth-century white women were expected to be delicate, with narrow ribs and tiny waists, to emphasize both their differences from men and their ethereal nature. Women wore corsets both to achieve a fashionable waist size and because of doctors' insistence that women's muscles were so delicate that a corset was needed to hold them in place. Extreme tight-lacing of corsets contributed to the fainting spells, headaches, and uterine disorders believed to be widespread among nineteenth-century white women. Contradictory medical claims about women's simultaneously animal and ethereal nature might have caused the damage that doctors were then called upon to alleviate.[29]

Medical doctors reinterpreted women's claims to a superior spirituality as proof of their subordination to their unstable, reproduction-oriented physicality. As one British doctor explained, "If the corporeal agency is thus powerful in man, its tyrannical influence will more frequently cause the misery of the gentler sex. *Woman, with her exalted spiritualism, is more forcibly under the control of matter. . . .* She is less under the influence of the brain than the uterine system . . . [I]n her, a hysteric predisposition is incessantly predominating from the dawn of puberty."[30]

In sum, mainstream Victorian thought viewed the relationship between mind and matter, or matter and spirit, as both gendered and adversarial. Middle-class men were to use their minds or will to control matter (or their bodies), their spending, and their women. Such efforts simultaneously brought them moral, physical, political, and economic benefits. In response, middle-class women asserted that their selflessness and passivity were evidence of their moral and spiritual superiority. They used such claims to distance themselves from matter (or their bodies). Yet women's power of spirit was at the expense of the strength of their bodies, and did not fully break their association with matter, nature, and spending—that is, with all that a man of character must repress.

EVOLUTIONARY THEORIES
AND ANGLO-SAXON DESIRE, 1870–1910

Older paradigms that based white middle-class male identity on will, independence, and the repression of desire were shaken by the economic and cultural changes of the post-Civil War years. In a society of increasing economic complexity, white men found that hard work and self-discipline bore little relation to economic success. Small-town manufacturers were relentlessly overtaken by corporate-run industries. As independent businesses failed in record numbers, white middle-class men found work as clerks or managers for large corporations. Mid-century ideals favored the independent male producer as the foundation of the republic. But what exactly did the corporate "brain worker" produce?[31]

Even the abundance brought about by the new industrial order posed threats to older ideals of middle-class manhood. A "manly" man practiced self-denial and kept his desires rigorously directed toward production. But as the fate of businesses began to lie as much in their ability to market their goods as it did in their ability to produce them, consumption was encouraged by advertisers, who increased their volume ten-fold between 1870 and 1900. Advertisers went beyond the sober description of a product's features and attempted instead to incite in consumers a generalized, omnivorous desire.[32] Did this imply that desires should be not denied, but, rather, expressed? Could it mean that economically, the consuming woman was more important than the producing man?[33]

The mushrooming growth of cities was another source of concern. Mainstream Victorian culture insisted that the "low" aspects of life, including sexuality, irrationality, passions, and even materiality, must be rigidly controlled. The goal was to achieve a world in which middle-class understandings of morality reigned supreme. But as cities filled with immigrants whose patterns of work, leisure, and sexuality sharply differed from those of middle-class white Protestants, some of the latter felt that this goal was threatened. They feared that the newcomers were creating an urban world of sensuality and vice that they, the high-minded portion of the population, could not control.[34]

A final challenge to the self-image of white middle-class men came from a more intimate source—namely, white middle-class women. Beginning in the 1870s these women competed with white men in higher education, asserted themselves in movements for social reform, and attempted to eradicate saloons, brothels, and other arenas of male pleasure. With the emergence of female typists, even business was no longer an exclusively male domain. White men could not always identify the economic forces that were undercutting their self-image as disciplined producers. They could, however, see that white women were infringing upon their turf. In response to women's unwelcome presence, some professional white men began to mobilize the arsenal of elite scientific discourse against them.[35]

The first attacks came, not surprisingly, from the medical profession. In 1873 Dr. Edward H. Clarke published a study entitled *Sex in Education.* Clarke revived the old claim that the development of women's minds would damage the health of their reproductive organs. Higher education would produce women with "monstrous brains and puny bodies," he insisted. His arguments were taken seriously and sparked a thirty-year debate over the question "does higher education unfit women for motherhood?"[36]

Clarke insisted that his findings were supported by science, which was the true and impartial arbiter of social questions. The "problem of woman's sphere . . . is not to be solved by applying to it abstract principles of right and wrong. Its solution must be obtained from physiology, not from ethics or metaphysics," Clarke explained. British physician Henry Maudsley agreed that the claims of science superseded those of morality. Women's exclusion from higher education was "a matter of physiology, not a matter of sentiment," he seconded.[37]

Further scientific support for women's domesticity came from the new evolutionary theories of Charles Darwin and Herbert Spencer. At the heart of both men's theories were the ideas of Jean Lamarck (1744–1829), who believed that acquired traits could be inherited. Building upon this theory, Darwin and Spencer concurrently developed the thesis that over the past millennia, the physical forms and mental capabilities of human beings had changed in response to the actions of individuals engaged in a "struggle for existence." Those individuals who developed superior physical skills, mental abilities, or social institutions were most successful in this struggle. The accomplishments of superlative individuals were passed on to their descendants through the inheritance of acquired traits and thereby eventually altered the basic form and capability of human groups.[38]

Evolutionary theories challenged biblical accounts of creation and the Christian belief that nature progressed by an orderly divine plan. The theories nonetheless became immensely popular, at least partially because of the ease with which mainstream ideals could be recast in evolutionary language and so given a scientific grounding. Evolutionary science proved particularly useful in shoring up hierarchies of race and gender, which had been challenged by the abolition of slavery in the South and by the movement of white women into the wage labor force in the North.

Evolutionary science was quickly integrated with anthropological theory in order to support mainstream ideals of public manhood and private womanhood. Victorian anthropologists speculated that the earliest human societies had been characterized by sexual promiscuity, communal land ownership, and matriarchal family organization. Gradually both private property and a patriarchal family structure had emerged. The two grew in tandem because men would strive to accumulate goods or land only if they knew they could leave their possessions to their offspring. To leave private property to a descendant, the heir must be known; and heirs can be identified with absolute certainty only if men have monogamous, faithful wives. Women's faithfulness could be best ensured by their sheltered maintenance in the private home. Strict monogamy and separate spheres for men and women were therefore essential for private property to exist, and developed in tandem with it.[39]

This anthropological scenario depicted male desire—for money, offspring, fame, or success—as the driving force behind progress and civilization. The primary value of the domestic woman lay in her ability to motivate productive male desire. Yet women's own morality was seen as contingent rather than innate. Since women's virtue depended upon their domestic isolation, any movement of women into the public sphere would destroy the sheltering conditions that ensured their morality. Women would become competitive and worldly, like men, and thus no sphere of life would remain to both tame and reward male aggression.[40] Furthermore, these theories implied that the sexuality of the publicly active woman would be less regulated. Legitimacy would be less certain. Men's motives for personal striving, consequently, would decline. The public activity of women would leave men unmotivated and the world in chaos.

Herbert Spencer synthesized these Victorian anthropological theories into a biologically based evolutionary framework. He explained that not only had patriarchal family organization evolved historically, it was sanctioned by the law of natural selection. According to Spencer, children raised in patriarchal families were better guarded and therefore healthier. These children passed on their superior strength, as well as a tendency to form stable monogamous couples, to their own children via the inheritance of acquired characteristics. The sons of protective fathers also grew to become superior warriors. Societies who followed monogamous patriarchal family forms necessarily triumphed, therefore, over societies with "lower domestic arrangements." The mind and body of the sheltered woman increasingly differed from that of her bread-winning husband. The divergence between the active, public man and the passive, domestic woman was not merely one of the crowning features of advanced civilization, Spencer argued—it was also bred into the very minds and bodies of "the race," via evolutionary processes of natural selection.[41]

GENDER AMBIGUITIES IN THEORIES
OF ANGLO-SAXON SUPERIORITY

By the 1880s many middle-class white Americans identified the "Anglo-Saxon" tribes of early medieval Germany and Great Britain as the superior, patriarchal groups lauded by evolutionary theorists and anthropologists. With the doctrine of Anglo-Saxon predominance, evolutionary theories displayed their fullest ideological usefulness as a weapon of white male supremacy. At the same time, theories of Anglo-Saxon dominance revealed ambiguities within definitions of late-nineteenth-century white manhood. Middle-class white women would exploit these ambiguities in order to legitimize their claim that "woman," and not "the white man," exemplified the highest qualities of the Anglo-Saxon race. It is therefore important to examine the idea of Anglo-Saxon dominance in some detail.

Theories of Anglo-Saxon superiority originated as theories of Anglo-Saxon altruism. They were often promoted by white men who opposed the ways that survival-of-the-fittest doctrines were being used to overshadow Christian morality and sanction the power of robber barons. The linkage of altruism to "advanced" racial characteristics can be seen in the work of pioneering sociologist Lester Frank Ward. Ward was among the first to challenge social Darwinist views with a reform Darwinist perspective. He argued that theorists who applied the amoral, competitive laws of nature to society were overlooking "the true value of the *psychic factor*" or the power of "mind." Human beings used their mental powers to consciously shape their environment. They created abundance and progress by extending their protective care to agriculture and livestock. More important, humanity developed the desire to selflessly protect the weak, or the sentiment of altruism. If "nature progresses through the destruction of the weak, man progresses through the *protection* of the weak," Ward argued. Others seconded Ward's view. Men like T. H. Huxley and Henry Drummond countered Spencer's lauding of the "survival of the fittest" with their own call for the nobler "struggle for the life of others."[42]

Ward only hinted that altruism, the true motor of social advance, was the defining feature of Anglo-Saxon populations. "The sentiment [of altruism] is of recent origin, the product only of highly developed and greatly refined mental organisation," Ward explained. "It exists to an appreciable degree only in a minute fraction of the most enlightened populations." But others were quick to identify Anglo-Saxons as these "most enlightened populations." Social theorist John Fiske, for example, was initially disturbed by evolutionary theory because it seemed to contradict Christian teachings of selflessness. He eventually embraced Darwin after concluding that the most successful tribes in the "struggle for existence"—the Anglo-Saxons—were those whose members were most willing to subordinate their selfish desires to the needs of the group.[43]

This lauding of Anglo-Saxon altruism served as an effective counter to those who used Darwin to attack Christian ethics and laud the virtues of an unregulated economy. It meshed well with Victorian associations of manhood with high-minded rationality. On the other hand, altruism—an emotion of the feminine heart—had long been identified with white middle-class women. As Spencer declared, "civilized" women were characterized by altruism, while men of all races were characterized by egotism.[44] If altruism was the crowning feature of Anglo-Saxons, then woman would be closer to the racial ideal than man—an unsettling proposition in these days of crusading womanhood.

Perhaps this explains why some white male theorists began to argue that Anglo-Saxons were superior because of their selfless altruism *and* their competitive ruthlessness. John Fiske was again a pioneer of this sort of argument. Echoing Spencer, Fiske explained that because of their selflessness, Anglo-Saxon tribes thrived. Stronger and healthier, they were able to conquer other tribes militarily. Warlike but altruistic Anglo-Saxons then continued to advance, eventually developing higher intellect, self-government, self-control, and money-making power. According to Fiske, nineteenth-century Anglo-Saxons constituted the pinnacle of human racial development. They were destined to spread their superior political and economic system throughout the world—it was an act of altruism, not conquest. If in the short run Anglo-Saxon colonization brought warfare, disease, and death, in the long run it would surely bring peace, self-government, civilization, and true, spiritual Christianity.[45]

This was the mature theory of Anglo-Saxon predominance. It cast Anglo-Saxon men as superior because of their unique embodiment of opposites. As Congregational minister Josiah Strong asserted in his 1885 bestseller *Our Country*, Anglo-Saxons exemplified both "pure, spiritual Christianity" and "money-making power," both "civil liberty" and "an instinct or genius for colonizing."[46] These oddly mixed claims gave the discourse of Anglo-Saxon superiority great ideological flexibility. When African Americans and immigrants claimed rights to political participation, Anglo-Saxon men could argue that only men of Anglo-Saxon descent had the inherited capacity for democratic government. When white women claimed that they, even more than white men, exemplified the civilized traits of altruism, then the ruthlessness and competitive power that only white men had inherited from their warlike ancestors could be invoked. When social-purity leaders asserted that lowly instinct must be eradicated, devotees of Anglo-Saxon predominance claimed that primitive male instinct and high-minded male leadership of culture had evolved together and could not be sundered. Indeed, this version of Anglo-Saxon superiority emphasized that the "manliness" of the Anglo-Saxon was the basis of "the race's" power. This stress on manliness was reflected in the tendency, common by the 1890s, to use the term "the white man" as a synonym for civilization itself.[47]

White male theorists began to elaborate a new psychological paradigm to explain the mixture of ruthlessness and altruism that characterized the Anglo-Saxon male. Pioneering psychologist G. Stanley Hall had been raised to believe that all "lower" impulses were debilitating threats to manly character that must be rigidly repressed. By the 1890s, however, Hall theorized a more benign relationship between men's lower and higher impulses. He argued that savage impulses were the basis of the vitality that characterized Anglo-Saxon manhood. According to Hall, all men had savage and competitive tendencies. Men of "primitive" races did not have the ability to control or channel these energies to higher ends, while women of all races had no passion to channel. Only "the white man" had both primitive drives and the ability to transmute these lower tendencies into competitive energy or toward moral, altruistic, or intellectual ends.[48]

This was an entirely new interpretation of the interactions between mind and matter. Although earlier Victorians had valued male competitive impulses as important motors for economic productivity, they were also aware of these impulses' disruptive potential. Personal happiness and social progress could only be attained, they believed, if these male traits were tamed, either by the moralizing presence of mothers and wives or through the influence of men's own inner, womanly heart. The repression of low or savage emotions was central to the Victorian goal of rigidly separating the lower and higher aspects of life. Indeed, through much of the nineteenth century middle-class white men had used the characteristics they claimed to be typical of primitive races to define what they were not. Nonwhite peoples, they claimed, were childish, savage, emotional, irrational, and unrestrained. White men were mature, civilized, rational, intellectual, and self-controlled.[49]

According to Hall, however, the fruits of civilization—not only wealth, but republican forms of government and patriarchal norms of morality—were the product of savage male energy that was channeled by male will rather than repressed by female influence. This trumpeting of white men's "savage" inner desire undercut the role of white women as civilizers. Men no longer needed their mothers and wives to uplift them. On the contrary, beginning in the 1880s many white middle-class men became eager to prove that they still embodied the primitive daring that had enabled their ancestors to win primordial battles between the races. If middle-class men no longer embodied the virtues of economic independence, perhaps the republic's strength could be grounded in male virility. Increasing numbers of white middle-class men became enthusiasts of athletics, camping, hunting, and body-building. They joined fraternal orders and established organizations like the Boy Scouts to ensure the hardiness of their sons.[50]

These men's open embrace of their "savage" impulses challenged a Victorian worldview based on the rigid exclusion of all low behaviors. It constituted a "revolt against dualism." Instead of seeing manliness as high-minded and self-controlled, proponents of the new masculinity claimed that men could be, and ideally ought to be, both civilized and savage.

Some white middle-class men were not ready to jettison earlier ideals of manhood in favor of these radical new definitions. They continued to view primitive emotion as a threat to their identity as decent, controlled, altruistic Anglo-Saxon men. Discussions of intrinsic male savagery did not fill them with pride. Instead, it led them to consider more seriously whether the best symbol of Anglo-Saxon superiority might be the altruistic, passionless Anglo-Saxon woman.

THE ERA OF WOMAN

Many late-nineteenth-century middle-class white women involved in temperance, social purity, moral education, women's suffrage, and women's clubs were staunchly Victorian in their outlook. They did not challenge the idea that civilization required the triumph of the higher over the lower orders, or that civilization was a racial trait of white or Anglo-Saxon nations.[51] Instead, they modified evolutionary understandings of the relationship between male competitive desire, female purity, capitalist economic organization, and republican forms of government. They argued that pure, selfless women rather than aggressive, desirous men were the best hope for civilization, the republic, and the (Anglo-Saxon) "race."

Supporters of the woman movement denied that the true state of nature was Darwinian competition. Some insisted that the universe followed a "moral order [resting] upon Love." Love had long been allied with the "womanly heart"; clearly, therefore, women's values and not men's were the basis of the cosmic order. Others linked this faith in "Love" to Ward's claim that it was altruism, not competition, that was the motor of evolutionary advance. Since women were naturally altruistic, the spread of womanly traits would dramatically accelerate the development of civilization. As Charlotte Perkins Gilman explained, the "masculine characteristics" of "desire, combat, and self-expression" now threatened the race's development. The future of civilization rested upon "service," a characteristic that self-sacrificing mothers, not aggressive husbands, best exemplified. "To serve each other more and more widely; [and] to live only by such service . . . —this is civilization, our human glory and race-distinction," Gilman wrote.[52]

Some male evolutionary theorists argued that women could not lead in culture because they lacked passion or desire. Many woman movement supporters agreed that the development of women's intellect came at the expense of their passion. They viewed this as positive, however, since they believed that passions were destructive to civilization. As *Popular Science Monthly* editor William Jay Youmans explained, (refined white) women's "intellectual and moral influences" would soon modify the "primitive attraction" between men and women. This was why women's increasing power and a flowering of civilization went together. "[O]nce woman becomes an individual in the truest and highest sense, civilization will have reached the threshold of its most glorious period," he wrote.[53]

The image of the Anglo-Saxon man whose intellect was fueled by his inner savagery was challenged by woman movement leaders with a vision of the Anglo-Saxon woman whose advanced intellect was linked to her loving heart. This was the meaning behind their frequent lauding of one another as women of "head and heart."[54] Woman-movement leaders repeatedly stated that womanly moral ideals and womanly intellect were inseparable. As women's suffrage activist and moral education reformer Lucinda B. Chandler explained in 1902, "[t]he last half-century has developed the thinking woman—the woman learning self-dependence and cherishing the higher ideals of womanhood, of motherhood, and of life." The "thinking woman" differed from the rational man because her "mental force" was inextricably connected to her "heart force"—understood not as irrational emotion, but as high-minded love and spiritual morality. This was the reason, Therese A. Jenkins argued in an article entitled "The Mental Force of Woman," that women's suffrage would inevitably "raise politics out of its filthiness, corruption, and ignorance, and . . . bring in the reign of purity, patriotism and intelligence."[55]

Evolutionary theorists who opposed the woman movement insisted that female mental development would weaken women's bodies and lead to "race suicide." Intellectual women were shortsighted and selfish.[56] Woman-movement leaders countered that male selfishness, not female mental development, was the true threat to the race. Male lustful desire was responsible for racial devolution, the social-purity version of race suicide. Men who impregnated their wives against their will or, even worse, who made sexual demands while their wives were pregnant produced offspring who were sickly and doomed to inherit the sensual passions of their fathers, they argued.[57]

Pro- and anti-women's-suffrage leaders agreed that women's contribution to the race lay not in their biological reproductive function, but in the maternal *values* that all refined women embodied, regardless of their reproductive status. As one anti-women's-suffrage author wrote in 1897, "To fulfill the law of womanhood, one need not be a mother, but only to be motherly; one need not be a wife, but only to be loyal to the unselfish principle of wifehood." As Chandler more forcefully put it: "*Motherhood is not breeding and feeding, but the soul-energizing of the race*"; women's main contribution should be spiritual, not biological. These women denied that women who abstained from marriage or motherhood were sabotaging the race. On the contrary, such women were the (white) race's highest expression. As women's club leader and antisuffragist activist Kate Gannett Wells enthused, "Oh, the serene, self-poised, erect, free, brilliant, wise, unmarried society girls, whose very evolution has made them handsome!"[58]

According to the most recent evolutionary and anthropological findings, male sexual desire was a deeply ingrained aspect of male nature. But many woman-movement and social-purity leaders believed that male lust was destroying "the race." Therefore male nature would have to change, to become more like the desireless nature of pure, civilized woman. Indeed, the idea that male nature was learned behavior that could and ought to be changed was the underlying presupposition of moral education societies, mother's congresses, the kindergarten movement, and the social-purity movement as a whole.[59]

By calling upon men to become more like women, woman-movement leaders challenged the Spencerian view that advanced civilization was marked by increasing divergence between the sexes. They boldly claimed that in true civilization, man and woman would come to resemble one another. Just as women who developed their intellects and entered the public sphere were becoming more "manly," so ought men to develop within themselves the higher elements of "womanly" morality. As Elizabeth Boynton Harbert explained, "The two most important masculine virtues are courage and knowledge. Humanity will not be perfected either in individual character or social destiny by the greater separate development of these in the sexes, but only in their balanced diffusion in both, making woman wise and courageous, and man tender and pure." Women's Club leader Winnifred Harper Cooley agreed. "If there is a differentiation in the masculine and feminine intellect, then surely man needs the chastening sweetness of the feminine and woman the stimulating strength of the masculine," she wrote.[60]

White woman-movement leaders' challenge to male proponents of Anglo-Saxon dominance can be seen in their attempt to identify whiteness with pure womanhood, not with competitive manhood (see figure 2). While some white male intellectuals defined "the White Man" as the exemplar of both instinctual savagery and high-minded will-power, social-purity activists used the word "white" as a synonym for sexual purity. They called upon men to proclaim their purity by wearing white ribbons; the slogan of the "White Ribboners" was "The White Life for Two."[61] More generally, social-purity and woman-movement leaders often used the word "white" as a synonym for the eternal truths of love, mental purity, and spiritual power that they claimed were the foundations of civilization—and that (Anglo-Saxon) woman naturally possessed. For example, Mary Lowe Dickinson, the president of the National Council of Women, found the perfect metaphor for womanly "spiritual influences" in the famed White City of the 1893 World's Fair. She wrote,

> We women have it in our power to make a white city, whose foundations shall be laid, deep down in women's and children's hearts, of the everlasting principles of truth and justice. . . .
>   The stones of its buildings will be the white thoughts of white-hearted women. . . . If we are . . . true enough to keep our work white and clean from all touch of ignoble things, we may have by and by . . . a structure of character and life and glorious work, of which that White City was but an evanescent prophecy and dream.[62]

If (refined or Anglo-Saxon) women were innately spiritual and pure, then the enfranchisement of women would surely inaugurate a new era in the history of civilization. As Matilda Joslyn Gage wrote in 1881, "The male element has thus far held high carnival, crushing out all the divine elements of human nature. . . . The present disorganization of society

Figure 2. White woman as the highest expression of the Caucasian race.

warns us that in the disenfranchisement of woman we have let loose the reins of violence and ruin which she only has the power to avert. . . . All writers recognize women as the great harmonizing elements of the 'new era.'"[63] Benjamin Flower, editor of the reform journal *The Arena*, identified this new age as the "era of woman." "The era of woman has dawned," Flower proclaimed in 1891, "bearing the unmistakable prophecy of a far higher civilization than humanity has ever known." Indeed, discussions of the coming woman's era were so omnipresent as to be dismissed as commonplace. "It has become almost a cant phrase to call this the woman's age," one woman wrote in 1893.[64]

Woman-movement leaders had varying conceptions of what a world dominated by "womanly" values would look like. Many predicted that the coming woman's era would be marked by the final eradication of disruptive animal desire. As one speaker at the 1873 Woman's Congress explained, "We are living in that dread time when the beast and the angel within the human have closed in deadly conflict, each contesting for Sovereignty. . . .

We have so long known the moral history of human life to be one imperfect, yet ever constant endeavor to eliminate the animal from our instincts and passions, that we never dreamed of the dread grandeur and fearful tenacity of its death struggle."[65]

Other reformers, such as Frances Willard and Lucinda Chandler, followed mainstream theorists and linked male desire to private property, individualism, and laissez-faire capitalism. They therefore associated a world in which desireless womanhood was the norm of human character with an economic reorganization based on "mutualism" and "collectivism." They hoped to replace patriarchal society, in which lone men battled each other and dominated their families, with a social paradigm based upon the matriarchal family. They believed that once mother love became the organizing principle of the age, a rational organization of resources based on altruism and generosity, rather than on individualism and achievement, would take care of material necessity. Ultimately desire would be stilled altogether. This liberating end of competitive desire would result from both an increase in the supply of love (drawn from the bountiful goodness of the mother heart) and a decrease in the demand for gratification (an outgrowth of the stilling of desire—which motivates competition and aggression—under the tutelage of the powerful mother's eye). In sum, while patriarchy and the free reign of male desire led to an economy based on waste, scarcity, and demand, matriarchy and the curbing of male desire would lead to an economy based on altruism, satiety, and supply.[66]

These broader implications of the triumph of "woman" help explain why the Knights of Labor, the Farmers' Alliance, and Bellamyite Nationalists not only encouraged women's participation in their ranks, but also supported temperance, women's suffrage, and social purity. These alliances were possible because by the last quarter of the nineteenth century reformers of all sorts began to understand the social chaos around them in heavily gendered terms. The Knights of Labor, the Grange, the Alliance and Populist movements, the Single-Taxers, and the Bellamyite Nationalists all hoped to implement politically the ideals of cooperation rather than conflict, harmonious sharing rather than cutthroat competition, and rational planning rather than unimpeded personal greed.[67] As some woman movement leaders saw it, these were the values of refined womanhood, not of lustful manhood. If enacted, these ideals would bring about a new age of justice, peace, and harmony. As one woman proclaimed in a toast before the Illinois Woman's Press Club in 1891,

> "Pealing! the clock of Time has struck the woman's hour,
> We hear it on our knees."

All crimes shall cease, and ancient wrongs shall fail;
Justice returning lifts aloft her scales,
Peace o'er the world her olive wands extends,
And white-robed Innocence from Heaven descends.[68]

SCIENCE AND THE ERA OF WOMAN

Male scientists often opposed women's rights arguments based on "abstract principles of right and wrong" by drawing upon the amoral but unchallengeable laws of nature. In response, woman-movement supporters redefined the meaning of science itself. They claimed that science rested not upon the brute law of nature, but upon the higher law of spiritual morality. As Elizabeth Boynton Harbert explained, "all true spiritual processes are always scientific, while all true science rests upon a spiritual basis." Journalist Helen Campbell seconded this opinion. "[E]ach step of modern science . . . proves to us . . . that there is but one world and that the spiritual one," she wrote.[69]

Woman-movement leaders then claimed that just as immaterial and lawful science had proved its superiority over mindless matter or nature, so would moral and nonpartisan women triumph over the tradition-bound, brutish reign of men. Abby Morton Diaz, longtime president of the Women's Educational and Industrial Union, explained that science was the triumph of the immaterial over the material. "[S]olid implements, water and wind, steam, electricity; with each advance less of solidity, and increase of power," she wrote. Lucinda Chandler linked this triumph of the immaterial over the material, or the mental over the physical, to the triumph of woman. "[T]he evolution of brains . . . has unsettled [the traditional] standard of civilization and the relations of the sexes," she wrote. "The woman movement is demonstration of the power of thought beyond the power of muscle; it is evidence that the intangible forces of mind are superior to the external material powers of muscle, and sword, and bullet." Frances Willard agreed. To her, the proof that now is indeed "woman's century" is that the "value of physical force has been reduced to its lowest terms."[70]

These woman-movement leaders associated the new "social" science even more closely with the power of woman. They were not the only ones to do so. An identification of social science with moral principles that "woman" best represented permeated the work of Auguste Comte, the French Positivist and "father of modern sociology." Comte insisted that a new era would dawn when the principles of science, elucidated by a "scientific priesthood," were made the basis of society. True science was inherently moral and social. Therefore moral and emotional women, rather than

rational and aggressive men, were "the best representatives of the fundamental principle on which Positivism rests, the victory of the social over
selfish affections."[71]

Comte's vision of social science as inherently moral was embraced by
some reform-oriented men. Lester Ward argued that if natural evolutionary
science was brutish and inefficient, then social science, which was human,
was altruistic and moral. Josiah Strong believed that the world was plagued
with "selfishness," but that its problems could be remedied through religious renewal and the methods of science. "The truths of science are God's
truths . . . its laws are God's laws," he wrote. Economist Richard Ely agreed.
He explained that "the function of social science" is "to teach us how to fulfill the Second Commandment."[72]

In short, science was the study of universal laws. Universal laws must
by definition be the same as the laws of morality and Christianity. Since
refined women were the embodiment of spiritual Christianity, they had a
natural affinity with science. This was, of course, a controversial interpretation. For example, although Comte spoke of revering "Woman," he linked
this veneration to the civilizing trends that "render her life more and more
domestic. . . ." Woman could be the spiritual leader in human development,
he implied, as long as she remained barred from the sites of social power;
she inspired science but was not herself a scientist.[73] But activist women
found their own uses for theorists such as Comte. The National Woman's
Suffrage Association journal *Revolution* frequently published passages
from Comte's *Positive Politics,* and the applicability of Comte's theories to
women's rights activism were elaborated in numerous editorials by Elizabeth Cady Stanton. As her typical editorials described,

> We insist . . . that Comte's principles, logically carried out, make women
> the governing power in the world. . . . Comte makes man a personal,
> selfish, concentrating, reasoning force. He makes woman impersonal,
> unselfish, diffusive, intuitive, a moral love power. . . . He says intellect
> and activity, capital and labor, ruler and ruled, can only be harmonized
> through affection, which is the feminine element in woman. . . .
>   In the restoration of the love element, which is woman, capital and la-
> bor will be reconciled, intelligence and activity welded together, forming
> a trinity that shall usher in the golden age.[74]

As early as the 1870s the association of "woman" with social science in
particular was an organizational fact. The American Social Science Association (ASSA) was closely affiliated with the Association for the Advancement of Women, which sent delegates to ASSA meetings throughout the
1870s and early 1880s. The majority of local affiliates of the ASSA, whose

membership far outnumbered that of the parent body, were numerically dominated by woman-movement activists. The ASSA advocated causes dear to the hearts of club women and social-purity leaders, such as the kindergarten system and sexual hygiene. Some male social scientists agreed that women and "social science" were natural allies. Frank Sanborn, the head of the ASSA, described social science as "the feminine gender of Political Economy." He added that the "work of social science is literally woman's work, and it is getting done by them more and more."[75]

Radical women such as Charlotte Perkins Gilman and Elizabeth Cady Stanton believed that science could both justify the importance of "woman" as "a moral love power" and promote convention-defying rational thinking. Science could save women from the arguments of misogynist ministers and the dangers of their own self-sacrificing sentimentalism, they argued. But the rhetoric of womanly selfless "science" as a redeeming power permeated more conservative women's groups as well. The underlying argument of the social-purity movement was that once women gained access to scientific knowledge about child-rearing, education, and heredity, they would create a new humanity and so usher in the millennium.[76] They turned to science for support for their belief that womanly purity, not male competition, was at the heart of (Anglo-Saxon) racial evolution.

The late-nineteenth-century woman movement thus merged the antebellum image of the disembodied woman as moral savior with more recent images of spiritual science as savior. It presented science itself as both feminine and salvific. This appropriation of science enabled woman-movement leaders to argue for expanded political rights without fundamentally challenging older paradigms of womanhood. Arguments for women's rights based on women's maternal nature had previously been countered by the linking of women's maternal nature to animal reproduction, and of their spirituality to irrationality. By defining self-sacrifice and morality as "scientific," however, women activists translated motherhood and spirituality, their traditional sources of both power and oppression, into far less ambiguous symbols of moral progress and rationality.[77]

This strategy was dependent upon white women's assertion that they were pure and desireless. Woman movement participants had much to gain from such claims. Since the combination of "natural" sexuality and "cultural" labor unnerved Victorians, these women were eager to free themselves *to* labor by freeing themselves *from* sexuality.[78] By distancing themselves from desire, they attempted to maintain the dignity of woman's maternal essence while throwing almost every charge made against women back in men's faces. They characterized men, not women, as irrational, un-

Chart 2. Social Darwinist versus Woman Movement
views of gender oppositions.

SOCIAL DARWINIST VIEW
OF GENDER OPPOSITIONS

Masculine	Feminine
willful desire	sensual desire OR passionlessness
freedom	constraint
universal	narrow
individual thought	race-mind
self-denial	self-gratification
demand	supply
producer	consumer
capitalist	primitive
progress	stasis
scientific	emotional

WOMAN MOVEMENT VIEW
OF GENDER OPPOSITIONS

Masculine	Feminine
desiring	without desire
freedom	harmony
competitive individual	cooperative family
egotistical	altruistic
male lust	maternal purity
sensual/material	spiritual
self-gratification	self-denial
demand	supply
capitalist	socialist
changing	unchanging/universal
lawless/material	lawful/scientific

scientific, and possessing an ungovernable sensuality that could destroy "the race" (see chart 2). Furthermore, by linking brutish men's oppression of pure women to selfish capitalists' exploitation of workers, reform-minded women of the 1880s and 1890s made numerous allies in their crusade for women's rights and the elevation of "the race."

On the other hand, white middle-class women activists' commitment to battling desire could easily warp their political analysis. Their alliance with farmers, workers, and Socialists was tenuous because it was based less on a coalition of the economically exploited against exploiters than it was on the opposition of body versus spirit. Many woman movement leaders opposed the excessive selfishness and corporeality of the male elite rather than its disproportionate economic power. Because they cast the problem in symbolic terms, some tended to resolve the problem symbolically as well. If the poor suffered because their labor conditions encouraged animality, their pain could be alleviated as much by encouraging a refined atmosphere in their homes as it could by an increase in wages or political self-determination.[79] Furthermore, like many of their white populist and Socialist allies, white woman-movement leaders rarely questioned the assumption that "Anglo-Saxons" were the pinnacle of evolutionary advance and therefore uniquely qualified to lead the nation. Most did not protest the rising tide of white violence against African Americans, passively or actively agreeing with their white male compatriots that such violence was simply another example of the triumph of the civilized over the primitive.[80]

A political stance based upon the eradication of desire also problematized and essentialized white female selfhood. Only if refined women's selfless purity was innate, rather than merely the result of their domestic isolation, could they leave their sphere and remain pure. This meant a renewed emphasis on purging the "beast within"; women's ability to "cleanse" the world depended upon it. As women's club leader Charlotte Beebe Wilbour explained, "God calls women now to the work of purification, and *if they can sink selfhood,* ideas of personal aggrandizement, and come singly and solely to the work of human redemption, they will be blessed beyond what women have known before."[81]

White women's "selfhood"—their ambitions, desires, and indeed their physicality—was again highly problematized. Since most prominent women were unwilling to go against the grain of Victorian cultural logic and accept the material, they were forced instead to de-materialize themselves. Women therefore aligned themselves, as Lucinda Chandler indicated, with the powers of thought, mind, and the immaterial. They would invoke the one power unanimously granted to them—that of womanly influence. But how could women's ethereal influence have real power in a material world?

HYPNOTISM, NEURASTHENIA, AND THE PROBLEMS OF LATE-VICTORIAN GENDERED SELFHOOD

The very question of how the ethereal could influence the material was at the heart of an academic controversy raging in 1880s France, and reported in medical and popular presses around the world. "The Battle of the Schools" pitted the upstart Hippolyte Bernheim of the University of Nancy against the celebrated Jean-Martin Charcot of the Paris Salpêtrière. The two physicians were arguing over the meaning and uses of a newly discovered force they called hypnotism. Like other great scientific discoveries of the day such as the telegram and the telegraph, hypnotism was an entirely immaterial means of communication. But hypnotism went beyond technology by allowing one mind to communicate directly with another. It was a shocking new discovery in an already dizzyingly miraculous century.

In fact, hypnotism was not as new as the eminent French doctors claimed. It was the offshoot of mesmerism, a healing and cosmological system created by Viennese doctor Franz Anton Mesmer (1734–1815). Mesmer claimed to have discovered an invisible fluid or universal ether, which served as a medium to transmit various forces—heat, light, and magnetism or electricity—passing between and so linking all physical and celestial bodies. Mesmer claimed that the fluid moved between bodies in a manner analogous to the movement of currents between magnetic fields. The fluid responded to opposing poles of attraction or repulsion that all bodies contained, and needed to ebb and flow freely between these poles. Mesmer named this property contained within all bodies "animal magnetism." Animal magnetism quickly became a synonym for "mesmerism," the more common label for Mesmer's system.[82]

The ambiguities that would later plague both hypnotism and closely related Mind Cure or New Thought healing techniques were present in mesmeric healing. Mesmer initiated the practice when he used magnetized water to cure large numbers of Parisians in the 1780s.[83] The meaning of mesmerism was transformed, however, by Mesmer's pupil the Marquis de Puységur. When Puységur made mesmeric "passes" over his patients, they fell into deep trances, becoming "mesmerized." The behavior of these entranced patients seemed to open new meanings and applications for mesmerism. On the one hand, the mesmeric trance caused a state of unconsciousness so deep that surgery could be performed without anesthesia. As trance-subjects were reduced to soulless matter, the mesmerist seemed to epitomize the power of will over body.[84] On the other hand, mesmerized patients exhibited almost supernatural powers. Mesmerized subjects were reported to diagnose illnesses and demonstrate clairvoyance or vision at a distance. They thereby transcended the barriers of the human body and became pure spirit. Their miraculous gifts seemed to imply the power of spirit over both matter and the rational mind.

Despite or perhaps because of these complex implications, mesmerism quickly became the province of traveling showmen and alternative healers. Yet individual French and British physicians continued to experiment with the process. One such was Manchester's Dr. James Braid, who in 1841 decided to investigate mesmeric phenomena in order to expose fraudulent claims. Braid instead discovered that he could easily mesmerize or entrance his subjects by ordering them to stare at a bright object. Braid concluded that the trance state was caused not by "animal magnetism" or an etheric fluid, but by the operator's influence upon the patient's nervous system. Braid named his version of mesmerism "neuro-hypnotism," later simplified to "hypnotism."[85]

Braid wrote articles about his experiments that received only limited acceptance in medical circles. In the 1870s, however, Jean-Martin Charcot began to experiment with hypnotism. Charcot, head of the Paris women's asylum, the Salpêtrière, had already gained international fame as a result of his work with hysterics. When Charcot delivered a lecture in 1882 on the therapeutic potency of hypnosis as a treatment for hysteria, the world was ready to take notice.[86]

Charcot insisted that hypnosis was a condition closely related to hysteria. He deduced that his patients easily fell into a hypnotic trance because of the same general weakness of the nerves that had caused their illness. Hypnosis, however, could alleviate many of their symptoms. Charcot reported that hypnotized hysterics were able to move limbs that had been paralyzed for years. Eminent physicians breathlessly followed Charcot's presentations of his patients passing through the clearly demarcated hypnotic stages of "catalepsy," "lethargy," and "somnambulism."[87]

Meanwhile, Hippolyte Bernheim, Professor of Internal Medicine at the University of Nancy, began conducting experiments of his own. He concluded that hypnosis was not the result of "weakened nerves," but was simply a heightened form of suggestibility. Bernheim explained the Salpêtrière patients' wild yet predictable fits of hysteria as nothing more than the effects of hypnotic suggestion. The patients were merely acting out their physicians' subtle expectations.[88]

The result of Bernheim's challenge was the "Battle of the Schools," beginning in 1882 and only ending with Charcot's death in 1893. The debate over the causes and potentials of hypnotism dominated medical journals and international conferences as well as the popular press of Europe and the United States. Between 1884 and 1887 alone, nearly eight hundred titles on hypnotism were published.[89]

Hypnotism fascinated the American public for a variety of reasons. On the one hand, it gave a new, scientific validation of widespread fears of contagion. The germ theory of disease, introduced in 1876, had popularized the idea that illnesses were caused not by internal weaknesses but by external agents. It would be another twenty years before the theory produced workable methods of fighting disease, and late-nineteenth-century Americans felt newly vulnerable to physical contagion. Many middle-class Americans also worried that the railroads, streetcars, and telegraphs that circulated goods, people, and information might also be the channels through which immorality crossed the boundaries of class. Temperance and social-purity literature frequently invoked the threat of "moral germs" and "moral contagion" as part of their argument that purity within the home was no longer sufficient to combat a threatening urban environment. Reports of the ability of one mind to influence another by hypnosis made some middle-class Americans even more fearful of the "hundreds of different avenues by which depraving influences and temptations may reach their homes." [90]

On the other hand, hypnotism offered hope to those who were committed to moral influence as a strategy of social change. Fearing that the current social upheaval signaled the final triumph of beastliness over civilization, they sought a means by which powerful minds could directly influence society. Science seemed to be the hope of the future. Might hypnotism, the new science of the mind, herald the inauguration of a new reign of mind over matter? This was the hope of many. As the motto of the Chicago Columbian Exposition's 1893 White City proclaimed, "Not Matter, but Mind: Not Things, but Men." [91]

A faith in the near-hypnotic potency not only of "men" over "things," but of womanly influence over matter was implicit in the strategies of middle-class authors who investigated the new urban poor. As we have seen, Charity Organization societies seemed to feel that refined women could reopen the "moral conduits" between the civilized and the savage. [92] Pioneering muckraker Jacob Riis also made reference to this model of social uplift. In his study *How the Other Half Lives*, Riis blamed both greedy landlords and degraded tenants for the squalid conditions of New York's slums. Yet his text was rife with descriptions of moral "contagion" versus refining "influence" that appeared to be more than metaphorical. When Riis found a previously bad tenement "entirely changed," for example, he offered this explanation for the transformation: "the secret [was] the new housekeeper, a tidy, mild-mannered, but exceedingly strict little body, who had a natural faculty of drawing her depraved surroundings within the beneficent sphere of her strong sympathy." [93]

Perhaps most important, hypnotism attracted the attention of Americans because it seemed to offer a potential cure for neurasthenia, a disease that many feared was reaching epidemic proportions. The term neurasthenia, literally nerve (neuro) weakness (asthenia), was first used by George

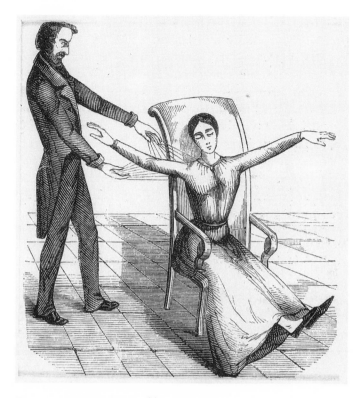

Figure 3. A mesmerist and his patient.
Male will controls the female body.

Beard, an American neurologist, in 1869. By the 1880s and through the turn
of the century, neurasthenia was a catch-all diagnosis for patients suffering
from symptoms ranging from exhaustion and body aches to "hopeless-
ness" and "fear of everything." It seemed so pervasive in the United States
that a common synonym for neurasthenia was "American Nervousness." [94]

Even as white male and female theorists confidently proclaimed their
competing views of Anglo-Saxon manhood and womanhood, the pervasiveness of neurasthenia indicated that many found each of the available
gender ideals problematic. Where the ideal Anglo-Saxon man was focused,
forceful, and active, neurasthenic men were passive and exhausted. Told
that the transmutation of desire was the key to manhood, neurasthenic
men instead so repressed their desires that they became immobile. The ideal
Anglo-Saxon woman was either ruled by her body with its delicate needs
or entirely separate from it. Neurasthenic women became so distant from
their bodies that their bodies no longer responded to their mind's com-

mands. Neurasthenic women exaggerated physical passivity until it became a kind of power; efforts to accommodate their delicate health became the organizing principle of their families' lives. Yet their illnesses only brought them tighter confinement to the family circle.[95]

Before the embrace of hypnotism as a form of therapeutics, medical treatment for neurasthenia simply reiterated faltering gender conventions about mental health. Physicians believed that each individual was born with a set amount of nervous energy that was determined by heredity. When too many demands were made on that energy, the result was neurasthenia. They argued that the nervous energy of white middle-class men was sapped by their excessive "brain work." Physicians advised these men to build up their inner nerve strength through a combination of rest, tonics, exercise, and perhaps travel to an invigorating environment. Such practices would recharge men's inner forcefulness. They then need only use their wills in order to "live within their means" of nervous and economic expenditure.[96]

Physicians had a different set of treatments for neurasthenic white middle-class women. They believed that these women, too, had a limited amount of nervous energy. Most physicians claimed that the demands of refined women's own reproductive systems left them weak and exhausted. Others insisted that women's nerves were weakened by their attempts at mental development. While treatments for male neurasthenics were designed to restore male energy, those for female neurasthenics attempted to eradicate the stimulations that overtaxed women's naturally low thresholds of nervous energy. Because some doctors assumed that women's reproductive organs regulated their energy as a whole, gynecological surgery, including clitoridectomies but more commonly ovariotomies, was used to treat neurasthenia in the 1870s and 1880s. Doctors proudly reported that the removal of women's sexual organs, which women neither needed nor missed, led to drastic improvements in their personal character. The other popular treatment for neurasthenic women, S. Weir Mitchell's "rest cure," encouraged women to accept their position as passive body. Under the rest cure, the neurasthenic woman's only activity was to fatten herself on a dairy-based diet. Visiting, reading, writing, or any activities that might stimulate women's mental energies were strictly forbidden.[97]

These treatments often failed. Men who were exhausted by the demands of their over-active consciences did not want to be told that they needed more will-power. Women who were sickened by contradictory injunctions that they must be totally spiritual yet relegated to the physical care of their offspring would not prosper under treatments that further problematized their physicality.

Physicians' high rates of failure led some doctors to question their own treatments. As one prominent American psychiatrist admitted in 1907, "[o]ur therapeutics is simply a pile of rubbish."[98] It led most, however, to question not their own methods of healing, but the nature, indeed the human worth, of their patients. If regimes based on rest and will-power could not cure many patients, it was because they were descended from inferior human stock. Such patients were suffering from "heredity," or the inheritance of their ancestors' negative traits. By the early twentieth century, American psychiatrists were diagnosing ninety percent of their patients as victims of heredity.[99]

In this context, a few bold physicians began to report that hypnotism, or "psychic suggestion, steadily and frequently applied" could restore the "mental equilibrium" of neurasthenics. One of the first to herald the potential benefits of "mental therapeutics" was George Beard, who caused an uproar at an early meeting of the American Neurological Society by suggesting that nervous disease might be caused—and cured—by emotions. But most late-nineteenth-century physicians who pursued hypnotism as a therapeutic agent viewed it as a method by which physicians could impose their will on recalcitrant patients. As one physician wrote in 1876, doctors can learn from "quacks, especially those belonging to the so-called Christian Science and faith-cure systems" about the importance of keeping a "secure mental grip" upon one's patients. Another seconded in 1901, "You must begin a system of mental education and start the mind moving along proper channels, and persist day by day until the power of your personality overbalances that of your patient."[100]

But as antebellum mesmerists had understood, a hypnotic or mesmeric paradigm was more complex than simply the imposition of one will upon another. The hypnotic trance could imply both the power of the operator's mind or will over matter and the superiority of the patient's spirit over both matter and mind. Furthermore, by the late nineteenth century the exact relations among the concepts of will, mind, matter, and spirit were themselves both heavily gendered and deeply contested. They were at the heart of the debate between the pure woman of "head and heart," who connected mind to spirit and believed in the conquest of "matter," and the new manhood, now divided between those who associated manliness with altruism and self-control, on the one hand, and those who grounded masculine mind and will in desirous passions and strong bodies, on the other.

As "regular" medical treatments continued to fail, chronic neurasthenics increasingly turned to the rising hosts of "mind curists" or "mental healers" for relief from paralyzing nervous illnesses.[101] Practitioners of the "Christian Science and faith-cure systems" realized that their patients' understandings of the relations between mind and matter, and spirit and desire, were linked to their conflicted feelings about ideals of gendered behavior. Mental healers therefore attempted to restore their clients' health by offering them revised understandings of the relationship between manhood and womanhood, mind and matter, and selfhood and desire.

2 The Mother or the Warrior

*Mind, Matter, Selfhood, and Desire
in the Writings of Mary Baker Eddy
and Warren Felt Evans*

Material hypotheses challenge metaphysics to meet in final
combat. In this revolutionary period . . . woman goes forth
to battle with Goliath.

Mary Baker Eddy, 1875 [1]

Spirit and matter sustain to each other the relation of male
and female; that is, one is active, the other passive or reactive.

Warren Felt Evans, 1886 [2]

As early as the 1870s, Christian Science and "mental" or New Thought
healers posed an active threat to mainstream medicine. Neurologists and
general practitioners could not understand why mental treatments, which
often consisted of a healer sitting quietly with a patient and meditating upon
uplifting statements, would succeed when their own more complex treatments failed. Historians too have had trouble understanding the popularity
of late-nineteenth-century mental healers. Some interpret their successes
as evidence of the personal neuroses of their patients. Others cite the mental healers' efficacy as proof that the nervous illnesses of late-nineteenth-
century middle-class Americans were rooted in economic anxieties. Mental
healers told their patients that they need only meditate, and their wishes
would be granted. This was comforting, historians argue, to an economically pinched middle class that felt both overshadowed by corporate giants
and guilty over their new consumer desires. [3]

A more complex understanding of the needs mental healers seemed able
to fulfill can be found in the writings of the two most influential early practitioners: Mary Baker Eddy and Warren Felt Evans. Evans, whose book *The
Mental Cure* (1869) was the first published mind-cure or New Thought
study, and Eddy, whose *Science and Health with Key to the Scriptures*
(1875) became the scriptural text of Christian Science, shaped the mind-
cure wave of the 1870s and 1880s. To understand their theological premises
and to decipher how ideas about gender structured those theologies is a de-

manding task. Their religious assumptions are quite alien to modern readers; yet we must explicate them if we are to perceive the pressing cultural tensions they addressed. We can then both understand why the writings of Eddy and Evans were hailed as revelatory by neurasthenic late-nineteenth-century Americans and have deeper insight into the draw of both Christian Science and New Thought.

Eddy and Evans were interested in a shared set of questions. What was the relationship between God and mind? Was mind masculine or feminine? Was it separate from or related to matter? Was matter masculine or feminine? Was desire an evil that woman must eradicate or the saving truth that man must embrace? How precisely did mind, body, and desire form the gendered human self?

Eddy's Christian Science condemned man, whom she saw as the symbol for "matter," or the sensuality that threatened civilized society. She equated the spiritual and the scientific, promoted salvific self-denial rather than aggressive self-assertion, and predicted the final triumph of spiritual "Woman" over manly desire. Eddy's theology was in keeping with the aims of the social-purity wing of the late-nineteenth-century woman movement. Evans's Mind-Cure or Mental Therapeutics associated man with spirit and woman with matter; linked the mental (rather than the spiritual) with the scientific; encouraged self-assertion; and lauded desire as the divine spark within man. He reworked both older and newer ideals of late-Victorian manhood.

The writings of Eddy and Evans went beyond simply reflecting the larger debate over manly desire versus womanly virtue. They posited new ways of understanding mind itself. Victorians generally pictured the mind as a single entity containing soul, will, and spirit. Eddy and Evans instead popularized the idea of multiple "minds" within humanity, thus preparing the groundwork for Americans' later acceptance of more academic psychological theories. They helped to create transitional, and, for some, energizing and healing forms of gendered selfhood. The apparent healing power of Eddy and Evans's writings indicates both the centrality of the issues to which both authors spoke—the need for new understandings of mind, self-control, self-assertion, and personal desire—and the confusions surrounding these core issues of Victorian identity.

By the 1890s the perspectives of Eddy and Evans would be institutionalized in two opposing wings of New Thought. An anti-desire wing would draw upon Eddy and valorize self-denial, the absence of desire, and the triumph of womanhood. A pro-desire wing would draw upon Evans, valorize

Figure 4.   Phineas P. Quimby, mesmerist and originator of New Thought.

desire, and laud matter or the body as a source of strength. A close look at their theologies reveals the diametrically opposed visions that competed for primacy in late-Victorian culture, and that formed the very foundations of the New Thought movement.

PHINEAS P. QUIMBY: THE BEGINNINGS OF NEW THOUGHT

Eddy and Evans were both the students of New Hampshire mesmerist Phineas P. Quimby (1802–1866), the first to elaborate a theory of mental healing. Although historians often refer to Quimby as the "founder" of the New Thought movement, the manuscripts in which he elaborated his methods were not available to the public until 1921. At that time, Horatio Dresser, a prominent New Thought leader whose parents had been healed by Quimby, published a heavily annotated version of his writings. Because

Quimby's writings were not widely available, they did not directly effect the development of New Thought during its crucial early decades. Quimby's influence was indirect, through his students, not through his writings.[4]

Quimby had been working as a clock-maker when French mesmerist Charles Poyen passed through his town of Belfast, Maine in 1838. Intrigued by Poyen's demonstrations, Quimby began to experiment. He discovered that he too had the power to mesmerize. Quimby found an ideal subject in Lucius Burkmar, a seventeen-year-old boy who claimed to diagnose diseases when in a mesmeric trance. Together, Quimby and Burkmar toured Maine and New Brunswick throughout the 1840s, giving popular demonstrations of mesmerism.

In addition to diagnosing diseases, Burkmar prescribed remedies. Some were absurdly simple—for example, drinking herb tea to cure advanced cancers—yet they seemed to be effective. Analyzing these healings, Quimby decided that Burkmar was not seeing into the body of patients, as he claimed, but rather was picking up the patients' own beliefs about the nature of their illnesses. His remedies seemed to work simply because Burkmar had his patients' complete confidence.[5]

Realizing that faith in health could cure, Quimby deduced that belief in illness caused disease. He concluded that at the root of disease were false opinions, and that the sick could be cured by simply reasoning them away from such false beliefs. This healing process, essentially a matter of logical argument rather than of the power of will or faith, could be undertaken either aloud or silently in the mind of the healer. In the latter case, the patient would pick up the healer's "scientific" or logically correct view through telepathy. Only here did Quimby maintain the older mesmeric focus on healing through impressing the subject with the mesmerist's superior will.[6]

Quimby shared the anti-professionalism common to antebellum sectarian healers. He believed that the two professions most responsible for erroneous, disease-creating ideas were "priestcraft" and doctors. "These two classes are the foundation of more misery than all other evils, for they have a strong hold on the minds of the people by their deception and cant," he claimed. Doctors caused disease by believing in illness and spreading their false beliefs to patients. Priests were even more deadly. Quimby believed that half the illnesses he treated were caused by fears implanted by Bible stories and church sermons. To free his patients from their fears of sin and damnation, Quimby provided his own reinterpretations of Bible stories. He found this method effective in curing thousands of people throughout New England in the 1850s and early 1860s.[7]

Quimby taught that the universe consisted of differently developed states of matter—mineral, vegetable, and animal. The level to which matter developed was determined by a spiritual force that Quimby identified as "Science" or the "revelation from God." Humanity must develop this inner "science" until humanity "becomes refined, and becomes the medium of this life of Science or everlasting life."[8] In other words, although matter was omnipresent and infused with spirit, the task of humanity was to escape matter and become transparent to spirit.

Quimby believed that woman was farthest from "matter," and therefore was the logical leader in human spiritual development. Referring to the story of Adam and Eve, Quimby wrote "man is of the earth earthly, yet in him was this Science in the form of a rib, or this higher power, and the Science called it woman. And this woman or wisdom is to lead man or ignorance to truth and happiness."[9]

Quimby made odd use of the term "science." On the one hand, he used science as a synonym for rationality as opposed to superstition. His identification of Christianity as a cause of disease, against which "scientific" argument was the only cure, hearkened back to an Enlightenment paradigm. On the other hand, Quimby equated science with the "revelation from God" or the divine itself. Furthermore, since science was equated with spiritual knowledge, and women were more spiritual than men, he depicted woman as the master scientist. "Like a chemist she . . . stands among all kinds of matter, which are under her control, and which she has the power of changing," Quimby wrote.[10]

Quimby assumed that spiritual woman was naturally selfless. Therefore woman readily taught her powers over matter to man, who then used his new gifts to subordinate the natural world. "Then she becomes a teacher of that Science which puts man in possession of a wisdom that can subject all animal life to his control." Quimby believed that with woman's aid, man could be "refined" to become the "medium of the life of Science," and so become more like woman. On the other hand, man's new understanding of "science" would enable him to control the very nature to which he, as male, was more closely aligned.[11]

Quimby passed away in 1866. His teachings bequeathed a confused legacy on the relationships between male and female, mind and matter, and spirit and science. His two most prominent students refined his theories in very different directions. Evans, a Swedenborgian minister-turned-mental healer, elaborated upon Quimby's depiction of man as master of nature. The widowed New Englander Mary Baker Eddy developed Quimby's vision of woman as man's selfless, scientific redeemer. Both elaborated theologies that were rooted in their own personally transformative encounters with Phineas Quimby.

MARY BAKER EDDY'S CHRISTIAN SCIENCE THEOLOGY

Until her meeting with Quimby in 1862, Mary Baker Eddy (then Mrs. Mary Glover Patterson) lived a wretched life. She was financially insecure, frequently isolated, and suffered from chronic "neuralgia in the spine and stomach." Eddy tried numerous health regimes to ease her condition, including hydropathy and homeopathy, and had dabbled in spiritualism and mesmerism.[12] Soon after her encounter with Quimby, however, Eddy regained her health. She was inspired by Quimby to begin developing the theories on mind, matter, and spirit that she would present to the world in her 1875 tract, *Science and Health.*

Eddy adopted many terms from Quimby's writings, such as "error," "science," and even the phrase "Christian Science" itself. Nevertheless, she transformed the meaning of those terms, and created a new religious framework for Quimby's method. Quimby was an influence upon—rather than, as later claimed, the originator of—Eddy's religious healing system.[13]

Mary Baker Eddy based her theology on the belief that the universe was entirely spiritual and entirely good. She reached this conclusion through syllogistic reasoning. Since God is all and God is good, therefore all is good and evil cannot exist. Equating "Mind" with "God," she wrote "all that Mind, God, is, or hath made, is good, and He made all. Hence evil is not made and is not real."[14]

If all is good and evil is unreal, how can one explain sin, sickness, and death? Here the concept of "Mind" became central. Eddy described God as a "divine Mind" whose purely spiritual thoughts created the spiritual universe. She believed that there also existed a second sort of creative mind, the human or "mortal mind." As the thought of divine Mind created all that was true, good, and eternal, so did human thought of "mortal mind" create all that was false, evil, and unreal. True reality was the "invisible universe and spiritual man." The material world and embodied person of daily life were "unreal," or mere illusions created by "mortal mind" or human thought. As Eddy explained, "Eternal things . . . are God's thoughts as they exist in the spiritual realm of the real. Temporal things are the thoughts of mortals and are the unreal, being the opposite of the real or the spiritual and eternal."[15]

Eddy therefore blamed evil on the human mind. The unregenerate human mind created an evil world by believing in evil and acting accordingly. People trusted the reports of their faulty senses. They then based conclusions upon these false reports which were not only sinful, they were deadly.

The most debilitating of these false beliefs, Eddy believed, was that humanity originated in matter rather than Spirit. She claimed that matter had no true existence independent of its creation by the false beliefs of mortal minds. Denunciations of the belief in the material world, or "matter," filled Eddy's writings. "Admit the existence of matter, and you admit that mortality (and therefore disease) has a foundation in fact. Deny the existence of matter, and you can destroy the belief in material conditions," she declared in a typical passage.[16]

Eddy's theology posited a universe divided between the spiritual and the material. She described Jesus Christ as a double-natured being who mediated between these two worlds. Jesus, she wrote, was human. The Christ, however, was "the divine image and likeness." Jesus used "the Christ" to dispel the illusions of the senses and take away the world's sins. In a similar fashion, Eddy saw humanity as encompassing both a material, human aspect and a more spiritual aspect which, like the Christ, was the "image and idea of God."[17]

Eddy's descriptions of the human-divine relationship are somewhat unclear. She seemed to suggest at times that human beings share divine attributes such as incorporeality and omnipotence. This view was supported by statements such as "man is the image and likeness of God, in whom all being is painless and permanent" and "because man is the reflection of his Maker, he is not subject to birth, growth, maturity, [and] decay."[18]

At other times, however, Eddy indicated that the "Spiritual man" was something entirely different from the "mortal man." She seemed to interpret the "mortal man" as the common person, condemned to sin, sickness, and death because of his or her mistaken beliefs about the nature of the world. She attacked as "a fatal error" the idea that "mortal, material man is the likeness of God." Explicitly countering what would soon become the standard New Thought belief that there existed a "divine within," or an aspect of God within each person waiting only to be recognized, Eddy wrote that "If He dwelt within what He creates, God would not be reflected but absorbed."[19]

Eddy was consistent, however, in her insistence that humanity must acknowledge an entirely spiritual reality in order to be saved. This goal was to be reached through the standard Christian method of repentance for sin. "Only those, who repent of sin and forsake the unreal, can fully understand the unreality of evil," she explained. Repentance was a demanding process. "Sin is the image of the beast to be effaced by the sweat of agony," Eddy wrote. Humanity received the strength needed for the mighty battle against the senses through reliance on God, or "immortal and omnipotent Mind," which alone was capable of "lifting humanity above itself into purer desires, even into spiritual power and good-will to man."[20]

Eddy's outlook was close to the orthodox Christianity of her day: one repented of sin by recognizing one's dependence on God's power. According to Eddy, salvation granted believers the unshakable assurance that omnipotent Mind could "control" all aspects of human life, and could be counted on to "defend" humanity against the false beliefs of mortal mind.[21]

EDDY'S CHRISTIAN SCIENCE HEALING

Eddy's ideas about illness and health were derived from her beliefs about the separation of divine Mind from mortal mind. Divine Mind or God created the true, spiritual universe, while mortal mind, or human thought, created the material world we inhabit. Mortal mind therefore also produced sickness. Our minds were beset by fears that weakened the body. On a deeper level, the human body itself was simply the "unconscious substratum" of the mortal mind. Deeply held beliefs literally externalized themselves in a diseased body. People could also pick up negative thoughts from the minds of others. One became ill not by catching people's germs, but by catching their mental fears.[22]

The claim that mind produces illness through false beliefs suggests that a change in beliefs could improve one's health. This was not exactly Eddy's view, however. She believed that although manipulating one's thoughts from illness to health could function as a cure, it ultimately strengthened mortal mind's hold over reality. To truly cure disease, Eddy believed the power of mortal mind must be broken and its false beliefs eradicated by immortal Mind. "The action of so-called mortal mind must be destroyed by the divine Mind to bring out the harmony of being," she wrote.[23]

Although Eddy wished to "destroy" the creative power of mortal mind, her healing technique seemed to depend upon mortal mind's susceptibility to the thoughts of others, as well as upon its ability to externalize thought into bodily changes. To heal, the Christian Scientist silently "argued" the patient out of her belief in the reality of illness, using the logical premises of "divine Science" as elucidated in *Science and Health*. The patient then mentally picked up the healer's argument and thereby realized that disease had no reality. When the patient became stronger, the healer explained aloud the "metaphysics" of Christian Science.[24] Rather than being healed by the mental power of the Christian Scientist, the patient was healed by the truth of the Christian Scientist's arguments, whether transmitted silently or verbally.

Eddy knew that many would interpret her healing method as a type of hypnotism or mesmerism. She emphatically denied this charge. "In reality there is no *mortal* mind, and consequently no transference of mortal thought and will power," she wrote. At the same time, Eddy implied that it was the mind of the healer, rather than the knowledge she imparted, which healed. "[B]e thoroughly persuaded in your own mind concerning the truth which you think or speak, and you will be the victor," she wrote.[25]

Although Eddy insisted that God or divine Mind was all-encompassing, mortal mind remained a powerful and problematic entity. Since the thought of mortal mind had creative power, Eddy believed that personal thoughts must be strictly controlled. "Stand porter at the door of thought," she advised. "Admitting only such conclusions as you wish realized in bodily results, you will control yourself harmoniously."[26]

The need to guard one's thoughts constantly was time-consuming but possible. The larger problem for Christian Scientists was how to guard against the intrusive thoughts of others. Eddy referred to the control that one person's thoughts could exercise over another as animal magnetism, mesmerism, or hypnotism. She had a special term, "Malicious Animal Magnetism" (familiarly known in Eddy's circles as "M.A.M."), for the thing she feared most: the intrusive power of evil thoughts.[27]

Eddy declared that, technically speaking, "animal mesmerism or hypnotism . . . is an unreal concept of the so-called mortal mind" and therefore did not exist. However, just as disease and sin, though unreal, nevertheless had to be "crushed" and "conquered," so the malicious mesmerists needed to be countered at every turn. Eddy blamed everything from minor irritants to major catastrophes on the "M.A.M." of her numerous opponents. When she succumbed to illness, she knew that her own thoughts could not possibly be at fault. She therefore organized round-the-clock vigils of her students, who silently "treated" her by directing their thoughts against the outsiders whose evil minds were responsible for Eddy's pains.[28]

Despite Eddy's vehement disclaimers, her healing process bore a family resemblance to mesmeric or hypnotic healing. Like the average "malicious mesmerist," she had to face the central conundrum of hypnotism: if your mental power can control the external world, what is to prevent the thoughts of others from controlling you? Eddy's group vigils were one solution to this problem. She apparently believed that the concentrated thoughts of a group would be more powerful than the malicious thoughts of wayward individuals.

On a deeper level, however, a fear of invasive hypnotic thought informed the very structure of Eddy's theological system. While some responded to the problem of hypnotic control by simply trusting in the high-mindedness of hypnotic "operators," Eddy's solution was to split the mesmeric mind in two. She claimed that there was a "divine Mind," which "controls" and "defends," and a lowly "mortal mind," which produces only evil, and which must be "destroyed." In Eddy's system, therefore, sickness or evil in one's life was a sign that one's "mortal mind" was active and unregulated. One suffered because one was not yet fully controlled by God or divine Mind— or, in other words, because one still had some (mortal) mind of one's own.

Eddy's creation of "two minds" would be made to serve wider ideological functions in the hands of her apostate students, many of whom were themselves of "two minds" about the relationship between womanhood, social power, and personal desire.

THE ROLE OF GENDER IN CHRISTIAN SCIENCE THEOLOGY

Eddy's Christian Science attracted disproportionate numbers of white middle-class women.[29] Such women found Christian Science healing a welcome alternative to ineffectual and sometimes brutal medical treatment. They appreciated Eddy's support for many goals of the woman movement. They found an outlet for their talents in the many positions within Christian Science that Eddy encouraged them to fill. Perhaps they enjoyed Eddy's occasional use of the term "Father-Mother" as a synonym for God.[30] These were only superficial manifestations, however, of a deeper, emotionally charged gender consciousness that permeated Eddy's writings. This gender consciousness was expressed in Eddy's vivid and sometimes violent language, in her apotheosis of "Woman," and in her association of men with matter and sin.

Eddy encouraged serenity and self-control among her followers. Her metaphors, however, frequently invoked a charged scenario of battle.[31] Indeed, violent imagery permeated Eddy's writings. "Instead of blind . . . submission to the incipient or advanced stages of disease, rise in rebellion against them," she declared. Humanity has been a "slave" to sin, and sin will be "conquered only by a mighty struggle." "Choke these errors [sins] in their early stages," she wrote, or they will "crush out" all human happiness.[32]

The "error" Eddy called her readers to revolt against was the belief in matter. Matter was the source of all discord, she insisted, and Adam, the first man, was matter's symbol. "Adam, the synonym for error, stands for a belief of material mind," Eddy wrote in a typical passage. More forcefully, she declared that "The parent of all human discord was the Adam-dream, the deep sleep, in which originated the delusion that life and intelligence proceeded from and passed into matter."[33]

Eddy presented a radical reinterpretation of Eve, the more conventional scapegoat for the world's evils. She frequently followed biblical usage, in which "Eve" is referred to as "woman." She then interpreted "Eve" or "woman" in a decidedly positive light. Drawing on what was then a common feminist interpretation of Genesis, Eddy wrote that God "names the female gender last in the ascending order of creation."[34] "Woman" was the first to confess her fault of eating the forbidden apple, and the first to realize that "corporeal sense is the serpent." As a result of her insight, Eve inaugurated a long line of salvific women, culminating, Eddy hinted, in Eddy herself. She wrote, "Hence she [Eve] is first to abandon the belief in the material origin of man and to discern spiritual creation. This hereafter enabled woman to be the mother of Jesus and to behold at the sepulchre the risen Savior. . . . This enabled woman to be first to interpret the Scriptures in their true sense, which reveals the spiritual origin of man."[35]

Eddy interpreted Genesis 3:14–15 (where the Lord God tells the serpent of the eternal enmity between its descendants and those of "the woman") not as a curse, but as a promise of woman's central place in the battle between spirituality and physical passion. She wrote, "The serpent, material sense, will bite the heel of the woman,—will struggle to destroy the spiritual idea of Love; and the woman, this idea, will bruise the head of lust" (see figure 5).[36]

Eddy's "Key to the Scriptures" covered only Genesis and the twelfth chapter of the Apocalypse, or the Revelation of St. John. These two biblical narratives happened to be among the few in which "woman" is a central actor. Explaining her decision to provide an exegesis of the Book of Revelation, Eddy wrote that it "has a special suggestiveness in connection with the nineteenth century."[37] She seemed to believe that her century would culminate in an apocalyptic battle, in which Woman would conquer the falsehoods of the Adam-dream. Describing her own era, Eddy wrote: "Material hypotheses challenge metaphysics to meet in final combat. In this revolutionary period . . . woman goes forth to battle with Goliath."[38]

The outcome of this battle was assured, since it was predicted in the book of Revelation. Woman, or the spiritual idea, triumphs, "matter is put under her feet," and human character is finally "purified." "This immacu-

Figure 5.   "Seeking and Finding." Mary Baker Eddy receives spiritual illumination. The image suggests that "mind" can triumph over lust, depicted here as a snake lurking in the background.

late idea [spirituality or Divine Science], represented first by man and, according to the Revelator, last by woman, will baptize with fire; and the fiery baptism will burn up the chaff of error with the fervent heat of Truth and Love, melting and purifying even the gold of human character." [39] The panorama of human history became for Eddy a simple drama between two warring actors—Woman on the one side and Matter on the other. While man was strongly associated with matter, it was matter, and not man, that woman battled. The question, then, is what precisely matter symbolized to make the concept so troubling to Eddy, and presumably to her followers as well.

Eddy offered no clear definition of matter. Her use of the term suggests, however, that although matter was explicitly linked with man (or "Adam"), it was also implicitly a code word for the body, and particularly for the female body with all its connotations of sexual vulnerability and social subordination. [40] Eddy attacked the association of women with mindless physicality in a chilling vignette in *Science and Health.* She told how a woman died from inhaling ether. "[H]er sister testified that the deceased protested against inhaling the ether and said it would kill her, but that she was compelled by her physicians to take it. Her hands were held and she was forced

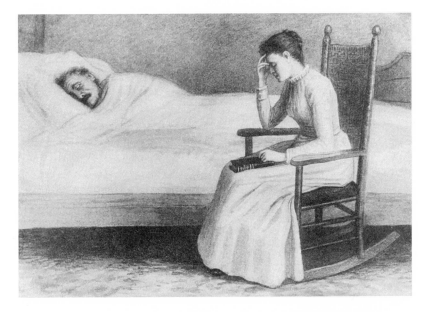

Figure 6. "Treating the Sick." Note how mind is again highlighted in this image.

into submission." The terrified woman died as a result. The autopsy indicated that the cause of death was not the ether, Eddy wrote, but the woman's fear of inhaling it. She condemned the doctors for their indifference to the woman's emotional state. "Is it skillful or scientific surgery to take no heed of mental conditions and to treat the patient as if she were so much *mindless matter. . . ?*" she asked.[41]

The story clearly upset Eddy, and seemed to sum up the medical beliefs and resulting practices that she opposed. Her own Christian Science cast women not as "mindless matter," but as warriors who would defeat the "Goliath" of matter, which Eddy linked metonymically with Adam. Adam in turn was linked to error, and error to the sins of "passion, selfishness, envy, hatred and revenge." It was not by chance that "passion" headed the list of sins. Eddy explained that Christian Science stood for "chastity and purity," not "sensualism and impurity." She asserted that women were not matter but mind or spirit and, furthermore, that Woman, who in the Apocalypse "symbolizes . . . the spiritual idea of God," can and must triumph over sensual, materialistic man.[42]

Eddy inverted the association of man with mind and woman with matter (see figure 6). Her depiction of man as the symbol for out-of-control sensuality and of woman as the force that would elevate humanity to its full spiritual potential placed her writings in the mainstream of woman movement ideology.

EARLY NEW THOUGHT THEOLOGY:
THE WRITINGS OF WARREN FELT EVANS

Warren Felt Evans's 1869 book *The Mental Cure* was widely read in the United States and was translated into several foreign languages. Evans published five more mental-healing texts, culminating in *Esoteric Christianity and Mental Therapeutics* (1886). His writings remained influential long after his death in 1889. Every major historian of New Thought and Christian Science agrees that Evans's ideas profoundly shaped the New Thought movement.[43]

Evans created a new philosophical framework for Quimby's healing method. His work incorporated Swedenborgianism, the German idealist tradition, and an eclectic array of world religions and esoteric traditions. Evans believed that his "Mental Medicine" or "Mind Cure" incorporated philosophy, religion, and science and so went beyond the parochial bounds of Christianity.[44]

Mary Baker Eddy bitterly opposed the teachings of Warren Felt Evans. The two authors nevertheless shared a number of premises.[45] Evans agreed with Eddy that since God was all and God was good, evil could not *really* exist. People believed in evil because they relied upon their senses rather than upon their spiritual perception. Humanity needed to rise above the senses to the realm of pure truth, or "science." "All genuine science consists in correcting the illusive testimony of our senses," he explained. Evans also agreed with Eddy that the evil from which "science" would deliver us was "matter." He promised the "termination of the reign of matter and sense, and the re-establishment of the dominion of the spirit" through the philosophy and practice of mental healing.[46]

Although Evans heralded the end of matter's dominion, he did not agree with Eddy that matter was intrinsically evil or unreal. Evans explained, "Matter is in itself not evil. In its reality and inmost essence it is divine— the second emanative principle from God." He added, "It is only when matter has dominion over spirit, that it is evil."[47] As an emanation of God, matter was naturally perfect. The role of the healer, and of humanity in general, was to realize matter's inherent goodness, rather than deny its very existence. Evans believed that matter, which he associated with nature and the body, was a passive, plastic force. Matter reacted to emotions, which were in turn shaped by thought. When our thoughts were dominated by wild emotions or animal needs, the inevitable result was illness. Illness was thus caused by a reversal of the natural order of things. Matter (or the body) was leading rather than following the dictates of the soul.[48]

The healer's role was to alter the patient's understanding of the origin of his or her illness. The patient must understand that "the deepest reality of the disease is not physical, but mental," Evans explained. The patient would then be cured by the combined power of God and the healer. Because the healer's mind was "surcharged with the . . . power of the Spirit," it could accelerate God's healing process by imparting its healing thoughts to the mind of the sufferer.[49]

A firm believer in thought transference, Evans suggested that healers modify their patients' thinking through a series of emphatic statements that he called "affirmations." The patient was to relax until he or she reached a hypnotic state. At this stage, affirmations rather than reasoned arguments were to be used by the healer because affirmations had proven more effective. "The influence of suggestion and positive affirmation upon a patient in the hypnotic state borders on the miraculous," Evans wrote.[50] A preference for "affirmations" over arguments would later become one of the features that divided practitioners of New Thought from those of Christian Science.

Evans's most radical departure from Eddy lay in his teachings about the "divine within." He claimed that within each person there existed an unchanging essence that he called the *Ego*, the *I Am*, or the *inner Self*. This inner Self was the divine spark within. The average person's Ego or inner divinity was smothered by the dictates of rationality, the pull of emotions, and the clamoring needs of the body. The task of humanity was to recognize and cultivate its inner divinity. This spiritual cultivation would give the individual tremendously increased personal power.

Evans's saving truth, then, was the very heresy that Eddy most feared— the claim that people need not abase themselves before God, since they contained their own divine inner spark and could cultivate Godlike power. As he explained, each individual was "not God but a God, possessed of all the attributes of its parent source, among which are omniscience and omnipresence." One uncovered one's divine inner spark by relying upon Jesus, whom Evans identified as "the principle or faculty of Intuition."[51] People must listen to their intuition, or the saving voice of Jesus within.

One strengthened the divine inner spark by slowing down external activities and letting go of worries. Conversant with the available Hindu writings of his time, Evans advised his readers to follow the Yogic practice of rhythmic, relaxed breathing. This technique would enable people to fall into a meditative state. He described this meditative condition as "going into the Silence," a phrase later adopted by every leading New Thought author.[52]

Evans described "the Silence," or the space one entered through meditation, as the storehouse of all power and knowledge. Jesus, or Intuition, was the conduit through which the cosmic repository of knowledge held in the Silence could enter the passive individual. "On the development of the intuition in us we can read the general record, and man is capable of knowing all that was ever known and of feeling all that was ever felt," Evans wrote. In an often-repeated metaphor, he pictured humanity as "imbibing" this knowledge from Jesus or intuition as one drinks from a "limitless fountain" or, more frequently, as a baby takes in milk from its mother's breast. "We need only to hold the soul passively open and upward to imbibe its [intuition's] life," he explained.[53]

Although Evans encouraged his readers to adopt an attitude of trust and passivity when they meditated, he also encouraged them to cultivate a very different emotion—namely, desire. "The sole condition of receiving this saving truth . . . is the *desire* for it," he wrote.[54] Here Evans was adding his own twist to a Swedenborgian theory of divine influx. He wrote, "The law which governs the influx of saving, healing truth . . . is given by Jesus in the Sermon on the Mount, 'Blessed are they who hunger and thirst after righteousness: for they shall be filled.'"[55] He restated this biblical precept using economic metaphors: "It is a principle which seems to extend through the whole universe, that a demand, a conscious need, creates a supply."[56]

Evans's simultaneous praise of both "mind" and "desire" was in stark contrast to the views of most woman-movement activists. In their view, an elevated mind was by definition untainted by desire; where desire was lowly, irrational, and selfish, mind was spiritual or scientific, lawful, altruistic, and womanly. As we have seen, Eddy pushed this oppositional relationship between mind and desire even further. She ensured the existence of a "mind" untainted by desire by separating the Divine Mind from the mortal mind and calling for the destruction of the latter. Because mind, the force that created the world's ills, was too closely linked to (masculine) change and desire, Eddy rejected mind as an impediment to purity.

Evans inverted Eddy's theology. While Eddy called for an iron-willed struggle against sin, Evans encouraged a relaxed passivity before a benevolent Intuition. Eddy envisioned salvation as the complete erasure of the self or "mortal mind" in favor of control by God, while Evans hoped to extend to humanity the power of divinity. Eddy believed that salvation required the eradication of desire; Evans lauded desire as the key to self-realization. Eddy's system was based on the will for passivity; Evans's system encouraged a passive desire for power.

EVANS VERSUS EDDY ON THE GENDER OF MIND, MATTER, SPIRIT, AND DESIRE

Evans's willingness to praise both mental power and the powers of desire was based at least partially upon the way in which he gender-coded key concepts in his theological system. While Eddy linked matter with "Adam" and spirit with "Woman," Evans gendered these concepts in a more conventional manner. "Spirit and matter sustain to each other the relation of male and female; that is, one is active, the other passive or reactive," Evans wrote. He viewed matter as passive and feminine, but also as divine; it was, as mentioned above, "the second emanative principle from God." Matter's holiness did not quite counter, however, its secondary status as feminine. While "in its place" it was *an invisible, divine, and immortal substance,* he also warned that "when matter has dominion over spirit . . . it is evil." When such a reversal occurred, Evans wrote, spirit must "break the reign of the senses and end their unnatural revolt."[57]

The idea that feminine attributes, although holy, must also be passive and subordinate, permeated Evans's writing. For example, Intuition, or the inner savior of humanity, was described as "the birth or evolution of the woman in man, that which is highest, and comes next to God." To highlight Intuition's important but nonthreatening aspect, it was also described as the "passive and feminine intellect."[58] Evans's Intuition resembled the salvific and self-sacrificing maternal conscience. He opposed Eddy's view that humanity was to be saved by the spiritual, battling Woman. Humanity was instead to be lulled to power by the safely contained woman, the woman *in* man.

Evans divided human nature into body (the temporary residence), soul (the true self), and spirit. "The soul should control the body," he wrote. Yet the "soul . . . has . . . no will of her own, since she is feminine and negative. And she is, therefore, by her nature, bound to obey the will of some[one] other than herself." The soul must obey spirit rather than body. Evans characterized the soul as a loyal wife, joined "as one" with her superior mate, the spirit.[59]

Evans seemed to alter this litany of gender hierarchy when he declared that "Perfected man is *androgyne;* that is, male and female in one personality." However, "man" did not become androgyne by valuing equally his masculine and feminine aspects. Evans described how the "union of the two

Chart 3. Mary Baker Eddy's Christian Science
and Warren Felt Evans's Mental Healing.

MARY BAKER EDDY'S CHRISTIAN SCIENCE

Cosmology

Divine Mind
(God, Spirit) (womanly, desireless)

CONQUERS

carnal mind
(human, false) (masculine, desirous, powerful, evil)

which creates

matter
(nature, body) (masculine, powerful, evil)

Salvation

Womanly Divine Mind eradicates masculine carnal mind. Result is a changeless, spiritual universe of peace and purity.

WARREN FELT EVANS'S MENTAL HEALING

Cosmology

God (Spirit)
1st Emanation = mind (contains divine spark) (masculine)

           aided by Intuition

                           (passive, feminine,

           aided by desire   good as long as subordinate)

2nd Emanation = matter (contains divine spark) (nature, body)
                     (feminine, good as long as subordinate)

Salvation

Masculine mind opens itself to womanly intuition and desire. This enables mind to enter the Silence. Result is strengthening of mind's divine inner spark, or "Ego"; increase in personal power; and greater control over nature (feminine), whose secrets are revealed. Progress is ensured.

regions of our being" resulted from "the submission of the lower to the higher."[60]

Here Eddy again offered an interesting contrast. While for Evans, the enlightened person was symbolized by a man who encompassed woman but kept her in her rightfully subordinate place, Eddy saw woman as the most appropriate symbol for redeemed humanity. "The woman in the Apocalypse symbolizes generic man. . . ." she wrote. She thus slanted her androgyny toward the feminine. "Union of the masculine and feminine qualities constitutes completeness," she wrote. Her description of the complete person more closely reflected Victorian ideals of womanliness than those of manliness, however. As Eddy explained, "Both sexes should be loving, pure, tender and strong."[61]

Evans's attitude toward his feminine-gendered concepts seemed ambivalent if not contradictory. On the one hand, he pictured God as a great comforting mother. "As an infant . . . sinks to rest in the maternal arms, so we must cease from our struggles, and sink to rest in the bosom of the manifested God," he wrote.[62] On the other hand, his attitude toward matter or nature, which he also gendered female, was often combative. He boasted that once the "outer senses are conquered and their reign broken," we will "wrest from all the objects of nature their hidden secrets." The "inward and real man" must be liberated from a "degrading bondage to the body and the senses," Evans declared in a typical passage.[63]

"Man" could be both a passive, relaxed infant on the "bosom" of divine Intuition, and a warrior-liberator against the "fetters of sense and the dominion of sin," not in spite of the fact that both intuition and the fetters of sense were gendered female, but *because* they were.[64] The equation would go as follows: We experience God through God's passive "emanations," intuition and nature or matter. These emanations, as passive, are by definition female; as females, they are like mothers. As mothers, they nurture and enrich, but ultimately bow down before, and serve, their sons, who are the rightful rulers of the universe. Thus matter and intuition are divine and nurturing, as long as they—again like women in general or mothers in particular—do not engage in an "unnatural revolt" and rule instead of serve, thus holding man in "degrading bondage." When this rebellion occurs, freedom is attained by a manful struggle to reassert the divine order, or to rightfully subordinate the feminine to the masculine. However, the revolt of the mothers, in the form of temperance, social purity, and woman suffrage campaigns, was precisely the context in which Evans's work appeared.

Eddy's and Evans's differing valuations of masculinity and femininity conditioned their approaches to matter, mesmerism, and desire. Evans saw matter as feminine; it was therefore passive and malleable, and needed only to be kept in its naturally subordinate place. Eddy, however, saw matter as masculine; as such, it was powerful and active, and had to be forcefully overthrown. Evans didn't seem concerned by mesmerism, or the power of "mortal" or lowly minds to influence the minds of others. Lowly minds were, after all, feminine and so "by nature" bound to obey the will of those with stronger moral temperaments. For Eddy, however, "mortal mind" was masculine. Its invasive, lowly thoughts were a powerful force that the spiritual person must constantly battle. Eddy's views, rather than those of Evans, more closely fit the outlook of the temperance, moral-reform, and social-purity movements.

Evans's celebration of motherhood and desire contrasted strongly with Eddy's distrust of both. This difference perhaps reflected the fact that Evans wrote about these issues from the perspective of a male child, while Eddy did so from the perspective of a woman who was herself a mother. Eddy rejected desire and motherhood; both in her personal life, by leaving her only child to be raised by another woman, and in her theology, in which she hopefully predicted the end of both passion and marriage. Paraphrasing Mark 12:25, she wrote, "[T]he time cometh of which Jesus spake, when he declared that in the resurrection there should be no more marrying nor giving in marriage, but man would be as the angels. Then shall Soul rejoice in its own, in which passion has no part."[65]

Eddy's hope for a future in which "passion has no part" was of a piece with her image of the ideal person as a spiritual woman, since Victorians defined "good" women as women who lacked desire.[66] Evans, on the other hand, viewed the all-giving mother from the perspective of an adored infant. For him, motherhood signified uncritical love. It was thus easily made an ideal.

The contrasting perspectives of Eddy and Evans related to more than their gender-determined positions vis-á-vis motherhood. Both authors were engaged in the consuming debate of their era: Did male desire create civilization (implying that women should remain in the home, in order to allow productive male desire to dominate the public sphere)? Or would female virtue redeem humanity (implying that women should enter the public realm in order to regulate or eradicate the evil of male desire)?

Eddy's position on this debate was clear. She called for Woman to aid divine Mind in the eradication of desire. Woman, or the "spiritual idea of Love," opposed both the external menace of men and the internal menace of one's own disruptive "mortal mind." Desire and divine Mind opposed each other since desire implied change (which Eddy associated with "matter" as well as maleness), and divine Mind implied permanence. The ideal state, in Eddy's view, would be a world without change, demand, competition, or reproduction, presided over by the passionless, spiritual woman. She hoped that with the end of passion and desire the very cycle of life would be stilled. As Eddy explained, the spiritual person would no longer be "*subject to* birth, growth, maturity, decay." Redeemed humanity would instead exist in the "painless and permanent" sphere of God.[67]

Evans's position was slightly more complex. It did not easily fit within either of the competing paradigms of late-nineteenth-century manhood. The mid-nineteenth-century ideal of manliness imagined the male self as containing both masculine desires and an elevating feminine heart. The roles of the feminine heart within man and of actual flesh-and-blood women were similar—both were to discipline, channel, and control disruptive masculine desires. The newer, late-nineteenth-century ideal of masculinity also pictured the male self as containing lowly desires, but it claimed that these "savage" desires must be drawn upon as a resource. Lowly male drives would be transmuted by the masculine will, not controlled or eradicated by the feminine heart.

Evans's version of male selfhood shared certain elements with both of these views. As mainstream Victorians held that woman's sheltered passivity enabled men to create progress and civilization, so did Evans picture a feminine Intuition that could, as long as it remained subordinate to male Spirit, lead men to power and dominion. Evans's Intuition functioned differently, however, from either the feminine heart or the masculine will. Unlike the feminine heart that tamed disruptive desires, Intuition was propelled by desire. Unlike the masculine will, which transmuted the raw material of savage masculine energy, Intuition simply opened the "conduit" to a pre-existing inner storehouse of knowledge and power. Evans's system implied that one need not discipline or mold one's inner impulses in order to progress in life. The intuitive impulse allowed one access to internal, already-complete forms of knowledge.

Evans's perspective was thus oddly modern. Woman-movement leaders, defenders of Victorian manliness, and heralds of the new masculinity agreed that the inner self contained bestial elements that must be disciplined. In contrast, Evans's view of the inner self as the "woman within man" was more akin to popular early-twentieth-century views of the unconscious. Anticipating later pop-Freudians who would hail the feminine unconscious as a source of truth, Evans presented feminine Intuition as a glorious, empowering, and unproblematic inner resource.

Evans's attitude toward desire was particularly iconoclastic. He proposed that men simply desire, and be satisfied. He claimed, very simply, that "a demand . . . creates a supply."[68] His perspective fit that of the new marginalist economists; they too saw (consumer) desire or demand as the force that dictated the creation of a supply.[69] Evans claimed that desire created the plenty that others believed would result either from competition and carefully channeled desire or from maternal selflessness and altruism. While Eddy taught that desire created chaos and so must be eliminated, Evans taught that male demand could create supply.

Evans could only liberate male desire, however, by challenging Victorian understandings of gender difference. Where middle-class male theorists pictured women as both subordinate to and inherently different from men, Evans portrayed the feminine (and, by implication, women as well) as sharing a basic essence with the masculine. According to Evans, the active, masculine mind or spirit, the feminine, enabling intuition, and dumb, plastic matter all existed along a continuum rather than in opposition to each other. Each were "emanative principles" from God.[70] Recasting the feminine as a (lesser) emanative principle of the divine made it far less threatening for men to accept matter, women, and desire—that is, the seemingly lower aspects of life. After all, these were simply the lesser emanations of one's truest, highest self. Instead of urging men to willfully control the alien "other" within, from "feminine" emotions to "masculine" drives, Evans advised men to accept the prompting of their intuition or their desire.

Evans's depiction of an enabling womanly intuition did not necessarily have positive connotations for women. Although Evans pictured the "feminine within" as a force that enabled man to "wrest from the objects of nature their hidden secrets," he stressed that the feminine within could have no independent existence. She had "no will of her own" and was "by . . . nature, bound to obey the will of some[one] other than herself."[71] Yet Mary Baker Eddy's perspective was not much different. In Eddy's view, the divine Woman leads humanity to the apocalypse. The price of this leadership, however, was the destruction of her own (mortal) mind.

Warren Felt Evans died in 1889, just before New Thought became a national craze. Mary Baker Eddy lived until 1910. She spent her final decades battling the New Thought leaders she accused of stealing and distorting her ideas. Yet Eddy and Evans were the two figures who most influenced the turn-of-the-century New Thought movement. Their highly ambiguous writings provided the basic intellectual framework for a generation of New Thought leaders. Most New Thought authors who wrote between 1885 and 1905 presented an amalgam of their two perspectives, simultaneously "affirming" and "denying" the power of woman, the importance of spirit, and the centrality of desire.

3 Emma Curtis Hopkins and the Spread of New Thought, 1885–1905

Dear child, listen to me: you are not suffering the consequences
of inheritance. You were not brought forth into the world of flesh,
from its lustful passions and sensual appetites.

Emma Curtis Hopkins, 1890[1]

I have found my Self, because I know my Self,
because I AM my Self.

Emma Curtis Hopkins[2]

In the mid-1880s mind cure flourished in New England.[3] Boston's Transcendental tradition made it a natural location for mental-healing practices. Boston was home not only to Mary Baker Eddy, but also to Warren Felt Evans, Julius Dresser, and Annetta Seabury Dresser, all of whom had, like Eddy, studied with Phineas Quimby. As if to celebrate their dominance over Eddy, New England mental scientists held their first convention in Boston in 1887, when Eddy's own movement was in shambles.

Despite this early attempt at organization, New Englanders did not dominate the mental-healing scene during the crucial formative decade of 1885–1895. The movement's heart and soul lay in the western states among dedicated teachers, healers, and missionaries, most of them female. These people were less educated and in more economically precarious situations than most of the genteel east-coast practitioners. While New England mental healers identified themselves as Emersonians and philosophical idealists, western mental healers more often presented their messages as outpourings of spirit. Their writings more rawly celebrated the New Thought promise that one's desires, whether spiritual or material, needed only to be expressed and their fulfillment would follow.

By the turn of the century, west- and east-coast healers alike had reason to feel confident that their beliefs would soon sweep mainstream America. In 1897, Ralph Waldo Trine's *In Tune With the Infinite* took the public by storm and became the first genuine New Thought bestseller. In 1902, a

Figure 7.
Emma Curtis Hopkins,
the "teacher of teachers."

richly illustrated article in the *American Monthly Review of Reviews* entitled "The Metaphysical Movement" claimed that "what is somewhat vaguely known as 'The New Thought' now numbers more than a million adherents." The article surveyed major New Thought centers in New York, Hartford, Boston, Chicago, St. Louis, Kansas City, Denver, San Francisco, Los Angeles, Seattle, and Sea Breeze, Florida, and told how the periodical literature of "the 'New Thought' . . . now numbers more than one hundred monthly and weekly publications in this country alone."[4]

This spectacular late-nineteenth-century growth of New Thought was primarily the result of the grueling labors of western-state leaders. Five dedicated individuals in particular created the institutional framework that enabled New Thought to spread—namely, Malinda E. Cramer (San Francisco), Nona Brooks (Denver), Annie Rix Militz (the Pacific coast), and Charles and Myrtle Fillmore (Kansas City). All five drew their initial inspiration from a single source: Emma Curtis Hopkins, the premier New Thought teacher of their day.

The teachings of Emma Curtis Hopkins would seem to provide a shaky foundation upon which to build a movement. She taught that desire was good and desire was evil; that the self was nothing and the self was God.

Hopkins's ambiguities may, however, have been the key to her importance. Many late-nineteenth-century middle-class Americans were deeply divided about the most important aspects of their lives. Family life, physicality and sexuality, and the drive for wealth seemed to both attract and horrify them. Hopkins allowed her late-Victorian followers to express both sides of their conflicting emotions. She also fueled her students' fervor by linking her ambiguous teachings about selfhood and desire to a new woman's era that would usher in a millennial reign of peace and harmony. With this goal in mind, her followers devoted their lives to promoting her ideas. Cramer, Brooks, Rix Militz, and the Fillmores were simply the most dedicated of Hopkins's numerous students who spent the last two decades of the nineteenth century criss-crossing the nation on missionary journeys, lecturing and healing the sick, establishing churches, schools, and seminaries, and producing journals, pamphlets, tracts, and novels elaborating what became known by the 1890s as "the New Thought" perspective.

BREAKING AWAY FROM EDDY:
THE RISE OF EMMA CURTIS HOPKINS

In 1883 Emma Curtis Hopkins was a sickly thirty-two-year-old housewife and mother married to a debt-ridden and violent husband.[5] That year, Hopkins, who lived in Manchester, New Hampshire, visited a neighbor, Mrs. Mary F. Berry, who was a follower of Mary Baker Eddy. Her neighbor had another guest as well—Eddy herself. Eddy spoke at length to Hopkins about Christian Science, and the chance encounter changed Hopkins's life. She turned to Berry for healing and was cured of her sickliness. In December 1883 Hopkins took a class with Eddy and distinguished herself immediately. Soon afterward she decided to devote herself to Christian Science and to Mary Baker Eddy. In January 1884 Hopkins put her new convictions into writing. She wrote to Eddy, "I lay my whole life and all my talents, little or great, to this work."[6]

An articulate, well-read, and beautiful woman, Hopkins rose quickly in the fledgling Christian Science hierarchy. In September 1884 Eddy appointed Hopkins editor of the *Christian Science Journal*. Hopkins held that position for a little over a year, and was then abruptly dismissed by Eddy and evicted from the Massachusetts Metaphysical College, Eddy's combination school and boarding house. The cause of Hopkins's dismissal was apparently her tendency to eclecticism, and, more specifically, her September 1885 editorial "Teachers of Metaphysics." The article began by praising

Eddy as "she whose life of cleansing sorrow left her the fit transparency for revelations straight from the infinite Source," but then described how Hopkins herself was "made to know Him face to face of whom I had heard . . . as a name only." This sort of talk was heretical to Eddy, who claimed a unique prerogative to meetings with God. Under strong pressure from fellow Christian Scientists as well as from Eddy herself, Hopkins resigned from the Christian Science Association on November 4, 1885.[7]

Hopkins did not go down in defeat, however. With the encouragement of another former student of Eddy's, Mary H. Plunkett, Hopkins moved to Chicago late in 1885. Her choice of this city was probably not random; in the mid-1880s, Chicago was host to a vibrant and eclectic mental-healing scene. Hopkins left her husband and son behind with this move. She never resided with either of them again.[8]

Hopkins's success in Chicago was nothing short of spectacular. In June 1886 she agreed to teach a class on Christian Science. Expecting no more than six pupils, Hopkins attracted a class of thirty-seven. This initial group included a number of loyal and able women who would soon become New Thought leaders in their own right, including reform journalist Helen Wilmans, British intellectual and women's suffrage activist Frances Lord, and Dr. Alice Stockham, an internationally known expert in women's health. The group formed itself into a permanent organization and named itself the "Hopkins Metaphysical Association." Hopkins's students then returned to their home towns across the midwest, where they started local Hopkins Metaphysical Associations. By December 1887 there were at least seventeen branches of the Hopkins Metaphysical Association in cities across the nation.[9]

The rapid spread of Hopkins Metaphysical Associations was fueled by Hopkins's missionary travels. In the spring of 1887 she taught a packed class in San Francisco. In October she taught in Milwaukee. In November she taught in New York City, where her class was attended by the nationally famous poet Ella Wheeler Wilcox, homeopathic physician Dr. Harriet Emilie Cady, and Boston author C. M. Barrows. By the end of 1887, Hopkins was said to have personally instructed six hundred students.[10]

Eddy's *Christian Science Journal* vilified Hopkins and Plunkett, who were described as "travelling over the land, professedly teaching Christian Science, and deluding their victims with the thought that they possess it."[11] Yet Hopkins was undoubtedly a more charismatic and successful teacher than Eddy. In 1887, Eddy's most productive teaching year up to that time, her classes averaged twenty-four students. That same year, a single class given by Hopkins was attended by two hundred and fifty students.[12]

Eddy became increasingly anxious over her former student's success. As she organized the first convention of her National Christian Science Association, Eddy was clearly worried about attendance. Her notice read:

> I have gotten up this N.C.S.A. for *you* and the life of the cause. I have something important to say to you, a message from God.
> Will you not meet this one request of your teacher and let *nothing* hinder it? If you do not I shall never make another to you and give up the struggle.[13]

As a result of such exhortations one hundred and fifty delegates from fifteen states, representing the strength of Eddy's Christian Science movement, attended the convention in April 1887. Yet by 1887 Hopkins was already a nationally recognized figure in mental-healing circles. The "mental science" convention in October 1887, also held in Boston, hailed Hopkins as "the star that rose in the East and has spread its glory through the West."[14]

In addition to teaching, Hopkins engaged in numerous other projects to spread her version of Christian Science. In 1886 she became the editor of the *Mental Science Magazine*. She left the magazine in 1887 and began writing for the *Christian Metaphysician*. In the pages of this journal the most active of Eddy's early opponents came together. Regular contributors included Warren Felt Evans, Alice Stockham, and Abby Morton Diaz, the well-known president of the Boston-based Women's Educational and Industrial Union.[15]

In November 1887 Hopkins's manager, Mary H. Plunkett, launched *Truth: A Magazine of Christian Science*. The journal was the organ of the Hopkins Metaphysical Association. That same year Hopkins launched the Emma Hopkins College of Christian Science. By September 1888, Hopkins had broken with Plunkett and agreed to write exclusively for a new journal, *Christian Science*, edited by her student Ida A. Nichols. Over the next four years *Christian Science* remained the primary outlet for Hopkins's writings.[16]

Women predominated at every level of Hopkins's numerous organizational endeavors, from students to ordained clergy to the presidents of local Hopkins associations. The handful of men who were involved understood themselves to be reverently following the lead of "woman." For example, mental healer Dr. Eugene Weeks spoke at Hopkins Metaphysical Association meetings only to pay "beautiful tribute" to "exalted womanhood."[17]

In 1888 Hopkins transformed her Christian Science College into the Christian Science Theological Seminary. On January 10, 1889, members of the first seminarian class of twenty women and two men completed their training and were ordained by Hopkins. The moment marked a key difference between Hopkins and Eddy. Hopkins received ordination from her followers and ordained women in return, while Eddy received ordination, but then appointed only men to positions of power within her church hierarchy.[18]

Hopkins quickly attracted the attention of a number of nationally prominent women. Novelist Clara Louise Burnham was an early participant in the Hopkins Metaphysical Association. Poet Ella Wheeler Wilcox continued her affiliation with Hopkins and published in her journal. Clara Colby, editor of the *Woman's Tribune* (the official organ of the National Woman's Suffrage Association), regularly advertised in the pages of *Christian Science* and visited the paper's offices when passing through Chicago.[19] Perhaps most impressive was the support of Elizabeth Boynton Harbert. As longtime president of the Illinois Woman's Suffrage Association, founder of the Illinois Social Science Association, the Illinois Woman's Press Association, and the Evanston Woman's Club, publisher of a women's suffrage paper, and weekly columnist for the Chicago *Inter-Ocean*, Harbert had extensive political connections. She attended meetings of the Hopkins Metaphysical Association, offered the group the use of her Evanston home, and was even offered the directorship of the Christian Science Theological Seminary (which she declined because of "over-pressure of duties").[20]

Harbert was probably instrumental in getting Hopkins to contribute "Bible Lessons" to the *Inter-Ocean*. Hopkins's *Inter-Ocean* Bible studies ran weekly from 1890 through 1898. Harbert also gave a warm speech at the ordination ceremony of Hopkins's first class of seminarians. Ignoring the two men among the graduates, she hailed the ceremony as evidence of a "glad new time come to us" in which "woman goes forth to proclaim the radiant realities of the Good." Suffrage and temperance activist Louisa Southworth had a similar interpretation of the ordination ceremony. "It was my privilege to be present at the Ceremony of the New Era, the ordaining of women by a woman, and the sending them forth to do both moral and physical healing by the power of the Spirit," Southworth wrote.[21]

Hopkins took concrete steps to align herself with the broader woman movement. The Hopkins Metaphysical Association sent representatives to the Woman's Alliance, a Chicago-based coalition of reform-oriented women's groups. The association also headquartered its "Columbian Congress of Christian Scientists," a group organized to participate in the 1893 Chicago World's Fair, at the fair's "woman's building," the Queen Isabella. (In contrast, Eddy chose to locate her group at the more gender-neutral World's Parliament of Religions area.) [22]

Hopkins was devoted first and foremost, however, to promoting her spiritual beliefs. She repeatedly expressed her "deliberate intention of converting the world to Christian Science," and under her guidance a missionary machinery was put into place. Hopkins established a Mission Fund to loan money for travel and worked out a routine whereby her most gifted students would travel to small towns and cities, give one or two free, well-publicized introductory lectures, and then sign up as many students as possible for a series of twelve purchased lessons. The healings that occurred in the course of these lessons helped spread the movement's fame. The talks attracted the elites of the towns they visited. Class gifts to teachers of diamond brooches were occasionally reported. [23]

Indeed, one explanation for the rapid spread of "Christian Science" lies in the fact that Christian Science teaching, writing, and healing was extremely profitable. Mary Baker Eddy had set the standard for amassing huge amounts of money through mental healing. Her Massachusetts Metaphysical College, founded in 1881, charged a phenomenal three hundred dollars for primary instruction (a class that probably ran six to ten lessons), and one hundred dollars for the normal class. [24] Prices charged by other New Thought teachers varied widely. Emma Curtis Hopkins's lessons were on the high end; she offered individual and group instruction at fifty dollars a course. Hopkins's student F. S. Van Eps gave a series of Christian Science lectures for twenty-five dollars, but delivered them over the summer months in Minnesota and advertised them as a combined package of spiritual enlightenment and cheap summer vacation. Mental healer and author Ursula Newell Gestefeld charged a mere one dollar a lesson, or eight dollars for a "term" of nine lessons. [25]

Fees received from teaching were not the only sources of income for many practitioners. Most also charged for "treatments" or healing services. Because of the practice of "absent healing" (the doctrine that since thought could not be restrained by space, there was no need for the patient to be physically present during treatment), healers could receive payment for limitless numbers of healings. Some of Hopkins's students became prolific writers, and sales from their writings might have generated a modest income. Those who didn't write acted as agents for those who did. Others earned money through loaning out transcripts of mental-healing lessons. Customers were usually charged twenty-five dollars for the privilege of receiving these lessons, copying them over by hand, and returning them to their owner.[26] Although the charges for teaching and healing varied greatly, it is clear that a charismatic and self-promoting healer could earn a very comfortable income. As E. Marion, a student of Hopkins and inveterate missionary traveler and healer, put it,

> When I see the beautiful workings of the spoken word of Truth, I almost shout aloud. . . . Just think of it; everything is mine, and I have the best of everything. Money flows to me through the mails; money comes to me in the classes; I have lovely people in the towns where I go in my classes; and I have the kindest families open their homes for me to stay in, and why is all this? Simply because I serve the Best.[27]

As Hopkins's newly ordained students traveled the country, the movement gained a firm national footing. In 1889 Hopkins's proposal that the Hopkins Metaphysical Association be renamed the Christian Science Association was accepted. Christian Science was spreading fast—but not the Eddy version.[28]

THE TEACHINGS OF EMMA CURTIS HOPKINS

Hopkins was able to captivate women and men of widely varying perspectives because her teachings incorporated the ideas of both Mary Baker Eddy and Warren Felt Evans. Finding a middle ground between them, Hopkins heralded both female virtue and manly desire. She thereby provided a flexible vocabulary that enabled her followers to create varying methods of healing and, more important, varying paradigms of gendered selfhood.

The "lessons in Christian Science" taught by Emma Curtis Hopkins began with syllogisms she probably learned from Eddy.[29] Because God is good, and God is all, therefore all is good, and evil cannot exist. Because God is Mind, and Mind is all, therefore all is Mind, and matter cannot exist. Health and spiritual redemption can be attained once people recognize that all is good, Hopkins explained. This truth of "science," rather than the lies of the "senses," must be followed.[30]

From here, Hopkins's teachings diverged from those of her teacher. First, Hopkins strongly opposed Christian teachings about sin. As she explained, Christianity taught that evil was a part of God's plan. Christianity was therefore responsible for the fact that people believed in and so mentally created evil.[31] These beliefs created the self-hatred and fear that resulted in disease. Hopkins declared, *"All disease is outward evidence of a belief in judgment against sin."*[32]

Hopkins's understanding of the relationship between Divine Mind and carnal mind also diverged from Eddy's view. Eddy argued that (womanly) Divine Mind must eradicate the lowly, masculine but powerful carnal mind. In contrast, Hopkins imagined the Divine Mind as masculine, and the carnal or mortal mind as weak, passive, and feminine. As if to highlight the insubstantiality of carnal mind, Hopkins depicted it as akin to a window or a mirror.[33] Most significantly, Hopkins agreed with Evans that the individual could have a "God-Self" within. According to Evans, this "Divine Within" was implanted by God and strengthened by (feminine) Intuition and desire. But Hopkins believed that one could receive this Divine spark from God only if one carefully disciplined one's unruly personality. For this reason she encouraged her students to meditate upon "affirmations" and "denials" that would reshape their characters. (There were meditations that "denied" the power of matter, for example, and "affirmed" the omnipresence of spirit.) By so doing, they were "cleansing" their glass- or window-like mortal minds of false beliefs. Such practices would enable the (masculine) Divine Mind to shine directly through the translucent mortal mind into the recesses of the individual heart.[34] They would enable the Divine Mind to impart a bit of itself to the individual—and to thereby provide the individual with a "divine Self." In short, Hopkins taught her students to "enter the Silence" or to meditate. Once in a meditative frame of mind they were to practice affirmations and denials. These would cleanse the mortal mind and increase the presence of the "God-Self or good self of us," the divine power within.[35] (See chart 4.)

Hopkins depicted this inner "God-Self" as a wise counselor within who could tell the individual what to do and how to live. As she described it, the God-Self "will teach us how to heal from sickness, how to conduct our business affairs, how to preach, teach, live exactly the right way, to make the most of ourselves here and now."[36] The development of a God-Self within would give the students Godlike powers. The student's own thought would become a "deathless, indestructible, invisible arrow, charged with the kind of mind you have, and [able to strike] out into other minds to change them to be more like you."[37] The student would then be able to "heal the sick by the word of [her] speaking." Furthermore, Hopkins promised, "there are other things besides sickness and sin that can be denied out of existence by our word. If we are in poverty, trouble, anxiety, name the state or condition and deny it."[38]

Hopkins described this God-Self as dominant and masculine. Her view of the God-Self contrasted with that of Evans, who described the divine inner spark as nourishing and maternal. Alluding to Revelations 12:1–5,

Chart 4. The Theology of Emma Curtis Hopkins.

COSMOLOGY

Divine Mind
(masculine, forceful)
↓
can shine into
↓
the disciplined mortal mind
(weak, malleable, feminine)
which is
subject to false "race beliefs"— original sin, heredity

Salvation

Weak mortal mind enters "the Silence" and is "cleansed," through affirmations and denials, of false beliefs.

Then Divine Mind can shine the "God-Self" or "Man Child" into the now translucent mortal mind.

Mortal mind or self is entirely controlled by the God-Self, who is all-powerful and whose desires are always good.

FROM EDDY:

"Two minds," Divine and carnal or mortal.

Matter has no reality.

FROM EVANS:

The Silence.

A "Divine within" (though only after mortal mind is disciplined).

Desires are good (though only if originating in the God-Self).

---

which describes how the "woman" brings forth "a male child" who will "rule all the nations with a rod of iron," Hopkins identified the "Man Child" with the internal God-Self: "Spirit . . . brings to exposure the Man Child, my I AM—who shall rule all nations with a rod of iron. The iron . . . is magnetic. It rules in the earth by holding all the particles together. . . . So all my being has moved because of my I AM."[39] This "child of dominion" was an internal but separate force that acted within the passive individual.[40] It was a masculine inner self that the passive, feminine individual could safely rely upon.

HOPKINS AND THE CREATION
OF A LATE-VICTORIAN FEMALE SELF

Hopkins's teachings had ambiguous implications for the white middle-class women who made up the majority of her followers. She argued that women were sickened by the belief that they were tainted by original sin. She also attacked "heredity," or the belief that one helplessly inherited the moral or physical ills of one's ancestors. The source of these debilitating beliefs, she taught, was the feminine, passive "mortal mind" itself. As Hopkins explained, "carnal mind" is dangerous because, through "personality," "it whispers subtly that we are weak, that we are ill, that we are inferior." [41]

Women were to transform their sickening "mortal minds" by using affirmations and denials to block painful encounters or offending "race beliefs" about sin, sickness, and death from their consciousness. As Hopkins explained, by practicing affirmations, "You are stating that what you can see with your own eyes and hear with your own ears is not true." Even those suffering from "what claims to be discord in the home" should apply this principle. "We should be so absorbed in looking at what is good that we couldn't see the bad," she advised.[42]

On the other hand, Hopkins's treatments did not simply entail the "denial" of one's problems. She helped her patients identify cultural beliefs in original sin or heredity that may have contributed to their feelings of helplessness. She also engaged her patients in a form of talking cure. She taught a six-step healing method that included not only verbal counsel and silent meditation by the healer, but also confessions of private sorrows by the patient.[43] "False beliefs" were admitted and then denied; the patient was broken down and then built up again. The healer was to

1. deny that the patient is ruled by the flesh (deny "matter," sin, and heredity);

2. deny any sense-evidence opposing the view that the patient is all spirit;

3. affirm that the patient is related to God the Good. At this stage, "chemicalization" occurred, as the patient's mortal mind rebelled against the idea that spirit rather than flesh had power. The patient would become weak, restless, and fearful. At this stage, the patient would sometimes pour out a confession of private sorrows, often related to fears about evil ten-

dencies inherited from ancestors.[44] The patient's state of fearful anxiety necessitated stage four:

4. deny the patient's fears, which will be roused by their "mortal mind" in opposition to the idea that All is Good;

5. deny any ideas that may contradict the statement that the patient is a child of God;

6. affirm that the patient is "the perfect creation of the living God— spiritual, harmonious, free, fearless."[45]

The result was that the deluded "carnal mind" would be destroyed and a new, more powerful self would emerge. This new character would be invulnerable to both "race ideas" and internalized voices that undercut one's feelings of self-worth.[46] As Hopkins explained, "People who are exceedingly sensitive to praise and blame, people who are made ill or weak by other mentalities, are not fully in the Science. . . . They must grow to such a strength that no one can darken or shake them."[47]

Hopkins's teachings could encourage rebellious behavior. Her depiction of the "God-Self" was particularly useful in this regard. The God-Self could function as a forceful, masculine ego for the gentle and retiring late-Victorian woman. By imagining their "personality" or "mortal mind" as a clear window through which a "Man Child" or God-Self radiated, Hopkins's students could behave in a forceful manner while still claiming to have stilled their unruly mortal "self."

Hopkins's teachings therefore permitted a great deal of ambiguity about self-assertion. If one conceived of one's mind as a window or mirror, it could be difficult to determine whether one's misguided "personality" or the external-but-internal "God-Self" was motivating one's actions.[48] As one student asked Hopkins, "When we do not know exactly what course to pursue, how can we be sure it is the true or false self that urges us into doing [*sic*] a certain way?" Hopkins's response was emphatic but hardly resolved the student's concern. She answered, "Do that which seems just right, or what you seem driven to do, and trust your choice. Trust that the Best, the Divine guided you. Never mind how far away from the Right it seems. *Trust that it is Right.* . . . Nobody is quite so wise concerning your own matters as yourself."[49]

Hopkins's admonition to "do that which seems just right," even if it seems "far away from the Right" could enable women who shared their culture's faith in womanly self-denial to engage in self-assertive behavior. Hopkins explicitly lauded self-love and self-assertion because she claimed to be speaking not of the mortal self but of the divine "Self." She wrote, "'Love thyself last' is poor policy, as the scorn and cringing of multitudes demonstrate. Unconsciously we have known that there is something wrong about such doctrine. 'I glorify myself' is Jesus Christ in you as Redeemer forever from poverty, foolishness, pain, grief, sickness. The Self is God."[50]

As we have seen, the ideology of sentimental selfhood portrayed white male character as a mix of inner morality and outer forcefulness; man's psyche contained both a feminine heart and masculine passion. It portrayed white female character as passive and moral without the balancing virtues of forcefulness and drive. Woman was thus inherently incomplete, and required a male partner or guardian if she was to function in society.[51]

The convoluted and ambiguous writings of Emma Curtis Hopkins record her efforts to make women whole instead of half. If men became whole by having a feminine heart within (as Warren Felt Evans's writings, traditional in this regard, had indicated), then women, externally gentle and passive, could only become whole by having a "Man Child" or masculine self within.[52] The creation of a masculine, Godlike inner self remained an imperfect solution to the problem of women's lack of ego, however. First, in order to incorporate the power of the "Man Child," Hopkins described complete identification with it; the Man Child became her "Self." She proclaimed that "I have found my Self, because I know my Self, because I AM my Self." As her phrasing makes clear, Hopkins believed that her "Self" was God's self and not her human female self. "I am glad to give myself to my Self and to give all my world to my Self," she wrote.[53] This differs from the workings of sentimental individualism. Men may have had a feminine heart within, but they did not then feel the need to erase their male selves in order to become one with their interior femininity. As we have seen, Evans posited the feminine within as a mere conduit leading to an empowered public male self. Yet Hopkins could not bring herself to describe the inverse relationship—that is, of an interior masculinity leading to an empowered public female self.

There was perhaps a more serious drawback in claiming a divine ego as a makeshift "self" and so a basis for activity in the world. God's self could know no obstacles, as Hopkins' "affirmations" and "denials" continually insisted. A world with no obstacle to one's desire is a world of delusion, however. Hopkins and her followers had to deny reality altogether, then, in order to feel they had a powerful "self" within. Unable to claim personal power, they instead claimed a Godlike power that forced them to systematically deny the realities of their lives.

HOPKINS AND DESIRE

Hopkins's merging of Eddy's doctrine of opposing minds and Evans's doctrine of the divine within allowed her followers to be of "two minds" about self-assertion. She was similarly divided on the question of whether womanly virtue or male desire was the basis of civilization. Eddy wanted to stop male desire, even at the cost of complete stillness. Evans hoped to liberate desire to the point where, unimpeded, it could itself create "supply." Hopkins took a middle course. She opposed the lustful desires of men. At the same time, she told her students that desire was good, but was not their own. She showed them how to desire while remaining passive.

On the one hand, Hopkins aligned herself with the desireless woman's era. She described the coming of a Mother God who would help "usher in the dawn of a new time," "wherein the poor may be taught and befriended, women walk fearless and glad, and childhood be safe and free."[54] This "new time" would reject the belief that men's sexual desires were medical "necessities" to which women must minister. As Hopkins explained, her students "know that the Mother God is the Holy Spirit of the Scripture. They discern the signs of the times in the uprising of woman and the spiritual interpretation she is giving to all words and movements. . . . They see that the rejection by the woman of this old false belief that evil is a necessity . . . is the second coming of the Christ."[55]

Echoing the major themes of the social-purity movement, Hopkins praised "the sacredness of marriage and the home" and proclaimed "the right of children to be rightly born and loved and tended by mother-father care." Alluding perhaps to her own unhappy marriage, she stressed that "the first sign of Eden returning will be the true home life, unspoiled by lawlessness or fear of evil dealings." Like Eddy, however, Hopkins expressed her ultimate hope that marriage and family would be reformed out of existence by citing Mark 12:5. "[W]hen we shall have perfected this symbol of life [marriage and the home]," then "there shall no longer be marrying, or giving in marriage, or giving of birth, for all shall awake to know they are as the angels of God in heaven."[56]

Unlike Eddy, however, Hopkins did not call for the eradication of all desire. She sometimes appeared to join Evans in an unambiguous lauding of desire. Citing Mark 11:24, she wrote that it was an "immutable and unvarying law" that "'[w]hatsover things ye desire, when ye pray, believe that you receive, and ye shall receive.'" She continued, "Why should you believe that you receive? Because health and strength and perfect living are the desires of the heart. Desires are . . . signs . . . of things that we have a right to. 'Wait patiently on the Lord, and he shall give thee the desires of thine [*sic*] heart.'. . . Not some things, but *whatsoever things*. Not sometimes receive, but always receive, provided you believe that you receive."[57] Hopkins also taught that desires would only be fulfilled if they were acknowledged. She explained that "exactly the blessing we want comes to us. But we must acknowledge it; that is, we must speak it."[58]

Some of Hopkins's students were puzzled by her praise of desire. As one of them asked, "How is the science consistent when in one breath it tells us we can have nothing to ourselves, and in the next breath tells us we can have the desire of our hearts?" Hopkins's answer referred back to the doctrine of two minds. She said, "nothing, nothing, *worse than nothing*, belongs to mortality. But *all things belong to the spiritual, or truly minded*." In another forum, Hopkins wrote "All things are yours because all things are God's. To think of them as yours separate from God would be a species of selfishness appalling to imagine."[59]

Hopkins taught a peculiarly passive version of desire. In numerous sermons she described women who would literally wait for the Lord to fulfill their desires, taking little action on their own behalf. As she described in a typical homily,

> There was once a woman who made up her mind that she would not work at all for her living. She sat down with her family of little children around her and said, "The Lord will provide for us." . . . She had made up her mind that the grim wolf named "want" should be kept from her door by the defending God. And she was the most miraculously lucky woman in the way help of all kinds was constantly rendered to her.[60]

Hopkins taught women to obey a self that wasn't their own. Women had desires that were not for what they appeared to be.[61] And they should fulfill these desires not through action, but through passive waiting. Hopkins hedged her assertion of women's selfhood on all sides, and so presented a highly ambiguous message. Her teachings therefore enabled her students to express both sides of their conflicting emotions. They also allowed her students to deny that their actions had any but the most spiritual motives. This perhaps explains why the behaviors that would typify later New Thought groups—millennial hopes and virulent infighting, praises of spirituality combined with grubby laudings of material wealth—were rampant among Hopkins's earliest followers.

LIFE AT HOPKINS'S CHRISTIAN SCIENCE
THEOLOGICAL SEMINARY

The promise of economic independence or even wealth; the excitement of travel; freedom from domestic life; the joy of healing; new circles of friends and comrades; a sense of self-respect and a newly won respect from others; and the conviction that one was helping to inaugurate a spiritual era of woman's power—these were the sparkling lures that drew women and some men into the world of mental healing in the 1880s and 1890s.

There were drawbacks to organizing one's life around mental healing, however. The experiences of students at Hopkins's Christian Science Theological Seminary (C.S.T.S.) demonstrated some of those difficulties. The C.S.T.S. was a rooming house as well as a school. In 1891 it housed sixteen permanent residents and eleven guests.[62] There, Hopkins taught her students that they could share the omnipotence of God as long as they relied upon affirmations and denials. As a result of this teaching, the rooming house/seminary became a hotbed of bitter infighting and barely repressed emotional chaos.

Conflicts arose as Hopkins's teachings flew in the face of people's lived experience. A prime example was her insistence that for those in "the science" there could be no poverty. "If you want to know how *'the Almighty is thy defense and thou shalt have plenty of silver,'* speak the truth concerning hunger and cold and nakedness. *Deny their reality,"* she exhorted. Given the profitability of mental healing, some accepted Hopkins's claim that all could have "plenty of silver" by divine "law." Others, probably those whose economic situations stubbornly refused to conform to the law of prosperity as well as those uneasy with the crass materialism the "law" implied, protested against the teaching. Yet Hopkins stuck to her position. "Some are hounding me, as if I originated the statement of Scripture that the fulfillment of the desire of the heart belongs by right to every one of us," she said at one meeting. But the text, she continued, reads "'Seek ye first the kingdom . . . and all these things shall be added.'"[63]

There may have been even more uneasiness over Hopkins's insistence that those truly following the "science" need never die. Hopkins frequently alluded to the "unreality" of "sin, sickness and death." She openly told her students that they would soon triumph over death. "Very soon we must raise the dead. Do not stop short of expecting to obey this last command of the risen Christ. All your work is secretly pushing you on to that final power," Hopkins exhorted.[64]

While the extremity of Hopkins's doctrines caused dissension among

her followers, other problems arose from the warping of personality—
the combination of paranoia, arrogance, and self-blame—that seemed
prompted by a belief in the absolute power of human thought. Some of
Hopkins's students lived in fear of contagious evil thoughts. Hopkins tried
to assuage these fears by telling them that "malicious mesmerizers" had no
power to hurt them.[65] Since she discouraged the belief in evil mesmerists,
some of Hopkins's students blamed their failure to attain health or wealth
on slight variations in the dogma taught by various teachers. Hopkins tried
to counter these fears, and the sectarianism that such fears produced, by insisting that no criticisms of other teachers be voiced at her seminary.[66]

Unpleasantness among the "scientists" also arose from the vicious
blame-the-victim attitude intrinsic to their belief that suffering could only
be produced by one's own mental attitude. Hopkins alluded to the "students
of Christian Science" who have become "quite conceited and hateful where
they used to be generous and gentle," and explained this behavior—as well
as the problems of continued sickness, poverty, and "sorrow in the home"—
as "chemicalization." In other words, she interpreted arrogance as well as
poverty, illness, and unhappiness as merely signs of the difficult transition
from a material to a more spiritually oriented life.[67] Yet Hopkins encouraged her followers to adopt a blame-the-victim attitude. She described a
visitor who "adroitly questioned many of those claiming to be Christian
Scientists, and got the admission from them that something was wrong with
nearly all of them." She explained that these illnesses were the Christian
Scientists' own faults:

> Those people ought to be invoking the power of God by speaking the
> word of God over and over and over till the power of God is demonstrated
> in them perfectly.
> There is surely some turning away from absolute faith in the power
> of the word while something is seeming to be wrong.[68]

To those suffering from poverty or unhappiness, Hopkins said, "Whoso
believes that it is Christian to be poor or in trouble, shows that he does not
understand Jesus Christ."[69]

Hopkins seemed to apply similarly exacting standards to her own conduct. Throughout the early 1890s she maintained a frenetic schedule of activity. She traveled and taught, published articles on healing and spirituality in addition to writing weekly Bible studies, preached Sunday sermons,
presented monthly addresses to the Chicago Hopkins Metaphysical Association, and oversaw her seminary's growth.[70]

In 1895, however, Hopkins abruptly withdrew from her seminary and moved to New York City. In a series of letters to her friends Charles and Myrtle Fillmore, she indicated that exhaustion and disillusionment with the infighting among her students had prompted her decision to abandon the seminary. "As you may imagine I am 'come at' from every quarter instantly. There is no describing my life," she wrote in the fall of 1894. "I have got between so many crossfires and have such personal weights to attend to that I have to let the cross firing alone."[71] In early December Hopkins again described her exhaustion, as well as the demands made upon her. "Do you know while I have been the guest of some people, in affluence, in luxury, they wouldn't let me go to bed nights—wanted me talking and smiling till midnight and felt I was an ungrateful one if I didn't?" She went on, "[Now] I am so tired that it seems as if I must die." Yet the letter also described her mystical feelings of omnipotent power: "Sometimes my dauntless divinity shines even through my bones and skin like glass, as if the sea [?]of glass mingled with fire were taking place in my body. The rags of environments, the rags of knowledge of thoughts, the tatters of weariness—doth the mighty me have reckoning with such garbage!"[72]

It was with these conflicting emotions that Hopkins retired from her seminary and moved to New York City. For the next thirty years she lived quietly in two rooms in the Iroquois Hotel. She continued to write and receive individual students, but she remained largely aloof from the New Thought movement.[73]

One other factor may have contributed to Hopkins's withdrawal. By the mid-1890s mental healers had footholds in almost every part of the nation, were becoming organized, and had begun to refer to themselves proudly as the "New Thought" movement.[74] Hopkins's personal efforts were no longer needed to ensure the spread of mental healing.

The actions of Mary Baker Eddy were partially responsible for the growth of a distinct movement known as "New Thought." In the early 1890s Eddy copyrighted the term "Christian Science" and began to sue anyone who used the phrase without her permission. By the mid-1890s, therefore, mental healers around the country were forced to rename themselves. Hopkins's *Christian Science* magazine, for example, was renamed *Universal Truth*, and her "Christian Science Association" became the "Truth Students Association."

Mostly, however, it was the dedication of Hopkins's students that led to the emergence of an organized New Thought movement. By the mid-1890s, her students formed the "western wing" of a thriving national movement. After Hopkins's retirement the key figures in the spread of this wing were Malinda Cramer (San Francisco), Nona Brooks (Denver), Annie Rix Militz

(Chicago and the Pacific coast), and Myrtle and Charles Fillmore (Kansas City). I now briefly survey the healing narratives and subsequent New Thought careers of these five early leaders.

Their healing narratives offer clues to what may have motivated late-Victorian women and men to devote their lives to New Thought. For some, New Thought beliefs about the power of the spiritual over the carnal appeared to offer an escape from compulsory heterosexuality. Others, those who had been born into the elites of their home towns but whose adult lives brought economic uncertainty, appear to have been drawn in by mental healers' promises that meditation would restore their "birthright" of economic security. Some also had previously believed that their illnesses were the result of an "inheritance" from an invalid mother. They were relieved to understand themselves now as children of God, with a "rightful inheritance" of health, rather than simply as children of women, inflicted with the curse of hereditary illness.

Their subsequent New Thought careers highlight the extraordinary influence of Emma Curtis Hopkins. Inspired directly or indirectly by Hopkins, each of these five former invalids embarked upon astonishingly active lives of writing, teaching, traveling as missionaries, and institution-building that laid the groundwork for the emergence of New Thought as a national movement. Through drawing upon each other's talents, they created a burgeoning national movement that promised its largely female following salvation through the "denial" of lowly desire.

MALINDA E. CRAMER AND THE HOME COLLEGE OF DIVINE SCIENCE (SAN FRANCISCO)

In 1902 Mrs. Malinda E. Cramer, the co-founder of Divine Science, published her own healing narrative. She had been an invalid for twenty-three years. Her case had "baffled the best physicians." Even the prominent magnetic healers she consulted had given up hope. As one told Cramer, "I would have hope of your recovery if you were not so . . . submissive to your sufferings; you are altogether too resigned."

Finally, in 1885, Cramer turned to prayer, asking, "Is there any way out of these conditions? Is there any Power in the vast Universe that can heal me?" She received "an immediate and all convincing reply" to her heartfelt plea. "Instantly Omnipresent Spirit was realized and everything was transformed into Spirit," Cramer wrote. "I at once saw the unreality of the conditions of dis-ease and was free from the belief that they had any power, or could control for either good or ill. Thus the axe was struck at the root

Figure 8.   Malinda Cramer,
Founder of Divine Science.

of the tree, and the old conditions passed away as fast as I disowned the old habits of belief." From this moment, Cramer's health improved rapidly. Within two years she was entirely healed.[75]

Despite Cramer's claims of divine revelation, she did not become an active mental healer until she attended Emma Curtis Hopkins's 1887 class in San Francisco. Almost immediately after that, Cramer immersed herself in the world of mental healing. In October 1887, just one month after the inauguration of Hopkins's *Christian Science* journal, Cramer began her own monthly journal, *Harmony.* She simultaneously began to teach and to call herself a "Spiritual Scientist." In March 1888 she and her husband Frank chartered the "Home College of Spiritual Science." Two months later Cramer changed the name of her school to the "Home College of Divine Science."[76]

In addition to teaching, healing, publishing, and editing *Harmony,* Cramer established a Divine Science church, where she preached regularly. She wrote several books on Divine Science and also undertook at least two cross-country missionary journeys. During these trips Cramer spoke to small groups of "Christian Scientists" or "metaphysicians" and organized them into new associations that became the nuclei of future Divine Science Colleges. The new groups' activities were then closely followed in the pages of *Harmony*. Cramer's students engaged in similar missionary travels. By 1900 Divine Science centers existed in California (Santa Rosa, Suisan, and Oakland), Missouri (St. Louis and Sedalia), Arizona (Phoenix), Colorado (Aspen and Denver), Kansas (Topeka), Iowa, Wisconsin, and Massachusetts, as well as in Chicago.[77]

Cramer affiliated herself with Hopkins and the Chicago-based Truth Students Association.[78] After Hopkins's 1895 retirement Cramer's group grew more dominant. Residents at Hopkins's Chicago center were listed in Cramer's "Harmony Scientists Directory" and participated in congresses arranged by Cramer.[79]

Cramer's "Divine Science," like Hopkins's Christian Science, was a predominantly female organization. Reports on meetings of her "Home College" mention women participants almost exclusively, and women contributors to *Harmony* typically outnumbered men by a ratio of six to one. About the same gender ratio prevailed among Cramer's ordained clergy. The listings in the Harmony Scientists Directory were generally two-thirds to three-fourths women.[80]

Cramer acknowledged the preponderance of women in her organization, writing in one article, "The question has been frequently asked: 'Why are women active in new religions?'" She explained that because women are "wondrously intuitive and susceptible to Truth," they could "tak[e] the lead in awakening the starving world to its greatest need." As the article continued, Cramer took an increasingly apocalyptic tone. She wrote, "The women of the present time . . . are sowing the seed that will . . . enrich the world and purify humanity of all the false and selfish elements that exist upon the earth."[81]

NONA BROOKS AND TWENTIETH-CENTURY
DIVINE SCIENCE (DENVER AND BEYOND)

After Malinda Cramer's death in 1907, a woman named Nona Brooks assumed leadership of Cramer's Divine Science movement. The chronic illnesses that led Brooks to Divine Science appear to have been caused by the fear that she had "inherited" weakness from her invalid mother, by anxiety over her economic instability, and perhaps most importantly, by a desire to escape heterosexuality.

Nona Brooks was born into a wealthy, orthodox-Presbyterian Kentucky family in 1861. Although both her mother and her sister were "chronic invalids," Brooks's health remained good until her father's sudden death left her financially dependent upon her sister, Mrs. Alethea Small, who then lived in Pueblo, Colorado, and with whom Brooks went to live. Upon arriving in Pueblo, Brooks discovered that her sister and brother-in-law had fallen upon hard times. She was compelled to join her sister in grueling household labor that had formerly been performed by the family's servants.

Brooks's only hope for financial security lay in marriage, yet she was unable to find a suitable spouse. She simply had nothing to say to the men who came calling. Even the best of them, Brooks's biographer Hazel Deane reports, "seemed to drug her into a sort of lethargy." Around this time she began to develop "ulcers of the throat." Her only social contacts were with the children in the Sunday school class she taught. Her health deteriorated rapidly. Soon Brooks was down to eighty-eight pounds and able to swallow only five types of food.[82]

At this point of crisis a neighbor, Mrs. Kate Bingham, entered Brooks's life. Bingham was an invalid who had attended a class given by Emma Curtis Hopkins. The class both healed and converted her. Upon Bingham's return to Pueblo in 1887 she immediately formed a women's Bible class based on Hopkins's teachings and insisted that Brooks and her sister Alethea attend. In the midst of one of Bingham's sessions, Brooks saw the room fill with light. She realized at once that she had always been well. From that moment on, Brooks was healed.[83]

Brooks eventually became a major Divine Science leader. Yet her involvement in Divine Science at first seemed overshadowed by that of another of her sisters, Mrs. Fannie (Brooks) James. Like Alethea and Nona, Fannie James suffered from both poor health and economic insecurity. In the late 1880s James, then living in Denver, was introduced to the new metaphysical thought by Mrs. Mabel MacCoy, yet another of Emma Curtis Hopkins's missionary students. James attended MacCoy's class and was immediately hooked. She convinced a large group of women to meet on a weekly basis at her home, where they listened to her expound on the Bible in light of Hopkins's teachings. Throughout the 1890s James's Bible classes attracted growing numbers of Denver women. James also corresponded with Malinda Cramer, and studied with her when Cramer passed through Denver. Since Cramer's ideas most closely matched her own, James decided to use Cramer's term "Divine Science" to describe her own teachings.[84]

Nona Brooks had meanwhile turned down her last two suitors and moved to Denver. There she worked as a school teacher and practiced mental healing. In 1898 Brooks and her sisters incorporated the "Colorado College of Divine Science," chartered "to prepare teachers and ordain ministers, and establish churches." Brooks then quit teaching and devoted herself entirely to the Denver Divine Science movement. She became one of

Figure 9.   Nona L. Brooks and her sisters Alethea B. Small and Fannie B. James, promoters of Divine Science.

the five-woman faculty of the Colorado College of Divine Science and a leader of weekly Divine Science meditation meetings. The turning point for Brooks, however, occurred in 1898, when she learned that "the ladies" who attended her prayer meetings wanted a regular church service and, furthermore, wanted her to lead it. Money was raised to send her to San Francisco, where she was ordained by Malinda Cramer. The Reverend Nona Brooks led her first service in Denver's Divine Science church on January 1, 1899, and so became the first woman pastor in the city of Denver.[85]

After the turn of the century Fannie James became less involved, while Nona Brooks became more active in the Denver Divine Science movement. In addition to teaching at the Divine Science college, "treating" the sick and unhappy, and delivering at least two sermons a week, Brooks edited *Fulfillment* magazine (1902–1906) and contributed to the *Divine Science Quarterly* (1906–1912).[86]

Brooks never married. Each summer she vacationed with her lifelong

"dearest friend," Mrs. Florence Hoyt, with whom she felt "a companion-
ship too deep for words."[87] Brooks's involvement in New Thought allowed
her to escape heterosexuality and to immerse herself in an almost entirely
female world. It also freed her from the economic dependence that would
have otherwise been her fate as an undereducated and unmarried middle-
class woman.

Indeed, Brooks's incessant labors brought her widespread fame. After
Cramer's death in 1907, Brooks's Denver college became the center of the
Divine Science movement. When east-coast New Thought participants organized the International New Thought Alliance in the early years of the
twentieth century, Brooks actively participated. She became a nationally
recognized New Thought leader.[88]

In 1917 Dr. W. John Murray, head of the largest New Thought group in
New York City, asked Brooks to occupy his pulpit for four months. She ac-
cepted, and also agreed to let Murray call his congregation the "First Church
of Divine Science." Meanwhile, Divine Science continued to spread. In 1918,
Divine Science churches existed in Oakland (California), Seattle, Boston,
Spokane, St. Louis, New York, and Oklahoma. By 1925, additional churches
had opened in California (Los Angeles, San Diego, and Sacramento), Kansas
(Topeka), Washington, D.C., Illinois, Iowa, and Ohio (Cleveland).[89]

Brooks resigned from the ministry of the Denver Church of Divine
Science in 1929, explaining that "the work would grow better under a
man." She remained active in the movement, however, even traveling to
Australia at the age of seventy to establish new centers there. Brooks lived
long enough to witness the triumph of Divine Science in the 1930s under
the leadership of Dr. Emmet Fox. Fox, who was ordained in Brooks's home
Divine Science church, took over Murray's New York City church on Murray's death in the early 1930s. Within a few months Fox had increased church
membership from fifty to five thousand, with meetings held at the Hippo-
drome. The enormous congregation was the largest single Depression-
era church audience in the country. Fox reached hundreds of thousands
more with his best-selling tracts, particularly *Power Through Constructive
Thinking* (1932) and *The Sermon on the Mount* (1934). Brooks died in 1945,
a revered leader of a national movement.[90]

Brooks's theology was similar to Cramer's, but contained fewer explicit
references to women's spiritual power. Nevertheless, as late as 1899 Denver
Divine Science was composed exclusively of women. In the early twentieth
century women represented from 75% to 90% of those most involved in
Divine Science. Even into the 1920s women made up the overwhelming

Figure 10.   Annie Rix Militz,
founder of Home of Truth.

majority of those actively promoting Divine Science.[91] Brooks's 1929 decision to pass Divine Science leadership to a man constituted a worried recognition of the fact that until that time, Divine Science was practically, if not
theologically, a women's religious movement.

ANNIE RIX MILITZ AND THE HOMES OF TRUTH (PACIFIC COAST)

The Home of Truth movement owed its existence to the efforts of a single
woman: Annie Rix Militz. Like Brooks, Rix Militz found in New Thought
a release from both illness and heterosexuality. In her hands, the ambiguous doctrines of Emma Curtis Hopkins became a straightforward "denial"
of the necessity of heterosexual desire.

In 1887, Annie Rix was a thirty-one-year-old unmarried school teacher
living in San Francisco. She was plagued by sick headaches she believed to
be an inheritance from her mother, a chronic invalid. When Emma Curtis
Hopkins taught a class in San Francisco that year, Rix attended. In the midst
of her instruction a sick headache came on. Rix applied Hopkins's teachings
and immediately cured herself permanently of both the sick headaches and

deafness in one ear. After her third lesson with Hopkins, Rix told her sister Harriet Hale Rix, "I have found my life work." She would promote the metaphysical truth that had restored her health.[92]

Rix's first step was to join Mrs. Sadie Gorie, another member of Hopkins's San Francisco class, in establishing a "metaphysical bureau" (a combination metaphysical bookstore and healing and teaching center). The bureau expanded quickly. It soon included a kindergarten, a school, a "Christian Science Bazaar" (a labor exchange), and a "charitable branch" that distributed goods to the poor. All activities at the bureau, which was called "The Christian Science Home," were paid for by free-will offerings.[93]

In 1889 Hopkins asked Rix to join the faculty of the Christian Science Theological Seminary in Chicago. Rix remained committed to her own Christian Science Home, but for two years she commuted to Chicago twice a year to officiate at Hopkins's class reviews. In 1891 Rix finally broke her three-year association with Gorie and permanently joined Hopkins's seminary. In Rix's absence, the work of the "Home" continued under the direction of Rix's sister, Harriet Hale Rix, and three other San Francisco women. In the 1890s, when Mary Baker Eddy won the exclusive right to the term Christian Science, Rix's Christian Science Home was renamed the "Home of Truth" and continued to expand. Meanwhile, Annie Rix spent the early 1890s teaching in Chicago, New York, and Colorado Springs. She met her husband, Paul Militz, when both were in residence at Hopkins's theological seminary. They married shortly after they met. The marriage was purely spiritual. The two lived and taught together in Sierra Madre, California in 1894 and 1895. After 1895 they lived apart for the remainder of their lives.[94]

Annie Rix Militz spent the period from 1895 to 1911 nearly incessantly teaching, writing, and traveling. She published regularly in *Universal Truth* (the successor to Hopkins's journal, *Christian Science*), and in 1899 established Chicago's "Truth Center," a variation on her "Home of Truth" idea. She taught in Kansas City, Minneapolis, and New York, and participated in New Thought summer retreats at Lake Geneva and Manitou. As a result of her efforts, by 1903 Homes of Truth dotted almost the entire length of the Pacific coast and had also spread to Minnesota (Minneapolis), Illinois (Peoria), Wisconsin (Geneva Lake), Missouri (St. Louis), Colorado (Denver), Kansas (Holten), Massachusetts (Boston and Worcester), Pennsylvania (Philadelphia), and New York.[95]

In addition to organizing scores of Homes of Truth, Rix Militz published six New Thought books between 1899 and 1918. She began her own journal, *Master Mind*, in 1911. *Master Mind* published numerous articles telling readers how to set up their own "Truth Centers." These do-it-yourself instructions resulted in the further spread of Homes of Truth.[96]

Rix Militz's theology closely followed Hopkins's teachings. She spoke of a "carnal mind" that must be "cleansed" and made "translucent" so that the Self or Divine Mind can shine through.[97] But while Hopkins's attitude toward desire was ambiguous, Rix Militz's was not. She taught that desire, and especially sexual desire, must be "stilled" if spiritual growth was to occur. She argued that once people conquered their sexual desires, they would be "regenerated" and never die. She associated desire with chaos and its opposite, purity, with "the immaculate Virgin that all womanhood typifies."[98] Rix Militz's "Homes of Truth," like the Divine Science centers of Cramer and Brooks, attracted an almost exclusively female following. Long after Hopkins's retirement, Rix Militz continued to claim that crime, intemperance, and "everything that militates against the progress of the human race" would soon be abolished as a result of the development of the powers of "woman."[99]

THE UNITY SCHOOL OF CHRISTIANITY (KANSAS CITY)

Rix Militz's "Homes of Truth" declined rapidly after her death in 1924. The most direct beneficiary of her labors was the Kansas City–based "Unity School of Christianity." This religious empire was constructed by Charles Fillmore, the "father" of Unity, through a series of strategic alliances with Hopkins, Cramer, Brooks, and Rix Militz.

Fillmore was born in 1854 in northern Minnesota. His father abandoned the family when Fillmore was seven. His only brother, Norton, left home when Fillmore was twelve. Around this time he had a skating accident that left his right leg weakened into his adulthood. He left Minnesota for Texas at the age of nineteen. There he met Myrtle Page, the daughter of the founding family of Pagetown, Ohio. She had come to Texas in search of a better climate to cure her tuberculosis. The two married in 1881.

Over the next five years, following land booms, the couple moved to four different locations in Colorado, Nebraska, and Missouri.[100] Each boom quickly became a bust. In 1886 Myrtle Fillmore, now the mother of two young children, found herself facing her husband's fourth business failure and, perhaps not unrelated, a flare-up of her old tuberculosis. Seeking relief for her ills, Myrtle attended a mental-healing seminar in Kansas City. She was particularly struck by one of the speaker's phrases: *"I am a child of God and therefore I do not inherit sickness."* Soon Myrtle Fillmore was attending the lectures of every metaphysical healer who passed through

Figure 11.   Charles Fillmore,
founder of Unity School
of Christianity.

Kansas City. By 1888 she had not only regained her health, she was healing others.[101]

Charles Fillmore at first remained aloof from his wife's growing interest
in spiritual healing. Two events spurred his further involvement, however.
The first was his encounter with Emma Curtis Hopkins. In 1886 Myrtle
convinced Charles to accompany her to Chicago, where the couple studied
with Hopkins. They developed a close and lasting friendship with her.
Charles in particular was almost awed by Hopkins. He described her as
"undoubtedly the most successful teacher in the world," adding that "[s]he
dwells so continually in the spirit that her very presence heals, and those
who listen to her earnest words are filled with new life." Charles Fillmore
began applying the principles he had learned, treating himself for "catarrh,
indigestion and other ailments." He also treated his lame leg. Within a decade Fillmore would pronounce the leg healed.[102]

The second impetus to Charles Fillmore's involvement was financial.
Kansas City's real-estate market bottomed out in 1889, leaving the Fillmores deeply in debt. With no real-estate deals to distract him, Charles decided to join with Myrtle in the publication of a metaphysical journal,
Modern Thought. The journal was successful from the start. Soon the Fill-

mores added classes, prayer meetings, and a publishing branch to their operations.[103]

Modern Thought's early issues included articles on an array of occult, eastern, and metaphysical beliefs. Soon, however, the journal focused on Emma Curtis Hopkins's version of Christian Science. In 1890 the Fillmores invited Hopkins to Kansas City, where she held a hugely successful class attended by eighty-seven pupils. That same year the Fillmores changed the name of their journal to *Christian Science Thought*. They were ordained by Hopkins in 1891. In the course of their ordination studies, the Fillmores cemented their friendship with many of Hopkins's more prominent students, especially Annie Rix.[104]

The Fillmores' publication expanded through the 1890s. Rebuffed by Eddy for their use of the term "Christian Science," the Fillmores renamed their journal *Thought*. A major turning point for *Thought* occurred in April 1890, when Myrtle Fillmore published an article announcing the formation of the "Society of Silent Help." Myrtle explained that members of the society would meet nightly at 10:00 P.M. to meditate upon set "affirmations." She wrote that because the "wonderful success of absent healing demonstrates that bodily presence is not necessary to those in spiritual harmony," readers could join this meditation circle in spirit. To partake of the society's healing power, readers needed only to sit quietly in their own homes at 10:00 P.M. and mentally concentrate on the groups' affirmation, published in *Thought* magazine.[105]

Myrtle Fillmore's "Society of Silent Help" caught on immediately. In the spring of 1891 the Fillmores began to focus their energies on *Unity*, their new metaphysical journal. In 1895 *Thought* was merged with *Unity*, which became the center of their ministry.[106] The society was renamed the "Society of Silent Unity." A notice in *Unity* explained its workings:

> All persons may become members "without money and without price" who will sit in peaceful mind for a short time, at nine o'clock each evening, and invite in . . . the conscious presence of the Holy Spirit. . . . For its centralizing potency a "class thought" is given each month, which all members hold in consciousness for a few moments; . . . then "ask what ye will in my name and it shall be done unto you."
>   . . . All who wish to be fully identified with us are invited to send in their names with a brief description of their trouble. We cannot undertake to answer such letters personally, but will respond in the Silence as the Spirit directs.[107]

In 1894, a year before the renaming of the society, the Fillmores had instituted yet another innovation. Those who sent in prayer requests were given certificate numbers. These numbers were then published in *Unity* alongside affirmations directed to the person's specific complaint (for example: "4987. Vinceland, N.C. 'You are free from the belief in sin. Wisdom and purity are yours by Divine Right'"). This ensured that those wishing to participate in Silent Unity would purchase *Unity* magazine (even though the Society of Silent Unity was based exclusively on "free-will offerings"). The society's promises of health and happiness spurred *Unity*'s growth. By 1894 *Unity* had subscribers in every state and territory in the country. Local branches of "Silent Unity" proliferated. There were 10,000 by 1903 and 15,000 by 1906.[108]

After 1894 Myrtle Fillmore dropped out of active participation in what she and her husband now called the "Unity School of Practical Christianity."[109] Charles Fillmore's activities more than picked up the slack. He arranged for prominent New Thought teachers to publish in *Unity* and offer classes at the Unity offices. He began teaching his own classes in "Practical Christianity" in 1897 and, beginning in 1905, published his spiritual writings. After World War I Charles Fillmore and his sons Lowell and Rickert bought fifty-eight acres of land in Lee's Summit, just outside Kansas City. By the 1970s the area, now called "Unity Village," comprised over 1,400 acres and included resort facilities, Unity's printing department, and Unity's teaching, healing, and administrative centers.[110]

The organizational genius of Charles and Myrtle Fillmore was not solely responsible for their phenomenal success. The Fillmores relied more than a little on the help of their friends. They drew heavily upon Hopkins's network during the crucial first decade of their work.[111] They were also close to Malinda Cramer, who taught classes in their offices, sold Unity tracts in San Francisco, and published Charles Fillmore in *Harmony*.[112] Most of all, the Fillmores drew upon the talents of Annie Rix Militz. Throughout the 1890s Rix Militz's "Bible Lessons" were the centerpiece of each issue of *Unity*. Many of her books first appeared in *Unity* in serial form. Rix Militz in turn helped spread Unity literature throughout the country. Charles Fillmore was deeply influenced by Rix Militz's perspective. In a 1902 interview Fillmore spoke at length about Rix Militz's favorite theme, "regeneration." He described his efforts to enact regeneration in his own body, with the ultimate aim of "immortality in the flesh."[113]

After the turn of the century the Fillmores disengaged themselves from the Divine Science milieu of Cramer, Brooks, and Rix Militz. Their relations with Rix Militz cooled after she launched her own journal, *Master Mind*, in 1911. Charles Fillmore gradually dropped his interest in immortality, and even in healing. His writings instead emphasized the need to regard all beings with love and to rely on God for all things. "If you want a dress, a car, a house, or if you are thinking of driving a sharp bargain with your neighbor, going on a journey, giving a friend a present, running for office, or reforming a nation, ask God for guidance," he wrote in a typical passage.[114]

The period of greatest cooperation between Cramer, Brooks, Rix Militz, and the Fillmores was undoubtedly during the mid-1890s. All were promoting ideas derived from Emma Curtis Hopkins. They taught that God was all and that matter did not exist. They claimed that the Divine Mind must triumph over the mortal mind. They explained how one could go "into the Silence" and use affirmations and denials to "cleanse" the mortal mind, thus allowing the Divine Mind to shine through. They believed that thought had creative power, necessitating the careful monitoring of one's thoughts. Overlooking Hopkins's ambiguity on the topic, these women and men emphasized the importance of overcoming "desire." They equated "woman" with desirelessness and hinted that the conquest of "desire" would mean the triumph of "woman."[115]

The alliances among this "anti-desire" school of New Thought leaders were strengthened through International Divine Science Association congresses, organized by Malinda Cramer and held in 1894, 1895, 1896, 1897, and 1899. These conventions attracted New Thought leaders from around the nation. By the late 1890s conventions of east-coast New Thought leaders were held as well. They culminated in the formation of the New Thought Alliance in 1904 and of the International New Thought Alliance in 1914.[116]

The Divine Science congresses predated the east-coast–oriented International New Thought Alliance and brought together the national leadership of the 1890s New Thought movement. The high point of the International Divine Science Association was probably the St. Louis Congress of 1897. It was attended by many of the stars of the movement. In her congress address, Malinda Cramer gave a "conservative estimate" of three million "liberal Scientists" at present. She gave the movement's history, starting with Phineas Quimby's teachings and continuing through the teachings of Eddy, Evans, Mental Science, Spiritual Science, Christian Metaphysics, and Practical Christianity, "and then showed that Divine Science is all inclusive."[117]

The International Divine Science Association was not the only large, female-dominated congress of the mid-1890s. On the contrary, the decade was rich with such assemblies, from the Biennial Conventions of the General Federation of Women's Clubs, which began in 1892, to the National Purity Congress in 1895 and the National Congress of Mothers in 1897.

The meetings of New Thought leaders and of mothers, purity activists, and club women were connected by more than a shared predominance of women and even by more than the existence of some overlapping membership. All were obsessed with the same concerns: Where did women's power lie? What was the role of womanly influence? What could women legitimately desire? What specific actions would help bring about the new "woman's era"? All agreed that this new era would only come about if the "carnal" or material was crushed by an assertion of spiritual power. Could a new era be constructed upon the foundation of a simple but heartfelt "denial" of desire?

4 Sex and Desirelessness

*The New Thought Novels
of Helen Van-Anderson,
Ursula Gestefeld, and
Alice Bunker Stockham*

Yes, it was to cost her dear, the love and the freedom for which, all
her life, she had longed. Were these really not to be found in the
world of men?

Ursula Newell Gestefeld, 1892 [1]

. . . the best could be worst, as the worst could be best
You must thank your own worth for what I grew to be
For the demon lurked under the angel in me.

Ella Wheeler Wilcox, 1901 [2]

There was a kinship between New Thought and the woman movement of
the 1880s and 1890s. Proponents of the woman's era hoped to purify the
self and contain desire. New Thought meditations offered an exciting new
means by which desire could be eradicated and selfhood reshaped. The New
Thought novel highlighted these connections and interrogated the vision
of white women's desireless selfhood that was the cornerstone of the "woman's era." Of particular interest in this regard are New Thought novels by
three female authors: Helen Van-Anderson, a student of Emma Curtis Hopkins; Ursula Newell Gestefeld, a student of Mary Baker Eddy; and Alice
Bunker Stockham, a student of Hopkins who also embraced the work of
Warren Felt Evans. To appreciate the cultural centrality of the issues explored in the work of these three novelists, we must first re-examine the
woman movement's concern with selfhood, sexuality, and desire.

THE LATE-NINETEENTH-CENTURY CONTEXT
FOR NEW THOUGHT LITERATURE

Historian Nancy F. Cott has demonstrated that the late-nineteenth-century
woman movement was based on three sometimes overlapping strands of
thought: "service," or the belief that women ought to aid their less fortu-

nate sisters; "rights," or the claim that women ought to have the same legal, political, and economic rights as men; and "emancipation," or opposition to oppressive male-defined structures and conventions. Yet at another level all three strands were aimed at containing lustful desire and encouraging a more elevated form of selfhood in both men and women.[3]

The more conservative of the "service"-oriented activists felt that society was threatened by personal immorality. Missionary women might trace this crisis to heathenism, temperance women to alcohol, club women to lack of cultural refinement, and charity-organization women to slum dwellers' lack of contact with the elevating influences of the well-to-do. But all claimed that the behavior they opposed promoted lustfulness, while the behavior they encouraged would help purify the self. As a late-nineteenth-century YWCA manual explained, they aimed to mold their charges "into all that is pure and excellent in character."[4]

Activists interested in women's rights also hoped to end disruptive sensuality and to uplift male and female selfhood. Some, like Elizabeth Cady Stanton, argued that it was only by achieving full social equality that women would free themselves from "hideous outrages on the mothers of the race" such as marital rape and enforced motherhood.[5] Others called for an expansion of women's rights so that women could bring their purifying "mother-heart" into wider areas of society. Frances Willard explained that woman "came into college and humanized it, into literature and hallowed it, into the business world and ennobled it. She will come into government and purify it, into politics and cleanse [it] . . . for woman will make home-like every place she enters, and she will enter every place on this round earth."[6]

The emancipation school challenged those who promoted womanly service. Matilda Joslyn Gage proclaimed, for example, that "not self-sacrifice, but self-development, is [woman's] first duty in life." However, they agreed with more conservative women activists that male lust damaged society, and that female virtue would improve it. Radical woman movement theorists were also concerned, therefore, with the nature of the self and the meaning of desire. As Eliza Burt Gamble explained, although conservatives claimed that "the stage of human society that we call civilization is an outgrowth of masculine energy stimulated by masculine desire and directed by masculine will," the opposite was actually the truth. According to Gamble, "Maternal affection . . . [is the] root of all our later ideas of justice and duty; and our present Utopian dream of the brotherhood of man . . . is but an extension of this early acquired character of the female."[7]

Social purity crusades were an important strand of the late-nineteenth-century woman movement in part because they directly addressed this issue of containing male desire and promoting female virtue, and in part because they encompassed service, rights, and emancipation perspectives. More conservative social purity leaders hoped to curb male lust by censoring the press, raising the age of consent, and shutting down houses of prostitution. The movement's more radical leaders encouraged sex education as a means of elevating attitudes toward sexuality. They attacked the economic basis of prostitution through promoting better pay for women. They also supported kindergartens, which they believed would produce boys and girls who were equally moral and spiritual beings. The entire spectrum agreed, however, that "unchecked" male lust degraded women, damaged their offspring, and weakened the race. If men were brought to women's high standard—or if social and economic conditions were changed so that every woman could achieve this standard—then a new race, and a new civilization, would emerge.

At the heart of the woman movement, then, was a wish to reform selfhood by moderating desire. The overt issue was the transformation of male character. But female character was also an issue. Many woman movement activists agreed with former U.S. president Grover Cleveland's claim that women had, "through their nurture of children and their influence over men, the destinies of our Nation in their keeping."[8] Woman's self had to be moral, therefore. Indeed, doubts about the worth of the female self were occasionally voiced by woman movement leaders, especially in the early years of the movement. As Jane Cunningham Croly, the founder of the woman's club Sorosis, wrote in 1869, "Suppose . . . that some of us did begin to realize that we were growing more and more stupid, and more and more 'dull,' and more and more 'inane' every day, and determined to do something to help ourselves, and that something was Sorosis, would not even that be accomplishing a little?"[9]

By the 1880s, women's organizations no longer claimed that they simply helped women become less "inane." Rather, they took credit for awakening women to their full potential as people of "head and heart." As one woman explained, temperance work "startled [her] into an active thinking life" and gave her a "broader view of woman's sphere and responsibility." This was why, according to Frances Willard, "[t]he WCTU [was] doing no more important work than reconstructing the ideal of womanhood." Unitarian minister and suffrage, purity, and temperance activist Anna Garlin Spencer even argued that since women were so rapidly achieving "intellectual and moral development," perhaps they should now work in groups that included men, so that men would not be left so far behind.[10]

This confidence in women's emerging character of high intellect and morality formed the basis of the millennial hopes of the 1880s and 1890s woman movement. Given woman's superior character and her powers of influence, there was no limit to what "organized mother-hearts" could achieve. The prestigious Chicago Woman's Club defined its goal as "a united effort towards a higher civilization of humanity." The 1888 International Council of Women declared that their aim was "the overthrow of all forms of ignorance and injustice and . . . the application of the Golden Rule to society, custom and law." Frances Willard hinted that reform-minded women could bring on the millennium. "[T]o help forward the coming of Christ into all departments of life is, in its last analysis, the purpose and aim of the W.C.T.U," she explained.[11]

The concern of woman movement activists with perfecting the self explains why many were interested in New Thought. New Thought was a tool that could reform the self by controlling disruptive desire. It could therefore help bring about a new woman's era. As Eliza Burt Gamble explained, "selfishness, sensuality, and inordinate greed are sapping the very foundations of society. It is to be hoped, however, that the beneficent influence of the New Thought will emancipate man from the thralldom of past errors, and that by it humanity may be saved from the dangers that threaten it."[12]

By looking at several New Thought novels, I will examine more carefully the shared goal of the woman movement and New Thought of creating a purified, desireless selfhood. What were the social conditions that made male desire such a troubling issue for some late-nineteenth-century middle-class women? What did they hope to gain by eradicating desire? What might they lose? What sort of human relations did they envision in a world without desire? What convinced them that a denial of desire was the best way to bring about a utopian woman's era? Did they really believe that the female self was pure, high-minded, and free of disruptive desire? What role, if any, could female desire play in the desireless utopia they envisioned?

The social context for these concerns was the economic instability that threatened the late-Victorian white middle class. The late-nineteenth-century U.S. economy was racked by frequent depressions. Small businesses failed in record-breaking numbers; formerly fluid paths to professional status for white males began to harden; and even the most powerful businessmen in small towns across the nation found themselves overshadowed, and frequently crushed, by newly emerging corporations.

If the consequences of this economic upheaval were sometimes dire for white middle-class men, they were also ominous for white middle-class women. In these years before the large-scale opening of clerical jobs to white women, undereducated white middle-class women had few alternatives to marriage. As wives, they were helpless before their husbands' economic decisions. Their lack of control extended to their bodies as well, since mainstream ideology both sanctioned men's unrestricted sexual access to their wives and condemned birth control and abortion.

As we shall see, this world of economic instability and female sexual dispossession informed the narratives of New Thought novels. The novels starkly illuminated the harsh conditions of late-Victorian middle-class marriages and thereby revealed the functions that an embrace of desirelessness could serve. Echoing and deepening the themes contained in the healing narratives of such New Thought leaders as Brooks, Rix Militz, and Fillmore, the novels described how a middle-class woman's "denial" of desire and faith in mind over matter could both buffer her emotionally against downward economic mobility and justify her rejection of marital heterosexuality.

Just as important, the very literariness of New Thought fiction enables us to examine the tensions within the ideology of desirelessness that was central to both New Thought and the woman movement. As literary scholars have explained, novels—and particularly novels of lesser literary quality— present the dominant cultural narratives of their day. The places where the narratives "slip" or become tangled are therefore revealing. They can be analyzed to show unresolved tensions in a culture.[13]

It is in search of such tangles that I analyze these New Thought novels. Although evidence indicates that the novels of Helen Van-Anderson, Ursula Gestefeld, and Alice Bunker Stockham were well received,[14] their importance does not rest with their popular reception. Rather, it lies in their unique ability to reveal tensions surrounding the issue of desirelessness.[15] The novels tell us both why middle-class women wished to "deny" desire and why this goal was ultimately futile. They help us understand why New Thought, and the broader culture as well, would so quickly turn from the "denial" of desire to its celebration in the early years of the twentieth century.

HELEN VAN-ANDERSON

Helen Van Metre was born to a family that traced its ancestry back to the Puritans, or so she later claimed. In 1885, the twenty-six-year-old Helen, now married and going under the name of Nellie V. Anderson, went to a mental healer and was treated for a "severe affection [*sic*] of the eyes." Nellie then studied with Emma Curtis Hopkins, and in January of 1889 she was among Hopkins's first ordained class of twenty-two students.[16]

Figure 12.   Rev. Helen Van-Anderson, pastor
of the Church of the Higher Life.

Nellie was described as having a cold, "somewhat retiring and sensitive nature." Nevertheless, by 1888 Nellie V. Anderson had become one of Hopkins's star missionaries. Between 1888 and 1890 she undertook missionary travels to Michigan, Ohio, Iowa, Colorado, Nebraska, and Massachusetts (Boston). In 1891, possibly to assert her new sense of worldliness, Nellie V. Anderson renamed herself Helen Van-Anderson.[17]

Van-Anderson moved to Boston in 1894.[18] Her husband, L. J. Anderson, does not appear to have moved with her, and after 1894 his name drops out of the historical record. Within a year, Van-Anderson was ordained to preach "without regard to sect or doctrine" by the Reverends Minot J. Savage, Florence Kollack, and Antoinette Brown Blackwell, all well-known figures in the Unitarian and Universalist churches. Van-Anderson became the minister for the "Church of the Higher Life," the first New Thought congregation in Boston. Under her leadership the church attracted overflow crowds and twice outgrew its headquarters.[19]

Throughout the 1890s Van-Anderson kept in close contact with Malinda Cramer's Divine Science group.[20] Van-Anderson also worked with Sarah Farmer to establish "Greenacre" in 1894. A combination New Thought summer school and vacation ground, Greenacre was intended, in Farmer's words, "to demonstrate that it is possible to live in the kingdom of heaven *now*." In addition to religious leaders from a variety of faiths, Greenacre attracted reformers and literary figures, including Helen Campbell and Edwin Markham. Van-Anderson spoke regularly at Greenacre. She also frequently contributed to the popular New Thought journal *Mind*.[21]

Van-Anderson also aligned herself with the woman movement, and particularly with the social-purity movement. As a missionary in the 1880s she had targeted temperance and social-purity activists, since she believed that she and they were "working for the same end." In 1895 Van-Anderson joined the Boston Honorary Committee of the American Purity Alliance.[22]

Van-Anderson's years of entrepreneurial, literary, missionary, and pastoral activity, as well as her connections with New Thought groups in San Francisco, Chicago, and Boston and her position as a columnist for *Mind*, the most prominent New Thought journal of the early twentieth century, all mark her as a major New Thought leader. While Van-Anderson published numerous tracts and books, most influential were two of her novels: *The Right Knock* (1889) and *The Journal of a Live Woman* (1895). Both novels illuminate the ways in which unhappy but deeply conservative women may have used New Thought to alleviate their experiences of class insecurity, male domination, compulsory heterosexuality, and compulsory motherhood. At a deeper level, they explore the meanings and functions of stillness, desirelessness, and love—the ostensible aims of both New Thought and the woman's era.

THE RIGHT KNOCK (1889)

The heroine of *The Right Knock* is Mrs. Marion Hayden, a society woman who becomes a "nervous invalid" after a fire destroys her home and her husband's business. Mrs. Hayden suffers from sick headaches and dyspepsia (a stomach ailment) and finds herself, at the age of thirty-five, becoming a "crass, crabbed old woman." She feels cramped in the smaller home she must now inhabit. There, unnerved by her children's noise, she can only escape by retiring to a quiet room for days at a time. She bitterly envisions "long years of uselessness stretching out before her."[23]

Marion Hayden's life is changed when she is healed by a female "Christian Science" practitioner. She decides to seek further training in the new metaphysics. Mrs. Hayden journeys two hundred miles to participate in a three-week course offered by Mrs. Pearl, a woman widely hailed as "'the' best teacher in the world" and clearly based on Emma Curtis Hopkins.

Much of the book describes Mrs. Pearl's lessons, which are summarized in Mrs. Hayden's letters to her husband, John. The book concludes with Mrs. Hayden's joyful homecoming. She is not only perfectly healthy, she has lost weight and her complexion is improved, all as a result of "denying matter."[24]

An important subplot involves two of Mrs. Hayden's young friends. They are Kate Turner, a deeply spiritual music teacher, and her house-mate Grace Hall, a "keenly intellectual and very independent" artist.[25] The two women become interested in the new "science." The novel consists of alternating chapters of Mrs. Hayden's letters (which transcribe Mrs. Pearl's twelve lessons) and scenes of Kate and Grace reading, debating, and ultimately accepting the letters' teachings.

A final subplot concerns Grace Hall and her suitor, Leon Carrington. Grace initially rejects Leon because she has heard rumors that he was engaged to another woman. After studying Christian Science, however, she decides that she ought to think generous rather than critical thoughts about him. She gives him a second chance, apparently discovers the rumors were false, and then agrees to marry him—after Leon assures her that she will still have her "individuality" after marriage.[26]

The Right Knock can be read for the content of Mrs. Pearl's lessons, which duplicated those of Emma Curtis Hopkins.[27] More interesting, however, is the narrative in which these lessons are embedded. That narrative describes how class instability, isolation, and male dominance are overcome by New Thought. Van-Anderson indicates that New Thought can grant married women protection from the economic incompetence of husbands. It can also deliver them from stifling domestic isolation into an emotionally charged world of homosocial bliss.

Christian Science ostensibly cures Mrs. Hayden of headaches and dyspepsia. However, the larger problem cured by Christian Science is downward social mobility. The connection between illness and economic instability is obvious, since Mrs. Hayden's invalidism and the demotion of her husband, John, from merchant to shopkeeper share a common genesis in the fire that destroys their home. The novel blames John for the economic downturn. He had engaged in "unfortunate speculation" and had failed to renew his insurance. It is these actions, rather than the fire alone, that lead to his family's economic downfall.[28]

The Right Knock portrays downward social mobility as a blessing in disguise, however: it restores Mrs. Hayden to the company of women. Before the fire, Mr. Hayden had pushed his wife to enter "society" in order to help his business prospects. Having done so, Mrs. Hayden had become the isolated object of other women's gossip. After moving to a "modest but comfortable" neighborhood, however, she finds her life filled with women.[29] She is frequently visited by Kate and Grace, by her neighbor Mrs. Reade, and, most importantly, by Miss Helen Greening, a cousin of Mrs. Reade.

Helen Greening is the first to introduce Mrs. Hayden to mental healing. This circuitous spread of mental healing through all-female networks matches accounts in letters to New Thought journals. *The Right Knock* implies that Miss Greening would have been ignored by Mrs. Hayden before the fire on account of her social status. As Mrs. Hayden tells her husband, "What would we have known or cared for Miss Greening, had we been living in the mansion on the hill?"[30] Hopkins's Christian Science must have spread not only among the prominent citizens mentioned in *Christian Science*, but also among the "middling" women depicted in *The Right Knock*.

New Thought teachings may have helped downwardly mobile married women adjust to their new economic status. After studying with Mrs. Pearl, Mrs. Hayden realizes that "the material are but emblems or symbols of the spiritual"; therefore money is not as important as spiritual wealth. Other teachings promise believers an inner wealth that changing circumstances or their husbands' risky investments cannot take away. Mrs. Pearl explains that one can regain the high status of one's birth. "We now claim our inheritance, the privilege to enter into the kingdom and possess the land, our royal birthright," she decrees. Through Christian Science we are reborn and "find . . . the palace doors open to receive us, and the insignia of royalty written upon our faces."[31] These promises to restore one's "royal birthright" may have been soothing to women who suffered the consequences of economic decisions but who were excluded from economic decision-making. An emphasis on one's high position at birth can also be read as an implicit critique of the family women married into as opposed to the family they were born into. The claim that "the insignia of royalty [is] written upon our faces" may have served as an oblique reminder of white middle-class women's belief that their class superiority was racially inscribed. The vicissitudes of marriage could not destroy their "birthright" as white or Anglo-Saxon women.

The Right Knock contains no explicit critiques of marriage. On the contrary, Marion Hayden defends Christian Science from charges that it disrupts family life. She writes, "You know, some people say (in their ignorance, of course) that Christian Science breaks up families. Oh, if they could only know, on the other hand, how it strengthens the bonds, . . . how it teaches us the sacredness of family relations."[32] Van-Anderson supports her character's claim that Christian Science strengthens the family by frequently describing Mrs. Hayden's love for her husband and children.

Odd slips in the narrative express Mrs. Hayden's ambivalence toward her husband, John, and her children, however. The first such slip occurs in Van-Anderson's characterization of John. Despite his fiscal irresponsibility, John is depicted as a model husband. He is "kindhearted," "upright," and "honest." He encourages his wife's interest in the new doctrines and eventually accepts them himself. Van-Anderson writes of Mrs. Hayden, "she had her husband's full sympathy and cooperation. Afterward, when she . . . knew more about other women's lives, she realized the value of it. . . . Oh, the sweet influence of a sympathy that unites and harmonizes two natures, no matter how opposite in character and tendencies." In another part of the book Van-Anderson forgets that Mrs. Hayden has perfect harmony with her "opposite in character" husband. Mrs. Hayden, she writes here, felt pure gratitude that her husband "had at last allowed her to try this [Christian Science] without ridiculing or scolding her."[33]

Other aspects of the text point to Van-Anderson's less-than-enthusiastic feelings about John. All of Mrs. Hayden's letters are addressed to "Dear John," yet the bulk of each chapter depicts Kate and Grace, rather than John, studying the letters and wrestling with their meaning. In keeping with the almost ritualistic assertion of John's wisdom and goodness, Mrs. Hayden tells him to send her his opinions of Mrs. Pearl's lectures: "You have such a clear way of expressing yourself," she writes. Yet in the entire 307-page novel, John's opinion of the teachings is expressed only once, when he interrupts Kate and Grace to present his exegesis of the Lord's Prayer. Similarly, although Mrs. Hayden ends her letters with "tell me of the children," the children are thereafter barely alluded to.[34]

The most striking evidence that Mrs. Hayden might wish to escape her family is a dream she describes to her husband:

> I dreamed of being at home last night, and . . . you were all so busy and happy. You did not see me. . . . a vague white something like an invisible net was spread between you, and the thought came that you and Anna [the family servant] were weaving something, and even the children had a part to fulfill. . . . When I awoke I was deeply impressed that this was a symbol of the united effort in making the seamless robe of Truth, and the family group represented the members of one body . . .

Oddly, Mrs. Hayden doesn't seem to notice that in this symbolic representation of the united family, she is invisible, her role ably filled by the family servant. The dream indicates that the "family group" could proceed quite well without her. In another episode, Mrs. Hayden learns that Mr. Hayden and the children have learned to heal each other of minor illnesses. Her presence at home is now even less necessary.[35]

While Van-Anderson describes John as functioning quite well without his wife, she also depicts Kate and Grace as two halves of a perfect, self-sufficient whole. Indeed, the novel's overt story of Mrs. Hayden's devotion to her husband provides only a flimsy cover for Van-Anderson's deeper fascination with intense and romantic female relationships. Because Kate represents intuition and Grace represents reason, for example, Van-Anderson argues that the two women can fully understand Christian Science. Together they are "head" and "heart," or the ideal of white womanhood promoted by woman-movement leaders. Kate and Grace debate philosophy, religion, and reform. Their compatibility is more than intellectual. They share friends and activities and sob in each other's arms when upset. They speak to each other in romantic, even erotic terms. "[I]t seems to me you are like a pure white lily bell, and I want to creep into your heart and live in its fragrance," Kate tells Grace.[36]

Toward the end of the novel Grace becomes engaged to Leon Carrington. Yet in the novel's final pages, it is Grace, Kate, and Mrs. Hayden who form a new family. Within the first hour of Mrs. Hayden's return from her weeks studying with Mrs. Pearl, Kate and Grace show up at her door.

> "I think you will have to include us in your family, Mrs. Hayden, for we could not resist the family welcome," said Grace, smiling with happiness, as she grasped Mrs. Hayden's hand and drew Kate close beside her with the other.
>
> "You *are* included my dears. There is but one family, you know," was the cordial reply grasping the hand of each.[37]

The Right Knock concludes with Mrs. Hayden, Kate, and Grace circled together in an enclosed, all-female family.

The Right Knock portrayed Christian Science or New Thought as a cure for illnesses triggered by economic downturns that forced women into too-close quarters with their children. New Thought compensated for economic instability through promises of divine inheritances that no circumstances could take away. It taught men and children self-sufficiency, and brought women together in tight communities. Judging from Van-Anderson's text, early New Thought was the ideal faith for the wife who knew that her husband was "scolding and belittling" her, but who could not admit this even to herself; for the mother whose children annoyed her, but who could only justify inattention to them by making herself ill; and for the woman who believed in the "family group" but who at some level wished that it excluded men and children.

THE JOURNAL OF A LIVE WOMAN (1895)

In Helen Van-Anderson's *Journal of a Live Woman* the subtexts of *The Right Knock*—incompatibility with one's husband, unhappiness with one's family, and a belief that the model for love should be love between women— are made more explicit. As the book opens, the novel's heroine, Victoria True, is miserably unhappy. She lives with her husband, Sanford—a drunkard whose cruel words leave her speechless with pain—and her elderly aunt Delia, who behaves as the "general dictator of the whole family." Completing the family are Victoria's three squabbling children: Marjorie, age six, who has "screaming fits"; Beatrice, age eight, who is "willful"; and Donald, age thirteen, who annoys Victoria with his "whistling and scuffling and constant questioning." [38]

Victoria blames herself for her unhappiness. "Oh, that I might master this petty, foolish self that suffers and makes others suffer!" she writes in her journal. Instead of turning to a mental healer for help, Victoria relies upon her intuition, represented as an inner "Voice." The Voice answers her heartfelt cries for self-mastery with blank-verse sentences that Victoria transcribes into her journal. Her Voice dispenses standard New Thought advice. If Victoria wishes to create "perfect character," she must speak only high-minded and loving words. These words will then create a positive reality, the Voice promises. [39]

Through meditating, withholding all negative judgments of others, and practicing nonresistance, Victoria transforms her life. She heals her dying sister Alice, earns the love of Aunt Delia, teaches her children "self-government," guides and comforts various neighbor women, and wins the "grandest of all victories," the reform of her husband. In the book's final pages Sanford approaches Victoria as she is sitting in her meditation corner, announces that he has given up drink, and begs, "Teach me, Victoria. . . . I want to be worthy of my noble wife." [40]

Victoria's Voice describes emotional engagement as filthy, dangerous, and exposing. The Voice promises that only emotionally distanced nonresistance—the ability to "stand unmoved amid mind elements that clash and roar"—will leave one feeling cleansed and clothed.

> After storm comes calm, . . .
> So doth the naked soul find

Wondrous raiment for its hard-earned cleanliness
The rich wrought seamless robe
Of Love shall . . . fasten
Near the heart. . . .
those who once put on this
Robe shall be as angels are.[41]

Meditation provides not merely clothing for "the naked soul," but armor as well. The Voice promises that if one thinks exalted thoughts,

the fear
That holds the woman-heart like chained and helpless
Slave will melt away.

Then, "Woman" will grow powerful and warrior-like:

A new
Strength will steal upon her, and that
Which appears benumbed and stunted and inefficient
Will grow to the fullness of a perfect stature.
. . . she will spring
Forth like Minerva, full armed with life.

Victoria soon feels this armored power. "I have made Love my shield and breastplate. . . ." she joyfully exclaims.[42]

According to *The Journal of a Live Woman,* the cleansed, clothed, and armored New Thought woman can float above the pain of her life. As Victoria exhorts, "Soar like a bird on the pinions of thought, into this radiant realm and there from your shining height look down and see the clouds of doubt and sadness and disappointment melt and disappear. . . . Or if you find yourself entangled in the cloud, stand still until it passes by and take with calmness what it has to give, knowing *all is good.*"[43]

In short, the gift that New Thought meditation brings, whether likened to clothing, armor, or physical distance, is protection. Surprisingly, shelter from the violence of "hot and low desires" as well as from one's own sense of being "benumbed and stunted and inefficient" comes from immobility. Women must "stand still" amid unhappiness, Victoria emphasizes.[44] This stillness could easily be read as self-sacrificing passivity. Yet woman-movement activists, intent upon the millennial transformation of society, also lauded stillness. Associating desire with change, they imagined a heaven of desireless stasis.

The goal of desireless stillness of the social-purity and woman movements could be read as a critique of ugly industrial expansion and disorienting social change. Yet stillness could answer more intimate needs. Within a stifling domestic world, "stillness" could be a form of resistance. The context was a world in which men's desires were sanctioned as the source of progress. As Gillian Brown points out, the role of the middle-class woman was to accommodate her husband's desires, economically (by adjusting their home life to his income) as well as sexually and emotionally. The "still" or motionless woman rejected desire, or rather, announced her refusal to mirror man's desire. No longer subject to economic or emotional fluctuations beyond her control, she achieved total emotional self-sufficiency. Stillness could be a form of self-possession, not of passivity. Many nineteenth-century Americans also believed that the highest ideals were permanent and unchanging. Martha Banta argues that by remaining "still," women were symbolically enacting their kinship with these higher ideals.[45]

The Journal of a Live Woman supports these arguments that stillness could be a form of resistance. The book details the practical benefits that Victoria receives from stillness, or from the refusal to emotionally engage with those around her. When her husband Sanford says cruel words to her, Victoria meditates on "Infinite Love" and is comforted: "then the peace came—*such* peace. *All condemnation was gone!* . . . I realized he was living his own life and I could give him freedom to live it in his own way. And then and there I let go of him. I really *did give him liberty* (in my mind, I mean)."[46]

Victoria "lets go" of her children as well. She teaches her son affirmations, and tells him to "govern *yourself* . . . ; instead of waiting for mamma to tell you what to do . . . , think for yourself." The need to teach her children self-governance helps Victoria justify her absence from them. When spending three weeks visiting her sister Alice, Victoria momentarily feels the "old foolishness about being away from the children." She rejects these anxieties, however: "If I could never leave them, how could they prove so well their self-reliance, and how could I prove my trust in them? Besides, are they not ever with me in my . . . loving thoughts?"[47]

New Thought meditations enabled Victoria to interpret her emotional and even physical withdrawal from her husband and children as a sign not of rebellion, but of love. This love differed from the older sentimental version. Maternal sentimental love depended upon direct engagement with the child. Complete, even suicidal self-abnegation for the sake of the child's soul was lauded as woman's highest ideal. Women were to act as salvific mothers to their husbands as well. They were to sacrifice health, strength, and even life to save men from their innate bestiality.[48] Van-Anderson, however, defined love very differently. Love was woman's "shield," "breastplate," and "seamless robe." She associated it with protection rather than with sacrifice.

Love could be transformed from self-sacrifice to stillness and safety through aligning it with the other major goal of the woman's era—the absence of desire. Victoria argues that the highest form of love is desireless love when she counsels a young woman named Violet Mercer about marriage. Violet tells Victoria that a man has proposed to her, but that she hesitates to accept him: "I hesitate because I know so little about the requirements of such a relation. . . . I have two friends who were so bright and happy and beautiful before they were married, and now, though they have never said a word, yet they both look so different—and—I cannot help feeling that they are terribly disappointed. . . . What does it all mean?"

Touched by Violet's "pathetic ignorance" and hoping to "shield her from the common fate" of women, Victoria resolves to teach her about true love and marriage. The key to true love, Victoria explains, is the absence of desire. Love is the opposite of the feeling that "continually longs for the presence of the body." That longing is not love, it is "selfishness," since it "demands self-gratification and causes all manner of diseases of both mind and body." In contrast, true love is so complete that the presence of the loved one is not needed. Both partners must have such "mental equilibrium" that "whether present or absent from the person of the loved one, the joy [is] complete." "In love there is no absence, and therefore no longing," Victoria concludes.[49]

In essence, Victoria insists that the only true marriage is a marriage without heterosexual desire. The model for love should be the emotional relationships between women, rather than the sexual relations between man and woman. Again, Van-Anderson presents love between women as superior to heterosexuality. As Victoria tells "Violet," "The meeting of two people who love in this way is like the bending toward each other of two flowers instead of the meeting between the bee and the honeysuckle."[50]

Helen Van-Anderson's *Journal of a Live Woman* repeats some of the subtexts of *The Right Knock,* including uneasiness with married life and the hope that absence from one's family can be redefined as the best way to love one's family. It goes beyond *The Right Knock,* however, in depicting the uses of New Thought denials of desire. While Victoria's desire for her husband's love leaves her feeling naked, dirty, and vulnerable, New Thought denials of desire promise to cleanse, clothe, and armor her. Victoria is uncomfortable not only with her husband's desire for drink, but also with his sexual desire, the desire that "demands self-gratification and causes all

Figure 13. Ursula Newell Gestefeld, founder of the Science of Being.

manner of diseases of both mind and body." If he wishes to be worthy of his "noble wife," he too must learn to repress desire. Only an absence of desire in both partners will ensure marital happiness, the novel implies.[51]

URSULA NEWELL GESTEFELD (1845–1921)

Ursula Newell Gestefeld's level of involvement in New Thought easily rivaled Helen Van-Anderson's. Gestefeld was married to Theodore Gestefeld, a Chicago newspaper reporter, and was the mother of four children when, in the early 1880s, she healed herself of an unspecified illness by reading Eddy's *Science and Health*. Shortly thereafter, in 1884, Gestefeld joined a class on Christian Science taught by Eddy. For the next four years she remained affiliated with Eddy while writing articles on Christian Science for a variety of mind-cure publications.[52]

In 1888 Gestefeld quarreled with Eddy and was expelled from her Christian Science Association. She went on to become a major New Thought leader.[53] After the death of her husband in the early 1890s, Gestefeld traveled the country, lecturing and teaching mental healing. She created her own religious system that she called the "Science of Being." By 1897, Gestefeld had settled in Chicago, where she preached her Science of Being regularly to a congregation of five hundred to eight hundred people.[54]

In 1903 Gestefeld renamed her Science of Being congregation "The Church of 'The New Thought.'" Over the next decade she was involved in various attempts to form New Thought churches into a national federation.[55] Like Helen Van-Anderson, Gestefeld also aligned herself with the woman movement. In 1893 she spoke on "Woman as a Religious Teacher" at the World's Congress of Representative Women. In 1895 she joined the Revising Committee that worked with Elizabeth Cady Stanton to publish *The Woman's Bible.* Gestefeld was a supporter of women's suffrage, a member of the Woman's Club of Chicago, and a founding member of the Illinois Woman's Press Association.[56]

Gestefeld wrote at least fourteen New Thought tracts. She also published two novels, *The Woman Who Dares* (1892) and *The Leprosy of Miriam* (1894). Like the novels of Helen Van-Anderson, Gestefeld's novels depict a woman's struggle to improve her domestic life through New Thought. While Van-Anderson promoted desirelessness as a means of shielding women from the financial ineptitude, emotional cruelty, and sexual demands of their husbands, Gestefeld problematized this faith in desirelessness by exploring the nature of female desire. The inner selves of both men and women were full of lustful desire, Gestefeld implied, but only men had the forcefulness to control their desire. Her novel *The Woman Who Dares* describes a terrible double bind that threatened to undermine the New Thought and social-purity ideal of desireless womanhood. The late-Victorian middle-class woman couldn't behave willfully without negating her womanliness. But without a forceful will she could not contain her own lowly inner desires. By exploring this double bind, Gestefeld's novel sheds light on the reasons why white middle-class women were so willing to "deny" selfhood and desire in favor of self-sacrifice and womanly "service."

THE WOMAN WHO DARES (1892)

The complex plot of Gestefeld's *Woman Who Dares* must be summarized in some detail. The novel's heroine is Murva Kroom, a passive, dreamy young woman who longs for "love and freedom."[57] Murva lives in Millville with her harsh father and her cruel step-mother. She has only two friends—John Wilson, an invalid whose heart is broken when his niece Haddie Wilson runs away to the city, and Kate, who becomes an invalid as a result of a carriage accident on the day of her wedding to Donald Crawford. Murva feels lonely and unloved. She periodically falls into meditative states. Her "inner visions" then guide and sustain her.

Murva escapes her oppressive home when she meets Harold Deering, a worldly young man who marries her and takes her to New York City. On the surface Murva's marriage to Harold is happy. Nevertheless, she begins to feel constrained in her wifely role. One day she suggests to Harold that she might want to engage in reform work with prostitutes. To Murva's surprise, Harold forbids this activity. With this decree, Harold asserts his authority over her for the first time.

Murva's uneasiness with married life grows when her friend Kate Crawford admits to Murva the true cause of her invalidism. Kate is wasting away with grief because her husband Donald is unfaithful. Kate deduces that he is unfaithful because, as a result of her carriage accident, she cannot "minister" to his "requirements." This means, according to "natural laws," that Donald must find sexual satisfaction elsewhere. Horror-struck by this revelation of the centrality of sexual intercourse to marriage, Murva angrily insists that "physical requirements" have nothing to do with the "essence of marriage." [58]

To prove that sex is not the basis of marriage, Murva tries to sleep alone one night. To her dismay, Harold insists that she return to his bed. Harold's sexual desire disgusts Murva: "Love! Was this wild passion . . . which held her fast in a palpitating grasp, breathing a hot turbulent breath upon her so that she was half suffocated, love? . . . This ferocious thing was not a man, but an animal, and it *loved* her!" [59] Desperate to prove that women's sexual services are not the essence of marriage, Murva consults a minister and a doctor. Both men insist that according to the word of God and the laws of science, woman's role is to satisfy men sexually and to satisfy them on demand. These discussions lead her to the earth-shaking realization that marriage is not the bulwark of civilization. It is instead the "original sin," since it allows unlimited gratification of the beast in man. Woman's role, Murva realizes, is to act as a Moses, and lead man to the "promised land of freedom from physical necessity." She therefore refuses to have sexual relations with Harold until he agrees to her terms, declaring that not until he "acknowledges that my person is my own, not his, and that he, as my husband, has a right which none other can possess, the right to request, but not to demand, will I resume the relations now suspended." [60]

Harold's response is to throw Murva out of their home. She returns to Millville, where she encounters Haddie Wilson, the niece of her friend John Wilson. Haddie has become a prostitute. Partially for Haddie's sake,

Murva moves back to New York and opens a home for women "of every kind and condition," where she offers them emotional support. (How the penniless Murva finds the money to open this home is not addressed.) A year later, Harold accidentally observes Murva in the act of saving a young girl from prostitution. He realizes that Murva is "an angel," and in the book's final scene begs her to lead him to the spiritual heights she has obtained.[61]

Gestefeld's *Woman Who Dares* is unusually outspoken for a New Thought tract.[62] Where most New Thought writings only hint at "sorrows in the home," Gestefeld explicitly names women's lack of control over sexual intercourse as the central problem of married life. Her novel also describes how male-defined ideologies provide interlocking support for male power. As Murva concludes, "religion, science, politics, however antagonistic . . . to each other," all nevertheless "stand arrayed in a solid phalanx" to support male sexual access to women. The novel's condemnation of the role of religion in women's sexual oppression is particularly bold. Murva describes how woman has "died for centuries that man may live, and religion has nailed her to that cross." She insists that "the world needs a new religion, one for women. Christianity is for men."[63]

The Woman Who Dares is memorable less for its critique of male dominance, however, than for its depiction of Murva Kroom's passionate search for freedom and selfhood, and of her failure to find either. The novel implies that because of women's powerful lusts, on one hand, and, on the other, the sanctions against their forceful behavior, women can never achieve freedom or self-expression.

Throughout *Woman Who Dares* Murva Kroom searches for freedom and selfhood. Her struggle begins within her family, where her father belittles her, overworks her, and emotionally stifles her. His constant demands leave Murva feeling alienated from her very self. As she explains, "It is not I who am seen from day to day watching every word I speak and everything I do so as not to give my father cause for more harshness and condemnation! It is a mask behind which I hide, longing for love and freedom!"[64]

The freedom Murva longs for is less a room of her own than a "self" of her own. As she tells Kate, "With all my heart and soul . . . I long for freedom! Long for the time to come when I can draw one free breath. . . . Shall I never have the chance to be myself?"[65]

The problem, however, is that freedom and womanhood are so antithetical that a free womanhood is unimaginable. Murva's vision of freedom is inseparable from her musings about manliness. She enjoyed listening to her fiancé Harold describe his life because his stories "gave her in some degree a sense of freedom. . . . Roaming from place to place as one willed, no one to say 'Come here!' or 'You must go there!'—seeing all manner of people and customs . . . master of one's self and subject to no authority, surely this must be delightful. And this is what it is to be a man, she thought to herself and sighed."[66]

Murva tries to envision woman's freedom but falls just short. Before she meets Harold, Murva contemplates running away from her father. But she decides not to slip away from him "as if she had no right to herself. No: her place was there until she was her own mistress and then—."[67] The fact that this sentence remains incomplete is significant. Murva cannot finish the sentence because she cannot imagine what comes after she becomes "her own mistress."

At one point Murva offers a tentative picture of what a free woman's life would be like. She tells Kate, "When I leave my father's house I shall take some situation which will enable me to earn my own living. . . . It will be nothing to work hard, if, when the day is over, I can be mistress of my time, and spend it as I like without interference from anyone. It will be a little heaven to be able to sit down quietly with my books and not have to dread angry looks and unreasonable demands." Even this simple dream is interpreted as so unnatural that it transforms the gentle Murva into a fierce, warrior-like being. As Kate responds, "By the time you have been able to be yourself six weeks nobody will recognize you. You will grow so strong and brave and become so formidable that perhaps even I shall be afraid of you." Kate imagines that the independent Murva will "battle with life" and "devour" her books.[68]

Kate implies that a woman who acts independently is by definition engaging in battle. Battling is by definition masculine. Therefore the woman who behaves independently and so battles the world is "mannish" and unlovable. Kate is not the only one to follow this line of reasoning. As Murva's fiancé Harold muses after witnessing her father's overbearing ways, "No wonder she wants to be free. . . . But how little she can know of what that means. Women need protectors. They are not fit to battle with the world. It makes them hard and aggressive, and gives them a masculine cast. . . . Such a none [sic] is not fit for a wife, and wifehood is woman's only legitimate office."[69]

Unable to become independent without appearing masculine, Murva seeks freedom by marrying a man. But while Murva had felt "hedged about" by her father, as a married woman she feels "swallowed up" by her husband's arbitrary rules and animal-like embraces. She concludes that marriage is "a bondage more far-reaching and deadly than the old [status as daughter], for in that she had, at least, the right to herself, the right to be alone." Confronted with the insistence of "ecclesiastical and civil law" that woman must "minister to [man's] necessities" and with the fury of her husband when she refuses, Murva despairs. Is the "love and freedom" she'd sought, she asks, "really not to be found in the world of men?"[70]

The question of whether women's "love and freedom" could exist in the man's world is explored further when Murva encounters the prostitute Haddie Wilson. Haddie tells Murva that "this world is what we're in, and we've got to make the best of it." Haddie had tried to earn her own way in the "world of men," only to find herself "drudging one half of the time and starving the other half. . . ." She therefore chose the only freedom available, which was to accept social ostracism and sell her body to men. Yet even the prostitute's minimal independence "unsexes" her. As Murva describes, there was "nothing soft and feminine about Haddie."[71]

Despite her knowledge that a struggle for independence is not womanly, Murva briefly considers active resistance to male dominance. She imagines that she might "hew out a new road for herself" outside the "time-worn path of tradition, conservatism and custom." Murva rejects open resistance, however, because she recognizes its futility. "One woman's opposing instinct to conditions accepted as right and necessary, her repudiation of these in the name of justice, . . . what could that do?" she asks. She realizes that the "woman who should dare" to "openly resist" would "find the world against her."[72]

Murva then has her epiphany about the role of women in marriage. Woman must deliver man from physical necessity and, as his divinely appointed "helpmeet, . . . show him to himself as he was before the fall into sense consciousness."[73] Murva's revelation that woman's mission is to show man his true divine nature is a deeply contradictory response to the constraints she experiences. She resolves the dilemma of how to achieve freedom without fighting for it—and so turning into a mannish freak—by casting her struggle not as a battle for women's freedom, but as womanly self-sacrifice undertaken to elevate and empower men.

Murva insists that her refusal to sleep with her husband is a form of self-sacrifice—not of her sexual desire, of course, but of her high social status. After her husband expels her from their home, Murva wonders "[c]ould she face the world with this stigma? For herself alone she would not have endured it. . . . but it was for him. It was to save the one given her out of all the world to save, through helping him to save himself. It was to help him put out the mark of the beast, and bring forth the image of God instead."[74]

Murva also casts her resistance as merely the *absence* of action. Rather than "daring" society, she simply refuses to fulfill one aspect of her wifely duties. She stands completely still until her husband and the world changes around her. As in Van-Anderson's text, stillness is a form of self-possession. It offers protection and emotional independence, as well as an acceptable means of altering a disturbing status quo.[75]

By casting her actions as self-sacrifice to restore men's mastery rather than as self-assertion to gain women's freedom, Murva is able to get what she wants while retaining her womanliness. While refusing her husband his "rights," Murva performs her other wifely duties without the slightest hint of "strongmindedness"; she is "pure, sweet, dignified, a very woman." Murva also repeatedly affirms her commitment to marriage throughout her "rebellion." "Do not think for a moment that I am condemning marriage!" she insists, and explains to her friends, "I am not deserting him! Oh, no! I am waiting for him!"[76]

Murva's turn to self-sacrifice is also related to the novel's ambivalence about womanly purity. Although explicitly depicting men as lustful brutes and women as desireless angels, *Woman Who Dares* also describes the female body as the embodiment of lust. Womanly self-sacrifice is therefore essential to maintaining order, the book suggests.

The association of women with the lustful body is vividly depicted in one of Murva's meditative visions. She sees two figures who embody animal lust and angelic spirit. Animal lust is dark, naked, hot-breathed—and female. Lust's body is described in lurid detail. Her breasts are serpents "whose heads were the nipples," thorns line the insides of her arms, and behind her "panting, pulsing, beautiful lips" Murva can see "cruel, strong, white teeth, which held between them human flesh." The angelic spirit, in contrast, is serene, with white hair and clothing. Its gender is not stated, but it carries a flaming sword and, in the absence of female characteristics, appears to be male. Murva is almost drawn into the deadly arms of lust. At the last moment, however, her way is barred by the angelic spirit's flaming sword. At the sight of the angel's "transcendent" countenance, Murva's "soul leap[s] from her body" and kneels before the angel. Her soul is thereby saved from the "consuming fire" of passion.[77]

Gestefeld unmistakably depicts lust as a woman. Murva can only escape lust by leaping out of her body altogether. For all their brutish ways, men are still closer to angels than women are, since lust is embodied in a woman's form. Manhood is associated with purity elsewhere in the text as well. The book's most spiritually advanced character is Murva's invalid neighbor, John Wilson. Once John's male body has been crippled, his manly soul can represent the highest aspects of humanity.[78]

Indeed, an active struggle against lust seems to be an exclusively male prerogative. This is illustrated by one of Harold Deering's dreams, in which he holds Murva in an embrace so tight that she is smothered to death. She is then reborn as a disembodied face that floats above him, leading him up a mountain that he climbs, strangling serpents as he goes. Serpents in this novel are associated not only with lust, but also with women's bodies. Harold actively destroys these "serpents." In contrast, Murva only escapes lust by literally escaping her body, through death. Her ghostly face, rather than her living body, inspires Harold to destroy lust, or the tempting female body. Murva engages in no activity beyond that of inspiring Harold.[79]

John Wilson and Harold Deering ultimately represent spiritual conquest and purity. This is because Gestefeld could not accept the social purity claim that the woman of "head and heart," or the woman whose rationality was inextricable from her morality, was the paradigm of human development. Women could not represent perfected humanity because their bodies, even more than men's desires, represented lust, and because lust could be defeated only through active struggle. Struggle and womanliness were a contradiction in terms, however. Gestefeld seemed to accept the Darwinian view that the "best" men could be both high-minded intellectuals and aggressive conquerors. Woman could use passive stillness to shield herself and perhaps to influence men. But her passive nature could not successfully eradicate her own lustful desire. For all of men's overt demands for sexual satisfaction, there lurked a terror that woman's self, if asserted, would be lustful. As Murva's friend Kate warned her, "by the time you have been able to *be yourself* six weeks nobody will recognize you." Murva would become, like the female image of lust she envisioned, a "devouring" monster.[80]

Given the restrictions that "hedge" Murva on all sides, her ultimate choices are less surprising. Freedom and selfhood are altogether too fraught with risk. Murva therefore decides to give up her quest for freedom and selfhood and instead, as she tells the prostitute Haddie, try to "forget myself" through serving others. In serving others, she is doing what she wants—that is, leaving her husband and joining the company of other women. Yet she does not "dare" to "hew out a new road for herself," as she had briefly imagined doing. Instead, she survives through inward-looking transcendence. In the book's final pages Murva realizes that by stoically holding to a higher vision "beyond the senses," she can "[open] for herself that starry pathway in which she could walk, though in the world of men."[81]

Murva's vision of a "starry pathway" that allowed her to be in yet above the "world of men" echoed the words of Van-Anderson's Victoria True, who longed for "the highway that leads upward and onward."[82] The tensions depicted in *Woman Who Dares*—the conflicting desires for "love" and for "freedom," the hope to alter men's sexual prerogatives as well as the fear of women's own sexual desire, and the deep ambivalence about openly challenging a world one recognizes as oppressive—all help explain why some women were drawn to the contradictory and nonconfrontational doctrines of New Thought.[83]

ALICE BUNKER STOCKHAM (1833–1912)

The novels of Helen Van-Anderson and Ursula Gestefeld illuminated the ways in which desirelessness could benefit some late-Victorian women. The context was an industrial economy that gave middle-class women no economic alternative to marriage, and medical and religious ideologies that supported men's unrestricted sexual access to their wives. In such a world, women could use desirelessness to construct a form of selfhood that served them in certain ways. As Van-Anderson showed, desirelessness and the conviction that one had a "divine inheritance" offered women shelter from downward economic mobility, cruel husbands, and demanding children. As Gestefeld revealed, stillness and desirelessness enabled women to feel they were impelling others to change without acting and thereby undercutting their claims to passive, womanly moral authority. Both women also hinted that an embrace of desirelessness could free women from compulsory marital heterosexuality and restore them to all-female communities.

What remains unclear, however, is the relationship of desirelessness to the utopian dreams of the woman movement. As we have seen, many woman-movement leaders hoped to "eliminate the animal" within humanity. Women's triumph over lust would allow them to become "the great harmonizing elements of the 'new era.'"[84] But what would a world without animal desire actually look like? How would the essential elements of late-Victorian ideology—the womanly self-sacrificing service and the manly, desirous competitive energy that fueled economic progress and evolutionary development—be reconfigured in a new woman's era?

The writings of Dr. Alice Bunker Stockham give insight into this question. Stockham was primarily an author of books on medicine, sexuality, and women's health. In 1893, however, she published a utopian New Thought novel. In it she attempted to envision the world of desireless purity that was the aim of the social-purity wing of the woman movement.

Figure 14. Dr. Alice Bunker Stockham, publisher and authority on sexuality and women's health.

By turning to fiction, Stockham was able to imaginatively create this world and thus explore how it would actually function. Ironically, the fictional world she created only demonstrated that the social-purity ideal of desirelessness was untenable. While desirelessness could help some women avoid aspects of marital heterosexuality, as a new model of selfhood it was doomed to failure. Her novel revealed the fault lines in the social-purity vision—instabilities that would lead Stockham to embrace a new ideal of womanhood that lauded passion as the heart of both male and female selfhood.[85]

Alice Bunker received her medical degree in 1854, thereby becoming one of the first women in the United States to practice medicine. She married Gabriel H. Stockham in 1857. The couple had two children, William and Cora. For the next twenty-three years Alice Stockham practiced medicine in Kansas and Indiana, specializing in the treatment of women and children.[86]

In 1883, Stockham published a manual on women's health entitled *Tokology: A Book for Every Woman.* It offered straightforward discussions of the physiology of human reproduction and practical advice on pregnancy, childbirth, the care of infants, "the diseases of women," and menopause. *Tokology* was equally notable for its bold stand on sexual politics.

Stockham denounced the sexual double standard, or the idea that "sexual union is a *necessity* to man, while it is not to woman." Men who believed this subjected their wives to excessive sexual intercourse. Women who were raised to equate womanly modesty with sexual ignorance found themselves loathing the sexual demands of their husbands.[87]

In short, Stockham argued that warped ideas about male and female sexuality poisoned marriage. The solution was to raise young men and women with a single high moral standard of sexuality. Once married, the couple were to "*take time for the act, have it entirely mutual from first to last*"; the result, Stockham promised, would be that "the demand will not come so frequently," and women's hatred for their husbands would be replaced with love. Most important, married couples were to remain chaste during pregnancy. This would produce children in whom "a life of purity and self-control will be natural," Stockham promised.[88]

Tokology was an immediate hit. By 1891 it had sold 160,000 copies. By 1897 it was on its forty-fifth edition and was becoming the standard work on women's health, sexuality, pregnancy, and childbirth for literate Americans. *Tokology* received high praise from women as diverse as Mary Livermore and Mary Gove Nichols. It was translated into German, French, Finnish, and Swedish. Count Leo Tolstoy was so impressed with the book that he arranged to have it translated into Russian as well. Tolstoy's preface to the Russian edition gives a sense of how radical Stockham's writings were in the context of late-Victorian culture. "This book is one of those rare books which does not deal with what everybody talks about and nobody needs, but about what nobody talks about and everybody needs to know," Tolstoy wrote, adding that "it immediately transports the reader into a new world of living human activity."[89]

In 1886, just as Stockham's book was winning her international fame, she and her friend Lida Hood Talbot joined Emma Curtis Hopkins's first "Christian Science" class in Chicago. In 1887 Stockham participated in the mental-science convention held in Boston and wrote articles on mental healing for the Chicago mind-cure press. She became the vice-president of the Hopkins Metaphysical Association in 1889. Yet the New Thought author Stockham appeared to admire most was Warren Felt Evans. His insights, she wrote, "should have made his name immortal."[90]

Hopkins's class seemed to inaugurate a new chapter in Stockham's life. She embarked on a flurry of entrepreneurial activities. In 1887 Stockham, then fifty-five years old, started the Alice B. Stockham publishing company. The company published *Tokology*, the writings of Warren Felt Evans, and a variety of books on health, sexuality, and education. By 1893 Stockham was employing a dozen clerks and bringing in several thousand dollars a month. She also recruited women to act as door-to-door book agents for *Tokology*. Stockham cast these business activities as forms of womanly philanthropy.[91]

In 1890 Stockham moved to Evanston, a suburb of Chicago, where she lived with her daughter, two nieces, and three servants. (Her husband did not move with her to Evanston. His fate is unknown.) There, Stockham became involved in a wide range of reform activities. She promoted women's suffrage and social purity. She was a founding member of the Illinois Woman's Press Association and represented the organization at the 1891 National Council of Women. She publicized the kindergarten movement and successfully petitioned to have the Finnish handicraft system "sloyd" implemented in the Chicago public schools.[92] She was also a prolific author. In 1893 she co-wrote with Lida Hood Talbot *Koradine Letters,* an epistolary novel about a young girl's growth into "spiritual law." In 1894 she wrote a health manual for girls entitled *Creative Life.* In 1896 she wrote *Karezza: Ethics of Marriage,* which promoted sexual intercourse without orgasm as a means of enhancing marital love and personal character.

By the mid-1890s Stockham's fame was international. Tolstoy continued to praise her work in Russia. She was a close friend of the Baroness Alexandra Gripenberg of Finland, the famed Parliament member and newspaper publisher who was also the leader of the Finnish women's movement. British sex radical and Socialist Edward Carpenter was a friend as well as a professional admirer of Stockham. Stockham cemented her international connections by traveling to Europe and Russia as well as to India, China, and Japan. By the mid-1890s British papers casually referred to Stockham as "Dr. Alice, whom everybody loves." Indeed, Stockham's works were praised by "everybody," from the WCTU *Union Signal* to the "weekly Anarchist-Freethought Journal" *Lucifer.* Admirers described her as "a woman of . . . activity, energy . . . breadth of mind, . . . [and] largeness of heart," or as the ideal woman of "head and heart." In later years she was called the "original 'new woman' of the West."[93]

Stockham's New Thought beliefs permeated all of her published writings. She even appended a section headed "Mind Cure A Reality" to later editions of *Tokology.* Stockham was herself a New Thought healer. She published Helen Van-Anderson and frequently cited the writings of Ursula Newell Gestefeld. She remained loyal to Hopkins until her retirement, and then affiliated herself with Malinda Cramer's Divine Science group. In 1897

Stockham began her own New Thought "college," the Vrilia Heights Metaphysical School in Williams Bay, Wisconsin. It was still in operation by 1908.[94]

The continuity of Stockham's New Thought involvements mask a deeper discontinuity in her intellectual outlook, however. Until the mid-1890s Stockham promoted the dominance of spirit over matter, the eradication of self and the containment of desire. Then Stockham shifted her approach. She began to explore the commonality of matter and spirit, and to celebrate sexual desire. Her 1903 volume *Lover's World* presented "affirmations" designed to awaken and accept, rather than still, sexuality: "I am not a child of evil; I am not begotten in sin; . . . all my inheritance is from the union of wisdom and love . . . ; thus that which gives a sign of this union—the sexual instinct—is good and not evil . . . I welcome it as the insignia of life."[95]

Stockham's shift to blessing rather than "denying" sexuality was an early example of a pattern that would become common among turn-of-the-century New Thought authors and, increasingly, in the larger culture as a whole. Insight into Stockham's reasons for changing her outlook can be found in her 1893 novel, *Koradine Letters.* The novel, which she wrote with minor assistance from Lida Hood Talbot,[96] attempted to use a narrative of female self-sacrifice as the basis of a social-purity utopia. Yet ultimately the novel questioned whether the female self was naturally pure; whether "service" and "love," rather than selfishness and (transmuted) savagery, could be the defining features of white or Anglo-Saxon identity; and whether the white woman, rather than the white man, could be the paradigm of humanity. Stockham's writings, both early and late, reveal the economic and psychological ambiguities that would haunt New Thought—and the woman's era.

KORADINE LETTERS (1893)

The novel's heroine, Koradine, is not the average thirteen-year-old. Her parents have raised her to believe that "any good thought held with tenacity . . . will surely come to pass." Koradine's life is further enhanced when a mysterious group led by a woman named Dr. Goodrich establishes the "Arcadian Institute of Development" nearby. The Arcadians practice a radical form of childhood education that combines the New Thought approach to meditation (which uses "affirmations" to ensure that high thoughts become habitual), François Delsarte's philosophy of theater (which uses a repertory of poses to ensure that elevated gestures become habitual), and Friedrich Froebel's philosophy of education (which uses specially designed games to instill in children the divine attributes of maternal love). Through training children in these techniques, the Arcadians believe they will "spiritualize the race into the fulfillment of the Apocalypse."[97]

Koradine is sent to be educated at the Arcadian Institute. The book details Koradine and her fellow students' experiences at Arcadia (mostly through letters written by Koradine to her cousin Edith). It is a momentous year for all concerned. The children effortlessly learn foreign languages, handicrafts, the secrets of nature, and the traditions of different nations. New Thought meditations are used for everything from healing sick children to saving sea travelers from shipwreck. The children grow in wisdom and poise. By the book's conclusion the students, now approaching their mid-teens, begin to pair up for what promise to be pure and eugenic unions.[98]

Koradine Letters was published one year after Gestefeld's *Woman Who Dares*, and it seems to offer a solution to the horrors portrayed in Gestefeld's novel. Gestefeld's Murva was raised in a harsh, patriarchal household where she was "never . . . free even to have a feeling." In contrast, Koradine and her fellow students are taught "to be free in our minds, that we may also be free in every bodily movement" and, specifically, that "'your bodies belong to you.'" The result is that Koradine becomes a "girl . . . who thinks and feels." She will grow up to be a woman of head and heart, the epitome of social-purity womanhood.[99]

Yet the most striking thing about *Koradine Letters* is the extent to which it duplicates the themes of both Gestefeld's *Woman Who Dares* and Van-Anderson's *Journal of a Live Woman*. Like Murva and Victoria, Koradine struggles to eliminate her "bestial" selfishness and her passionate desires (in this case, for pretty clothes and the love of her female friends). By the novel's conclusion Koradine has eliminated her passions and become "an angel." Yet her transformation does not make her the leader of humanity. Like Murva, Koradine uses her angelic power to make man "more a master." In the book's final pages, Koradine's meditations restore sight to a blind boy, Tommy Merton. Koradine imagines she is setting a "sparkling crown" upon his head. She dreams of Tommy "walking upon the water," thus likening the boy to a god.[100]

Stockham's novel also echoes Gestefeld's by presenting a *crippled* man as the epitome of human development. In Gestefeld's *Woman Who Dares*, a male invalid, John Wilson, is the novel's most spiritually advanced character. Similarly, the spiritual leader of Gestefeld's novel *The Leprosy of Miriam* is Paul Masters, a cripple whose face, "guiltless of beard," combines "a man's strength and dominance with a woman's gentleness and beauty."[101] Stockham seems to follow both of Gestefeld's novels in implying that because true purity requires "strength and dominance," it is available only to men whose bodies have been weakened.

The other striking aspect of *Koradine Letters* is Stockham's almost obsessive use of the word "white." The term "white" was highly contested in the 1890s, as white middle-class Americans debated whether it signified womanly purity or Anglo-Saxon manliness. To uncover the wider resonances of *Koradine Letters*—and to understand why blind Tommy is the hero of Koradine's novel—we must take a closer look at the way in which Stockham deploys the term "white."

In *Koradine Letters* Stockham attempted to break the association of whiteness with manly Anglo-Saxon aggression and instead align it to womanly qualities. The novel's female characters have "white, holy" spirits. Whiteness is linked to "love." Stockham also associates whiteness with sensitivity; male characters turn "white" from emotion or illness. This does not negate the alignment of whiteness with womanly qualities, since rarified emotions, nervous illness, and heightened sensitivity are the qualities of refined white womanhood.[102]

Koradine Letters hints, however, at a problem with the character of women. Were they really naturally "white"? Koradine's struggle to eliminate her selfishness implies that they are not. The experiences of other female characters support this sense that women's whiteness is quite precarious. A "pretty, pink-faced" girl named Estelle, for example, is so interested in being attractive that she applies cream to her face after the dormitory lights have been turned off for the night. The next morning, Koradine reports, Estelle has a shock: she is now "black as Flop, my cat. She had rubbed her face with black shoe polish instead of the white cream, and looked too funny for any use. The bed and pillows were a map of Africa."[103] Estelle's response is to amuse the other girls by playing "negro minstrel" for them. The teacher's response is to warn the girls that "the more light we had when we made our toilets the better; that 'dark rooms were for developing photographs, not girls.'" But the scene's underlying message was that white women were capable of selfishness and sensuality. They needed to be strictly monitored, since any eruption of their sensual vanity could revoke their "whiteness" and transform them, literally overnight, not only into an African, but into an animal and a failure, like "Flop, my cat."[104]

Stockham agrees with Gestefeld, then, that women's apparent purity only thinly conceals their savage lust. The fragility of (middle-class white) women's "whiteness" perhaps explains social-purity leaders' emphasis on womanly "service." More than providing a means of contesting the Darwinian emphasis on competition, it assuaged their own fears that white female nature might be bestial and selfish rather than high-minded and spiritual.

Stockham argues that women's dedication to "service" will keep them white, or negate their inner bestial selfishness. When an Arcadian student named Gertrude decides to become an actress, for example, she invokes "service" to offset fears of female selfishness. "Once I had an ambition . . . to be seen and known, to become famous for self. I know better now," Gertrude explains. Her "desire" has changed from "what I thought I wished, to that which . . . I may serve best in."[105]

There is a problem with basing one's high status on one's willingness to serve. Service is lowly; it is associated with matter, not spirit. As Dr. Goodrich explains, "spirit is that which thinks [and] has feelings." It is "served" by "matter or body," which is "negative" and presumably without thought or feeling. Since spirit has "feelings," and white signifies emotional sensitivity, spirit is aligned with whiteness. Since matter is spirit's opposite, it is presumably not white.[106] Matter is destined to serve. Service, the equation implies, is not white.

Like many woman-movement leaders, Stockham elevated service by associating it with love. Love is equated with service in the case of Matthew, a violent, animal-like child adopted by the Arcadians. When Matthew finally engages in an act of kindness, Dr. Goodrich explains that "love has surely awakened in his heart if he has begun to serve." Yet Matthew's loving service does not raise him from matter to spirit. It simply makes his animal nature more tractable. "[H]e is taming," one Arcadian notes.[107] The tamed, loving Matthew holds approximately the same position in the Arcadian social hierarchy as Leo, the Arcadians' dog; in the novel's final, Delsartian-tableau scene Matthew lies with the dog on the floor. This makes sense. If matter could so easily be transformed into spirit, then the basic rationale for the Arcadian system—the inculcation of methods by which spirit could dominate matter—would collapse.

These issues have relevance for the behavior of women, since women must serve in order to prove that they are white and not beasts. Women, even if elite, are in an ambiguous social position, therefore. As women they are people who serve, which means they are low—but because they serve out of love, they are high. Motivated by love, they have feelings and are aligned to the spiritual. Their acts of service, however, align them with matter, which does not think and feel. Love ought to bridge the gap between matter and spirit. Yet love cannot elevate matter. It simply "tames" matter and makes it a better servant. Despite the claims of woman's-era supporters, therefore, love does not triumph over violence. Instead, love functions as violence. It enforces hierarchy and compels matter, or the lowly, to more willingly serve spirit, or the socially elevated.

Social-purity leaders' insistence that (refined) women were committed to "service" rather than to selfhood was only one part of their strategy to elevate womanhood. They also insisted that boys be raised to be as pure as girls. This would ensure that the married woman would never be dirtied or diseased by the lust of her husband. Stockham used the "sweet" and "beautiful" blind boy Tommy Merton to illustrate the idea that properly raised men could be as passionless as women. Because Tommy is blind, he is a model of what man can be if cut off from "unnatural" influences that inflame desire. Tommy and Koradine fall in love. But Koradine will not suffer the sexual fate of women described in *Tokology*, since Tommy is entirely without sexual desire.[108]

In creating the feminine Tommy as a romantic hero, Stockham appears to offer a new paradigm for marital relations. Yet the novel suggests that raising boys to be more womanly will not solve the problem of compulsory heterosexuality. Even the most "tamed" heterosexuality is tinged with violence, Stockham implies. She also hints that heterosexual interaction with even the most gentle man cannot match the emotional and erotic satisfaction of love between women.

Stockham had described heterosexual intercourse as a form of violence against women in *Tokology*, when she explained that the sexually put-upon wife ended up with "[e]very organ in her body . . . diseased, and every function perverted." Similarly, when Koradine witnesses a man attempting to seduce an Arcadian student named Dorothea, she compares the man's sexual interest to a violent blow: "Her face was white and she looked as though some one were about to strike her. I saw a man strike a woman once . . . and there was something in Dorothea's expression that made me remember that woman's frightened face."[109]

The violence of heterosexuality and its inferiority to love between women can be further highlighted by contrasting two teary scenes in which Koradine receives flowers. The tears are significant, because in Stockham's sex manual *Karezza* she equates tears with sperm or sexual fluids. She spends three pages describing how "spermatic secretion" is analogous not to "bile, which, once formed, must be expelled," but to "tears," which "do not accumulate and distress the man because they are not shed daily."[110]

In the first teary scene, Koradine receives flowers from her beloved friend Elizabeth on her thirteenth birthday. As Koradine lay in bed, "some one came and laid something cool and damp upon the pillow close to my face. I

opened my eyes and there stood my beautiful Elizabeth, . . . looking like
our rose bushes up at Hill Farm. . . . She put her arms around me and kissed
me twelve times, and "for the sacred thirteen" she kissed me on my lips."
The cool, damp objects on Koradine's pillow were flowers. As Koradine describes, the flowers "were so fresh and dewy and Elizabeth so beautiful,
that I felt as though the sun had come into the room, and—and—well, I
cried a little; but just then the girls piled onto my bed and began pounding
me thirteen times."[111] The scene, then, describes Elizabeth, who looks like
flowers, putting damp flowers near Koradine's face, and then further moist-
ening her face with kisses. Koradine then cries, making her face even tearier
(after which she is pounded). If flowers are linked to women, and tears to
sexual fluids, then the sexual content of this scene becomes clear.

In the second scene, Tommy gives Koradine a white rose. As Koradine
describes, "A white rose has fallen in my lap. Tommy is below waiting for
me, the rose is his card. It struck me as he tossed it up, and has left a drop
of dew upon my cheek that lay hidden in its heart. It is the joy tear of an
angel, I am sure."[112] In comparison with Elizabeth's use of them, Tommy's
use of flowers to communicate is more physically distant and entails a hint
of violence—the flower "struck" Koradine's face, recalling her earlier memory of a man striking a woman. In contrast to the excesses of liquid generated by the flowery encounter with Elizabeth, Tommy's flower leaves only
a single "drop of dew" or "joy tear." It draws forth no corresponding tears
from Koradine. The scenes suggest that in heterosexual encounters, the
tears of emotion or sexuality must be constrained. Only in encounters between women can emotion and sexual feeling flow freely.

There is perhaps an even more serious problem with presenting the passionless man as the appropriate mate for the service-oriented woman. The
desireless man would not engage in the competition for wealth. According
to mainstream Victorian thought, however, wealth was the precondition
for civilization. As Josiah Strong and countless proponents of Anglo-Saxon
dominance insisted, "money-making power," as much as morality, love,
and service, was a defining attribute of civilization. As popular novelist
Joaquin Miller bluntly put it, "All civilized peoples . . . are comparatively
rich; and when this world shall be all civilized we shall all be very rich." In
Koradine Letters Stockham agrees that wealth is a crucial component of
civilization. The Arcadian teacher Dr. "Goodrich" elaborates upon her own
name by stating that "the truth of our way is proven by the goodness and
riches flowing in."[113]

The problem was that wealth was created, according to social Darwinists,
by the very male desire that social-purity leaders hoped to eliminate. If

wealth was to be part of utopia, it had to originate in something besides male drive. Stockham therefore associated wealth with the natural warmth of the sun that poured out "gold for the world to grow rich and happy in." [114] This is a crucial alignment. Only if wealth flows like sunlight can social-purity principles create utopia, a world with no desire but with plenty of wealth.

Yet hints remain that wealth is the product of violence and exploitation, not of sunlight and love. The Arcadian "cooperative" is funded by a banker named Jack Gatling. "Gatlings" were machine guns that were used by federal troops against strikers. By the 1890s these guns had become a symbol of capitalist oppression of workers. [115] With "Gatling" bankrolling Arcadia, their "spiritualized human race" is supported by capitalists' violence against workers.

The Arcadians condemned social Darwinist values of violence, racism, militarism, and even private property. [116] Yet Stockham also suggested that these values were in fact "natural." As Koradine stares out the window one morning, she reminds herself to think communally; she looks through "my—no—our window." But immediately after checking her tendency to think in terms of private ownership, Koradine interprets the behavior of nearby birds as a spectacle of race and class warfare in defense of private property. She observes a dozen blue jays engaging in a "bird battle" with "several thousand black-birds." The blue jays are angry at the "black rascals" because they are "trespassing upon [the blue jays'] property." [117] This episode presents military aggression against "blacks" in defense of private property as natural, "lovely," and linked to the creation of "fruit" or riches.

In a second bird parable Stockham suggests that aggression against outsiders is nature's use for seemingly "pesky" men. As Koradine watches, "brisk, busy little English sparrows" unite to drive off a cat that has been stalking baby robins. She describes the sparrows' efficient use of violence: "They all arose in a body and swooped down upon the cat picking at its eyes and body so fiercely and making such a noise that it was glad . . . to scamper back to the farm yard . . . while the merry rescuers went flying and chirping away." Koradine describes this as "a beautiful true story," while another Arcadian observes that English sparrows are not "little pests," but have an important role to play in nature. [118]

The "English" sparrows' "brisk" and "busy" demeanor marks them as Anglo-Saxon men. Such men naturally use violence to ward off threats to the family—significantly a cat, previously associated with blackness, animality, and "Flop" or failure. Men are not simply "pests" after all. [119] Stockham suggests that the violent Anglo-Saxon male ensures wealth, safeguards private property, and rescues Anglo-Saxon women and children from economic failure.

Given that Tommy is neither "brisk" nor "busy," Stockham must have realized that his asexual image could not mesh with the view that Anglo-Saxon male drive created wealth, whiteness, and civilization. Perhaps this is why Stockham repeatedly insists that Tommy is in fact a white man. Indeed, he is the whitest figure in the book. He has "white hands," a "white and shining" face, and even "eyelids that look like white rose petals." Stockham associates Tommy with wealth as well as whiteness. Koradine dreams of Tommy floating "out into the path of gold" formed by the sun's rays upon the water.[120]

Stockham hoped to convince her readers that Tommy—a man who lacked sexual desire—was the true "white man" who trod a "path of gold." But this strategy apparently didn't convince even Stockham herself. She equated male energy with animality and female degradation, on the one hand, and with competition and wealth on the other. Male sexual energy could not be separated from male energy in general. This is why Tommy, although perfect sexually, is a disaster in terms of energy. His desirelessness only increases once his vision is restored. Koradine explains that "things around do not seem to attract him. He sits as one entranced." Tommy's desirelessness spreads to enfold Koradine. As she describes her reaction to Tommy's renewed vision, "My heart beats slow and I am stifled with the awe that creeps over me like some living thing, freezing me into . . . stillness."[121]

Instead of exemplifying utopia, Tommy and Koradine illustrate the impossibility of the social-purity strategy. If both halves of a couple are "entranced," who creates the wealth that is a precondition of civilization? Stockham's text implies that white women were in a problematic position because whiteness connoted riches as well as purity. But riches were created by energy that was inseparable from sexual desire. White women could not display either sexual desire or an interest in wealth without being seen as uncivilized.[122] Women could acquire riches, the prerequisite for civilized life, only through association with men. But the male sexual desire that created wealth also had the potential, as *Tokology* indicated, to turn women into beasts. Yet educating men to be more like desireless women would not work either. Heterosexual relations remained tinged with violence and inferior to love between women, no matter how "womanly" the man behaved. Just as important, desireless men lacked the male drive that created riches in the first place. How then could (white) women be leaders of civilization?

STOCKHAM AND SEX RADICALISM:
KAREZZA AND *THE LOVER'S WORLD*

Stockham's attempt to imagine a desireless social-purity utopia in *Koradine Letters* failed. She did not give up her quest to elevate the role of advanced womanhood, however. She turned to new intellectual sources: the writings of Edward Carpenter and, to a lesser extent, those of Havelock Ellis. These men challenged both social-purity and social-Darwinist perspectives by claiming that women had a sexual nature. Yet Ellis and Carpenter agreed with social Darwinists that men and women had very different sexual natures. They argued that the male sex drive was aggressive; it had to be transmuted as society became more civilized. But women should not transmute their sexual instincts. Their instincts were already, in Carpenter's words, "so clean, so direct, so well-rooted in the needs of the race" that they need only be expressed. Both men argued that in women, the sexual instinct was spiritual. Devotion to sex and maternity was therefore the best way for women to spiritualize the race. Women who attempted to transmute their sexual energy into intellectual achievement would only warp their holy instincts.[123]

Stockham seems to have drawn upon these ideas in order to resolve the problems that plagued *Koradine Letters.* In her sexual-advice manuals *Karezza* (1896) and *Lover's World* (1903), Stockham accepted the sex-radical view that (white) women were sexual beings. "Passion belongs to the . . . healthy woman as much as to the healthy man," she now argued. But in order to make sex-radical ideas more consonant with social purity ends, Stockham altered the sex-radical view of sexual passion. First, she argued that men were like women, in that all passion was spiritual. Second, she argued that women were like men, in that they too could transmute sexual passion. In all of her post–*Koradine Letters* writings Stockham gave women directions on how to "master," "appropriate," and "transmute" their sexual energy.[124]

Stockham used this vision of sexual passion as pure, transmutable, and essentially the same in men and women to shore up the social-purity position on sex, maternity, and human nature. She explained that there was no need for women to channel their sexual energies into marriage and maternity. Passion was simply creative power. Therefore "[i]t does not follow that this creative power shall be devoted to procreation, but it may be used in any good work."[125]

Women who did marry were simply presented with a different sort of opportunity for the transmutation of sexual desire. Stockham advised married couples to engage in "Karezza," or motionless sexual intercourse. Couples following this technique would find that *"the demand for physical expression is less frequent."* The goal of *Tokology*—sexual relations that are mutual, controlled, and infrequent—was thus given a more solid grounding. Through Karezza, women would spiritualize sex—not by more fully following their reproductive instincts, but by transmuting sexual energy into intellectual strength. "[I]n the Karezza relation the creative principle becomes active in both husband and wife. . . . [and] ideas of great moment are conceived," Stockham explained.[126]

Stockham continued to support the social-purity position that in the "perfect personality . . . both the male and the female principles are harmoniously developed." She provided "affirmations" that would help realize this goal of a human character modeled on "womanly" values. She advised her readers, whether male or female, to meditate upon the following:

> "I am a creator, not merely of human children, but a creator of thoughts, of ideas and of resources. I devote my great heart-love to the interests of the world. There is no task too onerous for my devotion, no service too difficult for my undertaking. All children are mine, all interests are mine, gladly and cheerfully do I answer the call to serve those who need me. I am both father and mother. In joy and gladness do I consecrate myself to the world." [127]

Appropriating the sex radicals' idea that sex was holy and adding that it was transmutable enabled Stockham to imagine (white) women as both sexual and civilized. But the problem of, on one hand, white women's embrace of love and service and, on the other, their dependence upon wealth that originated in violence remained unresolved.

Stockham never lost her suspicion of female selfhood, and so never deviated from her insistence that women's self must be contained through love and service. She implied that the most dangerous aspect of male lust was that it destroyed women's love—the love that compelled womanly service and so contained the lowly female self. Stockham repeatedly quoted women who claimed to despise their husbands because of their husband's sexual demands. In a typical letter, a woman wrote that her husband "is kind and provides for his family," but went on that because of his brutish sexual demands, "now—(will God forgive me?)—I *detest*, I *loathe him*, and if I knew how to support myself and children, would leave him." If men's sexual selfishness threatened marriage, Stockham promised that men's "mastery" of their sexual drives would restore women's natural love for their husbands. A husband's sexual self-control would enable his wife to "proudly say 'I love' where previously she said 'I hate,'" Stockham explained.[128]

Since female discontent, like male selfishness, created emotions that barred women's "love and service," Stockham presented affirmations designed to stifle women's discontent. To a woman who wrote that despite having "a kind husband, plenty of means, [and] plenty of leisure," she was still unhappy because "her children were so cross and irritable that she daily wished to go away from them," Stockham replied that the woman had "made her own discontent." She ought to meditate upon her blessings of "a kind husband, the pleasant home and dear children." Stockham recommended the writings of poet Ella Wheeler Wilcox, who advised women that their "restless discontent" would vanish if they repeated to themselves, "'I am happy, busy, useful. I am a reflection of God's mind—I love, rejoice, and am happy.' . . . Look at your husband and children and say, 'I love them—they are blessings; they are gifts from God and I am happy and grateful.'" [129]

By the early twentieth century Stockham had shifted from denying sexual passion to blessing it. Yet she still defined women by their "love and service." The purpose of elevating sexuality was to ensure that male lust would not generate hatred and discontent, rather than love and service, among women. But what of the problem of wealth? Would the sexually considerate husband still be able to engage in the brutish competition that created wealth?

Stockham's solution to this quandary was to redefine the creation of wealth as a problem of eugenics. She claimed that if men exercised self-control during sexual intercourse, and women guarded their thoughts during pregnancy, then the couple would "conceive children superior to themselves." Such tactics would ensure wealth for all. Stockham explained that controlled sexual relations would eliminate the "unregenerate rabble of poverty and vice" as well as the racially unfit, the "nerveless deformities of drunkenness and debauchery." [130]

Stockham might have promoted these eugenic ideas because they helped to keep (middle-class) women "white." Proponents of Anglo-Saxon dominance believed that wealth depended upon the competitive drives of white men. These male drives could both make women "white" by giving them wealth and make them "black" either through turning them into "breeding animals" or through eliciting women's own sexual desire. But if wealth was instead the natural result of moral goodness, then it would no longer be problematic for women. Stockham's version of eugenics, which called for race improvement either through controlled sexual union or through the creation of "child thoughts," gave women a means of creating moral people. If all were good, all would be rich—since Stockham believed that poverty was the product of moral failure. No immoral people means no poverty. Stockham's eugenics implied that wealth was not the product of male desire, which women couldn't control; it was the product of morality, which women could control. White women would no longer be faced with the impossible choice of either being pure (celibate) but impoverished or rich but sexually degraded.

Stockham's solution, which was common among both sex radicals and social-purity leaders, simply shifted the responsibility for spiritualizing the race to the intellectual and procreative Anglo-Saxon woman rather than the violent and productive Anglo-Saxon man.[131] The meditative mother became the means by which the "lower races"—the poor as well as the "uncivilized"—would be destroyed; social Darwinist goals by other means.

Stockham's writings reveal additional factors that subverted white women's dream of a higher civilization, or a "woman's era." The problem was broader than women's own insecurities about the purity of their inner selves. White middle-class late Victorians equated civilization with three contradictory elements: spiritual growth, material wealth, and aggressive Anglo-Saxon predominance. White social-purity and woman-movement leaders' acceptance of these linkages (between wealth, spiritual power, and Anglo-Saxon supremacy) sabotaged their efforts to reconceptualize sexuality in a way that would enable them to be full participants in civilization. White women's efforts to claim the mantle of civilization were fatally compromised by the racial and economic hierarchies inscribed in the discourse of civilization itself.[132]

The problematic interrelations among, on one hand, love, desirelessness, service, and female selfhood, and, on the other, money, violence, and racial and class identity would be reworked by a new set of New Thought leaders at the turn of the century. Prominent among them was Helen Wilmans. Wilmans's writings would help to reorient New Thought by spotlighting the weak links of the woman's era—the source of wealth and the nature of desire.

5   Money and Desire
Helen Wilmans and the
Reorientation of New Thought

Dependence is degradation. This is an aphorism I challenge the world to contradict.

Helen Wilmans, 1884[1]

The poor man is *not* honest. The honest man is *not* poor.

Ida A. Nichols, 1891[2]

WOMEN, WEALTH, AND DESIRE

Until the turn of the century, women's New Thought texts only ambiguously praised desire and wealth.[3] They could not be too overt, because late Victorians linked desire and wealth with manliness. They believed that the acquisition of money was rooted in aggressive desire. While the male self could be trusted to create wealth by channeling desire, both mainstream and New Thought authors implied that female desire was dangerous and incapable of transmutation. Indeed, for some late-Victorian women, the horror of life without money was not as great as the horror of a female self in which desire and aggression were liberated. Discussions about whether women could or ought to desire therefore led to troubling questions about the nature of white middle-class women's selfhood, on one hand, and their relationship to money and power, on the other.

The relations between late-Victorian constructs of female selfhood and beliefs about money and desire were plagued with further ambiguities. Money represented the force that woman counterbalanced; yet it purchased the haven-like security that woman represented. Many acknowledged at some level that woman's selfhood—the cultural construct of the feminine self as delicate, spiritual, and uplifting—was dependent upon her access to money. Heaven was reached on a "path of gold," Stockham had written. A woman without money was hardly a woman. She would end up, like Gestefeld's Haddie, either "drudging," "starving," or prostituting her body. A woman's active pursuit of money would "unsex" her. Efforts to attract money indirectly by luring men into marriage transformed the pure woman into a grasping animal.

New Thought tracts addressed this tension between the need for money as a precondition for pure womanhood, on the one hand, and the ban upon women's open pursuit or desire for it, on the other. Yet they did not overtly challenge the fear of female desire that underlay much of their culture's anxiety about women's relationship to wealth. Instead, most New Thought authors of the 1880s and early 1890s tried to reconceptualize desire in order to make it better fit the conventional view that good women lacked desire. Some offered women tips on how to contain their desires, so that they would not suffer when, like Van-Anderson's Mrs. Hayden, they found themselves cast into a lower economic class. Others, like Alice Stockham, insisted that women who pursued careers that might, incidentally, bring them financial rewards were motivated solely by their natural desire to serve.

A final means of containing women's unseemly desire was to follow Hopkins and draw upon the theory of two minds. Hopkins's student H. Emilie Cady typified this approach. Like Hopkins, Cady described a carnal mind that must be stilled so that the Divine Mind or "Father in us" could shine forth. This Divine Father, whom Cady called "the central 'I' of our being," was the source of our desires. "The hunger we feel is but the prompting of the Divine within us," she wrote. Desire was good, but its object was not what it seemed. "[A]lthough to the ignorant mind it may seem that it is more money as money . . . that [the person] wants, it is, nevertheless, more of good (God) that [one] craves; for all good is God," she wrote.[4]

This "two minds" strategy allowed women to redefine their desire for luxury as not their own, but God's. The writings of Hopkins's student Ida B. Nichols, a wealthy former invalid who used inherited money to start Hopkins's *Christian Science* magazine, epitomized this approach. Nichols admitted that one biblical "statement, in particular . . . appealed to me: 'The Almighty shall be thy defense, and thou shalt have plenty of silver.'" Yet she insisted that her love for gold was really a desire for "good," that her inherited wealth was a sign of God's love, and that she pursued her desires only because God wanted her to. She wrote, "As material things are symbolic of the good . . . it is the highest good which gives them to me. I can make what I choose, because God made me a maker. As I am a maker, why should I not make the things which are symbolic to me of Absolute Good? . . . Gold is the symbol of good. Pure gold is the symbol of Absolute Good." Writing in the early 1890s, Nichols offered her readers, largely female, "affirmations" of wealth that made scarce reference to the spiritual. "You are rich. You are abundantly rich. Millions upon millions are yours. God is your support," she wrote. Yet she continued to urge her readers to cleanse "the human self that claims for itself, that desires for its own gain," and to insist that the acquisition of gold was really nothing more than a desire to "manifest the glory and omnipotence of God."[5]

By the early 1900s, this sort of indirection was becoming less common. A new generation of New Thought leaders emerged who openly lauded wealth and desire. They insisted that woman and man must equally learn to "exalt" themselves, and that "[t]here isn't a greater, grander, more Godlike thing to do than to *make money.*" They horrified older New Thought leaders, who condemned the "many unscrupulous persons who have . . . entered the New Thought ranks for the sole purpose of 'conquering poverty at some one's else [*sic*] expense.'" But the younger generation mocked those who held themselves above that sort of thing. As one New Thought author wrote in 1902, while such leaders may "talk beautifully of . . . 'drawing on the infinite supply,' . . . you will notice that they move around very briskly after the nimble dollar."[6]

HELEN WILMANS (1831–1907)

The younger generation's prime inspiration was Helen Wilmans, author of *The Conquest of Poverty* (1899). Wilmans was a reform journalist who started her career praising the woman's era and concluded it asserting that wealth, the product of bloody competition and unleashed desire, was the "birthright" of all. Although she was known for her unabashed praise of money, the heart of Wilmans's New Thought philosophy was an assertion of selfhood. "Next to the word God comes that limitless and unconquerable word 'I'. . . . We must refuse to believe that an assumption of humility is pleasing to God. . . . Let us begin at once to exalt ourselves," she insisted.[7] As we have seen, Wilmans was not the first New Thought woman to laud money—or desire. But she refused to pretend that her desires were not for wealth, and were not her own. This is partially the reason the younger generation revered her.

Like virtually every major New Thought leader of her time, Helen Wilmans was a student of Emma Curtis Hopkins. Yet Wilmans used the vocabulary she learned from Hopkins to proclaim that desire, matter, and the animal will formed the heart of healthy female selfhood. She broke through Victorian gender ideologies to articulate a sense of self that for all its crudity was notably modern. Why was Wilmans the first to so radically interpret Hopkins's ambiguous teachings? How did she thereby help lay the groundwork for the spread of New Thought in the twentieth century?

Answers to these questions can be found in a source that Wilmans made sure to provide—her life story. Wilmans viewed her life as a parable whose

Figure 15.   Helen Wilmans,
founder of Mental Science.

meaning she needed to discover. That is why she wrote and rewrote her autobiography in a wide range of political and theological essays between 1884
and 1905. This record shows that Wilmans's experiences differed from those
of most of Hopkins's other students in several important ways. Wilmans
was a full generation older than most New Thought leaders; she was born
in the 1830s, so her formative years occurred before the full flowering of
late-Victorian culture. Her youth on the frontier (Illinois, at that time) further distanced her from high Victorian gender ideology. Wilmans was also
from a different economic class than many female New Thought leaders.
Her marriage brought her not tedious domesticity, but the grueling labor
of an impoverished farm wife. This is perhaps why her early political ties
were not to the social-purity or temperance movements, but to the labor
movement, populism, and the radical wing of the woman movement—all
of which insisted upon the importance of economic self-determination.

But we cannot reduce Wilmans's perspective to her age or her class. It is
equally important to reconstruct the ways in which Wilmans herself understood her situation. Her personal letters, political essays, theological texts,

and autobiographical musings reveal that her precarious economic status did not exempt her from the gender norms of her day. Contemporary ideals of womanhood were strikingly discordant with her most pressing daily needs—yet it took years of intellectual struggle to reject them. Her writings provide an invaluable record of the process by which some women would finally discard their era's ideal of spiritually powerful but economically helpless womanhood. They highlight the role that ambiguous New Thought teachings played in enabling Wilmans, and others like her, to revolt against womanly ideals in the final decade of the nineteenth century.

Wilmans's writings are also significant in relation to the broader philosophical trends of the late nineteenth century. She insisted that the achievement of healthy selfhood in both men and women was dependent upon their realization that matter and mind were interdependent, equally alive, and capable of growth.[8] Her popular writings thereby paralleled those of early pragmatist philosophers who made similar points. This should come as no surprise. As Harvard philosopher George Santayana explained in 1913, the feelings of common Americans, or "the moods of the dumb majority," were voiced by turn-of-the-century philosophers like William James who engaged in a "revolt against formalism." Yet the life of Helen Wilmans, an author whose writings have been condemned by historians as particularly crude examples of New Thought as a cult of success, provides new insight into this broader philosophical revolt. It highlights the ways in which challenges to mind-body dualism were intertwined with a rebellion against the confining dualities of late-Victorian constructs of manliness and womanliness.[9]

HELEN WILMANS: FROM FARM WIFE
TO REFORM JOURNALIST, 1831–1882

Helena Ridgeway Lloyd Longstreet Wilmans was born in Fairfield, Illinois on June 14, 1831. Her father, Caleb Wilmans, ran the general store that served their town of three hundred. Her mother, Elizabeth Ann Ridgeway, was proud of her descent from a wealthy East-coast family. The family viewed themselves as "quality folks." The Wilmans were big fish, however, in a very small pond. Fairfield in the 1830s and 1840s had a distinctly frontier quality. Violence, illness, and death were common in the town. For entertainment, Wilmans and her siblings would watch the drunken brawls in the saloon across the street from their home. Serious epidemics often attacked three-quarters of the town's residents at once. Wilmans recalled the routine sight of children with distended abdomens and shrunken limbs. The one garment worn by such children was "so short and narrow that it did not conceal the shape of the distorted little bodies. It goes without saying that most of them died in childhood, and that funerals were so common as to make no impression on my mind at all." In contrast to this level of misery, the Wilmans were aristocrats. The sign that they were "high livers" was that they wore store-bought clothes and "had meat three times a day, and wheat bread, and plenty of preserves and other sweets."[10]

Despite the rural poverty that surrounded her, Wilmans recalled a happy childhood. She was the second of nine children, and as the oldest girl, she was expected to look after her younger siblings. She adored them, and later recalled their antics with great affection. She grew up believing that within her small world, she was a figure of importance.

Wilmans hoped to attend college and pursue a literary career. Her dreams were threatened when her father followed the gold rush to California in 1849. He never returned. The family heard of his death by fever six years later. Caleb Wilmans's death left the family in dire financial straits, and Helen's future looked bleak. She received a second chance, however, when her brother came up with twenty dollars. This was enough to send her to the Methodist Episcopal Conference Female College in Jacksonville, Illinois.

Wilmans graduated from college in the early 1850s and moved with her younger sister to Griggsville, Illinois. There she became a teacher. While her fifteen-year-old sister Emma had many suitors, Helen, practically an old maid at the age of twenty-four, had fewer prospects. She fell in love with a medical student who rejected her. On the rebound, she agreed to marry another member of the medical profession, Dr. John Caldwell Baker.[11]

In 1856, at the age of twenty-five, the newly married Wilmans accompanied her husband to his farm in Solano County, California. For the next twenty years Wilmans lived the life of a poor farm wife. She worked from before dawn to midnight cooking, washing, ironing, sewing, and tending house for ten to twenty-five men. She bore two children who "never opened their eyes," as well as four living children. Despite Wilmans's constant pain caused by swollen joints, her husband refused to hire a servant to help her with her chores. "He seemed to consider me a machine with power to run day and night. He had consideration for his horses and for his men and for himself, but none for me," Wilmans wrote.[12]

Dr. Baker, whom Wilmans described as having a "wretched and self-tormenting" disposition, was also lacking in business sense. As his land declined in value Baker turned bitter and morose. Wilmans recalled that "my

heart quailed whenever I heard his step on the porch. His entire attitude re-
pelled me. . . . His indifference to the fact of my working so hard was a
growing hurt, and I came in time to almost hate him for it." [13]

During the early years of her marriage Wilmans clung to the evangelical faith of her mother. But at some point she violently rejected evangelical Christianity. According to her autobiography, Wilmans's anti-religious
epiphany occurred when she begged local preachers to tell her "how my
children are to be saved from hell." When they told her to leave the salvation of her children to God, she suddenly realized that they really didn't
care about the issue. Enraged, she ordered the preachers out of her home.
"It was in this act that I laid down the burden of a life time, though at that
moment I did not know it," Wilmans later recalled. [14]

In the late 1860s Baker's farm was mortgaged and sold for debt. The family moved to Lake County, California. From there Wilmans sent her daughters Ada and Florence to school in San Francisco. Soon after, Wilmans and
her two youngest children joined them in the city. She lived in the city with
her four children for two years. There, Wilmans was determined to fulfill
her girlhood ambition of earning her living by her pen, but her efforts were
unsuccessful. Dr. Baker frequently visited Wilmans and her children in San
Francisco. The two apparently reconciled; by 1875 Wilmans had returned
to Lake County with Baker. [15]

It was difficult for Wilmans to return to the farm. She held to her dream
of becoming a "literary woman," and struggled to write articles after her
twelve-hour day of household labor. Her articles continued to be rejected.
Meanwhile, Baker reverted to his old ways. "The doctor gave me no encouragement and no sympathy. He had no hesitation in piling more and
more work on me," Wilmans wrote. He had discovered quicksilver on his
land, and now compelled Wilmans to keep house for a crowd of miners in
addition to carrying out her work for the farm.

The turning point in Wilmans's life came in 1877. That year her youngest
child, Jenny, a "most angelic little girl," died at the age of nine. After this
tragedy Wilmans made her final break with Baker. For years she had struggled at Baker's side in order to ensure that her children would do better than
she had done. Now Jenny was dead, Wilmans had sent her daughters Ada
and Florence to San Jose to learn the printing trade, and her son Claude was
at school. She wrote, "I [realized that I] was really in a position where I could
assert my freedom for the first time in my married life." [16] According to her
later accounts, one morning in 1877 Wilmans prepared breakfast for the
miners as usual, then packed a valise, borrowed ten dollars from a neigh-

bor, and caught a coach for San Francisco. She never saw Baker again. He died in 1879.[17]

Wilmans arrived in San Francisco determined that she would "find something besides slaves' work to do." "I was a first-class cook and housekeeper, and I could have gotten dozens of such situations, but I would not have them. I would starve first," she insisted. Wilmans found a job writing for a four-page weekly devoted to the sale of patent medicine. When the paper folded after six months, she got another writing job, and then another, until she ended up working for the San Francisco reform journal the *Overland Monthly*.[18]

In the late 1870s Wilmans "believed that certain social and political reform was all that was necessary to enable men and women to rise in the scale of being." She attended union meetings and became close with Charles F. Burgman, one of the five members of the first Executive Board of the American Federation of Labor. Burgman married Wilmans's daughter Florence, and eventually joined Wilmans in rejecting the labor movement in favor of New Thought.[19] During these years, however, Wilmans was known as a supporter of labor.

In the early 1880s Wilmans moved to Chicago to accept a job at the *Chicago Express*, which she described as the "leading reform paper in the world." There she met Charles Cyril Post, a fellow journalist and labor activist. Fifteen years younger than Wilmans, Post was described by contemporaries as having a "lean, hungry look as if in pursuit of something." They were married in 1883, while Post was writing his first novel, an exposé of railroad scandals entitled *Driven From Sea to Sea, or Just Campin'*.[20]

The early 1880s were confusing years for Wilmans. She was sometimes attacked for her controversial editorials. More disturbingly, she found herself growing away from the labor movement. She decided that workers were not worth supporting since most wanted nothing more than to change places with their employers. The refusal of many workers to support women's suffrage also angered her. Deciding to be "recklessly obedient" to her own ideals, Wilmans quit the *Chicago Express* and in 1882 started her own journal, *The Woman's World*.[21]

Wilmans's paper covered subjects typical of the more radical wing of the 1880s woman movement. She protested the crime of forced maternity. She heralded women's suffrage and the importance of women's financial independence, whether pursued through small-scale entrepreneurial activities or through female labor unions. She praised women ministers but repeatedly denounced the Church for degrading women.[22]

From 1882 to 1886 Wilmans struggled to keep *The Woman's World* afloat. These were difficult years for her both financially and philosophically. To make sense of her situation, Wilmans drew upon discourses of womanly purity, manly violence, and occult transcendence. None of them helped her to make sense of her downward economic spiral. Her frantic search for a cosmology that would support her efforts to take action on her own behalf reveals the inability of existing discourses to accommodate the experiences of women struggling for economic survival. Wilmans's experiences during the mid-1880s help illuminate why she would be ready, by 1886, to accept the teachings of Emma Curtis Hopkins's Christian Science.

THE *WOMAN'S WORLD* YEARS: 1882−1886

Between 1882 and 1884 Wilmans put out *The Woman's World* only sporadically. She simply lacked the financial resources to run the paper. Her dire financial situation was not alleviated by her marriage. Like Wilmans, Charles Cyril Post was trying to run his own journal, entitled *Roll Call.* Their 1883 marriage cost them two dollars, which almost used up their joint savings. The couple struggled, often unsuccessfully, to make ends meet on a combined income of five dollars a week.[23]

Wilmans's financial straits were worsened by family tragedy. Wilmans and Post lived with Wilmans's daughter Ada Powers and Ada's two children, Jessamine and Helen. The baby Helen became ill. Her care ran Wilmans into debt and forced her to temporarily suspend publication of *The Woman's World.* The baby finally died in March 1885. Wilmans described the situation to a subscriber: "At last the darling died and the funeral expenses were added. By this time the dry season for newspapers had set in . . . and I found myself in debt and not making anything." She was grief-stricken over the loss of her granddaughter but determined to continue her efforts to remain independent. "I hope [the Lord] will not let me starve. However starvation is the penalty of those who work for masters," she wrote.[24]

Wilmans's economic struggles soon affected the content of *The Woman's World.* She tentatively explored the use of her readers as a source of money. In February 1885, when her granddaughter was desperately ill, Wilmans published a heart-rending story in *The Woman's World* about "Rose," a girl who been impregnated and abandoned by her employer. She urged her readers to send baby clothes to the *Woman's World* office, marked "for Rose," since "Rose's baby will be born not to one mother, but to the universal motherhood of the race." Shortly thereafter she tried the ploy again. This time the seduced and abandoned woman was named Mary, and Wilmans asked her readers to send not baby clothes but hard cash to relieve "Mary's" plight. Wilmans finished Mary off in her September 1885 issue, in which she provided a tear-jerking description of the death of Mary and her baby in childbirth. "Send no more money, friends," she concluded dramatically.[25]

Even with direct infusions of cash from her readers, Wilmans could barely keep *The Woman's World* afloat. She tried the high-pressure sales tactics she must have learned while working for a patent medicine magazine in the 1870s. But the subscription list continued to shrink. By May 1885 it had dropped from its high of 3,800 to 2,000.[26] In June 1885 Wilmans published "A Talk With My Subscribers," in which she confessed her financial problems. She announced that she would now run advertisements in the paper and that it might appear more irregularly. After this, advertisements for "Compound Oxygen" and "Magnetic Garments," often accompanied by testimonials from Wilmans, took up the body of the paper. "I was wretched physically and had been for years," she wrote in a typical endorsement; nothing had helped her except treatment by "compound oxygen."[27] Through ruses such as these she managed to keep the paper solvent.

THE PROBLEM OF WOMEN'S FREEDOM IN *THE WOMAN'S WORLD*

Wilmans was deeply conflicted during these years, and the paper's content reflected her confusion. She was unsure whether it was womanly love or manly conquest that was the key to "race" progress. She was torn between her allegiance to conventional ideals of womanhood and her sense that such ideals were not applicable to a woman in her position—one struggling for survival and living by her pen and her wits.

On one hand, Wilmans's articles promoted a social-purity or woman movement perspective. She wrote that woman, though man's counterpart, was still "finer than he." "She breathes a more etherial [*sic*] . . . atmosphere . . . and is by nature fitted for the reception of a class of truths which he can only receive through her." These "spiritual truths" would soon bring about the "woman's era," Wilmans predicted. She seemed to accept the association of man with mind and woman with love and spirit. "Men are intellectual centers, women are love centers," she wrote. "We have lived and are living in the intelligent age, though we are rapidly approaching the love age or women era." Woman is "pulling down the temples of the brain, and making religion the practical duty of the present hour," Wilmans proclaimed.[28]

Yet she also lapsed into the opposing view: that the violent Anglo-Saxon man was the "conqueror" and creator of race progress. From this perspective, woman's social oppression could only be a sign of her inferiority. She wrote that while it was true that man has "underrated [woman], and assigned her to the position in life which he did not care to occupy," yet man has also developed himself "into the most splendid being on the globe." She believed that man's oppression of woman was not his fault. "Man does not subject her; she subjects herself by remaining unfit for anything but subjection," Wilmans explained.[29]

Wilmans's *Woman's World* articles expressed the elite wing of the woman movement's approach to the problem of poverty. She claimed that the current age of man, or the "intelligent age," was marked by poverty, class inequality, and the "spirit of robbery." Male government "has degenerated into a huge nest of thieves," she claimed; as a result, the "rich, idle class is growing richer, while the poor working classes are growing poorer." Only woman's "motherly heart, her helpful hands and ministering influences" would abolish this "corruption and filth." Women's love would also end poverty, she declared, because "the mother influence looks after the weakest first." Echoing the Charity Organization movement, Wilmans praised women's unique yet ethereal ability to reach the poor. The poor, she wrote, live like "brutes," and "[n]o appeal to their slumbering intellects will reach them. . . . There is but one avenue to their comprehension, and that is . . . through their feelings, and only reached by Love."[30]

Wilmans wrote that womanly love would end poverty, while she herself lived at poverty's brink. She attacked corrupt male intelligence that used sharp business dealings to fleece the public, while it was only her own such dealings that kept Wilmans and her family afloat. Perhaps this is why arguments *against* the power of the loving and selfless woman over the intelligent and selfish man began to appear in her writings. In the midst of an article praising woman's love nature, for example, Wilmans suddenly stated that there were really no cut and dried differences between the sexes. "Blind trust is a womanly attribute," she wrote, "but there are womanly men and there are masculine women. Sex cannot make the dividing line with precision." She sporadically abandoned her call for the triumph of the "mother heart" over male intellect to describe the emancipated women of the future as "shining, resplendent and glorious in the exercise of their powers of intellect."[31] In one exceptionally bitter piece, Wilmans veered abruptly from condemning the fact that woman has been "defrauded of her position" as "love principle" and forced to serve man's "coarser inclinations," to instead mount an attack on the love or maternal principle itself. "Woman gives and keeps giving, asking nothing in return. She is a mother not only to her child, but to her husband and father and brother also." She continued, "Her position is such that her life becomes that of self-abnegation. . . . She abandons herself. Her life is mere giving, which is a dead loss to her, and eventually, ceasing to be appreciated, becomes a dead loss to her husband also. The numbness of death is the penalty of marriage under the system that enslaves and degrades woman."[32] This outburst against womanly sacrifice was telling. Yet it appeared, as did all of Wilmans's protests against woman as love principle, within an article whose larger message was that woman represented love and spirituality.

In her paper Wilmans declared that "[w]omen mean to be free." Yet her allegiance to selfless love as the foundation of female identity made it difficult for her to envision women's freedom. On one hand, she claimed that freedom was the ultimate goal of all living beings. "The determination to be free is latent in every heart. It is so all-powerful it will carry its devotee through the whole calendar of crime to gain its end. Freedom is the aim and the ultimate intent of evolution," she wrote.[33] But there was a problem here. Wilmans defined freedom as the "unfettered" expression of one's nature. Woman's nature was love, or the desire to care for the weak. Yet women were already engaged in selfless care for others. Did this mean that women, already expressing their deepest nature, were therefore already free?

Although Wilmans's paper denounced the many ways in which women were "enslaved," because she insisted that women represented love, she came close to insisting that they were already free. She wrote that women were rejecting housework and maternity. The problem was not that these labors were taxing, isolating, mentally deadening, and socially denigrated, or that they forced women into a position of economic dependence upon a male breadwinner. Housework and maternity were problematic only because they were "compulsory" (since most other professions were closed to women). "[W]oman is forced to accept such duties as men refuse to do. She has no choice. It is the being forced that I object to," Wilmans wrote, adding that "[t]he sense of compulsion . . . KILLS my natural desire." Women's natural desire, however, was for exactly the forces they now seemed in rebellion against—housework and maternity. "In a state of perfect freedom I believe that the great majority of women would prefer to do the household work," she wrote. As for maternity, Wilmans assured her readers that "[i]f women were free this instinct would be intensified a hundred fold."[34]

As long as Wilmans believed that women's deepest instinct was selfless maternal love, she was forced into a position similar to Alice Stockham's— that women must be "free" in order to express their deepest nature, which was loving service to others. Despite her occasional outbursts against maternal love as "mere giving, which is a dead loss" to all, still "freedom" for women remained a conceptual impossibility for Wilmans. "Freedom means manhood and godhood, too," she wrote.[35] Wilmans's efforts to envision women's freedom were blocked in part by her understandings of male and female nature. She likened women to plants, which grow slowly and without apparent effort. The "seeds of greater growth" in women were the very social oppressions Wilmans protested. "[T]his pressure brought to bear against [women] is only to force them up to a higher plane." But men's relationship to nature, she claimed, is different; they are aligned with the competitive violence of animals rather than with the natural growth of plants. If women grow passively, through suffering, men grow actively, through conquest. When men are confronted by danger they "become instantly strong, and face it joyously, and conquer it with animated hilarity," she explained.[36]

Yet Wilmans believed that freedom could only be won through a (manly) animal struggle. "[K]ick at the first hint of slavery to any man or woman," she exhorted; "Kick, but kick like a man, not like a mule." She sometimes invited women to participate in this violent struggle for freedom. "And you, my sisters, do not worry so much about the salvation of the heathen while you are afraid to claim your own soul or the value of your own labors. Be women, brave, earnest women . . . but do not think that it is unwomanly to kick when imposed upon."[37] But how did "kicking" fit the image of woman as "finer" and "more etherial" than man? Did suffering merely refine women and contribute to their natural growth, or must women "kick" when imposed upon? The two paradigms did not fit. One would have to go.

WILMANS'S SPIRIT-MATTER PROBLEM

The discourse of womanly spirituality and manly violence could not include a vision of women's freedom. Perhaps it was the dead-end quality of these discourses that led Wilmans to pursue a third—the spiritualist and Swedenborgian discourse of spirit and matter and their relationship to immortality.

In late 1884 Wilmans announced that henceforth articles on immortality would hold as central a place in *The Woman's World* as articles on the rights of women.[38] Soon her journal was filled with discussions of spirit, matter, and immortality. Wilmans's fascination with immortality may have been fueled by her grief over the death of her daughter Jenny. Yet she also clearly viewed "spirit" and "matter" as codes for male and female. In *The Woman's World* the social relations between men and women were simultaneously explored in two different vocabularies—on one hand, the "woman's era" rhetoric so typical of the woman movement, and on the other, the esoteric intricacies of "spirit's" relationship to "matter."

Wilmans's reliance upon conventional understandings of spirit and matter forced her to make statements that contradicted the stands she took in her political writings. In the latter, she praised woman as an ethereal force that would bring on the reign of spirit. But in her occult writings women represented not spirit, but matter. "Spirit and matter; father and mother; positive and negative," Wilmans wrote. That spirit and matter represented male and female was clear from her frequent invocation of "sex" as the force that brings them together. "[T]hrough the law of sex spirit and matter must enter into an equal marriage in order to perpetuate the individual," she explained. The relationship of (male) spirit and (female) matter or body was not really a "marriage" of equals, however. "Ignorance exists because matter is . . . not yet sufficiently infused by spirit to be obedient to the behests of spirit," she wrote.[39]

Wilmans claimed to be interested in the "marriage" of spirit and matter as a solution to the problem of mortality. She predicted a time when people would experience immortality for themselves rather than through their offspring. The exemplar of the horrors of physical mortality was the very force that she praised in her political writings—maternity. "The production of seed, or children, is nature's confession of failure, and her reserved resource against defeat. It is her . . . substitute for perpetuation." Wilmans's tone turned morbid. "The world has been an open sepulchre of one continued series of abortions in an effort to produce the man and woman who shall stand upon the border line of the visible and the invisible, prepared to FEED THEIR CONTINUED EXISTENCE FROM THE SEEN AND THE UNSEEN EQUALLY"—that is, who would nourish themselves equally upon spirit and matter.[40]

Wilmans's occult writings, like her political writings, were leading her to dead ends. Her paper was flagging and her finances were desperate. The paper's final edition was May 15, 1886. It contained Wilmans's bitter essay on women's "mere giving" that leads to the "numbness of death." Then, in June 1886, Wilmans took an action that changed her life: she signed up for Emma Curtis Hopkins's first Chicago class in Christian Science.[41]

WILMANS AS NEW THOUGHT ENTREPRENEUR, 1887–1901

Wilmans's earliest mental-healing articles praised not Hopkins, but Eddy and "still more the works of that great soul, Dr. Evans."[42] Hopkins's class nevertheless marked a turning point for Wilmans. She learned ambiguous doctrines concerning the power of thought and the power of woman, the necessity of selflessness and the godliness of desire. Equally valuable to Wilmans were the friendships she established with her classmates, who included Alice Bunker Stockham, Lida Hood Talbot, Ida B. Nichols, and Frances Lord, a British reformer who was a close friend of Elizabeth Cady Stanton's. Most important, the class gave Wilmans a solution to the problem that had bedeviled her adult life—the problem of poverty.

Wilmans's commitment to the new "science" was forged almost immediately, when in the midst of her lessons her husband, Charles Cyril Post, fell ill. According to her later accounts, Wilmans cured him through her newly learned powers. Later she would see this moment as the birth of her own system, which she named "Mental Science."[43]

Although Wilmans claimed that her mental healing had taken Post past the life-or-death stage, he remained too weak to work. Wilmans sold *The Woman's World* to Frances Lord and used the money to send Post to Douglasville, Georgia, where she joined him in 1887. There, her life-long battle against poverty continued. Wilmans attempted to support the couple through mental healing. Her efforts gained her notoriety in the small Southern town. But as she later described, "I soon got tired of the whole matter, especially since there was no money . . . in it."[44]

Wilmans's financial situation remained precarious until Post suggested that she write down a series of lessons in Mental Science and try to sell them. With no money to pay printing costs, Wilmans and her daughter Ada Powers prepared by hand six copies of the six lessons Wilmans wrote. They placed an advertisement in *The Woman's World* offering to lend the set to customers, who, for twenty-five dollars, would be allowed to copy the lessons by hand and then return them.[45]

The scheme marked another turning point in Wilmans's life. "The first twenty-five dollars that came surprised me," she recalled. "Then more orders came, and still more, until I was dazed with success." The money generated by her advertisement, along with money Wilmans received from "absent patients," quickly overshadowed the paltry sums she had been earning as a healer. Soon she was able to print her lessons and sell them more widely. Wilmans and Ada Powers then started a Mental Science paper entitled *Wilmans Express*.[46]

By this point Wilmans had refashioned Hopkins's "Christian Science" into a faith more fully her own. Its hallmark was the claim that humanity was nourished by an interior "fountain" of thought and will, which represented one's inner divine power. To promote her beliefs, Wilmans established the "Wilmans Metaphysical College," which offered classes leading to diplomas as well as "lovely accommodations for a limited number." Tuition was fifty dollars, and board cost from seven to ten dollars a week. Aided in her teaching, writing, and healing business by her daughters and their husbands, Wilmans was on her way toward building a small financial empire in Georgia.[47]

In 1892, after five years in Douglasville, Wilmans and Post moved to Florida. Wilmans explained that they moved because Douglasville was too small to accommodate the refined students attending her Metaphysical College.[48] She omitted a major part of the story—her husband's involvement with Tom Watson and the People's Party.

Post was a close friend and political ally of the notorious Populist leader Tom Watson. While Wilmans ran her Metaphysical College, Post was the managing editor of the *People's Party Paper*. In 1892 Post became the head of the Georgia People's Party. That year, Douglasville was the scene of a violent political battle between the Democrats and the People's Party, a contest that would help determine the future of Populism in Georgia. In April the Democratic State Central Committee attempted to discredit Post and the Populists, declaring that "[t]he chief of the Third Party in Georgia [C. C. Post] is a Republican and an infidel" who believes "neither in Democracy nor in our God." The attacks continued through the summer, culminating in a speech by state governor William J. Northen in which he called Post "the foulest of God's creatures" and denounced Helen Wilmans as "an atheist herself" who "makes $1,000 a month selling her damnable heresy." Soon after this speech, a mob attacked Post and W. C. Peek, the Populist candidate for governor. Almost immediately after this attack, Post and Wilmans fled to Florida.[49]

Wilmans and Post moved frequently during the next several years, but by 1897 had settled in Florida. There, Wilmans published a journal entitled *Freedom* and wrote several books on Mental Science, including, in 1899, *Conquest of Poverty* (which included two chapters by Lida Hood Talbot, coauthor of *Koradine Letters*). She continued to practice mental healing, and later estimated that she saw approximately 7,000 to 10,000 patients in the 1890s.[50]

Wilmans also perfected her mail-order business during these years, using a hard-sell approach to advertise her services. In her journal *Freedom* she asked her readers, "Do You Own the Wilmans Home Course in Mental Science? If Not You Surely Want It, and If You Want It You Can Surely Get It Now."[51] Even more lucrative were Wilmans's "absent treatments." A typical advertisement read:

> Have you not heard that through the power of *right thinking* you can be healed of every form of a disease whether it is physical or mental? . . . you can be healed in your own homes while the healer is hundreds of miles away. . . . Thought . . . goes from the brain of the healer to the brain of the patient and corrects the error existing there. . . . It not only cures disease, but strengthens the broken will, and plants hope in the breasts of the despairing, and opens the way to success in every undertaking.
>
> For particulars send for the Mind Cure circular. Circulars FREE. Consultations FREE. State your case and receive an early reply.[52]

Wilmans charged three dollars a week or ten dollars a month for these "absent treatments." She employed a staff of stenographers to answer the enormous volume of mail she received.

Wilmans also invested her money in Florida real estate, and strongly encouraged her readers to do the same. But perhaps the money-making scheme closest to her heart was her book-agent business. "A great many people are taking up the study of Mental Science 'for the money there is in it.' And there is money in it," Wilmans wrote. The book that would make her agents money was *Conquest of Poverty*. Belief in Mental Science was not a requirement, she promised. By 1900 almost 40,000 copies of the book had been sold; by 1901, over 60,000. "These have mostly been sold by solicitors, and as far as we know it is the only paper-covered book that has ever been successfully handled through agents," Wilmans boasted.[53]

Wilmans's money-making ventures bore remarkable fruit. By the turn of the century, when the average middle-class income ranged from $900 to $4,500 a year, she was earning $25,000 to $50,000 a year. Wilmans and Post used this fortune to buy property on the ocean, where they constructed a small town named Sea Breeze. In addition to a store and a palatial residence, they built the Hotel Colonnades, an "amusement pavilion" with a 1,200-foot pier into the ocean, and the Wilmans Opera House.[54]

Their most exciting project, however, was the "University of Psychical Research." This "school for the higher education of the race" would teach Oriental and natural history, religions, evolution, mental philosophy, Mental Science, music, and art. By the turn of the century Wilmans believed that her "little city by the sea," built by the "power of our thought expressed in creative action," was destined to help bring forth a new breed of humanity.[55]

Wilmans's faith in her new creed was shared by her many prominent friends in the world of reform. One of the first to visit Wilmans and Post in Sea Breeze was Benjamin Orange Flower, editor of the reform journal *The Arena*. Alice Stockham wrote to send her best wishes on the college. "I so rejoice for the world that [the college] is well in hand," she wrote. "Success to your idea. I know it is a big one, and if I can aid you about teachers or anything, command me. It is to be and will grow like Topsy. Bless your dear heart," Stockham enthused. Lida Hood Talbot came to stay with Wilmans in Sea Breeze for several weeks. Louisa Southworth, a prominent suffrage worker and close friend of Susan B. Anthony's, was also a frequent visitor. In 1900 Southworth contributed $1,000 for the purchase of lots for the school.[56]

In December 1899 Wilmans formed the Mental Science Association. Its goal was to promote the study of Mental Science and the formation of Mental Science "temples." Wilmans's son-in-law Charles Burgman then undertook a cross-country lecture tour that hawked both Mental Science and Florida real estate. By May 1900 temples had been formed in Sea Breeze, New York, and San Francisco. By October, there were temples in Los Angeles, Seattle, Portland, and Chicago. In July 1900 the first national convention of Wilmans's followers was held in Seattle. Estimates of attendance ranged from several hundred to 1,200. The group was greeted by the mayor of Seattle, who, while admitting his "ignorance of . . . [the] purposes and attainments" of Mental Science, yet welcomed them politely to his city.[57]

In the spring of 1900 Wilmans was asked to be an honorary vice-president of the newly formed, East coast–based International Metaphysical League. It was a sign of her acceptance by the national New Thought leadership. By early 1901 she was busy preparing for the second convention of Mental Scientists, which was to be held in the opera house that bore her name. She had come a long way from the dejected farm wife convinced of her own inferiority. Now, despite minor irritations from "doctors and Christians" who were harassing her about her journal *Freedom*, Wilmans was confident about the future. In October 1901, one month before the convention, she wrote to her friend Eugene Del Mar, "Now I tell you this convention is going to make history. You know . . . that we have by far the biggest idea that has ever come into this world—*the power of mind to control matter to absolute perfection*—until disease, old age and death are utterly abolished." She went on to predict that "the world will be redated from 28th November."[58]

THE THOUGHT OF HELEN WILMANS

The heart of Mental Science was Wilmans's claim that matter was alive and intelligent. "[T]he substance which . . . we have called dead matter *is a mental substance*," she insisted. Wilmans now attacked the idea that spirit must dominate matter. She insisted that all matter had life. Since to be alive was to be capable of thought, Wilmans concluded that "[e]very atom in the universe had power to think. . . . Animals think; plants think; even crystals think." The universe was a single, living mind that manifested itself in diverse material forms. Spirit, which Wilmans now condemned as "cold," "vapory," and "diffuse," symbolized false beliefs that led to death. She agreed with the common New Thought claim that "all is mind," but defined mind as inclusive, not exclusive, of matter.[59]

Wilmans's Mental Science incorporated the Darwinian view that desire propelled evolution. The cosmos was held together by the "Law of Attraction," she wrote, and the force that propelled attraction was desire.[60] For ages the suppression of inner desire had blocked human evolution. Mental Science would liberate humanity by teaching people to acknowledge the Law of Attraction, and to express their inner desire.

Wilmans believed that if people liberated their inner desire, they would awaken their divine intelligence. They would realize that their minds were one with the Universal Mind. This understanding would unlock for humanity the creative power of the universe and lead to limitless growth and fulfillment of every desire. In contrast to Eddy and many woman-movement leaders, who imagined "mind" as powerful only if it crushed desire, Wilmans followed Evans and other male theorists who claimed that mind was fueled by desire. Indeed, she claimed that desire was the basic building block of the self. "The desires I see in myself are evidence of my own selfhood. They form my ego," she wrote. She went further, insisting that God was not "spirit" but universal mind, or conscious, intelligent desire. "*[T]he law of attraction*" is "*what religious people call 'God,'*" she wrote.[61]

Wilmans claimed that if people accepted their inner desires, they would be transformed from dead matter to living mind. The difference between dead or unawakened matter and living mind was akin to the difference between an enslaved beast that suffers mutely and a free, cunning beast that hunts joyously. Drawing upon newer paradigms of animal-like masculinity, Wilmans described the "ripened man," writing that "the strength and character of his animal progenitors have passed into his brain and live there in disguise, or show forth in cunningly devised methods for the attainment of that power which the beasts—his forefathers—took by force." If liberated, one's "latent power" or "desire" would follow the laws of survival of the fittest. Desire, Wilmans wrote, is "utterly selfish; it is the ego; it is the 'I' in a struggle with every other 'I.'"[62]

Wilmans's Mental Science writings embraced "mind" and animal struggle. Yet in her *Woman's World* years, Wilmans had equated mind and violence with man and spirit and love with woman. This had forced her to imply that women could not be free. Freedom was an expression of one's nature, but woman's nature was to love, or to serve others. Woman could not be free because freedom was won by violent struggle, which was the prerogative of man. Woman's lot was oppression, since while man grew from conquest, woman grew from suffering. Wilmans implied that although woman was not "mind," she was also not "spirit," since the relationship of spirit and matter was like that of man and wife, in which matter must serve the needs of spirit.

Wilmans's shift to lauding "male" principles did not mean that she had abandoned her interest in freedom for women. On the contrary, her Mental Science seemed to allow for the assertion of an autonomous, intelligent, desirous female self, as conventions of womanly purity did not. Wilmans may have adopted her rhetoric of violence and mental power in order to resolve the problems of women's selfhood and freedom that had bedeviled her *Woman's World* years. That her conception of "matter" as alive, intelligent, and capable of thought had everything to do with the relationship between womanhood and freedom was clear from Wilmans's 1898 autobiography, *A Search for Freedom*.

DESIRE AS THE KEY TO WOMEN'S FREEDOM

In *A Search for Freedom* Wilmans recast her life story as a parable of how the female self could be enslaved by false "race beliefs." Only her rejection of deadly commonsense beliefs and the restoration of her natural animal self had saved her. The heart of *A Search for Freedom* was a shocking claim—that animal will was the savior of (white) womanhood.

Wilmans devoted much of her autobiography to the glory days of her childhood when her animal will was still intact. While during her *Woman's World* years she had equated women's nature with the passive growth of plants, she now described her own childhood nature as that of a wild, fighting beast. When a teacher had tried to beat her, Wilmans had "jumped on her and bore her down with [her] weight." She went on that she "tore her [teacher's] cap off and pounded her unmercifully." This freedom-loving animal spirit was godlike, and was the natural prerogative of girls as well as boys. Her childhood friend Kate, for example, had an "erect and divinely muscular" form. Kate's divine form was enlivened by her animal strength and courage. When the schoolboys gathered to "jeer and taunt" the schoolgirls, Wilmans recalled, Kate "springs . . . upon them with the agility of a tiger . . . digs her claws into [one], kicks three or four more, butts another with her head . . . until she puts them all to route."[63]

A woman's animal will was dangerous only if repressed. When Wilmans tried to repress hers, she recalled, it felt "as if some latent power imprisoned in my breast was tearing me to pieces in order to escape." The life of Kate exemplified the dangers of repressing one's animal will. Kate eventually married and became the mother of "extraordinarily fine children," Wilmans wrote. Yet although Kate could have become "a splendid woman and a social leader," she ended up insane. "Her strength, her force, the very majesty of her intellect, having found no outlet suitable to their grand character, had turned to rend her."[64] Wilmans's narrative stood in stark contrast to mainstream debates of the 1890s. Physicians insisted that women's intellectual development sapped their bodies and could lead to insanity. Many woman-movement leaders claimed that women's intellectual development was linked to their pure and selfless hearts, and so posed no threat to the established order. Wilmans's writings were perhaps unique in their unabashed lauding of an aggressive, intelligent female self.

Wilmans explained her misery as a farm wife as the consequence of the loss of her animal will, or her divine selfhood. The culprits were the very forces she had praised in her *Woman's World* years—religion and love. Religion did the first round of damage. Wilmans claimed that the idea of her own innate sinfulness had made her suffer physically. "[M]y heart weakened until it felt like lead within me. I am sure that in this one thing I laid the foundation . . . which made me a physical wreck later in life," she wrote. Her evangelical Christian beliefs transformed her from a free creature to a mistreated piece of livestock. "I see now what a profanation [*sic*] the religion of the age is," she claimed. "I did not see it then. My brain had not ripened to the power of such perception; so I simply suffered dumbly, as an animal might suffer from some dull, slow torture it could not get away from." Religion damaged her by destroying her selfhood. "I had come under the dominion of a great fear. I had lost the foot-hold of self, and was adrift," Wilmans wrote.[65]

Like religion, love robbed Wilmans of her freedom. Her childhood was spent caring for her younger siblings. "I was a slave to the little things, but did not seem to know it. It was my love for them that enslaved me," she wrote. But next to adult romantic love, youthful maternal love was mild in its effects. After falling in love with Harry Washburn, a young man who rejected her, Wilmans recalled that she "degenerated" into a state of "almost maudlin idiocy. What is there in life to compensate for such complete loss of self as this?" Like maternal love, romantic love "enslaved" her. Like religion, it stole her natural health and vitality. Even remembering her infatuation "I am taken back through the pain of the whole thing," she confessed. "My heart feels like lead in my breast, and my hand is too nerveless to write." Such weakness left her ripe for "conquest" by a stronger being. It was when she was suffering from her rejection by Harry that Dr. Baker proposed to her. "I was too heart-broken and too weak, both physically and mentally, to resist," Wilmans wrote.[66]

Wilmans described her first marriage as a period of "such slavery as would scarcely be thought possible for any woman to fill." The problem was less her poverty than her self-image. "I had been so unappreciated that I had come to regard myself as an inferior creature," she wrote. She suffered from her adherence to social convention. "If I had been brought up with any other idea than that of man's God-given right to lord it over woman, I could have changed the whole tenor of my life and of [Dr. Baker's] also." The result was that Wilmans regressed beyond the suffering of a dumb animal, to that of lifeless matter itself. She was "crushed to the earth," her "soul ground into the dust daily."[67]

But just as there were two sorts of animals—the enslaved creature who suffers dumbly and the cunning beast that fights for its freedom—so were there two kinds of "dirt"—a lifeless dust and a fruitful soil. Wilmans's maternal love, the very force that had enslaved her as a child, now helped spark her transformation from dead dust to living earth. When she turned out of her home the preachers she had been questioning about infant damnation, Wilmans felt "born into a new world." "Like the young plant I had burst the soil that lay so heavily above my head, and had come through into the realm of light above." Henceforth she turned not to a spirit-God, but to living nature for renewal. She studied "nature and her laws." "I became a veritable product of earth, submerged in her fruitful soil—so to speak—where, like some seed or bulb, I took root and began to feel the throbbing pulse of mother earth quickening the life within me."[68]

Instead of attempting to crush her lowly "carnal mind" so that the "Divine Father" or "man-child" within could provide a makeshift ego, Wilmans embraced fruitful and intelligent "matter" as the basis of selfhood.[69] She associated growing matter not with the passive life of plants, but with the animal will. Once Wilmans regained her "foot-hold of self," her animal will was liberated. As she wrote in her journal *Freedom*, "Lord, the kicking I have had to do in order to keep from under the waves. I did not know about the high, intellectual, reposeful position of unquestioned mastery; that has been a thing of evolution with me; and the root of it was this fighting, gouging, hair pulling animal will; this determination not to be wiped out of existence by the world's established beliefs in the weakness of woman."[70]

In short, Wilmans claimed that the essence of humanity was the clawing, animal will; a human essence that was shared by men and women alike. She rejected the view that while men grow from conquest, women are ennobled by suffering. "We must refuse to believe that an assumption of humility is pleasing to God; it has not made men and women of us, and never will," she wrote. Wilmans asserted that the struggling animal essence of man and woman empowered them both. Rejecting the common image of spiritual woman "crowning" man, she insisted that any "man or woman" could take their place "on the apex of creation." Following Mental Science will "change us from the weaklings we now are to men and women of glorious powers," she promised.[71]

Wilmans's approach to female selfhood differed dramatically from that of other New Thought authors. Mary Baker Eddy wanted to "destroy" all desire, which she associated with lowly, masculine matter. Woman symbolized the triumph of spirit—but only if she eradicated her "mortal mind," or selfhood, or desire. Warren Felt Evans believed that matter, women, and mothers were good as long as they did not engage in "unnatural revolt" and dominate, rather than serve, the masculine spirit. The desirous woman was acceptable only as long as she was "willing to obey the will of some [one] other than herself." Emma Curtis Hopkins could accept desire only if convinced that it was not her own, but God's. She insisted that women must distrust their lowly, mortal selves and instead rely upon the divine spirit. Helen Van-Anderson's "Victoria True" wanted to be rid of "this petty foolish self that suffers and makes others suffer" in favor of "stillness." Ursula Gestefeld's "Murva" imagined the liberated female self as a lustful, cannibalistic monster. Alice Stockham ultimately accepted passion within women, yet she continued to distrust the vain, sexual inner self that could in an instant transform a woman from "white" to "black." That is why Stockham insisted that women must continue to "love" and "serve."

Wilmans's ideas about female selfhood should also be contextualized in relation to those of more mainstream writers. As we have seen, the turn of the century marked a distinctive moment in the transition from Victorian to modern ideals of manhood and womanhood. During these years ideals of selfhood were unsettled and highly contested. Some lauded the manly man who based his identity on his willful self-control, and others the masculine hero who prided himself on his savage self-expression. Those who proclaimed that woman must be a "race mother" and conserve her mental energies in order to produce more hardy sons were challenged by those who lauded the intellectual and moral woman whose "mother heart" had little to do with her reproductive status. Popular and elite theorists alike debated the precise role that desire in general, and sexual desire in particular, played in male and female character. In the forefront of this discussion were radical late Victorians such as Edward Carpenter and Havelock Ellis, who shattered Victorian norms by depicting a continuum between tabooed and socially legitimated forms of sexuality, and by lauding sexuality as the "ever wonderful, ever lovely" key to life.[72]

Yet even these radical theorists did not fully challenge late-Victorian ideals of womanhood. Edward Carpenter agreed with Alice Stockham that women's "instinct" was to "serve" and "love." Havelock Ellis insisted that women's deepest desire was to be "conquered" by men. In contrast, Wilmans insisted that women's deepest instinct, like men's, was to engage in a savage struggle for freedom. She declared that for women, as for men, to be "conquered" was not pleasure but "slavery" and "torture." Wilmans was perhaps one of many turn-of-the-century female New Thought writers who drew upon the available discourses of their day to fashion unique, transitional paradigms of womanhood and manhood—paradigms that challenged not only the common gender norms of New Thought texts, but those of the broader culture as well.[73] Her views are thus important to resurrect, even though, as we shall see, they would be opposed and ultimately erased from popular memory during the early years of the twentieth century.

LOVE, SEX, AND MATERNITY

Wilmans's acceptance of a desirous female self led her to reinterpret love, sex, and maternity. Most New Thought women, like most woman-movement leaders, claimed that women's deepest instinct was love defined as self-sacrificing service. Therefore there could be no such thing as women's freedom. Wilmans took a different approach. Instead of rejecting freedom as a goal, she redefined the meaning of love. In place of love that led to self-abnegating "service," Wilmans elaborated a psychology of love that was rooted in self-love and desire.

Wilmans presented her theory of love in her 1893 volume, *Blossom of the Century*. There, Wilmans insisted that love ought to be based not on selfless service, but on assertion of self. "Every form of love rests on desire; rests on the basis of self," she wrote. She opposed the Christian interpretation of love which called for the "renunciation of one individual to another" and the "total sacrifice of the selfish principle as expressed in desire." This position was self-defeating because "no one who is weak in his own selfhood can give himself; and this is love." Real love only occurred with the "ripening of the ego." It emerges when people have power and freedom, *"For love is the overplus of strength,"* she insisted. True love for others always remained rooted in self-love. Once attaining strength and freedom, Wilmans explained, the individual finds that his or her "happiness is best served by . . . noble words and generous deeds. And thus, even in the execution of man's loftiest ideal for the universal good, we see that he acts in obedience to his self-love." [74]

Wilmans's praise of self-love in both men and women led her to challenge mainstream views on sex and motherhood. She never condemned men for their "selfish" animal desire.[75] She hated her first husband not because of his sexual demands, but because he overworked her. Indeed, she mentions sex only once in her autobiography when, perhaps alluding to Stockham's *Karezza*, Wilmans promises that in the "higher marriage" there will "still be sex interchange; but under the control of the intellect it will not result in creation on the animal plane." Wilmans's positive attitude toward marital sexuality may have been the result of her feelings of attraction toward her two husbands.[76] Her theoretical acceptance of the desirous female self may also have made sexuality less troubling for her. She could accept her sexual feelings because she did not fear that "animal" desire would negate her womanhood.

Wilmans reconceptualized maternal love as well. "The mother love, that beautiful and tender and holy feeling, is self-love," she asserted. Love for children is really a form of happiness for the mother, since the "child is the object of the mother's desire." She claimed that "the love of the child is but a projection of self-love" because "[y]our child is the latest and most vital part of yourself; how can you help loving it?" Wilmans argued that maternal feeling was the product not of self-sacrifice but of a strong ego. She wrote that "constantly strengthening individualism develops the *motherhood* of the person." Furthermore, "[t]rue motherhood is not confined to woman alone; the grandest, most god-like men I have known, have been magnificent representatives of this most just and loving and powerful feeling." [77]

One problem with Wilmans's view of maternity was women's lack of choice over when they would conceive. Love was the overplus of strength, she wrote, but women were just as likely to bear a child before they had developed self-love as after they had done so. And to love another before one had developed self, Wilmans believed, led to diffusion and even death. A second problem lay in the nature of the child. Wilmans praised the intense vitality of children, but was also aware that their energy could be directed against the mother. "What unflagging pertinacity these young folks have," she wrote. "Parents may resolve and re-resolve; but *they* only re-solve once; . . . *they* never let up; the mother's resistance wears threadbare in places; *they* perceive the weakening, and with that vitality which knows no need of rest they walk in and have their way at last." Yet this problem could be alleviated through a change in social conditions. "[T]here are scarcely any parents who have sense enough to raise their own children," Wilmans wrote. "Moreover, the system of isolated households is not con-ducive to the highest development of these gifted little creatures."[78]

WOMEN AND WEALTH: *THE CONQUEST OF POVERTY* (1899)

Wilmans was most widely known for her 1899 tract, *The Conquest of Pov-erty*. In tackling this issue she was treading on difficult ground. As we have seen, other New Thought women authors handled the issue of women and money with great indirection. Ida B. Nichols, who was already wealthy when she experienced her "Christian Science" healing, redefined wealth as a spiritual gift from God, and her desire for it as God's desire. Stockham, perhaps representing women who earned their own fortune, redefined her productive activity as service. Gestefeld and Van-Anderson, perhaps repre-senting women who were downwardly mobile, redefined poverty itself as unimportant when one lived in one's "thought world."

Wilmans refused all of these ruses. She was not interested in finding ways to soften the blow of poverty. As she wrote in *The Conquest of Poverty*, "I had borne poverty until I simply would not bear it any longer."[79] She would not recast her desire for wealth as a desire for service, nor claim that her desires were not her own, because she refused to base women's selfhood on selflessness, or to base women's freedom on service. Wilmans rejected self-lessness and service because she had no fear of woman's nature no matter how violent it might be. To her, the struggling animal within woman was the beast that fights back, and so wins freedom. Its cunning desire for survival was the motor of life, growth, progress, intelligence, and "race" evolution.[80]

Wilmans began *The Conquest of Poverty* by asserting that women and men had the right to strive for wealth. She dedicated the book to "working men and women everywhere . . . who long for greater wealth of purse and power and self. . . . Turn on the light of selfhood as you read this book and let the light be strong. Discover self!" Like her contemporaries, Wilmans linked "purse," "power," and "self." Unlike them, she had no fear of the fe-male self, and so felt no need to bar women from "wealth of purse." Wil-mans illustrated poverty's "conquest" not with the usual stories of strug-gling young men, but with her own transformation from dejected farm wife to successful author and healer. *"I made myself over,"* Wilmans bragged, and she would show her readers how to do the same.[81]

Wilmans's tract echoed what had long been standard advice for struggling young men. She told her readers to first awaken their desire and then channel their desires, through intellect, into the planning and execution of a business goal. Directly countering the common tales in other New Thought tracts, Wilmans wrote: "I never proposed that a purse, having five thousand dollars in it, should fall into my lap, nor anything else remarkable. I simply started with the assertion that my business would net me a certain amount. . . . I would then think out a plan of action by which my income would increase and diligently set to work to execute it." She stressed, however, that her "positive thought currents" were the key to her success. "Money comes from doing," she wrote. "But underneath the doing lies the mighty motor, thought."[82]

Wilmans's primary interest was the production of wealth, not the consumption of goods. She addressed "the man or woman who has no money *to start business with.*" But she viewed consumption as a precondition to business expansion. With this end in mind, Wilmans gave instructions on how to consume. She described "spending money as lavishly as [one's] desires prompt" as an act of mastery.[83] As previous mental healers had taught how one could command one's wayward body, so Wilmans gave tips on how to master one's spending. She described her own constant affirmation: "I am not afraid of poverty; I will not pinch down on my money spending; I will not economize as that word is commonly understood. I will live my life and not die all the way through it. I am bigger than money and a thousand times more positive. In the nature of things it is for me to command and it to obey. This is the law whose mandate is absolutely unchangeable."[84] This affirmation was meant to help her readers overcome the fear that Wilmans believed lay behind the craving to save money. Because spending was both a sign of self-trust and essential to the expansion of one's business, she presented it as a courageous step toward "conquering" poverty.

Wilmans claimed that her drive for riches was motivated by her craving for freedom. "I love money; and the reason I love it is because money has another name and that other name is freedom," she wrote. During her *Woman's World* years, Wilmans had found it difficult to assert women's freedom, since freedom meant the ability to follow one's nature, and women's nature was to serve. But even then she had asserted that money was a prerequisite for women's freedom. She had written that "pecuniary independence" must be the bedrock of the woman movement, because "dependence is degradation." The new women clerks, Wilmans had predicted, will be their husbands' "partners" rather than their "private property," and they will *"have only as many children as they desire."* Yet Wilmans had largely confined herself to encouraging "Profitable Home Industries for Ladies." She had also supported the view that women and men must take different routes toward freedom. As an article by Lucinda Chandler—one of the very few in *The Woman's World* not written by Wilmans herself—explained, "Man has wrenched his rights from despots by physical struggle. Woman must wrench hers from despotic custom and man's rulership by moral struggle."[85]

In *The Conquest of Poverty*, Wilmans no longer offered separate definitions of male and female freedom. She claimed to have escaped marital degradation not by changing her mind so that degradation didn't hurt, but by ending her dependence. Now she had freedom, she explained, because she was liberated from "anxiety and fear" as well as from a "crushing sense of duty." Just as significantly, her pursuit of wealth freed her because it strengthened her ego, or self, or desire. Wilmans was adamant that an "intense desire" coupled with "an implicit faith in self" was all one needed to conquer poverty. She had a simple explanation for those who "treated" themselves for wealth through affirmations and still remained poor; their "desire for money" was not "intense" enough.[86] Wilmans's financial advice thus built upon her beliefs about evolution and desire. Anything that stunted desire was enslaving and death-dealing. Anything that encouraged desire—including a craving for financial success—was aligned with growth, life, and freedom.

Hints remained that the "unfettered" desire for money could be something other than liberating. Wilmans wrote that in her pre–Mental Science days she had been "tortured day and night by fear of actual want." This was why "money represented a certain phase of freedom to me. . . . Therefore the desire for money was my leading desire. I was a slave for lack of it." But her next sentence implied that her craving for money, as much as her lack of it, was her jailer. "Every thought of my life was chained to it, and could not escape. How could my spirit (thought-life) try its wings in the clearer atmosphere of the ideal under such circumstances?"[87]

Wilmans clearly preferred the mental "chain" of craving for money to the "fear of actual want." But her incessant scheming throughout the 1890s for more agents, more subscribers, more patients, and more money indicates that desire could be as "enslaving" as the stillness of desireless selflessness. When an irate reader wrote to Wilmans, "If you can drop your foolishness long enough to give me a treatment I shall be glad. I am convinced . . . that you do nothing but fool away your time in useless amusements," Wilmans responded that she was "working like any slave" to keep up her Mental Science practice.[88]

More important than the possibility that Wilmans felt enslaved by her entrepreneurial activities is the question of her attitude toward the "slaves of capital," the working poor to whom she had previously been so devoted. The attitude of most New Thought authors toward those who obstinately remained poor despite God's "endless supply" could only be characterized as vicious. Ida B. Nichols's approach was typical. She insisted that while many sing the praises of "honest poverty," the truth was different: "The poor man is *not* honest. The honest man is *not* poor. The poor man does not know God. He does not speak Truth of the rich, unfailing storehouse of God. . . . The honest man is not poor, because he speaks Truth. He talks of the inexhaustible wealth of God, his Father, whose open hand . . . bestows every blessing he desires."[89]

Wilmans's *Conquest of Poverty* was addressed to these selfsame poor. She described her reader as a "man who is out of work, and who sees his children in rags and crying for bread." Such a man could change his condition simply by recognizing his own power, individuality, and ability to think. He must "recognize his manhood and his rights, the dignity of human nature and the godlike character of his own undying intellect, and be thereby raised in the scale of being." Or, she added, he can "fail to do this and be crushed out of life."[90]

Wilmans's approach to the poor recast New Thought religious sentiments in social-Darwinist terms. She lauded the brutality of unrestrained competition and saw no contradiction in heralding her own "freedom" while at the same time insisting that the suffering of others was what they truly deserved. "Your life depends upon your power to conquer. *Refuse to conquer and perish: conquer and become a god*," she stormed.[91] Wilmans's drive to escape poverty impelled her to reject the ideal of womanly service. It also led her to reject human compassion, as well as any consideration of structural causes of, and possible solutions to, the problem of poverty.

Perhaps the clearest elaboration of Wilmans's attitude toward the poor was in a piece she wrote for the *Chicago Express* entitled "Willing Slaves of the Nineteenth Century." She published the piece in the early 1880s, just before she started *The Woman's World* and well before her embrace of New Thought ideas. The article opened by asserting that the "slave-driver, selfish as he is, is a gentleman compared with the slave." The wealthy are criminal, yet "these men . . . have necessarily—without really intending to do so—benefited the race throughout by their enterprise." The poor are truly inferior. They allow themselves to be "kicked" and don't demand their rights. They are dazzled by the very wealth that oppresses them. Most egregiously, they use their privilege of citizenship to deny this same right to the "intelligent women of these States." "American women above all others are your sympathizers," Wilmans wrote, and yet "you turn up your noses contemptuously when reference is made to their political equality." The poor are "the obstacle—the only obstacle—in the way of race emancipation," because "you will not think. The moment one of you begins to do this, he ceases to belong to that class to whom these words are addressed." She called upon the poor to embrace the "full-grown manhood" of their "brother toilers" who are "organizing for protection"—or "die and give place to those who are susceptible to the noble impulse of a more refined age."[92]

Wilmans was extremely proud of the article, and reprinted it in its entirety in *Search for Freedom*. She was not the only one to admire it. In 1895 the piece was reprinted by the *Commonwealth Library*, a monthly that published "choice Socialist Works by Standard Authors." They reprinted Wilmans's essay in a series that included R. G. Ingersoll, University of Chicago professor Albion Small, William Morris, Sidney Webb, and Peter Kropotkin. The editors probably viewed the piece as an impassioned call for workers' revolt, and may have particularly relished its anger at workers for "ador[ing] the system" that oppresses them. The editors cut Wilmans's paragraph criticizing workers' disdain for women's suffrage, thus proving her point about labor's—or Socialists'—contempt for the issue. When Wilmans reprinted the piece in 1898, she cut the sentence about the need to organize for self-protection. She defined "manhood" instead as the "effort to comprehend the true situation and to arouse within your brains the thought that will meet it."[93]

What is interesting about the piece, however, is Wilmans's assertion that "thought" and action could erase not only conditions of poverty, but the people who lived in them. "The moment one of you begins to [think], he ceases to belong to that class to whom these words are addressed," she wrote. This was in line with her Mental Science cosmology, which held that all elements of life could transform themselves. Matter was alive, and therefore could think; thinking matter became a new form of mind. Women could escape their fate as slavish, dumb, regenerating matter if they would think; they would then be "made over" into a new being, a free woman. But if "dumb" and "slavish" workers would think, they did not become a new, emboldened form of worker. Rather, they transformed into their opposite— that is, entrepreneurs. As there had been no place for free womanhood under the older social-purity/social-Darwinist system, so Wilmans left no place for an intelligent, empowered working class in her Mental Science cosmology.

Wilmans's Socialist admirers presumably interpreted her essay as a call to action against capitalist enslavement. Yet they may also have agreed with Wilmans's insistence that workers must use their brains, or die and give way to a more refined "race of men." Hopes for a perfected "race" were pervasive among turn-of-the-century reformers and radicals. As we shall see, the belief that the race could be transformed drew countless reformers into the New Thought nexus. If the goal was race perfection, then New Thought, rather than Christianity or Darwinian science, could most effectively bring forth the new era.

6 New Thought and Early Progressivism

We believe that this world is large enough and rich enough . . .
to become the happy home of perfected humanity.

"Statement of Principles,"
Union for Concerted Moral Effort, 1892 [1]

. . . the New Thought . . . should be the feeding force, the
crystallizing center of all the new movements of the new era.

R. Heber Newton, 1899 [2]

From the 1890s through the early years of the twentieth century, scores of prominent white middle-class reformers came to believe that New Thought meditations, as well as hypnotism, telepathy, and other forms of psychic power, were important new tools that could help elevate society.[3] Some reformers were so taken with these ideas that they wrote their own New Thought tracts. Their embrace of New Thought did not generally interfere with their activism. Rather, New Thought claims fit seamlessly within their political worldviews.

Like other Americans, reformers were introduced to New Thought through a variety of means. Some initially encountered it as a treatment for nervous illnesses. Others were exposed to New Thought through the organizing efforts of more elite mental healers. In 1895, for example, east-coast New Thought leaders formed the Metaphysical Club of Boston for the express purpose of introducing New Thought to the broader intellectual leadership of the city. Reformers were introduced to New Thought through associates who embraced the movement. Perhaps some reformers were attracted by the progressive stance of a few high-profile New Thought authors, such as Ralph Waldo Trine, who argued that "socialism is the only basis . . . that can be deduced from [a] belief in . . . the Fatherhood of God and the brotherhood of man," and Ella Wheeler Wilcox, who told her readers that because competition generated hatred that "produces disease and misfortune," all Americans ought to "study socialism and cultivate thoughts of universal brotherhood." [4]

Whatever the route that brought reformers into contact with it, by the turn of the century the association between New Thought and reform was far from uncommon. In 1901 the New Thought monthly *Mind* reported that New Thought material was now "read with avidity in economic societies and social clubs, in political and moral reform organizations, in liberal Christian associations, and by individuals interested in the rescue of science from the pitfalls of materialism."[5]

Reformers who were sympathetic toward New Thought beliefs about the telepathic, creative power of thought included woman-movement leaders Frances Willard, Abby Morton Diaz, Elizabeth Boynton Harbert, Lucinda Chandler, and Clara Colby; liberal and radical Protestant ministers R. Heber Newton, Benjamin Fay Mills, and J. Stitt Wilson; socialist advocates Edward Bellamy and Josephine Conger; and investigative journalists Benjamin Orange Flower, Paul Tyner, and Helen Campbell. They were active participants in an interlocking network of organizations and journals that were at the heart of 1890s middle-class reform.

These reformers' enthusiasm for New Thought demonstrates the surprising pervasiveness of these beliefs among politically active people.[6] Not every Progressive embraced New Thought; no doubt many viewed it as outlandish. New Thought was both a popular *and* a marginal discourse. Rather like current claims that the "twelve steps" of Alcoholics Anonymous can cure an ever-expanding range of addictions, New Thought claims in the 1890s were both surprisingly widespread and somewhat disreputable.

The pervasive-yet-marginal character of New Thought does not lessen its interpretive significance, however. On the contrary, its very extremism—the ways in which it took commonsense ideas and pushed them over the boundary into increasingly fantastic claims—is precisely what makes the acceptance of New Thought by some reform leaders so revealing. New Thought was similar to perfectionist efforts in other periods of American history, from phrenology and water-cure in the 1840s and 1850s to rolfing, re-evaluation or co-counseling, and transactional analysis in the 1970s and 1980s. As in those cases, it is important both to identify the extent to which New Thought was adopted by nationally influential individuals and to understand what the embrace of New Thought reveals not simply about the psychology of individual reformers, but about the underlying beliefs of the broader culture.

Why then did some reformers adopt New Thought? What can their embrace of New Thought tell us about the cultural currents of the 1890s? At the most basic level, some embraced New Thought because they were committed to imagining a better world. New Thought taught that one's mental picture of a better world was the first step toward creating that world. Hence New Thought could sustain reformers as they strove to realize their visions.

But New Thought was also compatible with a more specific goal that was pursued by many turn-of-the-century reformers—namely, race perfection. Many reformers hoped to use telepathy and New Thought techniques to accelerate dramatically the evolution of a perfect race. They believed that morally and physically perfected people would help save the republic from moral, political, and economic ruin.

On the basis of arguments made in middle-class reformers' writings on hypnotism and New Thought, I offer a new label that explains their core beliefs: *evolutionary republicanism*. This worldview could place both New Thought and the woman of "head and heart" at the center of hopes for a renewed American republic. Though sharply revealed in the writings of reformers who ultimately embraced New Thought, an evolutionary republican outlook was also typical of many reformers who ignored New Thought. Reformers' New Thought writings enable us to see more clearly the workings of this ideology. My proposal of the concept of evolutionary republicanism is an example of the diagnostic possibilities afforded by marginal religious discourses such as New Thought.

I begin, therefore, by elaborating the evolutionary republican perspective. I will then identify specific reformers who both were motivated by this outlook and embraced New Thought beliefs. An outline of these reformers' extensive personal and professional networks clarifies how they were able to shape some of the most important institutions of the early Progressive era. A close look at their New Thought writings reveals that their marginal beliefs were of a piece with the broader worldview typical of turn-of-the-century white middle-class reformers.

EVOLUTIONARY REPUBLICANISM IN THE 1890S

Historians have long been aware that our understanding of the Progressive-era worldview is incomplete. Unable to find intellectual coherence in the period's disparate reform crusades, one historian has suggested that we simply sever early Progressivism into its three component discourses: the rhetoric of antimonopoly, the call for social bonds, and the language of scientific efficiency.[7] The early Progressive reformers who embraced New Thought were interested in social bonds and opposed to monopoly; they praised both morality and science. Yet none of these elements, or even their combination, fully captures their outlook. Nor can these three discourses explain the other defining characteristic of early Progressive reformers—their deep consciousness of "race," a concern manifested both in their frequent invocation of "the race" as the imagined beneficiary of their plans and, more generally, in the violent racism that characterized white American culture in the 1890s.

The term evolutionary republicanism, however, more accurately describes the political outlook of these New Thought reformers. Their vision was indebted, in part, to classic early American republicanism. According to this ideology, the government of a republic ought to be characterized by its selfless devotion to the public good. Such a government could exist only if the people who made up its citizenry were virtuous, self-sacrificing, and economically independent (and so incorruptible). Republican ideology thus emphasized the creation of conditions conducive to personal morality, rather than an expansion of the electorate, as the essential precondition for a viable democracy. The two greatest threats to a virtuous citizenry were excessive power at the highest levels of society and social chaos at the lowest levels of society. If these extremes were avoided and the citizenry remained independent and virtuous, then the republic, governed by a citizens' democracy, would flourish.

By the 1880s republican ideology had been reinterpreted by working-class radicals in the Knights of Labor and Alliance movements as a class critique of industrial society. They accepted the republican premise that the nation's strength was dependent upon the morality of its citizens. Arguing against those who viewed monopolists or self-made men as the source of the nation's power, they insisted that "producers" formed its moral and political center. This core was now threatened by unregulated capitalism. The "iron law of wages" decreed that employers had the right to decrease wages to the lowest point the market would bear. Workers were then compelled to work fourteen-hour days in order to survive. This damaged them physically, destroyed their domestic life, and prevented their moral and intellectual development. In short, "wage slavery" was incompatible with the development of personal virtue upon which a republic depended. As the Knights of Labor manifesto proclaimed, there was "an inevitable . . . conflict between the wage-system of labor and republican system of government." The republic would be saved, they argued, if unregulated capitalism was somehow modified—through Greenbackism, the Single Tax, workers' cooperatives, land nationalization, or unionism—so that workers, or producers, received a "proper share of the wealth they created."[8]

By the 1890s, white middle-class reformers were putting forth their own version of republican ideology.[9] These relatively comfortable journalists, novelists, ministers, and philanthropists did not suffer from fourteen-hour days of factory labor. They were disturbed by the wealth and ostentatious display of nouveau-riche robber barons, the apparent moral and physical degeneration of the industrial working class, and their own lack of economic self-sufficiency in an increasingly corporation-dominated economy. As true economic independence receded, they found a new grounding for the virtue of the nation's citizens in beliefs about Anglo-Saxon evolutionary superiority.

The hybrid belief system that resulted, *evolutionary* republicanism, was bound up with the claim that native-born white Protestants had inherited from their Anglo-Saxon ancestors the traits that were the prerequisite for political participation in a republic. They argued that their own morality was less a product of their status as producers than it was of their racial inheritance. Political corruption and economic exploitation would be overcome not by challenging the wage system, but by evolving a more virtuous race.

The language of turn-of-the-century middle-class reformers highlights this concern. They consistently spoke of their desire to save "the race." Their use of the term "the race" needs to be understood in its context. Turn-of-the-century white Americans commonly believed that economic and cultural differences among groups were racial differences that were the result of centuries of evolutionary development. Following mainstream scientific ideas of the time, they believed that there were three stages of human racial development: savagery, barbarism, and civilization. White reformers and conservatives alike agreed that Anglo-Saxon Protestants represented the highest evolutionary development of advanced civilization. (This is why the terms "civilized," "refined," "advanced," "high-minded," "Protestant," and even "the people"—all terms that peppered the writings of reformers—were racial markers that generally signified Anglo-Saxon.) Hence white reformers, like white conservatives, generally equated "the race" with native-born white Protestants of "Anglo-Saxon" ancestry. Some white turn-of-the-century authors used the term "the race" to connote both the Anglo-Saxon race and the human race—an ambiguity that encouraged the potential identification of the white race with the human race. And in this time of flux in racial definitions, a few specified that "the race" meant the "American" or even "human" race. These intellectuals nevertheless embraced an evolutionary framework whose ultimate goal was (human) race perfection.[10]

When the early or proto-Progressive reformers who are the subject of this chapter spoke of saving the race, therefore, their words could be roughly translated as "we must ensure the evolution, and prevent the devolution, of advanced or Anglo-Saxon characteristics." Race salvation was a question of pressing political concern, since the character of the race determined the future of the republic. The "race" was also the focus of utopian hopes. Reformers believed that Darwin had illuminated the laws of racial development. There was no reason, therefore, why this development could not be dramatically accelerated. Reformers need no longer be satisfied with encouraging simple virtue among citizens. Race perfection, and hence a perfected civilization, now seemed within reach.

White reformers' acceptance of their day's conventional wisdom about Anglo-Saxon evolutionary race development had two important implications. First, it meant that like most late-nineteenth-century white middle-class Protestants, white reformers were confident about their moral and intellectual superiority, which they believed to be the product of their familial and racial ancestry. Second, it meant that their primary object of concern was not the citizen, but the embodied, racialized individual who, in classic Darwinian fashion, was believed to be molded by his or her ancestry, on the one hand, and by the environment, on the other. The strength of the body, the health of the mind, and the specific traits that made up ideal manhood and womanhood were thus of central concern. Because reformers wanted to save "the race," they were fascinated by the question of how "higher" traits could be strengthened in individuals and transmitted across generations. They were interested in how refined environments could enhance racial development or, conversely, in how the debilitating effects of brutish environments could be overcome.

In short, by the 1890s some middle-class reformers had become intrigued with the questions of bodily health, mental and spiritual development, and environmental influence that had long been the focus of New Thought meditations. They believed that as Anglo-Saxons, there was no limit to the mental or psychical wonders they could eventually perform. It is no wonder that a significant number of them became fascinated by New Thought claims about the power of (advanced) minds to restore health, to perfect human character, and to influence the minds of others.

Reformers were also drawn to New Thought because its authors grappled with a debate that they believed had profound political ramifications—namely, raising the question of whether manly competition, selfishness, and desire or womanly cooperation, self-sacrifice, and love best epitomized, and fueled, Anglo-Saxon or race development. This debate went to the core of their battle with conservatives over the best means of developing and ultimately perfecting both race and republic. Social-Darwinist–oriented conservatives believed that only manly Anglo-Saxon desire and competition led to the "survival of the fittest." Monopolies were simply examples of the economic survival of the fittest. The resulting exploitation and suffering of the poor were nature's way of destroying the "unfit." For the sake of race improvement, therefore, poverty and suffering must not be alleviated by the state. State interference was also anathema since it hindered capitalism, which, like the law of evolution itself, was natural and automatically benevolent. Society must follow the laws of nature, not those of human morality.[11]

In contrast, reformers, or "reform Darwinists," tended to follow Lester Ward's school, whereby it was not manly competition, but womanly Anglo-Saxon altruism, self-sacrifice, and the conscious use of rational and spiritual powers to improve the environment that were the keys to race development. They therefore opposed laissez-faire economic practices that were based on, and rewarded, selfishness, competition, and greed. Such qualities, they believed, degraded the race. They also led to the development of excess power and luxury at the top of society and to landless, desperate, and hence corruptible masses at the bottom—the twin enemies of a virtuous republic.

White middle-class reformers of the 1890s promoted a variety of methods to accelerate the development of (womanly, "advanced" or Anglo-Saxon) cooperation, self-sacrifice, and love, thus ensuring the future of the republic. Some reformers called for a "cooperative commonwealth," or a Socialist system that encouraged altruism. Others stressed the importance of environmental change. Individual morality could be elevated if saloons were shut down and high-minded amusements encouraged; if the hours of labor were shortened, thus leaving workers time for moral uplift; and if urban housing and sanitation were improved. Because of the hereditary transmission of acquired traits, such reforms would ultimately improve the "people" or the various "races" of America as a whole.

A third approach to reform involved eugenics. Many reformers believed it was possible to breed out criminals and create a loving, high-minded, altruistic citizenry. They therefore advocated both education about sex as a divine racial responsibility and censorship of literature that inflamed the lower passions. These approaches were all means to the same end of a spiritualized society and a perfected race. This is why white middle-class reformers of the 1890s were frequently enthusiastic supporters of economic, environmental, and eugenic approaches to race uplift.

White reformers' evolutionary republicanism—their belief that race perfection could save the republic—explains their enthusiasm for "woman," for "science," and sometimes for New Thought, the scientific faith of the new woman's era. All three symbolized the new values of a perfected society. The very existence of pure, maternal womanhood was the proof that selflessness, altruism, and love could become the dominant values of the race. New Thought meditation practices promised to strengthen woman's already considerable moral influence. Recent scientific and technological breakthroughs were proof that the immaterial would inevitably triumph over the material. New Thought was an example of just this sort of true science, advocating not brutish, biological laws of jungle competition, but rational and immaterial methods that supported higher moral law.

Even more than "science" or "woman" did, New Thought thrilled some reformers because it offered concrete methods to accelerate the transformation of race and society. New Thought authors showed how negative qualities of selfishness and desire could be crushed and divine qualities of love and altruism strengthened. New Thought meditations could help rally public opinion behind the cause of reform. They could offset the evils of a degrading environment. Intensified through the powers of neonatal influence, they could accelerate eugenic race improvement.

Indeed, there was no reason to doubt that New Thought meditation would soon play a major role in society. Many middle-class reformers found it easy to believe that their inherited high-mindedness was but a stepping-stone to their development of pure telepathic power. The ability to communicate by mind, and to influence the mentality of "lesser" peoples, was simply the next, rapidly approaching evolutionary threshold of their magnificent race in its culminating era. It was a power that they could harness—and soon—as a means of elevating the race and so saving the republic.

HYPNOSIS AND EVOLUTIONARY REPUBLICANISM: THE SOCIAL THOUGHT OF BENJAMIN ORANGE FLOWER (1858–1918)

Perhaps the most forceful exponent of the occult-tinged, pro-"woman," reform-Darwinist perspective I call evolutionary republicanism was Benjamin Orange Flower. Though forgotten today, Flower was a major figure in the white middle-class reform world of the 1890s. He is best known to historians for his editorship of *The Arena*, a reform journal that he founded in 1889 and edited, with one four-year break, until 1909. Under Flower's guidance *The Arena* became one of the most influential reform journals of its time. It promoted Populism, socialism, campaigns for direct democracy, women's suffrage, social purity, and free speech. Flower published the earliest Social Gospel theorists. He was a personal friend and political ally of

Figure 16. Benjamin O. Flower, author and editor of *The Arena.*

almost every major middle-class reformer of his day. He considered them all to be members of the "Arena Family."[12]

In the contest over whether it was manly competition and desire or womanly cooperation and self-sacrifice that best characterized the (Anglo-Saxon) race, Flower clearly supported the latter view. He characterized "the people" as pure, attuned to nature, and unselfishly committed to service and love. In contrast, he characterized wealthy monopolists as men whose "moral nature" had been "eclipsed by the passions." Blinded by selfish greed, they dismissed "faithful workers" and hired women and children in their place. Unemployed men took refuge in saloons where alcohol "feeds the fires of animal passion as coal feeds a furnace." Monopolists then used their speculative, nonproductive riches to suppress liberty and democracy, which were, along with selflessness, hard work, and productivity, intrinsic aspects of Anglo-Saxon racial identity. From their initial greed, therefore, moral contagion spread to infect the body politic. In short, the newly rich were racially devolutionary. The battle against "privilege" was a battle for the moral character and political future of the race.[13]

Flower cast the struggle between the people and privilege as a cosmic battle between, on one hand, the forces of spirit, or purity, intelligence, and moral fervor, and, on the other, the forces of matter, or sensuality, selfishness, and corruption. Hypnotism, psychic research, Christian Science, and New Thought all had central roles to play in this battle. He believed that hypnotists and mental healers had stumbled upon new laws that would enable humanity to scientifically harness and direct psychic, moral, and spiritual power.[14] Hypnosis was a revolutionary new method that could make race perfection possible; and upon race perfection rested the hope for millennial democracy.

Flower wrote at length about the deeper implications of hypnotism. He argued that the present state of humanity was "the natural result of ages of education, when notwithstanding all talk to the contrary, the mind has in reality been subordinated to the appetites, the passions, and desires of the body." This situation, he claimed, could be reversed by hypnotism, which was proof of "the power not only of mind over mind," but also "of *mind over matter.*" Now we need only further develop "the value of hypnotism as a moral agent." Cases had already been cited, Flower reported, of drunkards redeemed and of "criminal propensities in children . . . greatly modified, and in many cases entirely removed" through hypnotic practice.[15]

Flower argued that New Thought and Christian Science healings had profound moral implications. As he explained, mental healers cure through "a direct appeal to the spiritual nature. . . . The older treatments have left the invalid where they found him; the newer treatment, . . . by awakening his moral nature, has led him from . . . sensual domination to spiritual supremacy."[16]

Hypnotism and mental healing had ramifications beyond the reformation of individual character. The united thought-force of the high-minded segment of the population could also lead to broad social change. "Thought is contagious and people are thinking," Flower explained. "Indeed, it is possible, if not probable, that in the near future it may be scientifically demonstrated that unspoken thought is a potent factor in influencing other minds; that from each individual there emanates a thought force that may infect others." From this it followed that when large numbers "are thinking earnestly along any certain line, the thought waves or mental emanations must necessarily become powerful factors in influencing public sentiment."[17]

Flower's understanding of his role as editor of a journal such as *The Arena* must be viewed in this light. "'The Arena' appealed to thought-molders," he wrote. Once influenced, such people would start "new centers for diffusion of the light of justice." Given his enthusiasm for hypnotism, Christian Science, and New Thought, it is likely that Flower meant the term "thought-molders" to be taken quite literally.[18]

Flower believed that the reform movements of his day had a valuable ally in (Anglo-Saxon) womanhood. Woman is "pure as the glistening snow-clad peaks in the midst of the moral degradation which taints manhood," he enthused, and flatly stated the "incontestable fact that woman is ethically, infinitely superior to man." Linking pure womanhood to a republican critique of excessive wealth, he frequently contrasted the pure spirit of woman with the "vicious spirit of the business world." He accepted the social purity claim that the nation's "best" women combined "head and heart," or rationality and spiritual morality. Female purity reformers were "women of intellectual and spiritual power" who acted as a "moral and intellectual force" in society, Flower wrote in typical passages.[19]

Flower viewed woman as the model of humanity toward which all others—that is, men—must aspire.[20] He also used women's reform organizations as the model for his political work. When, in an 1892 editorial, he listed the forces that were awakening humanity, the list was composed exclusively of women's organizations and groups that were numerically dominated by women; they were, in the order listed, kindergarten schools, industrial education, working girls' clubs, women's clubs, the Woman's Christian Temperance Union, the White Ribbon and White Cross movement, societies for home culture, summer schools of philosophy, college extensions, and the Associated Charities. Flower's own "Unions for Practical Progress" or Arena Clubs were modeled after 1890s women's clubs. He described how the "strongest and most efficient" of the Arena Clubs originated in the "dainty drawing room" of Mrs. E. C. G. Ferguson, a "powerfully minded" woman whose "graces of mind and heart" attracted "coteries of purely and thoroughly intellectual people."[21]

Flower applauded the presence of women in reform movements because he believed that "[i]n the various spheres of activity in which woman has engaged, her influence has been that of a purifying, refining, and ennobling power." Paeans to the power of womanly influence were standard journalistic fare throughout the nineteenth century. However, Flower argued that womanly influence could *directly* affect the political process, as opposed to operating indirectly, through husbands and sons. He seemed to view womanly influence as an almost hypnotic mental force that could have profound public effects. He explained the recent moral awakening against alcohol, prostitution, and child labor, and in favor of women's suffrage, as "the natural and inevitable results of the patient, determined work of a number of women, and some men, who were in a very real sense the sowers of virile thought-seeds throughout the land." If the moral forces of the land were awakened, the result would be a leap in human evolution. It would inaugurate, in Flower's words, a "new time," in which loving, pure, high-minded women and men used "thought power" to uplift the nation, and to spread their vision of a republican, cooperative commonwealth throughout the globe.[22]

There is abundant evidence that a broad sweep of 1890s reformers were fascinated by hypnotism, New Thought, and telepathy, and that this fascination was linked in their minds, as it was in Flower's, to an underlying hope for race perfection, on one hand, and a lauding of woman as the model for this perfection, on the other. Not surprisingly, a stronghold for this sort of thinking was the social-purity wing of the 1890s woman movement.

EVOLUTIONARY REPUBLICANISM
AND THE WOMAN MOVEMENT

A small group of white middle-class women, linked by ties of friendship and years of overlapping political work, formed the core leadership of the women's clubs and women's suffrage, temperance, kindergarten, social-purity, and working-women's aid societies that dominated the 1890s woman movement. Most were motivated by an evolutionary republicanism refracted through the woman movement's own version of Anglo-Saxon perfectionism. They believed that the republic was threatened from the "mob" below as well as from luxury above. Many were sympathetic to unionized workers' claims that those who did not produce were social parasites. But they also believed that the solution to society's problems ultimately resided in the perfection of the individual through perfection of the environment and so of the race. "Woman" played a central role in this perfection, not only through her cheerful industry, but also through her powers of pure, desireless rationality and neonatal and postnatal maternal influence. Many believed that the practices of New Thought healers represented an exciting new means by which woman could be purified, the race perfected, and the republic saved.

Prominent members of this network included Elizabeth Boynton Harbert, Lucinda Chandler, Abby Morton Diaz, Helen Campbell, Clara Colby, and Frances Willard. By outlining the political prominence of each of these women, their relations to one another, and their acceptance of an evolutionary-republican perspective, it is possible to understand why they were fascinated by New Thought. More broadly, it provides a new sense of the millennial worldview of the late-nineteenth-century woman movement.

According to historian Steven Buechler, Elizabeth Boynton Harbert (1843–1925) typified the mainstream woman movement of the 1880s and

1890s. She served as the president of the Illinois Woman's Suffrage Association for twelve years. Harbert was a founder of, and for two years the president of, the Illinois Social Science Association; a founder of the Illinois Woman's Press Association; the president of the Evanston Woman's Club; and a board member of the Girl's Industrial School of South Evanston. She was also an influential journalist. She wrote a column entitled "Woman's Kingdom" for the Chicago *Inter-Ocean* and published her own paper, *New Era*, which supported temperance, social purity, and women's suffrage. Harbert was the author of three woman-movement protest novels: *Golden Fleece* (1867), *Out of her Sphere* (1871), and *Amore* (1892).[23]

Harbert was also intimately associated with the New Thought movement. She studied mental healing in the 1880s and was soon using meditation to "treat" the ailments of fellow suffrage activists. She was an early supporter of Emma Curtis Hopkins, whose ordination ceremonies she described as evidence of a "glad new time come to us" in which "woman goes forth to proclaim the radiant realities of the Good." She even attributed the harmony that characterized the 1888 International Council of Women to the meditations of New Thought women. Harbert had close personal friendships with many New Thought leaders and supporters, including Frances Lord, Louisa Southworth, and her Evanston neighbor Alice Stockham.[24]

Harbert's final novel, *Amore* (1892), was published by the New Thought press of Lovell, Gestefeld and Co., and contained citations from Alice Stockham on the "proven law" that "holding to the thought with steadfastness and intensity, verily brings the good."[25] In *Amore* Harbert attempted to synthesize her political and spiritual outlook, and this novel is therefore worth examining in some detail.

Amore recounts the romance between Philip Ward, an orthodox minister, and Theodora Dwight. The lovely Theodora believes that Jesus came to save the world from "gross materialism" by revealing to humanity "its divine origin, its divine powers, [and] its divine destiny." She is devoted to temperance and reform and has the ability to heal by mind. Her combination of political and spiritual qualities mark her as belonging to a "new order of women."[26]

Philip marries Theodora, renounces orthodox Christianity, and adopts her creed. The couple organize a group called the "Truth Seekers." They believe that "in order to secure harmony we must combine differences," including the differences between manliness and womanliness. Also basic to their outlook is the faith that every child has the potential to become a "child-angel." Some Truth Seekers therefore propose that the nation devote itself to the nurturing of children and be presided over by a male and a female president. The group is also sympathetic to women's suffrage, socialism, prohibition, compulsory education, kindergartens, dress reform, the Chautauqua idea, and university extensions. Ultimately, however, they believe that "the universal recognition of the law of love . . . [will] usher in the millennium." The novel concludes with Philip and Theodora, or "philos" and "theos," garbed in white and appearing as "the typical young priest and priestess of the New Age."[27]

For all its occult trappings, *Amore* presents an outlook that was typical of 1890s middle-class reform. Harbert's republicanism comes through in her attacks on both the "selfish" "personal ease, luxury, and comfort" of the rich and the "wickedness, suffering and crimes" of the poor. A hierarchy of race morality is invoked in the text. Theodora always wears white, while the clothing of a sensual woman character has an "oriental" look. The novel emphasizes the importance of the environment in determining character, but within a hereditarian framework. Philip and Theodora's refined qualities are traced to the uplifting environment of their childhood homes as well as to the neonatal meditations performed by their mothers, while a rapist is the offspring of "an unwilling mother and a sadly ignorant father."[28]

Harbert argues that while reform work is important, ultimately human nature must be regenerated. It must become high-minded and spiritual, not lowly and material. This is why *Amore* argues that the "Golden Age" will only come about "under the inspiration and intuitional guidance of a great-souled woman." Woman can transform human nature because she embodies the "divinity of motherhood," or a pure, loving, spiritual, and self-sacrificing character. As a reformer she can inspire and uplift others. As a mother she can use neonatal influence to enlighten her offspring. As reformer or mother, woman's influence can be strengthened and consciously directed through New Thought meditation practices.[29]

Harbert's *Amore* provides a fascinating elucidation of the ways in which a spiritualist–Theosophist–New Thought perspective could alleviate the emotional turmoil of the white middle-class woman who hoped to "save" her "sister woman." Her problems were numerous. The reformer despaired over the magnitude of the horrors facing women, from "child-brides and slave mothers" to "the agony of outraged womanhood, and enforced motherhood." She wrestled with "fear of possible mistake in [her] plans for [humanity's] uplift." She suffered the mortification of being "sneered at" by the "very women for whom [she was] undergoing martyrdom."[30] (Harbert herself found the latter problem particularly trying. As she wrote in an autobiographical sketch, her "eyes have been closed to the ingratitude on the part of those for whom she has unselfishly labored, that a better spirit of cooperation might spring up among womankind.")[31]

A faith in New Thought meditation, telepathy, and reincarnation could solve all of these problems. The *"problem of evil"* was solved by faith that humanity was essentially spiritual, not material. This meant that all women were in fact free, since nothing could enslave the spirit. Faith in doctrines of reincarnation helped the reformer deal with the glacial pace of social change. The reformer's conviction that she inhabited a higher "sphere" helped her to cope with being misunderstood. Indeed, reformers who learned to enter the "silence" would become as powerful and imperturbable as the God of Love. They would not "faint, despair or die, although for a time misunderstood and unloved, so long as there remain[ed] to them the right to be loved, and the opportunity for service."[32]

Lucinda Banister Chandler (1828–?) was a friend and political ally of Elizabeth Boynton Harbert. Chandler first made a name for herself with her 1871 pamphlet "Motherhood, Its Power Over Human Destiny." This highly influential work argued that if pregnant women were freed from "polluting intrusions," then physical and moral "deformities" would vanish.[33] Chandler insisted that women could control maternity only if they had full economic, legal, and political independence. The parlor talks that she organized to discuss her ideas led to the formation of the Moral Education Society of Boston, the first of its kind in the nation. Dedicated to the promotion of "enlightened parenthood" and a single high standard of sexual purity for men and women, moral-education societies quickly spread to New York, Philadelphia, Chicago, and other major cities.

By the mid-1870s Chandler was publishing articles about enlightened motherhood in every major women's rights journal. In the 1880s, her ideas received even wider play when Alice Bunker Stockham quoted them extensively in *Tokology*. Chandler became the vice-president of the National Woman Suffrage Association, and after moving to Chicago in the early 1880s she became vice-president of the Illinois Woman's Christian Temperance Alliance and president of the Chicago Moral Education Society. During that decade Chandler published in Harbert's *New Era* as well as in Wilmans's *Woman's World;* Wilmans's office also distributed Chandler's pamphlets. In the 1890s Chandler joined the Illinois Woman's Press Association, where she served on committees with Alice Stockham, Frances Willard, and Emma Curtis Hopkins's followers, Ida B. Nichols and Helen Van-Anderson.[34]

By the 1890s Chandler had adopted "Christian Socialism" as well as a doctrine she called "Americanism." She argued that humanity only evolved in conditions of liberty. This is why Americanism, which is based on the idea of liberty, provides "the most complete opportunity yet opened up by human evolution" for the "perfection of the race." Women's freedom must be an essential aspect of Americanism, Chandler argued. While the "male man" is the "exponent of brute force," woman has a unique "susceptibility to psychical, mental and spiritual forces." If women were free, they could use their spiritual powers to "mold pre-natal life" and thereby promote the "race building" which is the true meaning of Americanism.[35]

Chandler made three concrete suggestions that would encourage race perfection. First, Americans needed to establish the "cooperative commonwealth." Second, Americans must reject the "savage theology" that sees human nature as "totally depraved" and blames "woman" as the "chief agency of its degradation." Finally, Americanism required a free motherhood. Woman must "control all conditions" relating to maternity; she must also "be environed by a social state" that ensured she would never face economic want. If human institutions were thus put "in harmony with the laws of being," Chandler argued, then "sordid, crafty, marauding savagery will be bred out of the individual and social state."[36]

Chandler's belief in woman's spiritual power, her faith in neonatal influence, and her desire to perfect "the race"—as well as her long association with Harbert, Stockham, Wilmans, and other New Thought advocates— perhaps explain why she ultimately embraced New Thought beliefs. In 1902 Chandler heralded "Mental Science" for providing the method by which "the race" could come "into its divine inheritance." Only since Mesmer have we understood "the power of mind in directing and controlling mind," Chandler wrote. But now that women have fully comprehended the "possibilities of soul energy and thought-force," her argument continued, they can "begin the transformation of civilization that will bring the new heaven and the new earth." "[F]or a Republic, . . . only the continuous progress, unfoldment, and growth of its citizens can be . . . a guaranty of its perpetuity," she concluded. Mental Science would save the republic and the race.[37]

Abby Morton Diaz (1821–1904) was another prominent late-nineteenth-century reformer whose New Thought beliefs were tightly interwoven with her woman-movement and socialist-political outlook. Diaz was a member of the New England Woman's Club, president of the Moral Education Association of Boston, and the founder and for twelve years (1881–1892) the president of the Women's Educational and Industrial Union. She was an early proponent of Bellamyite Nationalism, a suffrage supporter, a popular lecturer at women's clubs, and a member of the Boston Honorary Committee of the American Purity Alliance.[38]

Diaz was also deeply involved in the New Thought movement. In 1886 she published two New Thought pamphlets, *The Law of Perfection* and

Spirit as a Power. The following year she wrote numerous articles for the *Christian Metaphysician,* an early mind-cure journal. She attended the first "Mental Science" convention held in Boston in 1887. In 1893 she published *Only A Flock of Women.* This work, which has been described as "the only Nationalist tract written entirely from the perspective of the woman's movement," was in fact a Nationalist–New Thought tract. In 1895 Diaz helped to found the Metaphysical Club of Boston. Throughout the late 1890s and early 1900s she wrote articles for *Mind,* the most prominent New Thought journal of its time. In honor of her years of involvement in the movement, *Mind* included a biographical sketch of Diaz in its "portraits of New Thought leaders" series in 1902.[39]

Diaz seemed to follow the "anti-desire" school of New Thought. Her 1886 tract *Spirit as a Power* praised the advantages of "sinking self in God," thereby "becoming unobstructed mediums, through which supreme, ever-present God may overcome evil." Diaz attempted to prevent an identification with all-powerful spirit from creating arrogant or complacent behavior. She did so by elaborating upon the concept of "Obligation," or the duty to behave in ways that demonstrated one's spiritual character. The power of spirit meant that all humanity was one. Therefore people must feel, and act upon, their "kinship with the poor rag-woman on the street." Since they could, through meditation, learn to be one with God, they must manifest divine qualities. As God "gives forth," so should people give forth in time, money, strength, and sympathy. As God is love, so must they "create a sort of love atmosphere" in the world.[40]

Diaz's spiritual beliefs led her to endorse a political vision quite similar to that of the "Truth Seekers" in Harbert's novel *Amore.* In an 1895 article published in *The Arena,* Diaz wrote that "reforms, charities, philanthropies, missions, rescue works, tenement-house leagues, pauper institutions, watch and ward societies, good government societies, prison associations, prohibition schemes, and our innumerable legal and penal enactments" would never get to the core of the problem, which was our need to "come into line with the laws of the universe." These laws involved, first, the right of every being to fulfill its individual potential, and second, the substitution of the "law of Oneness for the competition and . . . *Selfness* now thought permanently established." Womanly self-sacrifice, not manly competition, was the key to a just and spiritual society.[41]

It would not be easy to "do away with selfness," Diaz admitted. But there were steps one could take. One begins by forming "a mental picture of our world as it would be with Truth, Love, Justice, in entire control." One then works to mold public opinion to the point at which the nation will demand a new educational system. At its heart, Diaz concluded, would be kindergartens and "an advanced department of *Parenthood Enlightenment,* whereby children shall be better born and better reared."[42] Once again, a New Thought–inflected race perfection was cast as the ultimate savior of the republic. But Diaz's emphasis on "obligation" made her religious system compatible with compassion, analysis, and political activism.

Helen Campbell (1839–1918) helped to launch the home economics movement in the 1870s. By the 1880s she had begun to investigate the condition of the urban poor in general, and the effects of low wages on poor women in particular. She became one of the nation's pioneering urban investigators. Campbell's studies helped to convince social-purity leaders that there was a link between exploitative economic conditions and prostitution. In 1891 she won an award from the American Economic Association for her monograph "Women Wage-Earners." In the mid-1890s, Campbell worked with her dear friends Charlotte Perkins Gilman (then Stetson) and Paul Tyner, a reform journalist, to put out a Populist-Socialist-woman-movement journal entitled the *Impress.* She worked at a Chicago settlement house and frequently contributed articles to the Bellamyite monthly the *Nationalist,* the *American Fabian,* and especially Benjamin Flower's *Arena.*[43]

Campbell was also a New Thought enthusiast. In 1896, she wrote a glowing article about Greenacre, the New Thought Chautauqua run by Helen Van-Anderson's friend Sarah Farmer. In 1897 Campbell co-edited a collection of writings by Horatio Dresser, a prominent New Thought author who was the son of Phineas Quimby's students Julius and Annetta Dresser. Horatio Dresser edited a magazine, the *Journal of Practical Metaphysics,* that attempted to strengthen the ties between New Thought and reform. Campbell contributed regularly to Dresser's journal. In one article she wrote that "the 'new thought' performs . . . the inestimable service" of helping the individual realize the "purpose of all life"—that is, "[t]o unfold from within." In 1904 Campbell served on the board of the New Thought Federation. Fellow board members included Nona Brooks, Horatio Dresser, Charles Fillmore, Alice Stockham, Ursula Gestefeld, Helen Van-Anderson, Sarah Farmer, and Ralph Waldo Trine.[44]

As Campbell understood it, New Thought helped spiritualize humanity. Therefore it could only speed the pace of reform. She explained that even though the "passion for money-making is strong in Anglo Saxon blood," an awareness that "spirit is the only real substance" could convince people that they are related to and responsible for one another. Then the wealthy would happily donate the money reformers needed if they were to provide the material services that helped prevent delinquency and crime. An appreciation of the power of intuition would also prevent younger settlement workers, most of whom had done postgraduate work in sociology, from treating with "superciliousness" the older settlement women (like Campbell herself) who had been "born too soon for college training." In sum, she viewed the joining of "intuition and reason," or head and heart, as the key to reform work. Campbell cited Dresser to support her view. "[I]deal and realization . . . feeling and thought . . . theory and practice . . . mind and matter are so many members of one whole," she quoted. Campbell's New Thought beliefs, like those of Abby Morton Diaz, were compatible with political activism. They helped Campbell to extend a lauding of the ideal character of "head and heart" to include a broader healing of society.[45]

Clara Bewick Colby (1846–1916) served as president of the Nebraska Woman Suffrage Association for thirteen years. A close friend of Elizabeth Cady Stanton, Colby contributed to Stanton's *Woman's Bible.* She was a delegate to the International Moral Education Congress in 1908 and a chairman of the National American Woman Suffrage Association's Committee on Industrial Problems Affecting Women and Children. Her most important contribution to the woman movement, however, was her editorship of the *Woman's Tribune.* She published the weekly journal, which became known as the official organ of the National Woman Suffrage Association, between 1883 and 1909.[46]

Colby's interest in New Thought dated at least to 1889, when she visited the offices of Emma Curtis Hopkins's *Christian Science* magazine. She was soon advertising her *Woman's Tribune* in New Thought periodicals. An advertisement she placed in an 1899 volume of Wilmans's *Freedom* was particularly striking. It presented endorsements for the journal by three lions of the woman movement—Frances Willard, Elizabeth Cady Stanton, and Helen Wilmans. Colby clearly hoped to bring New Thought women into the woman movement. She also used the columns of the *Woman's Tribune* to expose her readers to New Thought, Theosophy, and Eastern religious beliefs. When women's-suffrage amendments were about to be voted upon in several state legislatures in 1912, Colby wrote to Elizabeth Boynton Harbert that she hoped to organize a "world rally of New Thought forces" to ensure that the laws would be passed. Colby eventually became an honorary vice-president of the International New Thought Alliance.[47]

Although Woman's Christian Temperance Union president Frances Willard (1839–1898) was a committed Methodist, New Thought ideas were not far from her own evangelical perspective. In a manual for girls Willard published in 1886, she explained that she had long been "a steady student of the law of habit." "Repetition is the only basis of perfection," she wrote.

Therefore girls should never speak or think ill of others. "I have set out for sainthood and nothing less," Willard informed her readers, and they ought to do the same. Willard was friendly with many New Thought believers, including Elizabeth Boynton Harbert and Helen Campbell. She owned a copy of Alice Stockham's *Koradine Letters* and was, with Stockham, one of the founding members of the Illinois Woman's Press Association (IWPA). Willard served on a number of IWPA committees with Stockham, Lucinda Chandler, Emma Curtis Hopkins, Ursula Gestefeld, and Helen Van-Anderson. She had kind words for "Christian science mind-cure," as she sometimes called it. Willard wrote a supporting blurb for Charles Newcomb's 1897 New Thought tract, *All's Right With the World*. She commented that its "very title is an inspiration. I have it on my dressing bureau, and am looking it over with much solace of spirit."[48]

Willard's section on "The Mind Cure" in her 1889 autobiography *Glimpses of Fifty Years* revealed her detailed knowledge of New Thought and her hopes that it would help bring about the triumph of spirit. She wrote that just when the world

> had so largely become a victim to the theory that only seeing is believing, the Heavenly Powers brought in this great reaction, which declared that the invisible is all and in all, that thoughts are the real things and things are but effervescent shadows; that there is no escape from what is infinitely good and infinitely immanent in everything created; that evil is a negation and must pass away; that to be carnally minded is death, but to be spiritually minded is life and peace. I have never studied the question seriously, because I have not had the time, but from conversation with experts in this study, who are also among the best men and women I have ever known, I have certainly felt that it would be disloyalty to God and to humanity for me to speak against this new era.[49]

Willard's support was noticed by New Thought followers. Mary F. Haydon's *Bible Year Book of the New Thought, With Daily Affirmations for Every Day in the Year* was "dedicated with Love to my First Teacher in the New Thought, Frances E. Willard of Evanston Illinois."[50]

MINISTERS AND CHRISTIAN SOCIALISTS

In the late 1880s many woman-movement leaders, including Frances Willard, Lucinda Chandler, Abby Morton Diaz, Helen Campbell, Charlotte Perkins Gilman, and Mary Livermore (a prominent women's-suffrage leader who was also sympathetic to New Thought) became dedicated proponents of Bellamyite Nationalism, a form of socialism.[51] The Nationalist movement gave rise to Christian Socialism and "Applied Christianity." These in turn were the forerunners of the early-twentieth-century Social Gospel movement.

By the mid-1890s Nationalists, Christian Socialists, and woman-movement leaders often met together in congresses and worked together on reform journals. Their association was a logical one, since many Bellamyite Nationalists and Christian Socialists, like many woman-movement leaders, were inspired by an evolutionary-republican perspective. They believed that selfish monopolists were destroying the economic, moral, and racial character of the nation, and that only spirituality and altruistic self-sacrifice could reverse race-degeneration and save the republic. By tracing the emergence of Christian Socialism and highlighting its debt to an evolutionary republican perspective, we can better understand why a small but significant number of early Christian Socialists embraced New Thought.

The Nationalist and Christian Socialist movements were sparked by the work of Edward Bellamy (1850–1898), a fiction writer who specialized in stories about hypnotism, out-of-body hallucination, and other forms of altered consciousness. Bellamy was also a journalist who sympathetically covered the women's-suffrage and women's-club movements. As historian Mari Jo Buhle points out, Bellamy "captured the *mentalité* of women leaders." His empathy with the woman movement went beyond a shared disgust for competition and a shared appreciation of cooperation, service, and economic and political equality among men and women. He also subscribed to its belief that social and economic change could unleash the evolutionary potential of "the race."[52]

Bellamy's utopian novel *Looking Backwards* (1888) depicted a future in which the nation's corporations have consolidated into one "Great Trust" that is managed by the people themselves. Now all Americans work for equal pay in an "industrial army" that is modeled on universal military service. Their labor is motivated not by competitive greed, but by patriotic duty and love of service. Because women are economically independent, they are free to select mates on the basis of their eugenic potential. The result is a "race purification" that creates, in a few short generations, a nation of mentally, morally, and physically superior Americans.[53]

The moral of Bellamy's novel was clear. The United States needed an economic organization based on cooperation and service rather than on "greed and self-seeking." A changed economic structure, along with the empowerment of women as mate-selectors, would accelerate human evolution and lead to race perfection. Although Bellamy didn't discuss telepathy in *Looking Backwards*, his later writings indicate that he viewed the cultiva-

tion of psychic power and the reformation of the economy along cooperative lines as means to the same end—the creation of a morally perfect and
mystically unified "race."[54]

Bellamy's book sold hundreds of thousands of copies, was translated into
at least twenty-six languages, and served to make socialism, previously associated with anarchists and immigrants, respectable to some segments of
the middle class. It sparked the creation of "Nationalist Clubs" devoted to
implementing Bellamy's vision. Bellamy modeled his Nationalist Clubs after the structure of the women's clubs he had covered as a journalist. Like
women's clubs, Nationalist Clubs were nonpartisan and primarily educational in focus. Nationalist Clubs had unusually large female memberships
and many women in leadership positions. As mentioned earlier, Mary Livermore, Frances Willard, Abby Morton Diaz, and Charlotte Perkins Gilman
were among the earliest promoters of Bellamyite Nationalism.[55]

Bellamy's Nationalist movement helped to inspire a group of radical
Protestant ministers who promoted "Christian Socialism" in the 1890s and
who pioneered the early Social Gospel movement. These ministers rejected
the complacent and other-worldly focus of mainline Gilded-Age Protestantism. They attacked the claim that selfishness and competition were the
motors of progress, as well as the laissez-faire business practices that such
beliefs promoted. Early Social Gospel leaders encouraged the "solidarity of
the race" by elaborating a Christocentric theology that emphasized Jesus'
self-sacrifice as an appropriate model toward which all could aspire. They
argued that if people followed the "law of love," they could bring about
the "kingdom," or a perfected, sinless human society.[56] The more radical
among them linked the "kingdom" to a socialist commonwealth. As Congregationalist minister George Herron explained, "the resources upon
which the people in common depend must by the people in common be
owned and administered." If "organized love" rather than selfishness became the "real constructive force" in society, the result would be a "new
civilization," a "kingdom of heaven" on earth.[57]

In the 1890s the Bellamyite Nationalist and early Social Gospel movements became tightly aligned. A number of journals promoted the resulting "Christian Socialism," including *The Dawn, The Kingdom, The American Fabian,* and *The Social Gospel, a magazine of obedience to the law of
love.* An overlapping group of ministers, journalists, and intellectuals contributed to these journals. Prominent among them were Edward Bellamy,
George Herron, R. Heber Newton, J. Stitt Wilson, Benjamin Fay Mills,
Henry Demarest Lloyd, Frances Willard, and Benjamin Flower.[58] Many of
these leaders came to sympathize with or embrace New Thought. These in-

cluded R. Heber Newton, Benjamin Fay Mills, J. Stitt Wilson, and even George Herron—as well as, of course, Benjamin Flower.

New Thought may have been attractive to these intellectuals because many of them shared with New Thought proponents a confidence that the "race" could evolve to spiritual "perfection." Some Social Gospel ministers specified that it was Anglo-Saxon evolutionary development that would bring about the "kingdom." [59] Others spoke of a more general race evolution, from "muscle" to "cunning" to "intellect" and, finally, to moral and spiritual power as "the strongest force on earth." Most Social Gospel ministers agreed that environmental and economic changes were primarily means to accelerate evolutionary race perfection, which they defined as the strengthening of love, service, and sacrifice. Only such environmental-evolutionary changes would bring about the "kingdom," they believed. Most also hailed "science," which they defined as first-hand observation that supported divine moral law, as an ally in the quest for race perfection. [60]

Many therefore easily turned to New Thought and telepathy as a means of stamping out "selfishness," encouraging spirituality, and perfecting the race. The Reverend R. Heber Newton, whom admirers described as "[g]entle and sensitive as a woman" while also "courageous as a lion," exemplified their outlook. Newton was one of the "pioneers of American social Christianity." In the 1870s he attacked laissez-faire ideas and encouraged businessmen to embrace cooperative methods drawn from Christianity and sociological study. In 1883 he testified before the U.S. Senate Committee on Labor and Education, where he described how lack of education, the slum environment, and the increase in machine production were making labor thriftless, inefficient, and overly eager to engage in strikes. These problems would only be solved through the evolution of a "co-operative commonwealth," he told the senators. In 1885 Newton joined the fledgling American Economic Association—an organization whose founder, Richard Ely, opposed laissez-faire economic theories in favor of government intervention to protect the interest of all classes of citizens. In 1889 Newton became an associate editor of *The Dawn*. Meanwhile, his religious thought became increasingly liberal. In his position as the pastor of New York's Episcopalian All Soul's Church, Newton was among the first to advocate the methods of Higher Criticism. These led him to question the divine origin of the Bible. As a result, Newton faced a heresy trial in the early 1890s. [61]

By 1899 Newton had found a faith that better supported his political outlook—New Thought. That year he worked with Horatio Dresser, Ursula Gestefeld, and other New Thought leaders to establish the International Metaphysical League, a New Thought umbrella organization. Newton served as president of the league in 1900, 1902, and 1906, and as an officer of the New Thought Federation in 1904.[62]

Newton explained the centrality of New Thought to reform work in a speech entitled "The New Century's Call," delivered at the first International Metaphysical League congress. He cited scientific discoveries, eugenic knowledge, and the growing popularity of socialism as examples of the magnificent progress of the nineteenth century. We now needed to evolve "the moral force that is to . . . direct the new tools . . . of the coming man and turn his dominion over Nature into the kingdom of God," Newton explained. New Thought provided the means of directing and strengthening this moral force. Therefore "the New Thought" must be the "feeding force, the crystallizing center of all the new movements of the new era." Its practices would enable men to "escape the defilement of every appetite and passion and lust, and free himself in the life of the spirit." New Thought meditation could promote "the more rapid spread of a nobler public opinion." He explained, "[i]f a generation were trained to use the potencies of concentrated, systematized thought, along the lines of the new ideas and ideals, what a revolution could be effected!" The result would be a "new order" in civilization, Newton predicted.[63]

Other Protestant ministers came to similar conclusions. In the 1880s, Congregationalist minister Benjamin Fay Mills (1857–1916) was one of the nation's most famous urban evangelists. That decade he claimed to have addressed five million people, and to have converted 200,000. By the mid-1890s, however, Mills's thought began to change. He was influenced by George Herron's radical ideas and in 1894 joined the editorial board of *The Kingdom*. By 1897 Mills had "outgrown the narrower orthodox conception" and begun "gathering about him a great congregation of liberal thinkers in Boston, Massachusetts."[64]

Mills elucidated his new outlook in an *Arena* article entitled "Between the Animals and the Angels." There he attacked monopolies, slums, and unemployment as conditions that an enlightened people should not tolerate and praised socialism as a rational system appropriate for a rational people. Ultimately, however, social problems would disappear only if we evolved more perfect people. This would be primarily a spiritual or psychic process. Mills pointed out that today, the "more rational of us are moving . . . into the region of the mind, and even beyond it," to "spiritual intuition." Once the "most advanced" people awakened to the "germ" of God within, they would find that they had fabulous powers. "We say that we control our bodies and create our circumstances; but we will find that it is just as easy to create our bodies and control our circumstances. If this body does not suit my purposes, I will learn to create one." We would similarly be able to create new social institutions, which are, after all, merely "crystallize[d] social thought." We begin by looking within for images of better institutions. These interior visions are "the very substances of things hoped for, the fine, impalpable but unavoidably real and powerfully generative substance that you may voluntarily project into the world of matter."[65]

Like Abby Morton Diaz, Mills encouraged his readers to envision a better world as the first step toward political action. His description of "an impalpable . . . generative substance" that could shape "matter" hinted at New Thought sympathies. Mills eventually embraced a faith that was indistinguishable from New Thought, when he founded the Los Angeles "Fellowship" in 1905. The Fellowship's goal was the "general uplift of mankind." Members studied Ralph Waldo Emerson, Walt Whitman, and the Bhagavad-Gita. Soon Fellowships spread across the country. Clara Colby became president of the Portland, Oregon branch. Mills never called his faith New Thought. By 1910, however, the journal *The World's Work* reported that New Thought was the "body and bones" of Mills's Fellowships. Fellowship members apparently agreed; many societies dropped the name "Fellowship" and adopted the name New Thought instead. New Thought journals of the 1910s routinely included Fellowship groups in their lists of "New Thought Meetings, Teachers and Healers."[66]

Mills and Newton were but two of the leading reform-oriented Protestant clergymen who moved from liberalism to New Thought. Others included Hugh O. Pentecost, Henry Frank, J. Stitt Wilson, and George Herron.[67] All hoped that economic or environmental reforms would lead to the triumph of "altruism over selfism" and hence to the "perfecting of the human race."[68] All believed that New Thought meditations, which stamped out lowly appetites and encouraged high-minded influence, were essential tools to this end.

THE ORGANIZATION OF "MORAL FORCES" IN THE 1890s

An evolutionary republican perspective underlay a trademark of 1890s middle-class reform—the numerous attempts to "organize" the "moral forces" of society as a means of transforming the nation.[69] A survey of some of these efforts enables us to see how they were united by their goal of race perfection. It demonstrates that the female-dominated purity and mothers' congresses of the 1890s were an integral part of the broader reform milieu of their day. It highlights the reasons why New Thought leaders could so easily coexist with evangelical Protestants as leaders of the "moral forces" of the 1890s.

The women's-club movement helped inaugurate the organization of the nation's "moral forces" with the formation, in 1890, of the General Federation of Women's Clubs. Following quickly after were Frank and Walter Vrooman's "Unions for Concerted Moral Effort." These unions sought to organize the best elements of "the race," which the Vroomans specified as the human race. They invited all "friends of justice and humanity . . . without regard to color, creed or class" to join the struggle against "selfishness" and the unchristian environments that encouraged selfishness. The Vroomans' unions supported temperance, education, and uplifting amusements, opposed strikes, and attempted to mediate between labor and management. The unions' 1892 statement of principles sounded the usual themes:

> Recognizing the moral law as the supreme law of the universe, we believe that its supremacy should be enforced in all of the affairs of life. . . . man should not only harness . . . the material forces of nature, but . . . he should also direct and control all social forces and tendencies, [and] . . . all . . . institutions should be brought into harmony with the moral laws and made to secure the highest interests of our race. We believe that this world is large enough and rich enough . . . to become the happy home of perfected humanity.[70]

The Unions for Concerted Moral Effort spread to Worcester, Massachusetts, Philadelphia, and Baltimore, but they were shortlived. By the end of 1892 they had shut down, the victims of impolitic if not autocratic leadership by the Vroomans.[71]

The Vroomans' idea received a second life because of Benjamin Flower. In 1893 Flower published an *Arena* editorial that called for a "Union for Practical Progress," within which all who "love mankind enough to sacrifice self in the interest of humanity—will strike hands for a common good." Impressed by the editorial, Walter Vrooman offered his support to Flower. The result was the formation, in 1894, of the National Union for Practical Progress. It called, first, for "scientific reformers" who would give up their comfortable homes and live closely with the poor, and second, for a unification of society's "moral forces." As Walter Vrooman explained, "[t]he object of the Union for Practical Progress . . . is to make possible simultaneous action on the part of all religious and moral forces of society. . . . Our idea is to have one subject brought up at a time and induce all the clergymen, labor unions, reform societies and other organizations founded upon an unselfish idea to speak out upon the same day upon the same subject. This is to be repeated by raising of a new moral issue every month."[72]

The "moral issues" tackled by the Unions for Practical Progress (UPPs) were often quite practical. They included the sweating system, tenement reform, the "saloon evil," child labor, prison reform, unemployment, and political corruption. Yet the call for all "moral forces" to speak out on the same day on the same subject must also have had a telepathic component, at least in the mind of Flower and other UPP members who shared Flower's zeal for telepathy. These included Unitarian minister Minot Savage and novelist and Populist activist Hamlin Garland, who were both members of the American Psychic Society, and New Thought author Henry Frank, who was among the UPP's most committed organizers.

The UPP spread quickly. By July 1894, there were at least forty local unions. Ultimately, Flower estimated that there were eighty to one hundred active UPPs. Articles about local efforts were published in *The Arena*, and the UPP's progress was followed in the Christian Socialist journal *The Kingdom*.[73]

The 1895 formation of the American Purity Alliance marked another major step in the organization of "moral forces" for the perfection of the race. The American Purity Alliance united disparate groups devoted to fighting the state regulation of prostitution, ending the double standard, "purifying" the press, and raising the age of consent. It held its first National Purity Congress in 1895. Prominent participants included Mary Livermore, Frances Willard, Anthony Comstock, Benjamin Flower, William Lloyd Garrison, and Frances Harper. Theodore Roosevelt, then the popular police commissioner of New York, sent the Congress a letter of support.[74]

Many speakers at the 1895 National Purity Congress expressed anxiety about the moral effects of new communication technologies. They feared that the papers that "daily enter the home" would plant the "first seeds of morbid desire and impure sentiment" in innocent minds. Servants, mail, trains, and steamships all increased the likelihood of degrading influences invading the home, speakers insisted. Some hoped to halt sensual contagion by erecting moral barricades. Dr. Laura Satterthwaite called for a moral crusade to "kill erroneous ideas; to erect barriers for both man and woman against sullied associates; to fortify the pinnacle which the one sex now occupies, and to bring the other to her level." Others believed that only parents' constant vigilance over their children's waking and sleeping habits, their play, their clothing, and their associates could stem the tide of impurity.[75]

Other speakers argued that even constant vigilance would not necessarily control the ultimate source of moral contamination, which was thought itself. As J. W. Walton explained, "Thoughts of evil will come back to you, like foul birds, in your holiest moments, and no skill of necromancy . . . will put them down." Anthony Comstock agreed. "Corrupt publications" invade the "chamber of imagery" within the child's heart, he argued. "Once the re-imagining faculties of the mind are linked to the sensual nature by an unclean thought the forces for evil are set in motion which rend asunder every safeguard to virtue and truth."[76]

This concern with the dangers of thought itself perhaps explains why the favorite biblical passage of the New Thought movement, "As a man thinketh in his heart, so is he," was cited repeatedly by National Purity Congress speakers. Mary Travilla, a member of the American Purity Alliance Executive Committee, went further. She presented New Thought techniques as the answer to social-purity concerns without mentioning New Thought by name. Travilla described the advice she had given to a woman who complained of problems with her husband and son:

> Every morning take a half hour from your work, find a quiet spot in your home, then enter into the silence of your heart. Think *only* of the mother-love you have for your boy. Dwell on the truth and beauty in his character. . . . *Then* for your husband. Oh! dwell tenderly upon the early days of your love and marriage, seeing *now* the true nobility of his manhood. . . . When they come home meet them with a smile and kiss, a new trust and hope in your heart, born out of that daily silence. Scold or upbraid them not, but steadily expect the best.[77]

Travilla's New Thought advice provoked no uproar at the evangelically oriented National Purity Congress. Instead, New Thought and social-purity concerns were so closely aligned as to be indistinguishable. Both viewed control of one's own thoughts as well as the thoughts of others as the means to race perfection.

The first and second meetings of the National Congress of Mothers, held in 1897 and 1898, are rarely included in historians' discussions of 1890s reform. Yet they addressed the heart of the issue that intrigued Nationalists, Christian Socialists, and moral reformers of many varieties—how to alleviate "selfishness" and so "perfect" the race.[78]

The National Congress of Mothers took as its starting point the premises that had defined maternal ideology since the 1830s: that the child reflected the mother, who must therefore be Christlike and teach her child by example. The majority of Congress speakers agreed that only women's selfless control of their every thought and emotion could ensure the perfection of the race. As Mrs. Alice Lee Moque explained, "No woman has the right to be selfish, and least of all will the tender, loving, maternal heart forget that every sob, every tear, every sigh, every fear, is a crime committed against her own unborn child, and from which it will suffer throughout its whole life."[79]

Many delegates at the National Congress of Mothers believed that maternal influence could create "perfected human life." They therefore welcomed speakers who offered the latest scientific findings about maternal influence. Mrs. Sallie S. Cotten, a highly prominent club woman, told the congress that if women followed scientific laws, they would soon bring about "the elimination of selfishness, the death of oppression, the birth of brotherly love . . . and the control of hereditary weakness of mind and of body, all by prenatal influences." She explained, "By the light of scientific knowledge [woman] should climb the steeps to scientific motherhood, for it is through her that the Great Alchemist will transmute the dross of the human animal called man into the gold of a nobler creature, made indeed 'in the image of God.'"

Professor Elmer Gates used medical language to make similar claims. He told the congress, "I wish to reiterate that every conscious experience creates in some part of the brain a definite structure, that every evil emotion creates in you poisons and that good emotions create nutritive products, and you can regulate these conditions at will." Gates proposed that women cleanse their emotions "systematically" through a method that sounded remarkably like New Thought meditation practices. Gates advised the expectant mother to "go by herself an hour or more each day, in quiet and silence and away from all distracting influences, and call up each one of the desirable emotional conditions to the fullest possible intensity and joyousness and worshipful adoration."[80]

Like New Thought writers, many National Congress of Mothers speakers routinely merged images of "science" and "spirituality." They stressed that women's strict, systematic control of their thoughts and emotions could form a "bulwark" against the tides of evil. They expressed millennial hopes that the coming woman's era would not only elevate women's status, it would transform the very character of the race.[81]

At the second convention of the National Congress of Mothers in 1898, speakers engaged in the usual condemnations of the "hideous selfishness" that led some mothers to deprive their children of their "birthright." Representatives of New Thought were among these speakers. Ralph Waldo Trine, author of the New Thought bestseller *In Tune With the Infinite*, spoke on prenatal influences. His comments were inflected by New Thought doctrine, but were indistinguishable from those of other convention speakers. Two representatives of the "Don't Worry" movement, a New Thought spin-off group that advocated "trust in the Unseen" as an antidote to stress, also addressed the convention. They spoke about the "Indwelling God," explained that "thought is a force," and described the "power of silence" as well as the creative efficacy of the spoken word.[82]

The pervasiveness of a New Thought mentality at the second National Congress of Mothers was epitomized by the congress's closing benediction. The preceding year's devotional had drawn on psalm 103, verses 13–14. The psalm referred to humanity as mere "dust" that must "fear" the Lord. Its view of God as wrathful and of humanity as weak and wormlike epitomized all that New Thought leaders found most abhorrent about Christianity. At the 1898 convention, however, the benediction was presented by Sarah Farmer, founder of the New Thought/Comparative Religion summer school Greenacre. Farmer spoke on "Our Birthright"—that is, on "our right to peace in the soul, and our power to realize it and impart it to others."[83]

THE ARENA AND THE NEW THOUGHT PRESENCE IN 1890S REFORM

The Arena was a pillar of 1890s reform. By examining its history, we can see how *The Arena* functioned as yet another route through which New Thought ideas were introduced to the progressive-minded turn-of-the-century American public.

Benjamin Flower's *Arena* had stood firmly behind almost every major reform crusade of the 1890s. Essays in *The Arena* were used as organizing tools by Populist lecturers. As we have seen, Flower used *The Arena* to help create the National Union for Practical Progress. He opened the pages of *The Arena* to Laurence Gronlund and other early Socialists. Flower himself was one of the initial supporters of the Intercollegiate Socialist Society, the first pro-socialist campus organization in the United States that was the direct ancestor of the Students for a Democratic Society. *The Arena* published the earliest Social Gospel theorists, and was one of the first reform journals to promote women's suffrage. *The Arena*'s support for social purity was so unstinting that a historian of that movement has identified it as a "Social Purity" magazine.[84]

By the late 1890s, however, the journal's future looked uncertain. Benjamin Flower left *The Arena* in 1896, apparently because the magazine had not been financially solvent. In 1897 *The Arena* was sold to John D. McIntyre, a New York manufacturer; a historian, John Clark Ridpath, became the journal's editor. In 1897 Flower became a co-editor of *The New Time*, a

Chicago-based "Magazine of Social Progress." *The New Time* published Eugene Debs, Edward Bellamy, George Herron, Booker T. Washington, and other prominent reformers. It also published authors who had close ties with New Thought, including Lucinda B. Chandler, Helen Campbell, Abby Morton Diaz, J. Stitt Wilson, Theodore F. Steward (head of the "Don't Worry" movement), and J. A. Edgerton (a journalist and organizer of the Nebraska People's Party who later became the first president of the National New Thought Alliance and the founder of the *New Thought Bulletin*). The journal also featured large advertisements by Flower's old friend Helen Wilmans.[85]

In September 1898 Ridpath, who had been running *The Arena* at a loss, abruptly resigned. Just when *The Arena* seemed threatened with extinction, however, a hero emerged to save the magazine. As Flower announced in *The New Time*, "'THE ARENA' LIVES." He described how, apparently, "a conspiracy was formed to wreck and discontinue *The Arena*, or to divert it from its mission as a reform magazine, but happily this scheme has been frustrated and the publication is in the control of a man who may be relied on to deal valiant blows in [*sic*] behalf of the liberties of the people."[86]

The Arena's savior was journalist and reformer Paul Tyner. Tyner's reform credentials were impeccable. He was an impassioned advocate of Populist economic reform and the eight-hour day, and a critic of blacklisting and government corruption. In 1898 he became the president of the Union Reform League (URL), an organization dedicated to hastening the creation, in Tyner's words, of "the fairer civilization of the new order pictured by Bellamy." Perhaps as a result of Tyner's association with Helen Campbell and Charlotte Perkins Gilman, he was a staunch advocate of the woman movement. He fully embraced its vision of race perfection through the merging of the highest qualities of manliness and womanliness.[87]

Tyner was also, like Flower, a proponent of New Thought. In 1897 Tyner became the editor of the Denver-based New Thought journal *The Temple*, and he addressed Malinda Cramer's fourth International Divine Science Association convention that same year. In *The Temple* Tyner and his wife Mathilde advertised themselves as "Metaphysicians" and offered "Lessons and Treatments by correspondence in English and German."[88]

In October 1898 Tyner took over both the editorship and the ownership of *The Arena*. In November he merged his *Temple* magazine, Horatio Dresser's *Journal of Practical Metaphysics*, and Benjamin Flower's *New Time* with the new *Arena*. Dresser became *The Arena*'s co-editor and Flower contributed frequently to the journal. Tyner announced that the new *Arena* would cover business, work and the worker, science, philosophy, and metaphysics. He emphasized that "the grand racial movement of the century we call 'the woman movement,' will always receive intelligent and appreciative attention in its pages."[89]

The Arena thrived under Tyner's editorship. Top reformers and reform-oriented poets and novelists continued to publish in the journal, including Leo Tolstoy, George Herron, William Lloyd Garrison, Booker T. Washington, municipal reformer Samuel ("Golden Rule") Jones, poet Edwin Markham, and of course Helen Campbell and Charlotte Perkins Gilman. The presidency of Tyner's URL passed to Christian Socialist author W. D. P. Bliss, but Tyner remained involved in the organization. Tyner also ensured that the URL maintained close ties with *The Arena*. The methods of the URLs were nearly identical to those of Flower's Unions for Practical Progress. They aimed, first, to unite the forces of reform, and second, to educate public opinion through the publication of cheap tracts, each of which would first appear in *The Arena*. In 1899 tracts were prepared for the URL by, among others, radical academic Frank Parsons, economist Edward Bemis of the University of Chicago, Bliss, and Tyner.[90]

Later that year, the URL was expanded and renamed the Social Reform Union (SRU). The group resolved to hire four national organizers to help spread the movement's ideas. It would raise money to create the "People's College of Economics," a university that would be "absolutely free from political or capitalist control."[91] It would also follow the URL plan of issuing monthly pamphlets on reform issues, each published first as an article in Tyner's *Arena*.

The SRU's list of officers was a virtual who's who of turn-of-the-century reform. It included Social Gospel leaders George Herron, Bishop F. D. Huntington, and Benjamin Fay Mills; Populists Anna L. Diggs and Judge Frank Doster; socialists Eugene Debs, Laurence Gronlund, and J. A. Wayland, founder and publisher of the socialist journal *Appeal to Reason;* labor leader Samuel Gompers; women's-club and women's-suffrage advocates Caroline M. Severance and Charlotte Perkins Gilman; African American leader Booker T. Washington; reform municipal and state officials Samuel Jones, John Altgeld, and Hazen Pingree; radical academics Frank Parsons and Edward Bemis; novelist William Dean Howells and poet Edwin Markham; and investigators and journalists Henry Demarest Lloyd, Florence Kelley, Bolton Hall, and Ernest Crosby.[92]

Through his multiple organizational activities, Tyner succeeded in newly cementing the relationship between *The Arena* and the foremost activists of turn-of-the-century middle-class reform. Then in October 1899, exactly one year after he had taken up editorship of *The Arena*, Tyner abruptly resigned. He announced that he would henceforth devote himself "entirely to the practice and teaching of metaphysical healing."[93]

Tyner resigned his position in order to devote himself to organizing the New Thought movement. Along with former SRU members Ernest Crosby and Bolton Hall, Tyner became a major force behind the International Metaphysical League, the forerunner of the International New Thought Alliance. Tyner simultaneously promoted the ideas of his new spiritual guide, Helen Wilmans. In 1900 he joined the six-person Central Advisory Board of Wilmans's Mental Science Association. Tyner was also active in the New York City Mental Science "Temple," along with radical-minister-turned-anarchist Hugh Pentecost and about thirty other members. In the early 1900s Tyner wrote feature essays for Wilmans's *Freedom,* in which he elaborated upon his favorite ideas—immortality, health vibrations, and the importance of unifying manly intellect and womanly emotion.[94]

Tyner turned over *The Arena* to John Emery McLean, who promised that the new *Arena* would be "absolutely non-partizan [*sic*] and non-sectarian," devoted solely to "promoting the social and civic welfare of the race through a search for Truth." "[I]t is our belief, however, that what is called the 'New Thought' . . . has a possible application that is practical, concrete and objective," he added, and announced that part of the new *Arena's* task would be to introduce New Thought beliefs "more widely" to the thinking public. McLean's position was partially motivated by self-interest: he was also the editor of *Mind,* the most important New Thought journal of the period.[95]

McLean had launched *Mind* in October 1897 with the express purpose of unifying the New Thought movement. It opened with a bang, presenting the serial publication of Julian Hawthorne's "psychological" (occult) novel "A Daughter of Love" and offering free copies of Elizabeth Boynton Harbert's *Amore* to journal subscribers. The magazine published almost every major New Thought leader. Charles Fillmore, Malinda Cramer, Helen Van-Anderson, Horatio Dresser, Ralph Waldo Trine, Ursula Newell Gestefeld, and Annie Rix Militz were among the contributors.[96]

When McLean became the editor of *The Arena,* he turned *Mind's* editorship over to Charles Brodie Patterson. Patterson was a prolific New Thought author who was deeply involved in the organization of New Thought national congresses. In November 1900 the two men switched positions; McLean left *The Arena* and returned to *Mind,* while Patterson became both the editor-in-chief of *The Arena* and, with McLean, the co-editor of *Mind.* The two journals had an extremely close relationship, therefore. Both were owned by McLean and edited by Patterson, who was aided by McLean in his editorship of *Mind* and by Benjamin Flower in his editorship of *The Arena*.[97]

Patterson edited *The Arena* until March 1904, when Flower again took over the journal. During Patterson's tenure a sprinkling of New Thought essays appeared in *The Arena* alongside articles by the major literary and political figures of the day—radical academics such as Edward Bemis and Frank Parsons; religious reformers such as the Vrooman brothers and George Herron; and many, including Clara Colby, Ernest Crosby, Bolton Hall, and Edwin Markham, who had New Thought affiliations and also published in *Mind*. Under Patterson *The Arena* reached its peak circulation of 30,000 (greater than that of the *Atlantic* but smaller than that of *Harper's*).[98]

While *The Arena* thrived under the editorship of Patterson and Flower, *Mind* did so as well under the editorship of Patterson and McLean. In March 1901 McLean announced that the circulation of *Mind* had increased over the past six months "at a rate unprecedented in the history of metaphysical publications." That month McLean also announced that *Mind* was absorbing *Universal Truth*, the journal run by former students of Emma Curtis Hopkins in Chicago. *Mind*'s editors probably spoke without exaggeration when they asserted that its "leadership, in the literary world, of the great metaphysical movement . . . is acknowledged everywhere. Its supremacy among New Thought journals is conceded."[99]

The close ties between *Mind* and *The Arena* exposed reform-minded Americans to New Thought ideas. They brought New Thought and major reform leaders to one another's attention. Flower and Patterson's *Arena* promoted the interaction among temperance, purity, woman-movement, Christian Socialist, and New Thought leaders so characteristic of the 1890s.

By the early twentieth century, many former Populists, Bellamyite Nationalists, Christian Socialists, and radicalized WCTU and women's-club members became supporters of the newly formed Socialist Party of America. Among them were many who had subscribed to a millennial republican vision of a cooperative commonwealth. The creation of this commonwealth would accelerate the evolution of a spiritual and self-sacrificing race of Americans. Some believed that this racial evolution might include the development of telepathic powers that could then be directed through New Thought meditation practices. They now brought this faith in telepathic power to the Socialist movement. Indeed, some observers parodied early-twentieth-century midwestern radicals as consumers of "socialistic and new-thought literature."[100]

Some early-twentieth-century Socialists believed that the cooperative commonwealth would inaugurate a transformation of "the race." Others believed that the emergence of high-minded people must be the precondition for Socialist revolution. In either case, many were ready to accept hypnotic thought-force as a valuable ally in the struggle for a transformed society. Social Reform Union member J. A. Wayland's *Appeal to Reason*, a socialist paper that had the highest circulation of any Left publication in American history, ran a weekly New Thought column by former Populist Allen W. Ricker. Ricker used his column to promote "telepathy or the conscious transmission of thought" as a tool of socialist revolution. The *Appeal* also ran a women's column, edited by Josephine Conger, that presented New Thought meditation as an aid to womanly influence. "All the great men and women of the world have believed in what we call New Thought," Conger wrote. The *Appeal* featured Ella Wheeler Wilcox, Edwin Markham, and other authors who were sympathetic to New Thought. The paper also frequently exchanged articles with *The Arena*.[101]

Even Ernest Untermann, a Marxist theorist (and the translator of Marx's *Kapital* into English) who was hired by the *Appeal* in order to help make the paper's understanding of socialism more "scientific," seemed to view socialism and thought-power as kindred paths to race perfection. "The victory of the working classes opens a new era in the conquest of matter by mind," Untermann explained. "It sets the human mind free to begin the conquest of death in earnest, and will end in the victory of the collective human mind over terrestrial environment." Communication with "minds on other planets" would surely follow, he argued.[102] Nor was the *Appeal* the only socialist paper to promote New Thought ideas. The official organ of the Socialist Party of Kansas, *Social Ethics*, was a New Thought paper. The Oklahoma socialist paper *New Life* also stressed the relationship between socialism and New Thought. On the other side, early-twentieth-century New Thought journals were full of debates about socialism. They frequently published articles and letters-to-the-editor by self-identified "New Thought socialists."[103]

The subjects of this chapter were viewed as radicals in the 1890s. By the 1900s and 1910s, many of the "race improvements" they called for—such as child-labor laws, compulsory education, factory legislation, tenement-reform codes, prohibition, and women's suffrage—became popular crusades and were ultimately enacted through municipal, state, and federal law. Americans supported these laws because they were compatible with the republican conviction that productive and virtuous citizens formed the basis of the nation's strength. The reforms were also compatible with the pop-Darwinian belief that improved environmental conditions would strengthen the development of the race. Some Americans accepted new reforms because they believed that through adherence to the laws of science and sociological study (popularly understood as little more than evolutionary theory illustrated by first-hand observations of the poor), the race could be perfected. Some supported Progressive-era reforms because they seemed to promote (Anglo-Saxon) "womanly" qualities of love, purity, and sacrifice.

In short, many white middle-class Americans' outrage over the devastation wrought by industrialization, political corruption, and laissez-faire capitalism derived less from empathy for the poor or anger over injustice than from fears about the potential degeneration of the race and hence of the republic. The white middle-class vision of Progressive-era reform could embrace censorship campaigns, Jim Crow laws, eugenics, and even lynching, as well as sanitation and tenement reform, factory regulations, women's suffrage, and socialism. All were potential means of safeguarding the evolutionary development of the Anglo-Saxon or human race and hence of inaugurating a purified republic.

By the early twentieth century the major pillars of this worldview began to crumble. Republican ideals of an independent, virtuous citizenry faded as corporate capitalist economic structures grew more dominant. The first cracks in evolutionary racism were made by youthful reformers, pioneering anthropologists, and university-trained social scientists. Social science in general began to professionalize, and could no longer be breezily equated with "God's laws," or womanly intuition, or the evolutionary trend toward race perfection. The idea that womanly qualities represented the highest level of evolutionary development came under virulent attack from theorists across the political spectrum.

In this context of rapid ideological change, some radicals would turn to feminism, psychoanalysis, and the Socialist left; others would embrace scientific "efficiency." Still others, including Benjamin Flower and Ernest Untermann, would cling to the pop-Darwinian hierarchies that had always undergirded their political efforts, and emerge as leaders of early-twentieth-century campaigns against Catholics, Asians, and immigrants.[104] In this new world, the era of woman would decay—and New Thought, the religion of the woman's era, would transform into an almost unrecognizable religion of success for a corporate era.

7   New Thought and Popular Psychology, 1905–1920

The woman of the past is no more; the woman of the future
is not yet.

Marie Merrick, 1903 [1]

If the daughter has been brought up on the "don't" plan, and has
just kicked over the traces, and assumed her own individuality,
I say *"Bully for her!"*

Elizabeth Towne, 1915 [2]

By the early twentieth century, the social and cultural context within which
New Thought had flourished began to change. Technological and managerial innovations definitively pushed the United States from an industrial
producer to a corporate consumer economy. As the economic infrastructure
shifted, so did mainstream paradigms of gendered selfhood. The ideal of
the self-controlled man and the pure and spiritually influential woman lost
its hold on the younger generation. The "woman's era," within which Victorian ideals of morality and progress would flourish under the guidance of
the desireless woman, died before it dawned. And a new discourse, that of
psychology, gradually replaced evolutionary progress as the most common
language Americans used to interpret both politics and selfhood.

New Thought beliefs had been intimately tied to the Victorian faith in
evolutionary progress and desireless womanhood. At the same time, many
New Thought authors had expressed a protest—sometimes overtly, sometimes covertly—against the lauding of self-sacrifice that typified the woman's era. How did New Thought fare as this worldview began to dissolve?
Would New Thought, the women's faith of the new woman's era, find an
audience in a world in which consumption was prized over production, psychology over religion, and personal expression over the repression of desire?

New Thought continued to thrive in the early decades of the twentieth
century. But it was a new form of New Thought. Its consumers were no
longer neurasthenic women and high-minded men; instead, they were
their long-suffering offspring who wished to cast off the oppressive weight
of their parents' overactive consciences. Theological debate within New

217

Thought dwindled. Its publicists stressed only the essential tenets of thought power, meditation, and affirmations and denials. Yet within this more generic New Thought a distinct ideological strand still existed—one that was indebted to such authors as Helen Wilmans and that was guardedly pro-desire. In addition, many New Thought authors easily adopted the vocabulary of popular psychology. By the 1910s, New Thought ideas were both molding and being absorbed by this new discourse of selfhood.

A NEW CONTEXT FOR NEW THOUGHT:
CULTURAL CROSSCURRENTS, 1900–1920

During the first two decades of the twentieth century the nation's economic structure shifted dramatically. The turn-of-the-century wave of corporate consolidations enabled unprecedented mass production. Manufacturers enhanced their productive capacity further by adopting scientific management techniques. These offered workers initially higher wages in return for assembly-line monotony and more intrusive managerial control. As a result of both organized political pressure and the needs of corporations for cheap labor, new sales and clerical jobs as well as some professional positions opened to white women.

These economic changes had social and cultural consequences. In response to both higher wages and deadening work routines, working-class men and women flocked to dance halls and amusement parks. There they openly rejected middle-class ideals of self-restraint. Their rebellious behavior attracted the attention of fun-seeking middle-class youth, whose emulation of working-class patterns of leisure furthered the growing revolt against Victorian ideals. They also attracted the attention of purity crusaders, who renewed their attacks on dance halls, liquor, and prostitution in the first and second decades of the twentieth century.[3]

The early twentieth century was also marked by organized challenges to the new economic order of corporate capitalism. Workers in the coal, mining, lumber, and textile industries engaged in massive strikes. The Industrial Workers of the World, a radical labor organization, encouraged workers to organize into "One Big Union," engage in a massive general strike, and transform the nation into a "workers' commonwealth." Under the leadership of Eugene Debs the Socialist Party of America reached its peak in 1912. A new generation of women who called themselves feminists defied norms of womanliness and allied themselves with the Socialist left.

Progressivism, the umbrella term used by historians to cover the outlook of a disparate group of intellectuals, political activists, and social scientists between 1890 and 1920, perhaps best epitomized the cultural cross-currents of this era. The first-generation Progressives were fervently anti-monopoly and devoted to cooperation, self-sacrifice, and sometimes psychic development as a means of race perfection. By the 1910s they had given way to a second generation, one dominated by university-trained experts who wished to regulate, not abolish, monopolies and corporations. Some Progressives sympathized with the plight of working-class Americans, while others wished to control them. Some supported purity crusades while others were horrified by the crusaders' excesses. Reflecting the new faith in human and environmental perfectibility, some pushed for the expansion of the electorate. Others, reflecting a new upsurge in scientific racism, pushed for the further exclusion of African Americans and immigrants from citizenship rights.

CONSUMPTION, PSYCHOLOGY, AND THE RECONFIGURATION OF DESIRE

By the early twentieth century, the productive capacities of major manufacturers had reached unprecedented levels. The resulting market saturation meant that the survival of the largest manufacturers was now dependent upon an increase in mass consumption. Therefore, the desire of the masses had become as crucial to the new economic order as their productivity—if not more so. The new centrality of consumer desire found expression in turn-of-the-century marginalist economic theory. Classical economics had emphasized production as the key to wealth, and had valued commodities according to their material use. In contrast, marginalist economic theory moved consumption to center stage. It judged the value of commodities not by their practical use-value, but by the extent to which consumers desired them. Marginalist economists thereby reversed the classical view that consumption was merely a means to further production. They instead saw production as a means to expanded consumption.[4]

This emphasis on consumer desire rather than on productive self-denial had profound implications for ideals of manhood and womanhood. For most of the nineteenth century, white middle-class men had identified themselves as producers and had prided themselves on their ability to repress or transmute their lowly desires. Now the economic importance of production was secondary to that of consumption. "Manly" self-denial and productivity were overshadowed. Desire was viewed not as a threatening power to be diligently channeled, but as an unproblematic force that was the true determinant of an object's value.[5]

The new centrality of mass consumption problematized late-Victorian views of white middle-class womanhood as well. Nineteenth-century images of wage labor as cutthroat and competitive had been used to justify white women's exclusion from most forms of paid labor and more generally from the public sphere. But by the early twentieth century, many businessmen believed that the key to economic growth lay not in the expansion of business enterprise, which was lauded by the culture as manly, but in the expansion of consumption, which was denigrated by the culture as womanly. The fact that "womanly" desire was now critical to corporate growth was recognized by the new department stores, which directly addressed women as consumers by offering them luxurious surroundings and an array of helpful services. Department stores "feminized" the public sphere of the marketplace, thereby threatening a middle-class male identity based upon self-control and the repudiation of "womanly" desire and feeling.[6]

Against this backdrop of economic transformation, new models of healthy subjectivity gradually emerged. Victorians believed that maturity was reached only after one defeated one's instincts and internalized social conventions. Only the more advanced "races" could incorporate moral norms or social conventions fully. One's ability to attain healthy subjectivity was thus largely determined by one's ancestry.[7]

In contrast, modern psychologists taught that the mind was composed of conscious, subconscious, and unconscious elements. The conscious mind had only marginal control over its subconscious and unconscious aspects. Of particular importance here was the unconscious. Understood as a part of the mind that escaped conscious control, the unconscious undercut the confidence in male will that underlay nineteenth-century thought.[8] The rigidly controlled, self-denying individual who internalized all of society's norms was now viewed as neurotically repressed. The healthy individual acknowledged, and sometimes expressed, his or her unconscious or "subconscious" desires.[9] The gift of self-knowledge and self-expression was not determined by heredity. While mental health could be profoundly influenced by one's immediate family, the activities of one's remote ancestors were irrelevant to modern psychological thought.

The new image of selfhood that encouraged acceptance of one's "lower" desires had potentially profound implications. Older beliefs in the determining powers of racial heredity had legitimated racism, wars of extermination, and separate and unequal spheres for women and men. A new validation of individual expression over community norms could challenge racial bigotry, liberate women from obsessive concerns with purity and "race" degeneration, undermine hypocrisy and conformity, and free people from the self-flagellation that resulted from fruitless efforts to erase forbidden thoughts.[10]

These possibilities were not realized—at least in the short run. New ideals of selfhood that challenged evolutionary paradigms with psychological ones were initially ignored by most American neurologists and psychiatrists. In the early twentieth century they continued to diagnose up to ninety percent of their patients as victims of heredity. The diagnosis of heredity took an even more sinister turn with the work of British psychologist Francis Galton and Italian criminologist Cesare Lombroso. Galton claimed to have discovered a way to measure intelligence accurately (his tests showed that intelligence was the exclusive property of the British professional upper-middle classes). Lombroso argued that criminals as well as social and political rebels were degenerates, literally throwbacks to earlier stages of human evolution. During the first two decades of the twentieth century, such arguments led to calls for the sterilization of the "unfit," the establishment of mandatory psychological testing of immigrants (ultimately used to support immigration restriction laws), and a renewed discussion of whether higher education for women weakened their bodies and therefore resulted in racial degeneration.[11]

This renewed emphasis on heredity was a last-ditch effort, however. Even as calls for eugenics as a means of race purification reached a fever pitch in the first decade and the early part of the second decade of the twentieth century, late-Victorian ideals of pure womanhood and willful manhood were being discarded in favor of a new vision that trumpeted desire. As one well-known author would explain in 1926, the "key-word of psychology today is desire."[12]

THE END OF THE WOMAN'S ERA

By the 1910s, the woman's era was over. This does not mean that the level of women's activism declined. On the contrary, the first and second decades of the twentieth century saw the expansion of the women's-suffrage movement, the creation of new coalitions between well-to-do and wage-earning women, the growth of the black-women's-club movement, and the emergence of a small but vital group of women who called themselves feminists.[13] But these groups of women were not united by a vision of an era of purity and desirelessness, presided over by men and women of "head and heart." Instead, they acted within a cultural context that increasingly valorized aggressive masculinity and stigmatized as feminized and inferior all who were not hyper-masculine—including effeminate men as well as all women and most minority groups.

Middle-class white men had been trumpeting the importance of aggressive Anglo-Saxon manhood since the 1880s. By the early twentieth century, these men began to emphasize not their civilized manliness, but their "primitive masculinity." They embraced body-building, team sports, and "rough" working-class pastimes such as boxing and created fraternal orders for themselves and the Boy Scouts for their sons. Cultural arbiters followed suit. Editors castigated literary sentimentalism as womanish and lauded ostensibly masculine realism. Art critics suddenly insisted that only manly, "vigorous" art was true art.[14]

In the 1880s and 1890s, some social-purity and woman-movement supporters had called upon men to become more like pure women. The high-minded "New Woman" of "head and heart" had been presented as the model toward which both sexes ought to aspire. By the first decade of the twentieth century, the memory of this New Woman was buried under the onslaught of the advertisers' "New Woman," or rather new "Girl"—the famous Gibson and Christy Girls. Athletic and charmingly rebellious, the Gibson and Christy Girls were healthy enough to assuage fears of Anglo-Saxon race suicide, pretty enough to encourage consumption of beauty products, and giddy enough to assure white men that they alone had a monopoly on intellectual life.[15]

The memory of the woman's era was also erased as advocates of the new manhood systematically appropriated and redefined "womanly" ideals of love, service, cooperation, and self-sacrifice. Propagandists for the 1897 Spanish-American War redefined self-sacrifice as a militaristic trait rather than a maternal one. Turn-of-the-century male reformers recast political reform as the province not of women motivated by their "mother hearts," but of men who were tough enough to hobnob with party bosses and battle the "primitive" both at home and abroad. Through redefining womanly service as "public service" and "municipal housekeeping" as virile labor, these men shifted the discourse of reform in order to shut out women.[16]

Social Gospel leaders of the first two decades of the twentieth century also participated in the male recuperation of "womanly" ideals. They promoted an image of Jesus as a "man's man." The days when men like R. Heber Newton had been proudly described as "manly as a lion but gentle as a woman" were over. Now Social Gospel leaders claimed to model their religious and reform work on the teamwork, order, efficiency, and strict chain of command supposedly typical of the military and the corporation, and not on the basis of cooperative, loving, nurturing, and self-sacrificing qualities ostensibly typical of the female-dominated family. They still lauded "cooperation," but they treated it as a synonym for the manly militaristic quality of "coordination," not the womanly quality of domestic love.[17]

Early-twentieth-century male social scientists distanced themselves from the earlier linkage of social science with morality and altruism. Such associations had legitimized women reformers' claims that their morally motivated investigations constituted social science. As Helen Campbell had argued, social science, like reform, should be jointly fueled by intellect and emotion. Now social scientists argued that their work was only truly scientific if political advocacy and heartfelt concern for the downtrodden were banished.[18]

In sum, by the early twentieth century there was a rapid reworking of the most basic terms of the debate between those who promoted channeled male desire as the motor of evolutionary progress and those who condemned lowly male desire as the force that poisoned civilization. The high-minded late-Victorian woman who expressed her "mother-heart" by serving society was marginalized by early-twentieth-century male reformers, who appropriated for themselves the "womanly" qualities of service and cooperation.

This appropriation was the first stage of an attack on every aspect of the woman's era. Turn-of-the-century psychologists continued to trumpet the late-Victorian view that while men and women were similar in primitive societies, advanced civilization was marked by increasing difference between the sexes. They characterized as "an atavistic reversion to the conditions beneath birds and mammals" the "ideal of the female 'reformers'" that men and women could be intellectually equal. Radical sexologists such as Havelock Ellis accepted female desire, but argued that it was perverse unless directed toward reproduction. Swedish feminist Ellen Key explicitly attacked the woman's-era view that motherhood need not entail physical reproduction. She compared "the woman who refuses motherhood in order to serve humanity" to "a soldier who prepares himself on the eve of battle . . . by opening his veins."[19]

These early sexual modernists were so confident that women reformers' claims of high-minded rationality were bogus that they called for empirical studies to document the inalterable differences between the male and female mind. Early-twentieth-century social scientists complied by testing male and female motor, affective, sensory, and intellectual abilities. To the surprise of many, their studies demonstrated that there were either no significant differences between the sexes or that girls' skills were slightly superior. Psychologists then decreed that mental tests could not capture the real difference between "masculinity" and "femininity." This difference resided, they claimed, in the (by definition unverifiable) unconscious.[20] They turned to the theories of Sigmund Freud, who claimed to have mapped the laws of the unconscious.

Freud reduced all desire to a form of sexual desire. He insisted that women's desires, no matter what their apparent focus, were really sexual desires. But the libido, or sexual energy, was a masculine drive. There was no such thing as a sexually healthy woman, therefore. Freud presented convoluted paradigms of female sexuality that defined mature womanhood as the successful transfer of women's erogenous zone from the clitoris, which gave women sexual pleasure, to the vagina, which gave men sexual pleasure. The healthy woman accepted her true identity as a castrated man.[21]

Female desire took on a new symbolic meaning in the early decades of the twentieth century. In the late-Victorian era, the desireless woman had symbolized hopes for a pure and ordered society. By the 1910s, as Freudian ideas were gradually popularized, female desire began to be interpreted as a specifically sexual desire. The sexually active woman became the emblem of both the thrilling vitality and the threatening excess of a new consumer society. As the symbol of a new cultural order, female desire drew the attention of advertisers, physicians, and social scientists alike. These groups agreed that female desire was healthy as long as it was narrowed and directed toward consumption and heterosexual expression within marriage.

This lauding of heterosexuality helped to create a new physical intimacy between husbands and wives. It also led to attacks on the women's associations that had been the source of women's political power. An emphasis on heterosexual expression led to the stigmatization of all women who were perceived as withdrawing sexually from men, including single career women, lesbians, and wives who devoted themselves primarily to their children rather than to their husbands.[22]

By the 1920s, Freudian vocabulary was used to assert the existence of very different sexual natures for men and women. Pop-Freudians posited the existence of a rational, "conscious" self and a sexual, instinctual "subconscious" self. For men, the two could work in harmony; men were expected consciously to pursue their subconscious desires for sexual gratification. A woman's subconscious sexuality, however, was divorced from her conscious self. Indeed, psychology manuals and popular fiction alike depicted woman's subconscious sexuality as so dramatically severed from her conscious self that if a woman "consciously" rejected a male suitor, she could be accused of "subconsciously" attempting to attract him. Her "natural" sexuality was depicted as residing in her animal unconscious, and so by definition was beyond her control. Women could justify their sexual activity only by claiming to have been carried away by a romantic passion stronger than their conscious direction. Those who openly pursued sex for the purposes of pleasure, social mobility, or economic gain were punished as deviants or prostitutes.[23]

In short, early-twentieth-century psychologists created a new discourse of gendered selfhood that lauded a broadly defined (white) male desire, while narrowing and sexualizing female desire. As one historian explains, while men created "social support for their own self-expression," they "blocked outlets . . . for some of the same impulses in women." As another states, "[l]iberation, in any drastic sense, was for men only; women . . . were assumed to be naturally different."[24] White male selfhood was again "whole," containing sexual desire and intellectual ability. Women's selfhood was again half, characterized by a sexuality they could not fully control. As historian Pamela Haag explains, twentieth-century popular psychologists "replicated rather than transcended nineteenth-century assumptions of a proprietary male self and an unruly, sexually dispossessed female self."[25]

NEW THOUGHT IN A NEW CONTEXT

What role did New Thought, a popular discourse of selfhood that had long debated the gender of "mind" and the meaning of desire, play in the popular formation of new ideals of selfhood? What was the fate of New Thought now that the woman's era was over?

Despite the decline of the late-Victorian woman's era, New Thought continued to thrive in the first two decades of the twentieth century. Many of the New Thought schools or churches begun in the 1880s and 1890s, such as Denver-based Divine Science, California-based Homes of Truth, and the Kansas City–based Unity School of Christianity, continued to grow. By the 1910s, there were approximately three hundred and fifty active New Thought centers in the United States and Canada. The movement boasted six major journals with circulations ranging from ten to thirty thousand, led by Elizabeth Towne's *Nautilus* and the closely affiliated *New Thought*. The move to organize New Thought groups into national and international congresses continued apace. Meetings of the National New Thought Alliance were held yearly between 1906 and 1913. In 1914 the group's meeting was held in London, and the name of the organization was changed to the International New Thought Alliance. Through the 1910s the International New Thought Alliance met yearly.[26]

By the 1910s New Thought authors also reached huge audiences through mainstream periodicals. Horatio Dresser wrote for *Good Housekeeping;* Ralph Waldo Trine published in *Woman's Home Companion;* and Ella Wheeler Wilcox offered New Thought advice through her syndicated columns in Hearst press publications. New Thought ideas were also presented in popular novels, such as Frances Hodgson Burnett's *The Dawn of Tomorrow* (advertised as "A Charming Bit of New Thought Fiction"), and reached the public through Buster Brown cartoons (the cartoon's creator, R. F. Outcault, was a member of the World's New Thought Federation and a contributor to *New Thought* magazine). Playwrights Charles Klein and Augustus Thomas produced shows that were recognized for their New Thought content.[27]

Although New Thought thrived, however, it was a very different faith from the one that had attracted reformers of the woman's era. Its advocates were far more likely to be independents. Self-help writer Orison Swett Marden presented New Thought ideas in his books and in his *Success* magazine, which in 1905 had a circulation of 300,000. Such women and men as Annie Payson Call, Flora Howard, and Frank Haddock, who were connected with no known New Thought school, wrote best-selling books with titles like *Power of Will* and *Brain Power for Business Men.*[28]

This trend toward the independent production of New Thought bestsellers had begun as early as 1898, when Horatio Dresser complained that now that "a large proportion of those who are cured" had become New Thought writers, the output had become "decidedly crude." He added, "The market is now flooded with [New Thought] books, pamphlets and papers, in which the same doctrine is set forth in slightly varied language, and the time must soon come when this over-production shall cease." The market was not saturated, however. In 1902 the philosopher William James noted that New Thought had now "reached the stage . . . when the demand for its literature is great enough for insincere stuff, mechanically produced for the market, to be to a certain extent supplied by publishers." This over-production continued through the early decades of the twentieth century. As late as 1924, an article in *American Mercury* reported that New Thought presses "turn out carloads of metaphysics."[29]

The new New Thought sometimes reflected broader cultural trends and denigrated "womanly" ideals in favor of the manly world of business. "There is a feeling in the air that the New Thought is something unpractical—something for feminine enthusiasts merely—something vague; semireligious; vaporous, unreal; not for ordinary hard-headed business men," one author wrote in 1902. But in fact, he argued, New Thought was perfect for the man "whose coarser independence prompts him to get through life comfortably, careless of whether his blunt speaking offends or pleases."[30] This trend toward dismissing "feminine enthusiasts" grew stronger in the next two decades, as New Thought tracts aimed at business success sold hundreds of thousands of copies.

Perhaps the most telling indication of the masculinization of New Thought was provided by the changing statements-of-purpose of its national alliances. The 1899 constitution of the International Metaphysical League, for example, still voiced the outlook of the woman's era. Its goal was to "promote interest in and the practice of a true spiritual philosophy of life; to develop the highest self-culture through right thinking as a means of bringing one's loftiest ideals into present realization; to stimulate faith in . . . the higher nature of man in its relation to health, happiness and progress; [and] to teach the universal Fatherhood and Motherhood of God and the all-inclusive brotherhood of man." By 1919, however, the International New Thought Alliance's Declaration of Principles expressed a different perspective. It "affirmed" "the good," "health," and "divine supply," and stated that "he who trusts in the divine return, has learned the law of success." It concluded, "We affirm the teaching of Christ that the Kingdom of Heaven is within us, that we are one with the Father. . . ." The idea of the "universal Fatherhood and Motherhood of God" had vanished without a trace.[31]

Most histories of New Thought begin during this period. They present New Thought as a crass, commercial "religion of success."[32] The movement's earlier history as the faith of the woman's era, like the woman's era itself, has been forgotten. Yet the break between the New Thought of the woman's era and the one that promised businessmen success was not as sharp as this scholarly focus on the later period would suggest. Continuity between the two periods existed because early leaders of New Thought did not disappear in the twentieth century. They attempted to carry on, altering their messages in order to better reach their new audiences.

To complete the story of New Thought, I now turn to the final years of the movement's original leaders. New Thought had been closely aligned with the woman's era. Yet it had also been a divided discourse, within which various schools had debated the connections between mind and matter and, more heatedly, the merits of desire. Ultimately it was New Thought authors' approach to gender and desire that determined their relevance in the modern world. Their fates help illuminate the new parameters of female selfhood in the post-Victorian era.

THE ANTI-DESIRE SCHOOL: ANNIE RIX MILITZ, URSULA GESTEFELD, AND HELEN VAN-ANDERSON

Annie Rix Militz actively promoted New Thought throughout the first two decades of the twentieth century. She wrote monthly social commentary, sermons, and exegeses for her journal *Master Mind*. She participated in national New Thought congresses. In 1913 she and her "companion and secretary" Miss Florence Johnson embarked on a two-year world tour in order to arouse global interest in New Thought. In 1914 she was present at the foundation of the International New Thought Alliance in London. In 1916 she opened the University of Christ in Los Angeles to train teachers and healers in her version of New Thought.[33]

Yet until her death in 1924, Rix Militz continued to advocate an 1890s-style message of salvific womanly purity. She argued that the planet would be regenerated once men and women recognized their shared spiritual nature. She urged her followers to "hasten the day when woman's voice will be heard, a clear, strong note with the best of men, who are ever in the vanguard of the world's improvement." In Rix Militz's view, the "woman's voice" was the voice of sexual purity. By the late 1910s she was encouraging her students to "seal themselves to the Lord," or embrace celibacy. Her followers' attitude toward popular U.S. culture, which increasingly celebrated desire, became dismissive, even combative. In early 1924, Rix Militz's sister Harriet Hale Rix announced that Home of Truth members were dedicating one day a week to "denying [the] sensuality and materiality" that emanated from the "two . . . amusement producing states" of New York and California. Such an attitude was deeply anachronistic by the 1920s. The Home of Truth had by this point taken on the characteristics of a self-enclosed sect. It did not survive Rix Militz's death in 1924.[34]

Ursula Gestefeld also remained active during the early decades of the twentieth century. She spoke frequently at New Thought congresses, occasionally served as an officer of the National New Thought Alliance, and continued to write and lecture about her "Science of Being." In 1914, the sixty-nine-year-old Gestefeld went to London to attend the inauguration of the International New Thought Alliance. By then branches of her Science of

Being had spread to Great Britain, and several of her works had been translated into German.[35]

Gestefeld attempted to write crossover books that would capitalize on popular interest in New Thought as an aid to the struggling businessman. But she never resolved her fear of female selfhood or desire. Her success manuals contained little more than platitudes about male action and female passivity. Her tract *How to Control Circumstances* (1901), which offered advice on how to respond to downward economic mobility, was typical. On the one hand, echoing male New Thought authors, Gestefeld described poverty as a spur to effort and achievement. With confidence in one's thought-power, one could "[g]ird up [one's] loins" and "meet and conquer" all exigencies, she wrote. On the other hand, she promoted a power through passivity more typical of her earlier work. Describing the fate of a woman who must "leave [her] handsome house and live in a small one in an unfashionable neighborhood," Gestefeld advised retreat into an inner world where one could not be hurt. "You Live in Your Thought World," she insisted. There, "that poor, mean, unfashionable house has no power to make you miserable. It is your thoughts about it that make you miserable."[36] Gestefeld was not at home in the twentieth century. Her Science of Being did not survive her death from toxemia, in 1921.

Helen Van-Anderson followed a similar sorry path. Once a respected spiritual leader, ordained by the major Boston ministers and hobnobbing with prominent reformers, Van-Anderson ended up writing for the *New York Magazine of Mysteries: A "Cheer Up" Magazine.* The magazine offered subscribers a "Mystic Success Club" membership, as well as weekly meditations for "prosperity." Yet Van-Anderson was unable to wholeheartedly promote New Thought as a cult of success. Her 1906 tract *The Mystic Scroll* contained only one short chapter on "The Law of Prosperity." The rest of the book reflected the outlook of the Victorian pure woman, now aging and infirm, who remained beset by nerves, eager to distance herself from her family, and deeply ambivalent about the nature of her own desires. Of the *Mystic Scroll's* ten "Practical Applications," three dealt with the sufferings of the person who felt put-upon by alcoholic spouses or annoying offspring; four were directed to overcoming one's own "Nervousness" or "Secret or Vicious Habits"; and three concerned failing eyesight, rheumatism, and other illnesses typical of the aging woman.[37] Van-Anderson nevertheless continued her own quest for happiness. She remarried shortly after the publication of *Mystic Scroll,* and wrote a final book in 1912 under her new married name of Helen Van Anderson-Gordon. After that, no more information on Van-Anderson is available.

THE PROPHETS OF DESIRE: ALICE BUNKER STOCKHAM
AND HELEN WILMANS

Alice Bunker Stockham and Helen Wilmans differed from most of their New Thought peers by promoting complex and arguably more radical versions of female selfhood and desire. The two were also successful businesswomen. One might expect that they would thrive in an early-twentieth-century world that lauded the hardheaded businessman and rejected the repression of desire. Yet as a result of legal suits, the careers of both women were destroyed by 1905. Their legal troubles suggest that the unabashed praise of female desire remained unacceptable in modern America. While the anti-desire school of New Thought became irrelevant, legal authorities helped to silence those who promoted the positive force of female desire.

In the early 1900s Alice Stockham advocated women's suffrage, eugenics, and social purity. She was the president of the Alice B. Stockham Publishing Company and an internationally known authority on health and sexuality. She was also a practicing New Thought healer who regularly attended meetings of the National New Thought Alliance. Stockham continued to write as well. In 1903, she published her opus *The Lover's World: A Wheel of Life.* There she argued that both men and women were sexual beings who could transmute their passions into a wide range of social activities. Stockham's final work expressed both the radical and the problematic aspects of the woman's-era hope to redefine sexuality in the interests of reform, cooperation, and race perfection.[38]

But Stockham's career did not survive long into the new century. In 1905, a pamphlet by Stockham entitled "The Wedding Night" came to the attention of the Society for the Suppression of Vice. She was promptly arrested for "sending improper matter through the mails." Stockham engaged attorney Clarence Darrow for her defense. She received a great deal of support from local women, many of whom reacted in such an "overenthusiastic" way to Darrow's arguments that they had to be ejected from the courtroom. Nevertheless, the seventy-two-year-old Dr. Stockham was found guilty. She was fined $250 and her books on sexuality banned. Neither the Alice B. Stockham Publishing Company nor Stockham's previous writings on marital sexuality survived the ruling. Only four years after the court case (in 1909), attorney and free-speech activist Theodore Schroeder noted that Stockham's writings, "nor any like them, are now anywhere to be had."[39]

After the trial Stockham moved to California with her daughter. She continued to practice mental healing and to write occasional articles for the New Thought journal *The Nautilus.* But her career as a proponent of women's sexual and intellectual energy effectively ended. The idea that women and men were not only equally sexual but equally able to direct and control their sexuality was unacceptable to the jittery mainstream of the early 1900s.

Helen Wilmans also did not survive long into the twentieth century. Her downfall was more protracted. As it turned out, Wilmans's hope that the "world will be redated from [the Mental Science convention on the] 28th November" proved premature.[40] Beginning in the spring of 1901, Wilmans was engulfed in a four-year battle with the federal government to save her name, her business, and her fortune.

Wilmans's problems began in July 1901, when her "absent treatment" business was brought to the attention of the postmaster general. Since the 1870s the postmaster general had had the right to issue a "fraud order" stopping mail service to any addressee believed to be operating a "scheme . . . for obtaining money through the mails by means of false or fraudulent pretenses." Such a fraud order was enforced against Wilmans.[41]

Wilmans fought back with characteristic energy. She presented hundreds of sworn testimonials attesting to the benefits of her treatment. The postmaster general was unmoved. He retained the fraud order and added a hefty fine. With that decision, Wilmans's business as healer and publisher was destroyed.[42]

The postmaster's ruling was just the beginning of Wilmans's troubles. She appealed the case, and it was quashed on a technicality on March 5, 1902. That year she wrote to her loyal supporter Eugene Del Mar, "I am not afraid of efforts being made to ruin me. They won't succeed, you may depend on that." But she added, "I am not depending for my success so much upon external means as on the state of my own thought."[43] Within two years Wilmans was back in court, facing four new counts of soliciting money through the mail for healing services she did not provide. This time she was convicted on all four counts. The jury reasoned that any sane person would know the services Wilmans promised were impossible to perform. Wilmans must therefore have been intentionally engaged in fraud.

Wilmans appealed her 1905 convictions and won. The circuit court judge based his reversal on the nearly identical case of *School of Magnetic Healing v. McAnnulty*. He ruled that "[t]he court is not a society for psychical research," and therefore had no right to judge the truth of Wilmans's claims. Since there was no way to prove either that Wilmans's treatments were ineffectual or that she believed them to be, the mail fraud charges were dropped.[44]

Wilmans's trials sent shock waves through the New Thought community. Malinda Cramer leapt to Wilmans's defense, arguing that her legal difficulties were the result of the "injured thought and envy" of one of Wilmans's "millionaire" neighbors. "Helen Wilmans' ability to make money is what they would like to crush," she wrote, adding that "[n]o one can prove that Helen Wilmans did not give absent treatments . . . by proving that she was driving, fishing or walking . . . at the time appointed, for there is nothing to prevent any one giving . . . treatment regardless of place and surrounding circumstances." Despite his disdain for New Thought success authors, Horatio Dresser also publicly defended Wilmans. In a rare political act, the International Metaphysical League formed a special committee, headed by Wilmans's ally Paul Tyner, to protest post-office interference with mental healers.[45]

Although Wilmans was ultimately cleared of all criminal charges, the years of court battles took their toll. By 1905 her business was ruined and her fortune depleted. Now in her seventies, Wilmans interpreted her physical ailments in light of her belief in mental power and physical immortality. "It seems as if all the nerves of my body are waking up after years of half-deadness, and they are squealing about it like everything," she wrote to Eugene Del Mar. "It is something like the pain that comes from bringing a drowned or frozen man back to life, and I expect that it is really encouraging." In 1906 Wilmans asked Del Mar to sell her books at whatever cost he felt appropriate. "Make me an offer," she wrote, adding, "[r]eally, I didn't care very much for the result of the trial. I know very well there is a lesson for me to learn, and when I have learned it these apparent persecutions will cease." C. C. Post died the following June, and Wilmans died three months later on September 5, 1907. Both the Hotel Colonnades and the Wilmans Opera House were later destroyed by fires which many suspected were set by the Ku Klux Klan. The only memory of Wilmans's University of Psychical Research is the street on which it was to stand, which today bears the name "University Boulevard."[46]

Helen Wilmans was caught in a national backlash against patent medicine peddlers and medical and religious quacks. Yet she was also targeted because of more local concerns. Malinda Cramer was at least partially correct when she highlighted financial envy as a cause of Wilmans's troubles. Wilmans had proudly publicized her financial wizardry. When a convention of doctors in Jacksonville, Florida denounced her for fleecing the public of $20,000 in one year, she reacted with defiance. "He made a mistake. I took in double that amount, and I gave full value for every dollar of it," she asserted. There was a gender component to the trial as well. Wilmans's wealth was all the more threatening because it had been created by a woman. In Wilmans's rural Florida community, neighbors categorized unnaturally powerful women as witches. In 1898 Wilmans wrote of her healing abilities that some "unusually ignorant people thought [them] a species of witchery, and held me in great awe. It came to be believed that I could raise the dead, and do many other things that I was not able to do." These fears emerged full force during her lengthy trials. Sea Breaze residents offered horrified testimony about Wilmans's power to bring success to gamblers, aid criminals in escaping the law, give women the ability to lead men to propose, and procure "abortions by mental processes." While Wilmans had sought to deify desire and the "clawing animal will," that same female will was demonized by her Florida neighbors.[47]

Alice Stockham and Helen Wilmans had attempted to rework late-Victorian constructions of white female selfhood by redefining the meaning of womanly desire. Stockham recast passion as an expression of the searching soul, not of the lustful body; as being equally present in men and women; and as a force that both men and women could transmute to moral and intellectual ends.[48] Wilmans heralded a female self whose deepest instinct, like that of the male self, was to strive for freedom. Men and women were equally fueled by desire and oriented toward growth, self-expression, willful intelligence, and the economic conquest of others. She argued that true love and maternity were dependent upon strengthening the ego rather than sacrificing it.

Stockham and Wilmans had not been alone in their efforts to redefine female desire. For a few years at the turn of the century, many New Thought tracts and journals presented female-authored hymns to desire. In contrast to sexologists, who insisted that female desire be exclusively oriented toward sexuality and reproduction, and to Freudians, who interpreted all desire as sexual desire, these authors viewed desire as a fundamental craving for multiple forms of self-expression. In contrast to those who saw creative, heroic desire as a masculine prerogative, these women claimed desire as the "birthright" of "woman." As the 1901 poem "Dominion" described, the "woman" who had formerly "dumbly crushed desire" was today filled with an "Unrest divine." She longed for "progress, beauty, truth—For freedom, friendship, knowledge, travel, books."[49]

Even some male New Thought authors joined in the praise of female desire. One such in the early 1900s, for example, was William Walker Atkinson, a devoted follower of Helen Wilmans, who became the editor of the popular Chicago-based journal *New Thought*. Atkinson's journal argued that men and women alike should freely accept their desires for independent thought, sexual expression, and prosperity. He presented cautionary stories about the sorry fate of the sheltered married woman who had "repressed . . . her natural desire to think for herself and to judge for herself." "New Thought can do a whole lot for this woman, providing she will get to work and make herself over again," Atkinson wrote in a typical editorial.[50]

The trials of Stockham and Wilmans were indicative, however, of a change in public tolerance for the praise of broadly defined female desire. By the 1910s, most New Thought authors argued that marriage and consumption were the only appropriate ends for female desire. Typical was poet and author Florence Morse Kingsley. Her popular short stories depicted the Christian condemnation of desire and discontent as a class weapon wielded against the poor by refined ladies who already had their hearts' desires. Kingsley's New Thought heroines rebelliously accepted their secret desires—which were for pretty clothes and generous husbands. Though positioning themselves as daringly modern, Kingsley's short stories were in fact an expression of the narrowing of female desire from freedom and economic independence to sex, consumption, and marital dependence.[51]

LOVE AS ACCOMMODATION TO WAGE WORK: THE PRO-DESIRE WRITINGS OF ELIZABETH TOWNE (1865–1960)

The writer who most typified the ambivalently pro-desire New Thought of the 1910s was probably Elizabeth Towne. By 1910 her journal, *The Nautilus,* had become the major New Thought journal in the nation.[52] Towne was one of the top-selling New Thought authors, and her Elizabeth Towne Publishing Company was the number-one publisher of New Thought books. Her message was one of accommodation to corporate consumer society. She told men that they could indulge their appetites without negating their manliness. She told women that their sexual influence over their husbands and their own profit-generating activities were equally legitimate ways of attaining their goals. Her depictions of male and female selfhood retained hints of the flexibility characteristic of earlier pro-desire New Thought authors. Towne's writings nevertheless retreated from the goal of freedom that had animated women like Wilmans, Stockham, and Gestefeld. They reveal as well the emotional price that Americans paid for rejecting long-standing Victorian ideals.

Towne's inspirations were Warren Felt Evans and Helen Wilmans.[53] These authors were appropriate guides, since her writings addressed a culture that was entirely changed from that of Ursula Gestefeld or Helen Van-Anderson. Most late-nineteenth-century New Thought writings reflected a world of sickly women and nervous men who needed to "deny," or at least make peace with, their lowly bodies and unacceptable desires. They had

Figure 17.   Elizabeth Towne,
author and editor of
The Nautilus.

viewed money as the problematic creation of aggressive and competitive
male drives. A middle-class woman's only realistic response to her husband's financial losses had been to silence her troublesome, discontented
"self." For Towne, however, money was less problematic and more widely
available. She addressed not bitter and sickly housewives, but hopeful female sales clerks who dreamt of pretty clothes and possible future careers
in the arts. For this audience, the older New Thought admonitions to
"deny" matter and repress desire lacked healing efficacy. Towne summarized their perspective: "'[I]t won't work in my case'—'there are persons
who can't be healed'—et cetera." [54]

Towne's job was clear. She would retool New Thought and make it effective in a post-Victorian world. Drawing on the "pro-desire" school, Towne
counseled self-assertion, not self-denial. Echoing Wilmans, she demanded
that her readers learn to "exalt" themselves. Women must reject "the spirit
of self-depreciation, or self-effacement." Men must stop being "so anxious
[to do right] that they overdo the thing" and instead learn to accept their
"appetites." [55]

This advice was appropriate for the small-town Americans Towne addressed. The men were white-collar employees whose major complaint was
that they felt "sluggish" and "dead tired mentally." They needed to accept

their body's need for play and pleasure, Towne wrote. The women were eager to lead happily married lives, yet were aware that economic alternatives to marriage existed. Towne advised them to deal with hostile husbands by going into the "silence" and affirming "love." If that didn't work, Towne wrote, they should affirm their own abilities and leave the marriage. Above all, they must raise their daughters with a knowledge of how to save, manage, and increase their income.[56]

Towne recommended a relaxed attitude toward gender roles. Every family needs the "mother's way of softness and the father's way of discipline," Towne wrote. "Some women are the men of the family, and some men are the women. But the Divine Order remains the same," she added. She praised the role of sex within marriage. "We believe that sex is divine, inherent in every organism and in every atom in all creation." She advised the clever wife to be a "woo-man." "In plain English," Towne elaborated, "the more loving the woman the sooner she gets what she wants, especially when she has justice on her side." She also urged her readers, male and female, to accept their desire for money. "There isn't a greater, grander, more God-like thing to do than to *make money*," she explained. The desire for money was not selfish, but cosmic. "[I]t is *the Law of your being* which says 'I DESIRE [money].' And Desire is the Law."[57] Towne was a prophetess of the modern who taught her readers to relax, breathe deeply, and consciously make themselves over to fit a new economic order.

Towne's writings also indicate the difficulty of this endeavor. It was not so simple for people to reject their upbringing and suddenly embrace money, desire, physicality, and sexuality. Towne used various strategies to ease her readers (and probably herself) through the transition. She sometimes presented Hopkins's argument that desire was good because it was not really one's own. "The desires of my heart are *God's* desires," she wrote in 1902. She urged her readers to accept their longing for business success because the key to "success" was not competitive greed, but "love." The coalman who loved his work, the sales clerk who loved her customers would surely prosper, Towne promised.[58]

Towne handled the countervailing voices of instilled conscience by subjecting them to mockery. She openly attacked the now-troublesome New England conscience. Most people were raised on the "don't plan—especially if [they were] born in New England," Towne wrote, adding, "[But t]his is the *do* age; not the *don't* age." She mocked the dour aspect of those who bragged about a "grouchy or choleric old ancestor who happened to have 'come over in the Mayflower'." Their high moral sense was the source of illness, not salvation. The "intelligent and good men" who "have no bad habits and who are anxious always to do right" are simply wearing their "nerves to tatters" over trivialities. "No wonder he is dead tired mentally. No wonder he can't 'let go.' No wonder he develops nervous prostration," Towne explained.[59] She tried to undercut the demands of conscience by reminding her readers that conscience was entirely relative. She explained that "conscience is a matter of education. The Hindoo mother thinks she ought to drown her baby girls in the Ganges. . . . Roosevelt *et al.* thinks he ought to knock down Spain for being mean to Cuba and the Filipinos. Tolstoi thinks he ought to resist nothing. All these people are winners in their own particular races because they square their acts with their 'oughts.'" In case the reader missed the point, Towne reiterated the example of the mother drowning her baby girl. "The Hindoo must mind *her* conscience and she will win her races," she stressed. That, she wrote, defined "character."[60]

Towne attempted to link character to self-love rather than to self-denial. Her version of self-love was intertwined with self-commodification, however. Loving oneself meant "enumerating all the things worth money you can do," she wrote. Towne implied that one exchanged "self" for money. "The more thought force you *put in* to what you do the more Self you have ex-pressed—*pressed out* of yourself. See? *And the more money you will bring*," she bubbled. In an even odder analogy, Towne wrote that selling one's ideas for money was "like selling your child." This did not mean that the sale of ideas, like the sale of a child, was painful or unethical. Instead, she advised, "[k]eep mum till you can profit from it."[61]

Towne was committed to silencing what she viewed as a stultifying and outdated conscience, and to lauding desire. Yet the transition from Victorian to modern values was not always so easily made. Towne's odd discussions of "selling your child," killing infant daughters, and rejecting "choleric" ancestors hint that the transition to modern behavior involved wrenching breaks from tradition that were never consciously admitted in her sunny writings.

Towne acknowledged that the modern world did not allow the one thing Helen Wilmans had craved—freedom. She was quite explicit that freedom from bosses, from family, and from circumstance was impossible. Happiness "*never* comes as a result of fitting circumstances to your notions. *It comes from fitting* YOURSELF *to circumstances*," she emphasized. Towne used the prison as a metaphor to describe the human condition. We are all "in a prison of circumstances," she explained. We are there because we need to be. Our prison is "stocked with just the sort of things [the prisoner] needs to exercise his mind, will and muscles upon, to fit him for the next higher class *in the line of his desires*." She concluded this metaphor on an ominous note. "Will he *adjust himself* to it all and work happily, faithfull-y [*sic*], willingly; and thus *shorten his sentence?* Or will he kick the walls and curse his work—and *lengthen his sentence?*"[62]

Perhaps the biggest difference between Towne and her New Thought predecessors lay in her understanding of the relations between gender on one hand, and desire, wealth, and freedom on the other. Most New Thought authors of the 1890s, like most late Victorians, conceptualized freedom, wealth, and independence as the product of desirous instinct channeled into violent struggle. This association of freedom, wealth, and independence with instinct, will, and violence meant that freedom was for white men only. Late Victorians imagined middle-class white men as desirous and lustful, and middle-class white women as desireless and pure. Only white men had the will to transform their ugly desires into the productive competitive drives that created wealth and guaranteed independence. Since only white men had the drive and the will to engage in such struggle, only white men could be free.[63]

Towne articulated a more modern view. She rejected the idea that desire was evil in men or in women, or that money was the product of violent but channeled male energy. For her, the world of work was not a gloriously competitive arena, but a more mundane setting in which one *"pressed out"* one's time, energy, and selfhood. She therefore opposed the belief that only white men had the inner forcefulness to engage in profit-generating activity. Instead, she equated paid labor with "love" and desire, qualities that she believed to be inherent in both men and women. For Towne, therefore, love was no longer a value in opposition to desire or to capitalism, as it had been for the reformers of the woman's era.

Elizabeth Towne called for accommodation to corporate capitalism. It would be simplistic, however, to interpret her writings as evidence of an absolute loss of freedom. If freedom is defined in mythic Darwinian terms as the right of every man to struggle for existence, then Towne's world of happy employees is clearly less free. But if freedom is defined as independence, the question becomes, independence of what sort? As Helen Wilmans pointed out, "dependence is degradation." The new economy described by Towne assumed widespread dependence upon bosses, and hence degradation. But it also promised economic independence from one's domineering parents or overly controlling spouse, and hence a form of freedom. According to Elizabeth Towne, love was linked to desire and to the creation of wealth, and all three were open to women as well as to men. But she admitted that wealth was not attained without some loss of "self" or independence, no matter who attained it.

NEW THOUGHT AND POPULAR PSYCHOLOGY

Through popular New Thought authors such as Elizabeth Towne, as well as through "crossover" writers such as Florence Morse Kingsley and Ella Wheeler Wilcox, "pro-desire" New Thought ideas filtered through to the general public.[64] Many of the older New Thought schools also began to herald desire and, eventually, to incorporate a more modern psychological vocabulary. The Fillmores' Unity School of Christianity, for example, adopted as the textbook of its movement H. Emilie Cady's *Lessons in Truth*, a book that heralded desire. *"Desire in the heart is always God tapping at the door of your consciousness with his infinite supply,"* Cady wrote. Divine Science followed a similar trajectory. Its founder, Malinda Cramer, had lauded Divine Mind, "denied" matter and desire, and argued that "the body is not you." By the late 1890s, however, Cramer had changed her position. Instead of teaching her students to deny the body, she announced in 1896 that "No longer is the question unsettled as to whether there is both Spirit and matter, two substances, opposed to each other; or . . . two minds, Divine and mortal, the opposite of each other; or . . . whether there is, or is not a body. . . . For it is now . . . accepted that Spirit is All in All inclusive of the body, not all in all exclusive of the body."

Soon Nona Brooks and Fanny James also adopted the position that matter was real and that mortal and Immortal Mind were in fact one substance. Under the leadership of Charles Edgar Prather, who published the Divine Science journal *Power* in the 1910s, Divine Science became even more accepting of desire. "All progress is simply the working out of desire," Prather wrote. Divine Scientists also kept up with the times by incorporating psychological language. They referred to their teachings as "practical psychology" and heralded the "subconscious mind" as the "storehouse" of power.[65]

As more New Thought writers appropriated the language of psychology, the distinctions between the two discourses began to blur. In the early 1900s, for example, the books of Wilmans's follower William Walker Atkinson bore titles such as *Law of the New Thought* and *Nuggets of New Thought*. By the 1910s, his books had titles such as *Your Mind and How to Use It: A Manual of Practical Psychology*. The substance of his "practical psychology" was identical to New Thought, however. Many others followed suit, including Richard Ingales, a New Thought author and admirer of Helen Wilmans whose book *The History and Power of Mind* (1902) was in its tenth edition by 1905, and perhaps most successfully, Frank Channing Haddock. Haddock's manual *Power of Will* (1907), which promised to "vastly multiply the power of the man or woman" through efficient use of the "subconscious realm" and the "law of discontent," sold over 600,000 copies by the mid-1920s.[66]

Mass-market women's magazines such as *Good Housekeeping* and *Ladies Home Journal* also confused psychology with New Thought. In the early 1900s these magazines paid more attention than any other popular publication to the issue of "nervous disorders." They presented the views of physicians, Protestant ministers, early psychotherapists, and New Thought healers as equally valid schools of modern psychotherapy. Horatio Dresser's 1910 definition of New Thought as "the use made of suggestion, subconsciousness, methods of silence and meditation, and other psychological principles" was typical of the muddying of the waters between the two schools.[67]

By the 1910s, New Thought seemed about to be absorbed by the more powerful and scientific discourse of psychology. But the relationship between New Thought, a hybrid nineteenth-century religious-scientific discourse of selfhood, and popular psychology, the twentieth-century discourse of selfhood, was more complex than a simple one-way absorption of New Thought by popular psychology. The two evolved somewhat in tandem, with a constant mutual influence. Indeed, the meaning of psychology for Americans cannot be fully understood without the background of New Thought.[68]

New Thought authors were among the first to understand that the neurasthenic or nervous illnesses plaguing late-nineteenth-century Americans were rooted not in physical weakness but in emotional and cultural tensions. They knew that to regain their health, patients needed new understandings of the gendered relations among mind, matter, selfhood, and desire. They popularized the idea that within every individual there existed two warring "minds." They offered Americans strategies for either expressing or containing their troubling desires.

It is not surprising that these methods were popular with women, or, indeed, that they were first understood as the components of a new "woman's religion." Late-Victorian ideals of selfhood were more problematic for white women than for white men. The sickly women who transformed themselves into New Thought healers or authors were driven by the same wrenching personal and cultural tensions that motivated men like William James, George Herbert Mead, and John Dewey to study the nature of the mind with the top laboratory scientists of Germany and the United States.[69] New Thought women realized more quickly than these scholars did that the solutions they sought were to be found not in measuring the speed of motor reflexes, but in reconceptualizing mind's relation to matter, sexuality, and desire.

As we have seen, when the transition from a producer to a consumer society made white male selfhood as problematic as white female selfhood had been, academic psychologists created new models of healthy manhood that enabled white men to accept their inner desires more easily. These models of white male selfhood were defined as models of human selfhood. They tended to present healthy womanhood as a contradiction in terms. The earlier exploration of gendered selfhood presented in female-authored, turn-of-the-century New Thought texts was forgotten by or written out of most histories of psychology.

It is important, therefore, to reintegrate the parallel stories of psychology and New Thought. In so doing the popular context and the female contribution to modern psychology are restored; a fuller history of the transition from Victorian to modern ideals of manhood and womanhood is provided; and the implications of current understandings of the gendered self are clarified.

Historians of psychotherapy generally point to the hypnotic experiments of French physicians Jean-Martin Charcot and Hippolyte Bernheim as the source for American psychologists' interest in the unconscious. But Charcot's hypnotism, like Phineas Quimby's mind cure, had its source in mesmerism. Mesmerism had both a medical-scientific and an occult-popular history in France and the United States.[70] Charcot's experiments had a similar dual legacy. On one hand, they influenced a handful of pioneering neurologists such as Sigmund Freud and Prince Morrow. On the other, they were widely reported in the popular press and in New Thought journals such as *Mind, New Thought,* and the *Journal of Practical Metaphysics.*

The French experiments were initially hailed more warmly in popular and New Thought journals than they were in medical journals. In the 1880s and 1890s reports about the relation between hypnotism and hysteria were scoffed at by most neurologists, who believed that neurological illnesses had their basis either in heredity or in undetectable physical wounds or "lesions" in the brain. Only after Christian Science and New Thought healers began to cure patients whom neurologists had abandoned as hopeless—and thus offer serious professional competition to the still-fledgling neurological profession—did neurologists look more closely at French experiments with hypnosis.[71]

By the early 1900s, both medical and popular American journals contained discussions of the "hidden" or "subconscious" self. This did not mean, however, that modern psychological principles had triumphed over religious or New Thought understandings of mortal minds and divine minds. When Americans discussed the subconscious at this time, they referred not to the primitive subconscious of Sigmund Freud, whose works were still largely unknown, but to what should more accurately be called the "subliminal self." This was a transitional conception of the extraconscious mind that bore a close resemblance to the New Thought idea of the "Divine Mind" or "Internal Reservoir."

The concept of a "subliminal" part of human consciousness was first described by Gustav Theodor Fechner (1801–1887), a highly influential German experimental psychologist. Fechner believed that the natural world was a manifestation of the soul of God, and he called this soul of God the "subliminal." Human consciousness contained sparks of the subliminal or God's soul, he argued. Fechner's views informed British psychologist Frederic W. H. Myers's study *Human Personality* (1903), which proclaimed that "no Self of which we can here have cognisance is in reality more than a fragment of a larger Self." Fechner and Myers influenced William James, whose writings helped pave the way for Americans' acceptance of psychology as the dominant discourse of modern selfhood. According to James, the subliminal consciousness functioned as a reserve of energy as well as a potential link to a larger, cosmic consciousness. James often described this larger consciousness as a "reservoir," a term that peppered many New Thought writings. "There is a continuum of cosmic consciousness, against which our individuality builds but accidental fences, and into which our several minds plunge as into a mother-sea or reservoir," James wrote in a typical passage.[72]

William James was one of the few psychologists to acknowledge publicly the similarities between cutting-edge psychological research and the writings of popular mental healers. In his 1890 essay "The Hidden Self," James pointed out that "mind-curers and Christian Scientists" and the French neurologist Pierre Janet were practicing the same technique of hypnotic suggestion. In his essays "The Gospel of Relaxation" (1899) and "The Energies of Men" (1906), James presented the latest neurological explanations of the relationship between actions and emotions. He then explained that "those converts to 'New Thought,' 'Christian Science,' 'Metaphysical Healing,' or other forms of spiritual philosophy, which are so numerous among us today," were bringing forth the very "copious unlocking of energies by ideas" that was the goal of his own physiological investigations. James read New Thought texts (he was particularly drawn to Ralph Waldo Trine), consulted New Thought healers, defended the rights of mind curists and other alternative healers, and wrote sympathetically about New Thought in his classic *Varieties of Religious Experience.* He not only acknowledged a pre-existing overlap between New Thought and early psychological investigations, he helped further that merging through his own respectful discussions of both discourses of selfhood.[73]

Most psychologists were less willing to discuss the parallels between their ideas and those of uncouth and undereducated mental healers. But the parallels existed nonetheless. The connection between New Thought and the Emmanuel Movement, a pioneering church-based clinic for "nervous disorders" that opened in 1906, was typical. The Emmanuel Movement was founded by Elwood Worcester and Samuel McComb, two Episcopalian clergymen who each also held a Ph.D. in psychology. They admitted that they opened a mental-health clinic in their church in order "to stem the tide [of the mental healing cults] which is sweeping . . . tens of thousands from the medical profession and from the Church."[74] Worcester and McComb's treatments drew upon the latest ideas of Fechner, Myers, and James. But the source for their healing practices could just as easily have been the popular New Thought movement that was their primary competition as both churchmen and neurologists. Worcester and McComb taught their patients that the subconscious was an "inexhaustible" power with "roots in the Infinite." The subconscious could be drawn upon to heighten intelligence, will power, and spirituality, they insisted. They praised the ideas of "the so-called Metaphysical School"—citing Ralph Waldo Trine, *The Arena* editor Charles Brodie Patterson, and other New Thought authors—as being of "the highest value." Their methods of deep relaxation followed by suggestion or autosuggestion were practically indistinguishable from New Thought treatments. The writings of Worcester and McComb, in turn, were highly influential. Their 1908 volume *Religion and Medicine* went through eight editions in its first seven months and was reviewed in every major American newspaper.[75]

By the end of the first decade of the twentieth century and the beginning of the second, both academic and popular authors were flooding the public with books about "suggestive therapeutics." Suggestive therapeutics consisted of a mix of French hypnotism and New Thought affirmation techniques. Its proponents drew upon the Jamesian and Emmanuel Movement understanding of the subconscious as an empowering subliminal self. They produced hybrid tomes such as Dr. Henry S. Munro's *A Handbook of Suggestive Therapeutics, Applied Hypnotism, Psychic Science* and John Duncan Quackenbos's *Hypnotic Therapeutics in Theory and Practice.* Titles like these lent credence to Horatio Dresser's claim that New Thought and psychology were one and the same.[76]

By the mid-1910s suggestive therapeutics began to be overshadowed by the daring new doctrines of Sigmund Freud. Though both schools used a similar vocabulary, their approaches were very different. While followers of suggestive therapeutics viewed sublimation as a sure-fire method of transmuting and spiritualizing sexual energies, Freud viewed sublimation as a never entirely successful struggle between primitive subconscious forces and the legitimate needs of civilized society.[77]

The differences between their approaches were smoothed over in the popular press, however. Indeed, those who introduced Freud to America did so through the lens of suggestive therapeutics, the Emmanuel Movement, and New Thought. Typical was H. Addington Bruce, a journalist and Emmanuel Movement publicist who had a respectful familiarity with New Thought writings. Bruce told his readers that Freud's talking cure would help liberate the genius that lurked within the subliminal self of the average individual. His writings on psychology had titles that were indistinguishable from those of New Thought publications.[78]

Max Eastman and Mabel Dodge Luhan, two of the earliest and most prominent intellectuals to write about Freudian psychoanalysis, also approached Freud from a New Thought perspective. Max Eastman, the radical author and editor of *The Masses,* had sought treatment for mysterious back pains at New Thought sanitariums. There he learned that his pain was simply "an idea stuck in the subliminal, an obsession, and nothing else." When Eastman encountered the ideas of Freud, he viewed them through this New Thought–inflected view of the subliminal as malleable and perfectible. He then popularized Freudian ideas through a series of articles in *Everybody's Magazine* in 1915. There he wrote that "headaches, nausea, 'neuralgia,' paralysis, or any other mysterious disorder" could be cured by Freudian analysis. Freud spurned hypnosis or suggestion, Eastman wrote, in favor of a method by which one opened a "shaft into the subconscious region and tap[ped] it of its mischievous elements." But this view of a perfectible subconscious was more akin to New Thought than to Freudian understandings of the inner self.[79]

Author and Greenwich-Village salon hostess Mabel Dodge Luhan was a pioneering "new woman" of the 1910s. Although she was a wealthy woman, Luhan supported the most radical political activists of her generation. She also thwarted convention by openly pursuing a life of intellectual, creative, and sexual expression. Luhan became one of the earliest popularizers of Freudian psychoanalysis. She was among the first patients of Freud's followers Smith Ely Jelliffe and Abraham Arden Brill. She wrote about her experiences with psychoanalysis in nationally syndicated columns in 1917 and 1918.[80]

Luhan attributed much of her self-knowledge to psychoanalysis. But she also gave credit to another source—the personal counsel of Emma Curtis Hopkins. Luhan may have found Hopkins the more sustaining of the two sources; she supplemented her weekly psychoanalytic sessions with Brill with thrice-weekly meditation sessions with Hopkins. Luhan's language reflected a familiarity with New Thought ideas. She described her break-up with journalist John Reed in the following terms: "Loosed [sic] from Reed, my powers ebbed back into my own reservoir and fed me where before they had been feeding him." Luhan ultimately ended her treatments with Brill for religious reasons. "He tried to remove every vestige of my belief in an inner power," she wrote. Luhan's talk of reservoirs and inner powers may have come from William James, but a more direct and likely source is Emma Curtis Hopkins.[81]

Luhan's relationship with Hopkins was long and intimate. It brings us full circle, to the final days of the woman whose ambiguous discussions of spirit and desire so influenced the early New Thought movement. In 1895 Hopkins abruptly closed her seminary and moved to New York City. Her activities over the next twenty-five years are not clearly known. She appears to have spent some time in Europe. She wrote books and saw patients. Her fame in New Thought circles continued unabated, but she avoided the limelight. In 1918 Hopkins was voted honorary president of the International New Thought Alliance, but she ignored the honor. In 1919 she wrote that people "[f]rom the ends of the earth" traveled to receive lessons and treatments from her. She accepted this homage with modesty. Yet Hopkins's schedule of clients remained heavy in the 1910s and early 1920s. New clients often had to wait weeks for an appointment.[82]

By the 1910s, Hopkins's writings had became more mystical. Her students had changed as well. Instead of nervous housewives, she "treated" the bohemian artists and writers then flocking to Greenwich Village. In addition to Luhan, Hopkins's patients included the artist Maurice Sterne, Elizabeth Duncan (the sister of Isadora Duncan), actor and pioneering stage director Robert Edmund ("Bobbie") Jones, painter Andrew Dasburg, and art exhibitor Nina Bull, who studied with Hopkins and who considered herself a Divine Science practitioner.[83]

Hopkins's most loyal and influential student in the 1910s and early 1920s, however, was Mabel Dodge Luhan. The two maintained an intimate correspondence between the years 1917 and 1923, and it is from this correspondence that we learn about Emma Hopkins's final years. The elderly Hopkins lived a simple, even Spartan life. Her home was a two-room suite in the Iroquois Hotel. When Hopkins rented three rooms with a private family in 1919 in order to "feel the temptation to write," she had to ask Luhan whether she could rent Luhan's furniture. "I do not want to *own furniture*," Hopkins wrote to her.[84]

Aside from her friendship with Luhan, Hopkins appears to have had no close personal relationships during her later years. Yet in her solitude Hopkins found the happiness that had escaped her when she had headed the Chicago Christian Science Theological Seminary. Luhan once asked Hopkins how she tolerated being "so alone except for all these people who come to you for help." Her answer was ambiguous. It hinted at either a regressive desire to escape from reality or an inward-looking and self-nourishing spirituality. Hopkins replied,

> Oh, it is wonderful to be alone and feel your oneness with everything outside you!
> . . . Sometimes when I am waiting for a student I go in my room and draw the curtains, and I lie down on my bed and draw the blanket over me and I have the most delicious moments.[85]

Hopkins undoubtedly derived great satisfaction from her healing work, which she maintained throughout her final years. Luhan left a moving description of how it felt to be "treated" by Hopkins in her "dim room among her roses and lilies."

> She sat in her little drawing room, in the Iroquois Hotel, clothed in an exquisite gown all soft black lace and silk, a large-brimmed lace hat on her soft white hair, and she smoothed and relaxed one so that at the end of one's hour one was renewed and reassured.
> I sat before her in a comfortable armchair three times a week. The shades were lowered and fresh flowers filled the room. . . . her violet eyes held mine as she—really inspired quite often—rambled on. . . .
> The effortless way—that was the way she counseled. Not to try, not to work, not to struggle. "Be still and know that I am God"—that sort of advice. An emphasis upon the power within that knows all and does all without the interception of the poor little "wandering, lunatic mind," or the powerless, stubborn will.
> . . . She stimulated and renewed one—causing the love and faith that life congealed to flow again. And she was so flattering! She loved us all, or seemed to. . . . She looked at us in turn and saw only the undying spirit buried in us, and she cared only for that. She would gaze at us during our hour with eyes shining love and tenderness, enhancing in each of us our feeling of worth; and then at the end of the hour she would rise, go to the

door, and, smiling a little coldly, grown remote, she would blow us out, appearing loath to shake the grateful hand or continue the intimacy she had seemingly established.[86]

The elderly Hopkins, for long years the "repository of the profoundest personal secrets of many people's lives," adored by many yet jealously guarding her solitude, died on April 8, 1925 of chronic myocarditis. She was buried in her family lot in Dayville, Connecticut.[87] Hopkins's death marked the end of a generation. She was the last representative of New Thought as a millennial faith of a new woman's era.

Conclusion
New Thought in American Culture after 1920

By the 1920s, New Thought seemed finished as a force in American culture. Once taken seriously by leading reformers, ministers, poets, and novelists, New Thought was now mocked by cultural critics. The opening volume of *American Mercury* in 1924 featured a satirical sketch of New Thought, whose claims were summarized as follows: "A boy of twelve admires Charlie Chaplin. He sets his subjective mind to work that night, and wakes up in the morning with a fine little moustache." Sinclair Lewis depicted New Thought as one of the scams practiced by the corrupt evangelist hero of his novel *Elmer Gantry*. H. L. Mencken lambasted New Thought in specifically gendered terms. "What remains of Emerson . . . is . . . a debased Transcendentalism rolled into pills for fat women with vague pains and inattentive husbands—in brief, the New Thought—in brief, imbecility," Mencken wrote.[1]

Despite the mockery of critics, New Thought ideas were available to Americans in a variety of forms throughout the 1920s and 1930s. Some turn-of-the-century New Thought authors remained popular. Elizabeth Towne's *Nautilus*, for example, had an average monthly circulation of 85,000 in the 1920s. New schools of New Thought emerged—most notably Religious Science, founded by Ernest Holmes in 1927. According to historian Charles Braden, Religious Science taught that "there were not two minds, but one," that the conscious mind could make the subconscious mind more creative, and that only our belief sets limits to the power of our thought. There was little new here, and not surprisingly so. Ernest Holmes acknowledged Mary Baker Eddy, Nona Brooks, and especially Emma Curtis Hopkins as his greatest influences. His brother Fenwicke Holmes, who also wrote Religious Science texts, was inspired by the writings of Helen Wilmans's follower William Walker Atkinson. By the early 1960s the Religious Science journal, *Science of Mind*, still had a circulation of 90,000. Ernest Holmes's textbook *Science of Mind* remains in print today.[2]

New Thought ideas also reached Americans under less easily recognizable guises. The Swiss writer Emil Coué enjoyed an enormous vogue in the 1920s. Coué wrote that the subconscious was a "mysterious power that germinates ideas and affects their materialization in the conscious form of action." Individuals could tap this power by repeating the following mantra daily: "Day by day, in every way, I am getting better and better." Though one prominent historian of psychology has stated that this system of popular autosuggestion "was relatively new on the popular level," contemporaries knew better. As one Baptist minister commented, Coué's method offered "everything that was ever of any good in Christian Science." The 1920s vogue for "applied psychology" also popularized New Thought methods. Applied psychologists claimed that their methods had nothing in common with "telepathy, spiritism, clairvoyance, animal magnetism, astrology or witchcraft," yet as historian Richard Weiss points out, "'applied psychology' and New Thought were composed of identical ingredients." Both encouraged people to enter a state of deep relaxation, within which they were to "affirm" their desires.[3]

What did scholars make of twentieth-century New Thought? An early analysis of New Thought appeared in a 1921 *Living Age* article by Charles Thomas Hallinan entitled "My 'New Thought' Boyhood." Hallinan argued that New Thought addressed concerns that were "fundamentally economic."

> [T]he old traditional security, open to all thrifty, hard-working folks, had disappeared, and . . . in its place was a bewildering struggle to adjust rigid incomes to ascending prices. Not a pulpit in our suburb had addressed itself to this plebeian anxiety, this perpetual concern, until "New Thought" came in.
>
> Given the right attitude of mind, said [the New Thought teacher,] . . . you could tap the boundless resources of the Universe. . . . When . . . [he] declared flatly that security and health and abundance were the privilege of all, he struck a chord to which every heart in our town thrilled.[4]

This analysis of New Thought as "fundamentally economic" dominated scholarship from A. Whitney Griswold's 1934 article, "New Thought: A Cult of Success," to the most recent serious work on New Thought, Gail Thain Parker's *Mind Cure in New England*. All interpreted New Thought as a faith that enabled Americans, for better or worse, to reorient themselves to the changing economic structures of twentieth-century American life.[5]

The continued draw of New Thought principles might be more directly attributable to the fact that its central concepts—that God is Mind and that human thought, the manifestation of Creative Power, can affect circumstances—are fundamentally ambiguous and can be interpreted to fit almost any personal or political goal. New Thought's intrinsic ambiguity explains why it outlived its turn-of-the-century origins and remained a force in American culture.

In the 1920s and 1930s New Thought ideas were used by disparate groups for widely varying ends. United Negro Improvement Association leader Marcus Garvey, whose favorite poet was Ella Wheeler Wilcox, drew upon the works of William Walker Atkinson, Elizabeth Towne, and Nona Brooks to create "a black version of New Thought." He used their ideas to encourage black men to persevere in their business enterprises, "visualize" their own empire, and guard their "thoughts" from the thoughts of whites. Father Divine, the leader of the Harlem-based Peace Mission Movement, cast himself as the successor to Mary Baker Eddy. He used New Thought claims that "all is mind" to deny the existence of race difference, and hence the need for racial segregation. White New Thought-Divine Science author Emmet Fox, who viewed himself as a successor to Nona Brooks, soothed Americans through the Depression with his bestsellers *The Sermon on the Mount* and *Power Through Constructive Thinking.* "The normal mode of obtaining one's supply is following some useful business or profession. . . . Scientific prayer will put anyone into such a position if he does not already possess it," Fox promised. And according to Meridel Le Sueur's Depression-era classic *The Girl,* New Thought ideas continued to help some men and women accept their troubling sexual desires. In one scene a man describes how "psychology" allowed him and his wife to accept their sexuality:

> Well after I left the church I got a course from some magazine, a course in psychology. . . . Well it made a new man out of me. I learned that thought is all-powerful. You can make anything so by believing it's so. You can make your own good and cure your own evil. . . .
>
> You can laugh, . . . but it works for you. Why I used to give [my friend] an awful tongue lashing every time I caught him looking at the pictures outside a burlesque show. Now I go to one every time I can. Everything is good. Before me and my old woman used to cry and pray every time our flesh was weak. Now she's like me. We love each other up whenever we feel like it and never worry. Everything is good.[6]

The claim that "thought is all-powerful" seemed to recede during the years of World War II. New Thought ideas reemerged full force, however, with Norman Vincent Peale's 1952 bestseller *The Power of Positive Think-*

ing. Peale cited three major influences on his work: the Unity School of Christianity, Christian Science, and Ernest Holmes's *Science of Mind*. From the 1970s through the 1990s, New Thought claims about the creative effects of mental "affirmations" have become more popular than ever. They are preached in scores of metaphysical institutes around the nation. They are promoted on late-night "infomercials" that in 1994 alone brought in one billion dollars in sales. Most significant, a New Age self-help version of "thought-power" permeates bestsellers written from widely disparate political perspectives, from feminist Gloria Steinam's *Revolution from Within* to conservative evangelist Robert Schuller's *Peace of Mind Through Possibility Thinking*.

These works present ideas that can be traced to the late-Victorian New Thought movement, and particularly to the work of Emma Hopkins's student, Religious Science founder Ernest Holmes. Louise Hay, author of the 1980s bestseller *You Can Heal Your Life*, started her career as a Religious Science practitioner. Julia Cameron, author of the omnipresent 1990s workbook *The Artist's Way*, credits Holmes with changing her life. "What a revolution [Holmes's book *Creative Ideas*] caused in my life and in my thinking!" she writes. "I had never read prayers like those, prayers spoken with the confident assurance that God, or 'Mind,' was deeply, personally interested . . . in our lives—if we would just speak the word. . . . These prayers proclaim our birthright," Cameron explains.[7]

On the whole, scholars and journalists alike have responded to this recent wave of "thought-power" enthusiasm with withering disdain. The literary style of these popular authors is condemned as "drivel." Self-help and New Age writings are attacked as an escape from rationality and critical thinking, and as a mind-numbing form of self-indulgence that signals the end of America as an enlightened democracy. One critic even claims that by dwelling on weakness and victimization rather than on strength and stoicism, self-help and New Age authors create the unhappiness their books then offer to cure.[8]

One can easily condemn today's bestsellers as personally and politically pacifying. Undoubtedly some have the effect on readers that Elizabeth Towne's writings overtly stressed—convincing them of the need to accommodate themselves to the "prison" of circumstance. Yet a more nuanced analysis is also in order. For example, although sociologists Robert Wuthnow and Donald Stone assumed that participation in New Age groups would increase narcissistic self-involvement and decrease political awareness, their surveys turned up surprising evidence to the contrary: that people involved in New Age groups such as Synanon, Scientology, and Zen "tended to be more committed" or socially and politically aware than those of similar background who were not. A recent study by Wendy Simonds found that women who read self-help literature do not mindlessly accept the authors' grandiose claims. They read for comfort and for insight on how to manage their lives, not for a one-step method for changing the world. Self-help reading both expresses and contains women's dissatisfaction with the status quo, Simonds concludes.[9]

Analysis of today's self-help and New Age culture should move beyond, on the one hand, blanket condemnation, and on the other, suggestions that these writings do not entirely pacify their readers. A first step would be to focus on the language and imagery that permeates today's self-help bestsellers. Turn-of-the-century New Thought texts were obsessed with the relationships among mind, matter, spirit, and desire. Today's self-help authors are concerned with the *inner child, recovery,* and *codependence.* These terms hint at tensions quite different from those explored by earlier New Thought authors. Instead of condemning today's authors for their narcissism and poor writing style, we might consider how their obsessive discussions of childhood, recovery, and codependence, or the nature of interpersonal connections, magnify and so enable us to recognize the way in which similar concerns permeate current political discourse.

Like the terms mind, matter, spirit, and desire, the terms inner child, recovery, and codependence are ambiguous, multivalent, and politically charged. New Age authors explore the inner child, while politicians battle over abortion, child abuse, and the meaning of new forms of reproductive technologies. Alcoholics Anonymous and its numerous spin-off groups preach recovery—a term that politicians use to refer to economic growth, but that simultaneously invokes both a desire to recover a golden past and a hope to re-cover or repress an unsettled past. Self-help bestsellers counsel readers on codependence and attempt to delineate the extent to which individuals ought to care for or "invest" in one another. At the same time, Americans' responsibilities to one another are being reworked both personally, as they attempt to renegotiate obsolete nuclear family forms, and politically, as the scrapping of the welfare safety net, battles over school funding and health care, and, most broadly, debates about the function of government versus private industry circle around the question of just what level of concern or responsibility those at the top ought to have for those at the bottom. In short, we could interpret the concerns of New Age and self-help authors in the context of the broader cultural forces they seem to invoke. Today's New Age and self-help authors represent not a nation wallowing in self-indulgence, but an eerily accurate barometer of the nation's most pressing personal and political concerns.

New Thought authors understood that the slippery concepts of mind, matter, spirit, and desire were both central to late-Victorian understandings of private life and political order, and implicitly gendered. They attempted to rework these concepts to create new models of gendered selfhood. Today's self-help authors praise emotional investment as womanly and condemn it as smothering. They attack men for their coolness and praise them for their independence. They link recovery to separating from one's mother, or to reuniting with her. They encourage people to strengthen their inner child by becoming ideal parents not to their children, but to themselves.[10] In short, self-help and New Age authors also link central political and cultural tensions to gendered selfhood, or to ideals of manhood and womanhood.

This is another reason to take these writings seriously. Since the 1970s postmodern theorists have argued that gender and subjectivity are not innate but are externally constructed by a variety of cultural and political forces.[11] Popular writers of self-help books are among the most aggressive participants in the complex process of fashioning new forms of gendered selfhood to fit a changing political and economic order. Future historians might find in the messy, ambiguous, unsophisticated but massively popular writings of today's self-help authors the clues to how gendered selfhood was renegotiated in the closing years of the twentieth century.

Notes

INTRODUCTION

1. "Disciples of Mrs. Eddy," *Chicago Daily Tribune*, June 15, 1888; "Christian Scientists," *Daily Inter Ocean*, June 15, 1888; "Sickness an Error," *Chicago Times*, June 15, 1888. A reconstruction of Eddy's speech is included in Mary Baker Eddy, *Miscellaneous Writings: 1883–1896* (Boston: Trustees under the Will of Mary Baker Eddy, 1896), 98–106.

2. Sydney E. Ahlstrom's entry on Mary Baker Eddy in *Notable American Women 1607–1950*, edited by Edward T. James, Janet Wilson James, and Paul Boyer, 3 vols. (Cambridge, Mass.: Belknap Press, 1971), 1, 556; Robert Peel, *Mary Baker Eddy: The Years of Trial* (New York: Holt, Rinehart and Winston, 1971), 237–44.

3. Peel, *Mary Baker Eddy*, 141; Penny Hanson, "Woman's Hour: Feminist Implications of Mary Baker Eddy's Christian Science Movement, 1885–1910" (Ph.D. dissertation, University of California, Irvine, 1981), 109.

4. See Mary Baker Eddy, "Mind Healing History," *Christian Science Journal* 5, no. 3 (June 1887); "Things to Be Thought Of," *Christian Science Journal* 5, no. 12 (March 1888); Mary Baker Eddy, *Science and Health with Key to the Scriptures* (Boston: First Church of Christ, Scientist, 1971), 419; Stephen Gottschalk, *The Emergence of Christian Science in American Religious Life* (Berkeley: University of California Press, 1973, 126–27, 116; Peel, *Mary Baker Eddy*, 228.

5. On women's numerical predominance, see Hanson, "Woman's Hour," 2, 156, 193, 318; Donald Meyer, *The Positive Thinkers: Religion as Pop Psychology from Mary Baker Eddy to Oral Roberts* (New York: Pantheon Books, [1965] 1980), 46.

6. Charles S. Braden, *Spirits in Rebellion: The Rise and Development of New Thought* (Dallas: Southern Methodist University Press, 1963), 297–98.

The term "New Thought" did not come into use until the 1890s. I use New Thought rather than Mind Cure because it became the title most mental healers claimed for themselves, while "Mind Cure" was often used by the movement's detractors. In addition, current scholarly usage favors New Thought over Mind Cure.

Mental healers have been included in this study of the New Thought movement only if they meet at least two of the following three criteria. First, their writings express the basic tenets of New Thought theology; a belief in the power of mind over matter, the existence of a "divine within," and the use of affirmations and denials to structure thought and so mold reality. Second, they participate in New Thought congresses and publish in New Thought journals. Third, they are students of recognized New Thought leaders.

7. Mary Baker Eddy, *Science and Health with Key to the Scriptures* (Boston: First Church of Christ, Scientist, 1971), 119–20; Warren Felt Evans, *Esoteric Christianity and Mental Therapeutics* (Boston: Carter and Karrick, 1886), 159; Emma Curtis Hopkins, *Class Lessons 1888*, ed. Elizabeth C. Bogart (Marina Del Rey, California: DeVorss and Company, 1977), 200; H. Emilie Cady, *Lessons in Truth* (Kansas City, Mo.: Unity School of Christianity, n.d.), 32.

8. Eddy, *Science and Health*, 412.

9. Evans, *Esoteric Christianity*, 156.

10. Comparisons of Christian Science and New Thought can be found in Braden, *Spirits in Rebellion*, 14–21, and Gottschalk, *Emergence of Christian Science*, 124–29, 284–87. Also see debate in primary sources, such as William G. Ewing, "Why Not Be a Christian Scientist?" and Charles Brodie Patterson, "What the New Thought Stands For," in *The Arena* 25, no. 1 (January 1901): 1–16. My interpretation leans toward Gottschalk, but is based on my own reading of *Science and Health* as well as on a vast number of New Thought sources.

11. Gottschalk, *Emergence of Christian Science*, 180–93.

12. Gottschalk, *Emergence of Christian Science*, 121–26; Braden, *Spirits in Rebellion*, 170–229. The International New Thought Alliance is currently headquartered in Arizona. It publishes a quarterly journal called *New Thought*.

13. Peel, *Mary Baker Eddy*, 63; Ahlstrom, entry on Mary Baker Eddy, in James, ed., *Notable American Women*, 1, 556, 560.

14. Braden, *Spirits in Rebellion*, 170–229; Richard M. Huber, *The American Idea of Success* (New York: McGraw-Hill, 1971), 127.

15. William James, *The Varieties of Religious Experience* (Middlesex, England: Penguin Books, 1982), 95; see Nathan G. Hale, Jr. *Freud and the Americans: The Beginnings of Psychoanalysis in the United States, 1876–1917* (New York: Oxford University Press, 1971), 231–32. The Arena's peak circulation was almost 30,000. Marden's *Success* magazine's circulation was 300,000. See Braden, *Spirits in Rebellion*, 165, 331; Huber, *American Idea of Success*, 125–26, 153, 164. As of 1955, *In Tune with the Infinite* had sold 1,597,314 copies. Alice Payne Hackett, *60 Years of Bestsellers, 1895–1955* (New York: R. R. Bowker Co., 1956), cited in Louis Schneider and Sanford M. Dornbusch, *Popular Religion: Inspirational Books in America* (Chicago: University of Chicago Press, 1958), 162.

16. Meyer, *Positive Thinkers*, 42; Huber, *American Idea of Success*, 125.

Of the top religious bestsellers between 1875 and 1954, almost half presented a New Thought-style message of thought as power. Every decade since 1890 has seen at least one such bestseller. (To be included as a bestseller, hardback sales of each volume had to surpass the 500,000 mark.) See Schneider and Dornbusch, *Popular Religion*, 145–47, 160.

17. Aidan A. Kelly, "Twelve-Step Programs and the New Age," in J. Gordon Melton, Jerome Clark, and Aidan A. Kelly, *New Age Encyclopedia* (Detroit: Gale Research, Inc., 1990), 469; Robert Lindsey, "Spiritual Concepts Drawing A Different Breed of Adherents," *New York Times*, September 29, 1986.

18. Lynne Namka is quoted in Wendy Kaminer, "Chances are You're Codependent Too," *New York Times Sunday Book Review*, February 11, 1990; see Barbara Grizzuti Harrison, "The Importance of Being Oprah," *New York Times* magazine, June 11, 1989; David Singer, "The Crystal Cathedral: Reflections on Schuller's Theology," *Christianity Today* (August 8, 1980): 28–29; see the elegant fiftieth-anniversary volume of Ernest Holmes's *Science of Mind* and current editions of Emmet Fox's *Sermon on the Mount*.

On President Bill Clinton's interest in Robert Schuller's "possibility thinking," see Gustav Niebuhr, "Not All Presidential Advisers Dwell on the Political World," *New York Times*, March 18, 1997, and Niebuhr, "Putting Life's Trials in a Sacred Context," *Sunday New York Times*, February 9, 1997.

19. A. Whitney Griswold, "New Thought: A Cult of Success," *American Journal of Sociology* 40 (November 1934): 311, 313; Richard Weiss, *The American Myth of Success: From Horatio Alger to Norman Vincent Peale* (Urbana: University of Illinois Press, [1969] 1988), 14; see Huber, *American Idea of Success*; John G. Cawelti, *Apostles of the Self-Made Man* (Chicago: University of Chicago Press, 1965); Meyer, *Positive Thinkers*.

There are two institutional histories that uncritically portray New Thought as an idealistic and spiritually oriented faith. See Braden, *Spirits in Rebellion* and Horatio W. Dresser, *A History of the New Thought Movement* (New York: Thomas Y. Crowell Co., 1919). Also see J. Stillson Judah, *The History of Metaphysical Movements in America* (Philadelphia: Westminster Press, 1967). Sydney E. Ahlstrom offers a balanced appraisal of New Thought as part of the broader American tradition of "Harmonial Religion" in *A Religious History of the American People* vol. 2 (Garden City, N.Y.: Image Books, 1975), 536–39. Historians of Christian Science typically discuss New Thought as a shortlived heresy that Mary Baker Eddy successfully contained. See Gottschalk, *Emergence of Christian Science* and Peel, *Mary Baker Eddy*.

20. Meyer, *Positive Thinkers*, 124, 229–30; Gail Thain Parker, *Mind Cure in New England* (Hanover: University Press of New England, 1973), 10, 11.

21. See Dresser, *History of New Thought*, 309; Meyer, *Positive Thinkers*, 46; Huber, *American Idea of Success*, 131–32; Parker, *Mind Cure in New England*, 17; Gary L. Ward, "The Feminist Theme of Early New Thought," ISAR Occasional Paper no. 1 (unpublished paper, 1989), 9–11.

22. J[ohn] E[mery] M[clean], "Growth By Absorption," *Mind* 7, no. 6 (March 1901): 464.

23. Here and throughout this study I put parentheses around the phrase "white" or "Anglo-Saxon" as a modifier for "man" or "woman." In so doing I am following the lead of Louise Michele Newman, who points out that "in dominant discourses [of the nineteenth century] such terms as 'woman,' 'man' and 'the race' were almost always used without modifiers, even when the speaker clearly meant the statement to apply only to members of the group specified by the absent (parenthetical) terms. . . . To simply use the racial, gender or class modifiers (egs. white, female, middle-class) without parentheses . . . would give the false impression that the nineteenth-century discourse was nuanced in this way. To leave the parenthetical terms out altogether would perpetuate the racism and classism of the nineteenth century." See Louise Michele Newman, "Laying Claim to Difference: Ideologies of Race and Gender in the U.S. Woman's Movement, 1870–1920" (Ph.D. dissertation, Brown University, 1992), 4–5.

24. Historians have not fully grasped the contours of this debate. Carroll Smith-Rosenberg discussed the battling images of lustful manhood and unnatural womanhood that existed in the latter decades of the nineteenth century, but did not examine the relationship between these images and discourses of evolutionary race progress. Richard Hofstadter outlined the differences between social Darwinists and reform Darwinists, but did not indicate the ways in which their differences included opposing perspectives on manhood and womanhood. Gail Bederman elucidated the connections between social Darwinism and new constructions of racialized manliness, but did not investigate the ways in which purity-oriented woman-movement leaders recast evolutionary discourses in order to support new ideals of white womanhood. Many recent scholars have detailed the anti-"feminization" backlash of the late nineteenth century. None has examined the nexus of ideas that helped trigger this backlash—specifically, the claim that "advanced" womanhood represented the pinnacle of race evolution.

See Carroll Smith-Rosenberg, "The Abortion Movement and the AMA, 1850–1880" and "The New Woman as Androgyne: Social Disorder and Gender Crisis, 1870–1936," in *Disorderly Conduct: Visions of Gender in Victorian America* (New York: Oxford University Press, 1985), 217–96; Richard Hofstadter, *Social Darwinism in American Thought* (Boston: Beacon Press, [1944], 1955); Gail Bederman, *Manliness and Civilization: A Cultural History of Gender and Race in the United States, 1880–1917* (Chicago: University of Chicago Press, 1995); E. Anthony Rotundo, *American Manhood: Transformations in Masculinity from the Revolution to the Modern Era* (New York: Basic Books, 1993), 222–83; George Chauncey, *Gay New York: Gender, Urban Culture, and the Making of the Gay Male World, 1890–1940* (New York: Basic Books, 1994), 99–127.

25. Bederman, *Manliness and Civilization*, 108, 25; Cynthia Eagle Russett, *Sexual Science: The Victorian Construction of Womanhood* (Cambridge, Mass.: Harvard University Press, 1989), 144–48.

26. See Therese A. Jenkins, "The Mental Force of Woman," *Popular Science Monthly*, April 1889, in Louise Michele Newman, ed., *Men's Ideas/*

Women's Realities: Popular Science, 1870–1915 (New York: Pergamon Press, 1985), 219.

27. See Lucinda B. Chandler, "The Completion of Humanity," *Mind* 10, no. 5 (August 1902): 372, 371.

28. Nellie V. Anderson, *The Right Knock: A Story* (Nellie V. Anderson: Chicago, 1889), 122; Helen Wilmans, *A Blossom of the Century* (Sea Breeze, Florida: Freedom Publishing Company, 1898), 43–44; M.[alinda] E. Cramer, *Basic Statements and Health Treatment of Truth*, 2d ed. (San Francisco: M. E. Cramer, 1893), 52; H. Emilie Cady, *Lessons in Truth* (Kansas City, Mo.: Unity School of Christianity, n.d.), 57–58 (her italics); Abby Morton Diaz, *Only a Flock of Women* (Boston: D. Lothrop Co., 1893), 50; Helen Wilmans and Ada Wilmans Powers, *Back Numbers: Wilmans Express, Condensed* (n.p., n.d.) 62; see Eddy, *Science and Health*, 529, 306–7; Evans, *Esoteric Christianity*, 41.

29. See Christopher Herbert, *Culture and Anomie: Ethnographic Imagination in the Nineteenth Century* (Chicago: University of Chicago Press, 1991).

30. See Cynthia D. Schrager, "Pauline Hopkins and William James: The New Psychology and the Politics of Race," *The Unruly Voice: Rediscovering Pauline Elizabeth Hopkins*, ed. John Cullen Gruesser (Urbana: University of Illinois Press, 1996), 182–210; Cynthia D. Schrager, "Both Sides of the Veil: Race, Science, and Mysticism in W. E. B. Du Bois," *American Quarterly* 48, no. 4 (December 1996): 551–98; see, for example, James T. Haley, comp., *Sparkling Gems of Race Knowledge Worth Reading* (Nashville: J. T. Haley and Co., 1897).

Ellen M. Umansky has researched "Jewish Science," or a Jewish version of Eddy's Christian Science, in the 1920s and 1930s. Since her project covers a period outside the parameters of my study, I have not included a summary of it here. See Ellen M. Umansky, *From Christian Science to Jewish Science: Spiritual Healing and American Jews* (Oxford University Press, forthcoming).

31. See Rita Felski, *The Gender of Modernity* (Cambridge: Harvard University Press, 1995), 142–43.

CHAPTER 1

1. Birney's speech of February 17, 1897, is quoted in *Through the Years: From the Scrapbook of Mrs. Mears* (Washington D.C.: National Congress of Parents and Teachers, n.d.), 28.

2. Lester Ward, *Dynamic Sociology* (New York: 1892), vol. 1, cited in William Leach, *True Love and Perfect Union: The Feminist Reform of Sex and Society* (New York: Basic Books, 1980), 95.

3. Mary A. Livermore, *The Story of My Life* (1899), cited in Mari Jo Buhle, *Women and American Socialism, 1870–1920* (Urbana: University of Illinois Press, 1981), 49.

4. Louise Michele Newman, *Men's Ideas/Women's Realities: Popular Science, 1870–1915* (New York: Pergamon Press, 1985) 54–55, 254; Alice Kessler-Harris, *Out to Work: A History of Wage-Earning Women in the United States* (Oxford: Oxford University Press, 1982), 110–40.

5. Ruth Bordin, *Woman and Temperance: The Quest for Power and Liberty, 1873–1900* (Philadelphia: Temple University Press, 1981), 52–53, 140; David Pivar, *Purity Crusade: Sexual Morality and Social Control, 1868–1900* (Westport, Conn.: Greenwood Press, 1973), 57–63, 112–19, 228–29. Membership in the General Federation snowballed throughout the 1890s and early 1900s. By 1914, the organization had 1,600,000 members. Karen J. Blair, *The Clubwoman as Feminist: True Womanhood Redefined, 1868–1914* (New York: Holmes and Meier, 1980), 142 n. 22.

6. Nancy F. Cott, *The Grounding of Modern Feminism* (New Haven: Yale University Press, 1987), 3–7.

7. "Woman's Kingdom" scrapbook, vol. 5, 28 June 1883, Schlesinger Library, EBH papers, cited in Steven M. Buechler, *The Transformation of the Woman Suffrage Movement: The Case of Illinois, 1850–1920* (New Brunswick: Rutgers University Press, 1986), 116.

8. Blair, *Clubwoman as Feminist*, 40; Paul Boyer, *Urban Masses and Moral Order in America* (Cambridge: Harvard University Press, 1978), 151, see 149, 153; Charles M. Sheldon, *In His Steps* (New York: Grosset and Dunlap, [1896] 1935), 65; cover illustration for Consul Mrs. Booth-Tucker, *Rules and Regulations for Rescue Officers*, 1897. Also see Anne Firor Scott, *Natural Allies: Women's Associations in American History* (Urbana: University of Illinois Press, 1993), 107, 114, 133, for accounts of womanly influence.

9. Woman's Parliament pamphlet, 1869, cited in Blair, *Clubwoman as Feminist*, 42. Croly made similar comments about Sorosis, the first woman's club. The club's purpose was "to bring the moral force of all good women to bear in a given direction." See Jane Croly, *Sorosis: Its Origin and History* (New York: Press of J. J. Little, 1886), 23, cited in Blair, 42.

10. Sorosis minutes, October 20, 1873, cited in Blair, *Clubwoman as Feminist*, 46, also see 49.

11. For "teachers of science," see Malinda E. Cramer, *Lessons in the Science of Infinite Spirit and the Christ Method of Healing* (San Francisco: M.E. Cramer, 1890), iv, 100; "Hopkins Metaphysical Association," *Christian Science* III no. 3 (November 1889): 85. Affirmations and denials are from Nellie V. Anderson, *The Right Knock: A Story* (Nellie V. Anderson: Chicago, 1889), 122, and Annie Rix Militz, *Primary Lessons in Christian Living and Healing* (New York: The Absolute Press, 1904), 90.

12. Helen Wilmans, "The New Cult," *Christian Science Thought* (June, 1890): 10, cited in Gary L. Ward, "The Feminist Theme of Early New Thought," ISAR Occasional Paper no. 1 (unpublished paper, 1989), 9; Louisa Southworth, "The Baccalaureate," *Christian Science* 1 no. 6 (February 1889): 144; Elizabeth Boynton Harbert, *Amore* (New York: Lovell, Gestefeld and Co., 1892), 40, 185 (her italics), 189, 231, 237. Also see Horatio W. Dresser's claim that "The New Thought became in fact one of the signs that 'this is woman's day,'" in Dresser, *A History of the New Thought Movement* (New York: Thomas Y. Crowell, 1919), 309.

13. Thomas Laqueur, "Orgasm, Generation and the Politics of Reproductive Biology," and Londa Schiebinger, "Skeletons in the Closet: The First Illustrations of the Female Skeleton in Eighteenth-Century Anatomy," in Catherine Gallagher and Thomas Laqueur, eds., *The Making of the Modern Body: Sexuality and Society in the Nineteenth Century* (Berkeley: University of California Press, 1987); Stephen Jay Gould, *The Mismeasure of Man* (New York: Norton and Company, 1981); Mary Poovey, *Uneven Developments: The Ideological Work of Gender in Mid-Victorian England* (Chicago: University of Chicago Press, 1988), 11.

14. Laqueur, "Politics of Reproductive Biology," 27; Carroll Smith-Rosenberg and Charles Rosenberg, "The Female Animal: Medical and Biological Views of Woman and Her Role in Nineteenth-Century America," *Journal of American History* LX (1973): 334.

15. Charles E. Rosenberg, *No Other Gods: On Science and American Social Thought* (Baltimore: John Hopkins Press, 1976), 26–39.

16. G. J. Barker-Benfield, *The Horrors of the Half-Known Life* (New York: Harper Colophon Books, 1976), 175–88: Nathan G. Hale, Jr., *Freud and the Americans: The Beginnings of Psychoanalysis in the United States, 1876–1917* (New York: Oxford University Press, 1971), 34–35.

17. See Robert E. Shalhope, "Republicanism and Early American Historiography," *William and Mary Quarterly*, Third Series, XXXIX (1982): 334–56; Jan Lewis, "The Republican Wife: Virtue and Seduction in the Early Republic," *William and Mary Quarterly* XLIV, no. 4 (October 1987): 689–721.

18. Barker-Benfield, *Horrors of Half-Known Life*; Sarah Stage, *Female Complaints: Lydia Pinkham and the Business of Women's Medicine* (New York: W. W. Norton, 1979), 70–73; Sally Shuttleworth, "Female Circulation: Medical Discourse and Popular Advertising in the Mid-Victorian Era," in Mary Jacobus et. al., eds., *Body/Politics: Women and the Discourses of Science* (New York: Routledge, 1990), 57; John S. Haller and Robin M. Haller, *The Physician and Sexuality in Victorian America* (New York: W. W. Norton, 1974).

19. Shuttleworth, "Female Circulation," 56–57; see Stage, *Female Complaints*, 73–74.

20. Mary Ryan, *The Cradle of the Middle Class* (Cambridge: Cambridge University Press, 1981), 146–55; Jeanne Boydston, *Home and Work: Housework, Wages, and the Ideology of Labor in the Early Republic* (New York: Oxford University Press, 1990); see Shuttleworth, "Female Circulation," 54–55.

21. Barker-Benfield, *Horrors of Half-Known Life*, 193–96; Buechler, *Transformation of Woman Suffrage*, 48–49.

22. Nancy F. Cott, "Passionlessness: An Interpretation of Victorian Sexual Ideology, 1790–1850," in Nancy F. Cott and Elizabeth H. Pleck, *A Heritage of Her Own* (New York: Simon and Schuster, 1979); also see Michel Foucault, *The History of Sexuality, Volume 1: An Introduction*, translated by Robert Hurley (New York: Vintage Books, 1980).

23. Laqueur, "Politics of Reproductive Biology," 30. See also Barker-Benfield, *Horrors of Half-Known Life*, 41–44.

24. Kathryn Kish Sklar, *Catharine Beecher: A Study in American Domesticity* (New York: Norton and Company, 1973), 81–86; Barbara Epstein, *The Politics of Domesticity: Women, Evangelism and Temperance in Nineteenth Century America* (Middletown: Wesleyan University Press, 1981), 85. See Nancy F. Cott, *The Bonds of Womanhood: "Woman's Sphere" in New England, 1780 –1835* (New Haven: Yale University Press, 1977), 199–201; Barbara J. Berg, *The Remembered Gate: Origins of American Feminism* (Oxford: Oxford University Press, 1978); Carroll Smith-Rosenberg, "Beauty, the Beast and the Militant Woman" and "Bourgeois Discourse in the Age of Jackson," in *Disorderly Conduct: Visions of Gender in Victorian America* (New York: Oxford University Press, 1985), 79–89, 109–28; see Sally L. Kitch, *Chaste Liberation: Celibacy and Female Cultural Status* (Urbana: University of Illinois Press, 1989), 26–28.

25. Jan Lewis, "Mother's Love: The Construction of an Emotion in Nineteenth-Century America," in Andrew E. Barnes and Peter N. Stearns, eds., *Social History and Issues in Human Consciousness: Some Interdisciplinary Connections* (New York: New York University Press, 1989), 212–20; Linda Kerber, *Women of the Republic: Intellect and Ideology in Revolutionary America* (New York: W. W. Norton, 1980), 185–232.

26. Lewis, "Mother's Love," 212–20; Cott, *Bonds of Womanhood,* 46–47, 70, 91, 94–96, 195–96; Ryan, *Cradle of the Middle Class,* 155–65; Amy Schrager Lang, *Prophetic Woman: Anne Hutchinson and the Problem of Dissent in the Literature of New England* (Berkeley: University of California Press, 1987), 3, 111, 143–45.

27. Cott, *Bonds of Womanhood,* 160–68.

28. Lang, *Prophetic Woman;* Gillian Brown, *Domestic Individualism: Imagining Self in Nineteenth-Century America* (Berkeley: University of California Press, 1990), 1–7.

29. Richard H. Brodhead, "Veiled Ladies: Towards a History of Antebellum Entertainment," *American Literary History* 1, no. 2 (summer 1989): 274–75; Lois W. Banner, *American Beauty* (New York: Alfred A. Knopf, 1983), 47–48; Susan Bordo, "Anorexia Nervosa: Psychopathology as the Crystallization of Culture," in Irene Diamond and Lee Quinby, eds., *Feminism and Foucault: Reflections on Resistance* (Boston: Northeastern University Press, 1988), 107.

30. J. G. Millingen, *The Passions; or Mind and Matter* (London: J. and D. Darling, 1848), 157, cited in Shuttleworth, "Female Circulation," 55 (my italics). Also see Johann-Jacob Bachofen, *Myth, Religion, and Mother-Right,* translated by Ralph Manheim (Princeton, N.J., 1967), in Susan Groag Bell and Karen M. Offen, eds., *Women, the Family, and Freedom: The Debate in Documents* I, 1750–1880 (Stanford: Stanford University Press, 1983), 381.

31. Burton J. Bledstein, *The Culture of Professionalism* (New York: Norton and Co., 1978); Richard Hofstadter, *The Age of Reform* (New York: Vintage Books, 1955); Robert H. Wiebe, *The Search for Order, 1877–1920* (New York: Hill and Wang, 1967); T. J. Jackson Lears, *No Place of Grace: Antimodernism and the Transformation of American Culture, 1880–1920* (New York: Pantheon

Books, 1981), 34, 40–41, 56; E. Anthony Rotundo, *American Manhood: Transformations in Masculinity from the Revolution to the Modern Era* (New York: Basic Books, 1993).

32. Alan Trachtenberg, *The Incorporation of America* (New York: Hill and Wang, 1982), 136.

33. Rita Felski, *The Gender of Modernity* (Cambridge: Harvard University Press, 1995), 61–90; Lawrence Birken, *Consuming Desire: Sexual Science and the Emergence of a Culture of Abundance, 1871–1914* (Ithaca: Cornell University Press, 1988), 22–37.

34. Daniel Joseph Singal, "Towards a Definition of American Modernism," *American Quarterly* 39, no. 1 (Spring 1987): 9; John D'Emilio and Estelle B. Freedman, *Intimate Matters: A History of Sexuality in America* (New York: Harper and Row, 1988), 172–73, 181.

35. Rotundo, *American Manhood,* 250–53.

36. Clarke, cited in Regina Markell Morantz-Sanchez, *Sympathy and Science: Women Physicians in American Medicine* (New York: Oxford University Press, 1985), 54; "Does Higher Education Unfit Women for Motherhood?," *Popular Science Monthly,* April 1905, in Louise Michele Newman, ed., *Men's Ideas / Women's Realities: Popular Science, 1870–1915* (New York: Pergamon Press, 1985), 152.

37. Edward H. Clarke, *Sex in Education,* in Bell and Offen, eds, *Women, the Family, and Freedom,* 427; Henry Maudsley, "Sex in Mind and in Education," *Popular Science Monthly,* June 1874, in Newman, ed., *Men's Ideas,* 79, 86.

38. On the significant differences between Darwin's and Spencer's ideas, see Richard Hofstadter, *Social Darwinism in American Thought* (Boston: Beacon Press, 1958); Louise Michele Newman, "Laying Claim to Difference: Ideologies of Race and Gender in the U.S. Woman's Movement, 1870–1920" (Ph.D. dissertation, Brown University, 1992), 33–34.

39. Rosalind Coward, *Patriarchal Precedents: Sexuality and Social Relations* (London: Routledge and Kegan Paul, 1983), 40, 63–65; Elizabeth Fee, "The Sexual Politics of Victorian Social Anthropology," in Mary Hartman and Lois W. Banner, eds., *Clio's Consciousness Raised: New Perspectives on the History of Women* (New York: Harper Colophon Books, 1974), 86–102. This analysis set the terms for debate about the relationships among women's virtue, male desire, and the progress of civilization, and informed both popular culture and the perspectives of theorists ranging from Matilda Joslyn Gage to Friedrich Engels and Edward Carpenter. See Rosemary Radford Ruether, "Radical Victorians: The Quest for an Alternative Culture," in Rosemary Radford Ruether and Rosemary Skinner Keller, eds., *Women and Religion in America Vol. 3: 1900–1968* (New York: Harper and Row, 1986), 1–10, and documents following on 14–30. Also see Eliza Burt Gamble, "The Influence of Sex on Development," *Mind* VIII, no. 2 (May, 1901): 95–100; W. E. Clark, "Woman, Man and Poverty," *Mind* X, no. 4 (July, 1902): 278–85; Frances Willard, "Annual Minutes," 22nd Annual Meeting, 1895, 59, cited in Epstein, *Politics of Domesticity,* 137; Elizabeth Cady Stanton, "The Matriarchate," in Aileen S. Kra-

ditor, ed., *Up From the Pedestal: Selected Writings in the History of American Feminism* (Chicago: Quadrangle Books, 1968), 140–47.

40. Poovey, *Uneven Developments*, 114–15.

41. Fee, "Sexual Politics," 97–101.

42. Lester Frank Ward, "Mind as a Social Factor," 1884, in David A. Hollinger and Charles Capper, eds., *The American Intellectual Tradition*, vol. 2, 1865 to the present, 2d ed. (New York: Oxford University Press, 1993), 42, 45 (Ward's italics); Hofstadter, *Social Darwinism*, 45–48, 74–75, 96, 104, 110.

43. Ward, in Hollinger and Capper, 46; Hofstadter, *Social Darwinism*, 94, 176–78.

44. Newman, "Laying Claim," 38.

45. Hofstadter, *Social Darwinism*, 94, 176–77.

46. Josiah Strong, *Our Country*, excerpted in Thomas G. Paterson, ed., *Major Problems in American Foreign Policy* volume I: to 1914 (Lexington, Mass.: D. C. Health and Co.), 347–49.

47. Gail Bederman, *Manliness and Civilization: A Cultural History of Gender and Race in the United States, 1880–1917* (Chicago: University of Chicago Press, 1995), 49–50.

48. Bederman, *Manliness and Civilization*, 79–108.

49. See Singal, "American Modernism."

50. Rotundo, *American Manhood*, 240; David Axeen, "'Heroes of the Engine Room': American 'Civilization' and the War with Spain," *American Quarterly* 36, no. 4 (Fall 1984): 482–502; Bederman, *Manliness and Civilization*, 16–17.

51. Newman, "Laying Claim," 5–7; see Bederman, *Manliness and Civilization*, 121–69.

52. Benjamin Flower, "Edwin Markham: A Prophet-Poet of the Fraternal State," *The Arena* XXVII, no. 4 (April 1902): 392, 404, 395; Charlotte Perkins Gilman, *The Man-Made World, or Our Androcentric Culture* (New York, 1911), 22, and Gilman, *Women and Economics: A Study of the Economic Relation Between Men and Women as a Factor in Social Evolution* (Boston, 1898), 74, both cited in Bederman, *Manliness and Civilization*, 153, 143–44.

53. William Jay Youmans, "Individuality for Woman," *Popular Science Monthly*, September 1891, in Newman, ed., *Men's Ideas*, 306; see Kate Gannett Wells, "Why More Girls Do Not Marry," *North American Review* 152 (January–June, 1891): 181.

54. See Mary Livermore's call for women to be active with "hand and head and heart," in *Story of My Life*, cited in Buhle, 49; Frances Willard's description of Elizabeth Boynton Harbert's home as both an intellectual and a "heart" center, in Willard, *A Classic Town: The Story of Evanston* (Chicago: Woman's Temperance Publishing Assoc., 1891), 367, and her call for women of "brains" and "heart" in "The Dawn of Woman's Day," in Nancy F. Cott et al., eds., *Root of Bitterness: Documents of the Social History of American Women*, 2d. ed. (Boston: Northeastern University Press, 1996), 403; description of Alice B. Stockham as a woman of "breadth of mind" and "largeness of heart" in "In-

terview in 'The Woman's Penny Paper' (London) with Doctor Alice B. Stockham," in back pages of Alice B. Stockham and Lida Hood Talbot, *Koradine Letters* (Chicago: Alice B. Stockham and Co., 1893), copy located in Frances Willard's personal library, National Woman's Christian Temperance Union Archives, Evanston, Ill.; Kate Gannett Wells's constant invocation of women's "mind and heart" in her essay "Why More Girls Do Not Marry," 175–81; Helen Campbell's call for "the concerted action of women who . . . think and feel" in "Women and the Civic Sense," *New Time* October 1897: 199; Annie L. Muzzey's description of Charlotte Perkins Gilman as a woman of "spiritual insight and a keen analytic sense" in "The Hour and the Woman," *The Arena* 22 (August 1899): 269; see Carolyn DeSwarte Gifford, ed., *Writing Out My Heart: Selections from the Journal of Frances E. Willard, 1855–1896* (Urbana: University of Illinois Press, 1995), 7–8.

This praise of refined women's "mind and heart" sometimes became extreme. One male reformer described female temperance and social purity leaders as "women of intellectual and spiritual power" who were a "moral and intellectual force," commanding "intellectual power and moral enthusiasm," and in general "intellectually brilliant and morally courageous." Benjamin Flower, *Progressive Men, Women and Movements of the Past Twenty-Five Years* (Boston: The New Arena, 1914), 143–45, 150.

Southern African American seminaries and colleges used an altered version of this slogan. They encouraged their students to develop their "Head, Heart and Hands"—that is, their spirituality, morality, and practicality. See Glenda Elizabeth Gilmore, *Gender and Jim Crow* (Chapel Hill: University of North Carolina Press, 1996), 11, 40.

55. Lucinda B. Chandler, "The Completion of Humanity," *Mind* X, no. 5 (August 1902): 371; Therese A. Jenkins, "The Mental Force of Woman," *Popular Science Monthly*, April 1889, in Newman, ed., *Men's Ideas*, 219.

56. See *Popular Science Monthly* essays in Newman, ed., *Men's Ideas*, 150, 202, 226, 321.

57. Carroll Smith-Rosenberg, "The Abortion Movement and the AMA, 1850–1880," in Smith-Rosenberg, *Disorderly Conduct*, 243–44; Linda Gordon, *Women's Body, Women's Right: A Social History of Birth Control in America* (New York: Penguin Books, [1974] 1977), 121, 126–29; Alice B. Stockham, *Tokology: A Book For Every Woman*, rev. ed. (Chicago: Alice B. Stockham and Co., [1883] 1894), 158; B. O. Flower, "Leprosy of the Soul," *The Arena* III (1890–91): 637, 638.

58. Ellen Coit Elliott, "Let Us Therewith Be Content," *Popular Science Monthly*, July 1897, in Newman, ed., *Men's Ideas*, 318; Chandler, "Completion of Humanity," 371 (her italics); Wells, "Why More Girls Do Not Marry," 176, see 179; also see Willard, "Dawn," in Cott et al., eds., *Root of Bitterness*, 400; Elizabeth Boynton Harbert, "Woman Suffrage—Why It Would Prove Advantageous" (1878), cited in Buechler, *Transformation of Woman Suffrage*, 113.

59. Pivar, *Purity Crusade;* Gordon, *Woman's Body*, 125.

60. Elizabeth Boynton Harbert, "Woman's Kingdom," Chicago *Inter-*

Ocean, March 3, 1877, cited in Leach, *True Love and Perfect Union,* 97; Winnifred Harper Cooley, "The Future of the Woman's Club," 380. Also see Harbert, *Amore,* 13; Lizzie M. Holmes, "Woman's Future Position in the World," *The Arena* 20 (September 1898): 342; Paul Tyner, *Through the Invisible: A Love Story* (New York: Continental Publishing, 1897), 179, 180.

61. Freedman and D'Emilio, *Intimate Matters,,* 153. See Mariana Valverde, "'When the Mother of the Race is Free': Race, Reproduction, and Sexuality in First-Wave Feminism," in Franca Iacovetta and Mariana Valverde, eds., *Gender Conflicts: New Essays in Women's History* (Toronto: University of Toronto Press, 1992), 20; see "Address by Mrs. Mary A. Livermore," in *The National Purity Congress, Its Papers, Addresses, Portraits,* ed. Aaron M. Powell (New York, 1896), 380.

62. Mrs. Mary Lowe Dickinson, "Response to Address of Welcome," in *The Work and Words of the National Congress of Mothers* (New York, 1897), 13, 20.

63. Gage, "Series of Conventions of the NWSA," *Ballot Box,* June 1881, cited in Leach, *True Love and Perfect Union,* 388 n. 71; see Stanton in Leach, 147.

64. B. O. Flower, "The Era of Woman," *The Arena* 4 (1891): 382, 384; Cora Maynard, "The Woman's Part," *The Arena* 7 (March, 1893): 485.

Numerous late-nineteenth-century authors referred to the "woman's era." See Richard Ely, "Introduction" to Helen Campbell, *Women Wage-Earners: Their Past, Their Present and Their Future* (Boston: Roberts Brothers, 1893), cited in Newman, "Laying Claim,"18; Hazel Carby, *Reconstructing Womanhood: The Emergence of the Afro-American Woman Novelist* (New York: Oxford University Press, 1987); Evelyn Brooks Higginbotham, *Righteous Discontent: The Women's Movement in the Baptist Church, 1880–1920* (Cambridge: Harvard University Press, 1993), 1; Felski, *Gender of Modernity,* 160–61.

65. Augusta Cooper Bristol, "Enlightened Motherhood," *Papers and Letters Presented at the First Woman's Congress of the Association for the Advancement of Women* (New York, 1874), 10–14, cited in Leach, *True Love and Perfect Union,* 93.

Calls for women to triumph over the flesh were common in the late nineteenth century. See Gordon, *Woman's Body,* 118–20, 126; *Letters from a Chimney-Corner,* 1886, cited in Haller and Haller, *Physician and Sexuality,* 90; Pivar, *Purity Crusade,* 155–56; Kitch, *Chaste Liberation,* 138; A. J. Swarts, "What is the Lamb?" *The Mind Cure* (December 1884): 39–41; S. Annie Yates, "The New Day," *The Christian Metaphysician* (January 1887): 12.

66. Frances Willard, "The Coming Brotherhood," *The Arena* VI (1892): 321–22; see Brown, *Domestic Individualism,* 24, 31–32; also Gordon, *Woman's Body,* 118–20.

67. Buhle, *Women and American Socialism,* 70, 84, 88; Meredith Tax, *The Rising of the Women: Feminist Solidarity and Class Conflict, 1880–1917* (New York: Monthly Review Press, 1980), 32–33; Epstein, *Politics of Domesticity,* 142–43.

68. Josephine Locke, "Beauty, the King's Messenger," *Christian Science* III no. 6 (February 1891): 173.

69. Harbert, *Amore*, 85; Helen Campbell, "Social Settlements and the Civic Sense," *The Arena* 20, no. 5 (November–December 1898): 590; see Abby Morton Diaz, "The Human Problem According to Law," *The Arena* 6 (1895): 623.

70. Abby Morton Diaz, *Spirit as a Power* (Belmont, Mass.: 1886), 17, see 19; Lucinda B. Chandler, "The Woman Movement," *The Arena* IV (1891): 705–6; Frances Willard, "The Woman's Cause is Man's," *The Arena* V (1891–92): 718. Maria Montessori also believed that the triumph of technology over brute force meant that "the reign of woman is approaching." See Montessori, *Pedagogical Anthropology* (1913), cited in Gould, *Mismeasure of Man*, 107.

71. Leach, *True Love and Perfect Union*, 153; Auguste Comte, "The Influence of Positivism upon Women," in his *General View of Positivism*, translated by J. H. Bridges (London, 1875; reprinted., Stanford, Calif., n.d.), in Bell and Offen, eds., *Women, the Family and Freedom*, 223.

72. Ward, "Mind as a Social Factor," 42–43; Strong, quoted in Dorothea R. Muller, "The Social Philosophy of Josiah Strong: Social Christianity and American Progressivism," *Church History* 28 (1959): 185, see 195; Ely, quoted in Robert M. Crunden, *Ministers of Reform* (Urbana: University of Illinois Press, 1984), 13. Also see Susan E. Henking, "Sociological Christianity and Christian Sociology: The Paradox of Early American Sociology," *Religion and American Culture* 3, no. 1 (winter 1993): 51.

73. Comte, "Influence of Positivism," 224; see Lang, *Prophetic Woman*, 138–59.

74. Articles by Stanton in *Revolution*, August 13, November 26, December 17, 1868, and May 13, 1869, cited in Leach, *True Love and Perfect Union*, 148; see Leach, 141–43, 156–57.

75. Sanborn is quoted in Leach, *True Love and Perfect Union*, 316 (see 317–19, 321, 331); and in Arnaldo Testi, "The Gender of Reform Politics: Theodore Roosevelt and the Culture of Masculinity," *Journal of American History* 81, no. 4 (March 1995): 1,526.

76. See Epstein, *Politics of Domesticity*, 131–32; Bordin, *Woman and Temperance*, 135; Gordon, *Woman's Body*, 129; Pivar, *Purity Crusade*, 176; Leach, *True Love and Perfect Union*, 90; also Sheila Rothman, *Woman's Proper Place* (New York: Basic Books, 1978), 82.

77. See Kitch, *Chaste Liberation*, 136–41.

78. See Kitch, *Chaste Liberation*, 29–38.

79. See Rothman, *Woman's Proper Place*, 77, 85–93; Boyer, *Urban Masses and Moral Order*, 143–54.

80. See Ignatius Donnelly, *Caesar's Column: A Story of the Twentieth Century*, ed. Walter B. Rideout (Cambridge: Harvard University Press, [1890] 1960); John Graham, ed., *Yours for the Revolution: The Appeal to Reason, 1895–1922* (Lincoln: University of Nebraska Press, 1990), 52–3; Bederman, *Manliness and Civilization*, 65–67; Newman, "Laying Claim," 110.

81. *New York World,* March 23, 1869, cited in Blair, *Clubwoman as Feminist,* 37 (my italics).

82. Frank Podmore, *From Mesmer to Christian Science: A Short History of Mental Healing* (New Hyde Park, NY: University Books, 1963), 39; see Robert Fuller, *Mesmerism and the American Cure of Souls* (Philadelphia: University of Pennsylvania Press, 1982).

83. Robert Darnton, *Mesmerism and the End of the Enlightenment in France* (New York: Schocken Books, 1970); Fuller, *Mesmerism and the American Cure,* 2–3.

84. See Podmore, *From Mesmer to Christian Science,* 79.

85. Ibid., 134–35, 143, 150; George Frederick Drinka, M.D., *The Birth of Neurosis: Myth, Malady, and the Victorians* (New York: Touchstone Books, 1984), 133; Terry M. Parssinen, "Professional Deviants and the History of Medicine: Medical Mesmerists in Victorian Britain," in Roy Wallis, ed., *On the Margins of Science: The Social Construction of Rejected Knowledge* (Keele, Staffordshire: University of Keele, 1979); see Robert C. Fuller, *Alternative Medicine and American Religious Life* (New York: Oxford University Press, 1898), 28, 40–42, 47–48, 55–6, 67–89; see Ann Braude, *Radical Spirits: Spiritualism and Women's Rights in Nineteenth-Century America* (Boston: Beacon Press, 1989), 34.

86. Henri F. Ellenberger, *The Discovery of the Unconscious* (New York: Basic Books, 1970), 82; Parssinen, "Professional Deviants,"116; Drinka, *Birth of Neurosis,* 83.

87. Ellenberger, *Discovery of the Unconscious,* 750; Drinka, *Birth of Neurosis,* 134–45.

88. Drinka, *Birth of Neurosis,* 144–45.

89. Ibid., 146.

90. Mrs. J. H. Kellogg, "Purity and Parental Responsibility," in Powell, *The National Purity Congress,* 214; see Paul Starr, *The Social Transformation of American Medicine* (New York: Basic Books, 1982), 135; Boyer, *Urban Masses,* 146.

Social purity campaigns implied an undercurrent of concern over how "civilized" Americans could both increase economic circulation and maintain social barriers. See Peter Stallybrass and Allon White, *The Politics and Poetics of Transgression* (Ithaca, N.Y.: Cornell University Press, 1986); Pivar, *Purity Crusade,* 109, 150, 160–61, 181; Freedman and D'Emilio, *Intimate Matters,* 158–59; Chas. M. Barrow, *Facts and Fictions of Mental Healing* (Boston: H. H. Carter and Karrick, 1887), 153–54.

91. Cited in Trachtenberg, *Incorporation of America,* 213.

92. Boyer, *Urban Masses,* 149.

93. Jacob A. Riis, *How the Other Half Lives* (New York: Dover Publications, 1971), 216, 221.

94. George Beard, *American Nervousness, Its Causes and Consequences* (New York: G. P. Putnam's Sons, 1881) viii–ix, cited in F. G. Gosling, *Before Freud: Neurasthenia and the American Medical Community, 1870–1910* (Ur-

bana: University of Illinois Press, 1987), 14; see Tom Lutz, *American Nervousness, 1903: An Anecdotal History* (Ithaca, N.Y.: Cornell University Press, 1991).

95. Carroll Smith-Rosenberg, "The Hysterical Woman: Sex Roles and Role Conflict in Nineteenth-Century America," in *Disorderly Conduct*, 197–216.

The diagnosis of neurasthenia encompassed cases formerly diagnosed as hysteria. It seems appropriate, therefore, to draw upon Smith-Rosenberg's work on hysteria in order to interpret neurasthenia. See Gosling, *Before Freud*, 9.

96. Gosling, *Before Freud*, 87, see 109, 115–16, 132; also Hale, *Freud and the Americans*, 44, 55–56; and Lutz, *American Nervousness*.

97. Gosling, *Before Freud*, xi, 98–101, 112–13, 46, 23, 58–62. Also see Stage, *Female Complaints*, 79–81; Barker-Benfield, *Horrors of the Half-Known Life*, 120–32; Ellen L. Bassuk, "The Rest Cure: Repetition or Resolution of Victorian Women's Conflicts?" in Susan Rubin Suleiman, ed., *The Female Body in Western Culture* (Cambridge: Harvard University Press, 1986), 141–43; Lutz, *American Nervousness*.

98. Charles G. Hill, Presidential Address to the American Medico-Psychological Association, *American Journal of Insanity* 64 (July 1907), 6, cited in Hale, *Freud and the Americans*, 17.

99. Barbara Sicherman, *The Quest for Mental Health in America, 1880–1917* (New York: Arno Press, 1980), 343; Hale, *Freud and the Americans*, 76, 53.

100. Gosling, *Before Freud*, 40, 63–65, 109, 126, 130–31.

101. Mental healers claimed to heal all forms of illness, from poor eyesight to cancer. Diagnostic techniques were still highly inaccurate in the 1880s and 1890s, however. Patients with "cancer" or "tuberculosis" may have suffered from any combination of bacterial, viral or psychosomatic ills.

Many mental healers explicitly limited themselves to "nervous and chronic diseases." For example, see advertisement for C. B. Patterson's "Mental Healing Institute" in final pages of *Truth*, November 1887; Dr. Eugene Weeks's notice in *Christian Science*, 1 no. 6 (February 1889): 169.

CHAPTER 2

1. Mary Baker Eddy, *Science and Health with Key to the Scriptures* (Boston: First Church of Christ, Scientist, 1971), 268.

2. Warren Felt Evans, *Esoteric Christianity and Mental Therapeutics* (Boston: Carter and Karrick, 1886), 41.

3. Donald Meyer, *The Positive Thinkers* (New York: Pantheon Press, [1965] 1980); Gail Thain Parker, *Mind Cure in New England* (Hanover, New Hampshire: University Press of New England, 1973).

4. Horatio W. Dresser, *A History of the New Thought Movement* (New York: Thomas Y. Crowell Co. 1919), vi–vii, 19–170; Charles S. Braden, *Spirits in Rebellion: The Rise and Development of New Thought* (Dallas: Southern Methodist University Press, 1963), 47–88; Meyer, *Positive Thinkers*, 33–4; Richard Weiss, *The American Myth of Success* (Urbana: University of Illinois Press, [1969] 1988), 196–97; Richard Huber, *The American Idea of Success*

(New York: McGraw Hill, 1971), 128–29. See Robert Peel, *Mary Baker Eddy: The Years of Discovery, 1821–1875* (New York: Holt, Rinehart and Winston, 1966), 181–83, 231–33 for a detailed history of the Quimby Manuscripts.

Quimby's importance is questioned by Parker, *Mind Cure in New England*, 5, and in J. Gordon Melton's "New Thought's Hidden History: Emma Curtis Hopkins, Forgotten Founder" (unpublished paper, Institute for the Study of American Religion, August 1988).

5. Frank Podmore, *From Mesmer to Christian Science: A Short History of Mental Healing* (New Hyde Park, N.Y.: University Books, 1963), 250–51; Horatio W. Dresser, ed., *The Quimby Manuscripts* (New York: Thomas Y. Crowell Co., 1921), 30–5.

6. Dresser, ed., *Quimby Manuscripts*, 295–97, 301–5, 307–8; see Catherine L. Albanese, "Physic and Metaphysic in Nineteenth-Century America: Medical Sectarians and Religious Healing," *Church History* 55 (December 1986), 498.

7. Dresser, ed., *Quimby Manuscripts*, 328, see 351–55; see Braden, *Spirits in Rebellion*, 54, 65, 69–71, 78–9, 83.

8. Dresser, ed., *Quimby Manuscripts*, 386, 384, 395.

9. Ibid., 387, see 393.

10. Ibid., 394, see 386, 384. Quimby wrote, "It has always been the case that all spiritual wisdom has been received through the female. . . . As men's minds are more brutal and less *scientific or spiritual*, they never believe till they can see with the natural man's eyes. Science to them is a shadow" (387–88 [my italics]).

11. Ibid., 394–95, see 387.

12. Sydney E. Ahlstrom's biographical sketch of Mary Baker Eddy in Edward T. James, Janet Wilson James, and Paul S. Boyer, eds., *Notable American Women* (Cambridge: Belknap Press, 1971), see 552–53.

13. Robert Peel, *Mary Baker Eddy: The Years of Trial* (Chicago: Holt, Rinehart and Winston, 1971) 135–36; Edwin Franden Dakin, *Mrs. Eddy: The Biography of a Virginal Mind* (New York: Charles Scribner's Sons, 1929), 144; see Mary Baker Eddy, "Mind-Healing History," *Christian Science Journal* 5 no. 3 (June 1887): 109–18.

14. Eddy, *Science and Health*, 311; see 331.

Eddy produced approximately four hundred versions of *Science and Health* between 1875 and 1906. I have compared a number of early versions of *Science and Health* and have found the changes between these and later versions to be largely editorial. The following analysis therefore draws upon the last revised version, which is the text Eddy saw as the clearest enunciation of her beliefs. See Robert Peel, *Mary Baker Eddy: The Years of Authority, 1892–1919* (New York: Holt, Rinehart and Winston, 1977), 303, 382 n. 14.

15. Eddy, *Science and Health*, 337.

16. Ibid., 368, see 269.

17. Ibid., 332, 303.

18. Ibid., 414, 305.

19. "If life [the divine] were in mortal man or material things, it would be subject to their limitations and end in death," she explained. Ibid., 303, 331.

20. Ibid., 339, 327, 407.

21. Ibid., 377, 417.

22. Ibid., 396, 379, 409, 306, 411–13.

23. Ibid., 400, see 104.

24. See 1884 edition of *Science and Health*, 186.

25. Eddy, *Science and Health*, 103 (her italics), 412, see 375.

26. Ibid., 392.

27. Peel, *Years of Authority*, 393 n. 50; Eddy, *Science and Health*, 100.

28. Eddy, *Science and Health*, 102; see Charles Seymour, "Mortal Mind Cure Literature versus Christian Science," *Christian Science Journal* 5 no. 3 (June 1887): 144–46; Dakin, *Mrs. Eddy*, 186, also 129, 159–64, 175–76, 186–87; Peel, *Years of Authority*, 68.

29. The number of professional Christian Science healers who were women rose from 75% in 1890 to 89% in 1910. Penny Hanson, "Woman's Hour: Feminist Implications of Mary Baker Eddy's Christian Science Movement, 1885–1910" (Ph.D. dissertation, University of California, Irvine, 1981), 156. See "Sickness an Error," *Chicago Times*, June 15, 1888; "Men in our Ranks," *Christian Science Journal* 27 no. 12 (March 1910): 763; Charles S. Braden, *Christian Science Today: Power, Policy, Practice* (Dallas: Southern Methodist University Press, 1958), 108; Stephen Gottschalk, *The Emergence of Christian Science in American Religious Life* (Berkeley: University of California Press, 1978), 257; Peel, *Years of Trial*, 10.

30. See Hanson, "Woman's Hour"; Susan M. Setta, "Denial of the Female—Affirmation of the Feminine: The Father-Mother God of Mary Baker Eddy," in Rita M. Gross, ed., *Beyond Androcentrism: New Essays on Women and Religion* (Missoula, Mont.: Scholars Press for the American Academy of Religion, 1977); Susan L. Lindley, "The Ambiguous Feminism of Mary Baker Eddy," *Journal of Religion*, 64 (July 1984); Jean A. McDonald, "Mary Baker Eddy and the Nineteenth-Century 'Public' Woman: A Feminist Reappraisal," *Journal of Feminist Studies in Religion* 2 no. 1 (spring 1986): n. 47, 109.

31. A close reading of *Science and Health* seems an appropriate way to understand the movement's draw, since evidence suggests that early converts studied the text carefully. The majority of letters published in that volume report people being healed not by practitioners, but "through simply reading this wonderful book, *Science and Health*." See 607. On people reading the text numerous times in order to decipher its meaning, see 602, 613, 626, 622; also McDonald, "Mary Baker Eddy," 106.

32. Eddy, *Science and Health*, 391, 405–7, see 378.

33. Ibid., 529, 306–7; also see 214, 338, 579–80.

34. Ibid., 508. See Sally L. Kitch, *Chaste Liberation: Celibacy and Female Cultural Status* (Urbana: University of Illinois Press, 1989), 127; Ann Douglas, *The Feminization of American Culture* (New York: Avon Books, 1977), 151–52.

35. Eddy, *Science and Health*, 533–34.

36. Ibid., 534.

37. Ibid., 560.

38. Ibid., 268; also see 570.

39. Ibid., 561, 565.

40. That "matter" could stand both for "man" and for the female body is evidence of how contested the idea of corporeality was during this period. The newer idea that man stood for matter only thinly overlay the older claim that woman represented matter.

Christian Science and New Thought writings generally defined matter as the finite, changeable, and unreal, as opposed to spirit, which is infinite, unchanging and real. See Annie E. Rix, "There is No Matter," *Christian Science* 4, no. 1 (September 1891): 6–7; Frank H. Sprague, "What Do We Mean By Matter?" *Christian Science Journal* 27 (1909–1910): 719–24.

Scholars have offered their own interpretations of "matter." Gail Parker writes that "'matter' was machines, giant corporations, evolution interpreted as fated waste, cities, everything that made men uneasy by speed, noise, visual confusion, status uncertainty or the sensation of physical weakness." Parker, *Mind Cure in New England*, 24. Susan Setta argues that matter stood for the female body. See Setta, "Denial of the Female," 295–97. I find Setta's interpretation more convincing.

41. Eddy, *Science and Health*, 159 (my italics).

42. Ibid., 407, 272, 561.

43. Evans had spent twenty-five years as a Methodist minister when chronic nervous illness drove him to seek mental healing from Quimby in 1863. Successfully healed, Evans that same year quit the Methodist ministry and joined the Church of the New Jerusalem (Swedenborgian). In 1869 he and his wife M. Charlotte Tinker Evans began teaching and healing out of a Boston office. Between 1869 and 1886 he published six influential books on mental healing.

See Braden, *Spirits in Rebellion*, 89–128; Robert Allen Campbell, "Warren F. Evans," *Christian Metaphysician*, November 1888: 171–73; Dresser, *History of New Thought*, 71–96, 126–28; William Horatio Clark, "A New Thought Pioneer," *Mind* 9 no. 4 (January 1902): 283–85; Gottschalk, *Emergence of Christian Science*, 137; also Parker, *Mind Cure in New England*, 48–56 and John F. Teahan, "Warren Felt Evans and Mental Healing: Romantic Idealism and Practical Mysticism in Nineteenth-Century America," *Church History* 48 (March 1979): 63–80.

44. Braden, *Spirits in Rebellion*, 89, 92–93, 98, 103, 132–36; see Gottschalk, *Emergence of Christian Science*, 108–9; Peel, *Years of Trial*, 211.

45. The following analysis is based on Evans's final work, *Esoteric Christianity and Mental Therapeutics* (1886). Evans considered this study the culmination of his years of writings on the system he called "phrenopathic healing." It contained the essence of the twelve lessons he gave to his students.

46. Evans, *Esoteric Christianity*, 159, 6, see 57.

47. Ibid., 28.

48. Ibid., 36–37, 42.

49. Ibid., 156, 103, 54.

50. Ibid., 152. The affirmations he suggested in fact still made use of arguments. They generally stated that the human essence was divine. Therefore, since the divine could not be sick, we also could not really be ill (see 54).

51. Ibid., 17, 16, see 86.

52. Ibid., 18, 95–97.

53. Ibid., 103–4, 24, 13.

54. Ibid., 71 (his italics), see 100.

55. Ibid., 72. The Sermon on the Mount was to hold a continuing fascination for New Thought authors. See Annie Rix Militz, *The Sermon on the Mount* (Chicago: F. M. Harley Publishing Co., 1899); Horatio W. Dresser, "The Sermon on the Mount," in Dresser, ed., *The Spirit of the New Thought: Essays and Addresses* (New York: Thomas Y. Crowell Company, 1917); Emmet Fox, *The Sermon On the Mount* (New York: Harper and Brothers, 1934).

56. Evans, *Esoteric Christianity*, 73.

57. Ibid., 41, 28 (his italics), 44.

58. Ibid., 16.

59. Ibid., 43.

60. Ibid., 40 (his italics), 42.

61. Eddy, *Science and Health*, 561, 57.

62. Evans, *Esoteric Christianity*, 141, see 24.

63. Ibid., 19–20, 43, see 54.

64. Ibid., 54.

65. Eddy, *Science and Health*, 64. Eddy sometimes implied that with higher spiritual evolution, women would not need men in order to reproduce. When one of her followers proceeded to claim that she had had a virgin birth, Eddy was forced to discredit the idea. "The perpetuation of the floral species by bud or cell-division is evident, but I discredit the belief that agamogenesis applies to the human species," she wrote. As Phyllis Cole points out, however, Eddy's continued fascination with the idea is shown by her scattered references to Louis Agassiz, whose microscopic studies of a vulture's ovum seemed to indicate the possibility of spontaneously generated life. Eddy, *Science and Health*, 68, see 547, 561. As late as 1898, Eddy still implied that reproduction without heterosexual intercourse might be possible. She wrote that "The propagation of their species by butterfly, bee, and moth, without the customary presence of male companions, is a discovery corroborative of Science of Mind." See *Science and Health*, 33, 541, cited in Lyman Powell, *Christian Science: The Faith and Its Founder* (New York: G. P. Putman's Sons, 1907), 210.

66. Nancy F. Cott, "Passionlessness: An Interpretation of Victorian Sexual Ideology," in Nancy F. Cott and Elizabeth H. Pleck, eds., *A Heritage of Her Own* (New York: Simon and Schuster, 1979), 162–81.

67. Eddy, *Science and Health*, 305 (my italics), 414. As Eddy wrote in an essay entitled, "Man and Woman," "In the divine Mind there is no sex, no sexuality, no procreation: the Infinite Mind includes all in Mind" (cited in Peel, *Years of Authority*, 163).

68. Evans, *Esoteric Christianity*, 73.

69. Lawrence Birken, *Consuming Desire: Sexual Science and the Emergence of a Culture of Abundance, 1871–1914* (Ithaca: Cornell University Press, 1988), 22–37.

70. Evans, *Esoteric Christianity*, 28.

71. Ibid., 43.

CHAPTER 3

1. Emma Curtis Hopkins, quoted in *Christian Science* 2, no. 6 (February 1890): 184.

2. Emma Curtis Hopkins, *The Radiant I AM* (Putnam, Conn.: Emma Curtis Hopkins Publications, n.d.), 15.

3. See Gail Thain Parker, *Mind Cure in New England* (Hanover, New Hampshire: University Press of New England, 1973).

4. Paul Tyner, "The Metaphysical Movement," *The American Monthly Review of Reviews* 25 no. 3 (March 1902): 312–13.

5. Little is known of Emma Curtis Hopkins's early life. Emma Curtis had married George Irving Hopkins, a high school teacher whom she described as "discreet, reserved, [and] silent," in 1874, when she was twenty-four years old. Their son John Carver Hopkins was born a year later. At some point Emma Hopkins began to suffer an illness. It was rumored among New Thought leaders that her health problem involved difficulty with breathing. Hopkins's illness could also have been related to her troubled marriage. By the early 1880s her husband was in debt, and Emma Hopkins could not "command a single dollar" of her own. Many years later, in a private letter, Hopkins admitted a more disturbing aspect of her marriage. "My darling lamb went insane," she wrote in reference to her husband George. "He used to strike me. He did not know it. He had been always the soul of chivalry and loving kindness."

Letter, Emma Hopkins to Mary Baker Eddy, December 17, 1883, Archives of the First Church of Christ, Scientist, Boston, Mass., cited in Gail M. Harley, "Emma Curtis Hopkins: 'Forgotten Founder' of New Thought" (Ph.D. dissertation, Florida State University, 1991), 19, see 16–18; letter, Emma Curtis Hopkins to Mabel Dodge Luhan, October 26, 1917, Mabel Dodge Luhan Papers, Archives of Beinecke Rare Book and Manuscript Library, cited in Harley, 153–54.

6. Harley, "Emma Curtis Hopkins," 16; Robert Peel, *Mary Baker Eddy: The Years of Trial, 1876–1891* (New York: Holt, Rinehart and Winston, 1971), 177; see letter cited in Peel, 179 and Hopkins's article "Teachers of Metaphysics," *Christian Science Journal* (September 1885): 112–13. Also see "Hopkins Metaphysical Association," *Christian Science* 1 no. 6 (February 1889): 158.

7. Hopkins, "Teachers of Metaphysics," 112–13; Hopkins's November 4, 1885 letter to fellow student Julia Bartlett, cited in Peel, *Years of Trial*, 179–80; also J. Gordon Melton, "New Thought's Hidden History: Emma Curtis Hopkins, Forgotten Founder" (unpublished paper, Institute for the Study of American Religion, August 1988), 6–7.

8. Hopkins's husband George filed divorce papers against her for "abandonment" in November of 1900. Her son John Carver Hopkins died in 1905, probably in an influenza epidemic. See Harley, "Emma Curtis Hopkins," 14–15. On the Chicago mind-cure scene, see Peel, *Years of Trial,* 141, 160, 211, 231; Melton, "New Thought's Hidden History," 6, 10.

9. Mary H. Plunkett, "Annual Address," *Truth* 1, no. 1 (November 1887), 5–6; "The Hopkins Christian Science Associations," *Truth* 1, no. 1 (November 1887), 18–19; Melton, "New Thought's Hidden History," 11–13; Frances Lord, *Christian Science Healing: Its Principles and Practices* (London: George Redway, 1888), vii–vii; J. Stillson Judah, *The History of Metaphysical Movements in America* (Philadelphia: Westminster Press, 1967), 171.

10. Plunkett, "Annual Address," 5; "Christian Science Work in Milwaukee," *Truth* 1 no. 1 (November 1887): 20–21; Melton, "New Thought's Hidden History," 12–13.

11. "Beware of False Teachers," *Christian Science Journal* (June 1887): 157.

12. Peel, *Years of Trial,* 217; Melton, "New Thought's Hidden History," 12, 6.

13. Cited in Peel, *Years of Trial,* 224 (Eddy's italics).

14. Peel, *Years of Trial,* 228; Hulda B. Loud, "A Skeptic and the Mental Healers," *Truth* 1 no. 1 (November 1887): 23.

15. Peel, *Years of Trial,* 180; see *The Christian Metaphysician,* 1887; Loud, "A Skeptic," 23.

16. Harley, "Emma Curtis Hopkins," 67–73, and Melton, "New Thought's Hidden History," 8–9, 11; *Truth,* November 1887; Emma (Curtis) Hopkins, "To Readers," *Christian Science* 1, no. 1 (September 1888): 20.

17. "Hopkins Metaphysical Association," *Christian Science* 1, no. 7 (March 1889): 193.
In one listing of twelve new associations, all had women presidents. See "Hopkins Christian Science Associations," *Truth* 1, no. 1 (November 1887): 19.

18. Louisa Southworth, "The Baccalaureate," *Christian Science* 1, no. 8 (February 1889): 144; Gary Ward, "The Feminist Theme in Early New Thought," Institute for the Study of American Religion Occasional Paper #1 (unpublished paper, 1989). Hopkins also predicted that her successor would be a woman. See "Hopkins Metaphysical Association," *Christian Science* 2, no. 3 (November 1889): 83; Melton, "New Thought's Hidden History," 19.

19. Clara Louise Burnham, "A View of Christian Science," *Woman's World* 3, no. 6 (June 15, 1887); see entry on Burnham in Frances E. Willard and Mary A. Livermore, *A Woman of the Century* (New York: 1893), 139; Ella Wheeler Wilcox, "The Creed" and "Christmas Carol," in *Christian Science* 1, no. 2 (October 1888): 32 and 1, no. 4 (December 1888): 83; "Hopkins Metaphysical Association," *Christian Science* 1, no. 8 (April 1889): 231.

20. Harbert asserted that "it was the silent meetings of the believers in harmony [Hopkins's followers] which preserved the wonderful harmony of the . . . thousands of women" attending the 1888 International Council of Women.

See "Hopkins Metaphysical Association," and Harbert, "Health: Its Requisites for Continuance," *Christian Science* 1, no. 8 (April 1889): 221–31, 206–08; "Hopkins Metaphysical Association," *Christian Science* 1, no. 9 (May 1889): 256; untitled poem, and Harbert, "Ordination Address," *Christian Science* 1, no. 6 (February 1889), 141, 143; see Steven M. Buechler, *The Transformation of the Woman Suffrage Movement: The Case of Illinois, 1850–1920* (New Brunswick: Rutgers University Press, 1986), 108–9.

21. Harbert, "Ordination Address," 141; Southworth, "The Baccalaureate," 144; see Ferne Anderson, "Emma Curtis Hopkins: Springboard to New Thought" (M.A. thesis, University of Denver, 1981), 75.

22. Ward, "Feminist Theme," 11–12. See *Christian Science* 1, no. 9 (May 1889): 256; see *Christian Science* 3, no. 6 (February 1891): 173, and no. 7 (March 1891): 218.

23. Hopkins, "C.S. Ordination Address," *Christian Science* 1, no. 7 (March 1889): 177; see "Advisory Council" report for year ending June 1, 1889, in *Christian Science* 1, no. 12 (August 1889): 344; see "Christian Science Work in Milwaukee," 20–21.

For gifts of pearls and diamonds, see *Christian Science* 1, no. 10 (June 1889): 282; also see *Christian Science* 2, no. 9 (May 1890): 303; "Personal Notes," *Truth* 1, no. 1 (November 1887): 30; and Florence Morse Kingsley, *The Transfiguration of Miss Philura* (New York: Funk and Wagnells Company, 1901).

For first-hand accounts of aggressive "Christian Science" proselytizing see Nellie V. Anderson, "A Call on Mrs. Steele," *Christian Science* 1, no. 6 (February 1889): 147–48, and Myrtle Fillmore, "A Christian Scientist Among Reformers," *Christian Science* 2, no. 12 (August 1890): 384–86. Edward Eggleson's *The Faith Doctor: A Story of New York* (Ridgewood, N.J.: Gregg Press, [1892] 1968) presents an outsider's account of pushy Christian Science or New Thought missionary women.

24. Peel, *Years of Trial*, 161. Peel points out that Eddy admitted many students for a reduced or entirely waived fee.

25. "Theological Seminary," *Christian Science* 1, no. 7 (March 1889): 200; "Jackson Work," *Christian Science* 2, no. 11 (July 1890): 357; "Personal Mention," *Christian Science* 1, no. 7 (March 1889): 200.

Mental healer A. J. Swarts also charged one dollar a lesson. See Peel, *Years of Trial*, 161. Malinda Cramer offered her primary class (eight lessons) for five dollars, her theological class (twelve lessons) for ten dollars, and her normal class, including diploma, for twenty-five dollars; the total thus came close to Hopkins's charge of fifty dollars. See *Harmony* 8, no. 11 (August 1896), opening page. Annie Rix Militz, on the other end, relied entirely on freewill offerings for her healing, teaching, and preaching services.

26. On absent healing, see healers's advertisements in *Christian Science*, including Mrs. Florence C. Gilbert ("The Absent Treated Successfully"), Dr. Chas. W. Close ("Absent Patients Preferred"), and A. D. and A. J. Fairbanks ("Absent Treatment a Specialty"). Back pages of *Christian Science*, 1 no. 1 (September 1888); no. 3 (November 1888); no. 7 (March 1889). For agents, see ad-

vertisements for Helen Van-Anderson's *The Right Knock* in *Christian Science*. See *Harmony* 2, no. 9 (July 1890): 304, 318; see calls for agents in back pages of *Freedom*, 1900. For manuscript copying, see *Christian Science* 2, no. 7 (May 1890): 241; Helen Wilmans, *The Conquest of Poverty* (Sea Breeze, Florida: Wilmans Publishing House, 1901), 63–64.

27. "Christian Science Healing," *Christian Science* 2, no. 9 (May 1890): 303.

28. As early as 1887, Hopkins Christian Science Associations existed in Illinois, Ohio, California, New York, Iowa, Maine, Nebraska, Wisconsin, Michigan, and Minnesota. Soon other branches were reported in Kentucky, Louisiana, Colorado, and Missouri. See "The Hopkins Christian Science Associations," *Truth* 1, no. 1 (November 1887): 19; Melton, "New Thought's Hidden History," 23–24; also reports in *Christian Science*, September 1888–August 1892.

Eddy eventually wrested the name "Christian Science" back from Hopkins. Her Christian Science rebounded over the next twenty years. However, the story of Eddy's achievements within her own church lies outside the boundaries of this study. See Robert Peel, *Mary Baker Eddy: The Years of Authority* (New York: Holt, Rinehart and Winston, 1977); Steven Gottschalk, *The Emergence of Christian Science in American Religious Life* (Berkeley: University of California Press, 1978).

29. My source for Hopkins's twelve lessons in Christian Science is Emma Curtis Hopkins, *Class Lessons 1888*, compiled and edited by Elizabeth C. Bogart (Marina del Rey, California: DeVorss and Company, 1977). Bogart found the contents of *Class Lessons 1888* in a scrapbook given to her by Mrs. Carpenter, the sister of Emma Curtis Hopkins. Bogart writes that the lessons "were used solely for private instruction and were never published in any form." However, each of the twelve lessons in Bogart's collection was published separately as pamphlets in the mid-1880s. The lessons were also published serially in Hopkins's *Christian Science* magazine (not to be confused with Eddy's *Christian Science Journal*), and were reprinted in mind-cure magazines of the late 1880s.

Bogart adds chapter headings not present in the earlier, separately published lessons. In one case, Bogart's version omitted a few sentences from the 1880s version. Otherwise, Bogart's edition and the earlier lessons are the same. See pamphlets, such as *Tenth Lesson in Christian Science, from the Lessons of Emma Curtis Hopkins* (Chicago: Christian Science Publishing Company, 1891).

30. Hopkins, *Class Lessons*, 13–14, 17, 87–88, 200.

31. Ibid., 176.

32. Hopkins, *Tenth Lesson*, 13 (her italics), see 176, 206; see Emma Curtis Hopkins, "The Atonement," *Christian Science* 1, no 2 (October 1888): 25–32. ("Perhaps nothing has disgusted the honest skeptics of our time with the Christian religion like its fundamental dogma of atonement.")

33. Hopkins, *Class Lessons*, 167, 201.

34. Ibid., 38, 46, 104; also Hopkins, *Tenth Lesson*, 8, 19.

35. Hopkins, *Class Lessons*, 204, 93, see 201–2.

36. Ibid., 93.

37. Ibid., 27.

38. Emma Curtis Hopkins, "Baccalaureate Address, Chicago 1891," in her *Bible Interpretations* (Pittsfield, Mass.: Sun Printing Co., 1925), 18; Hopkins, *Class Lessons*, 106.

39. Emma Curtis Hopkins, *The Radiant I AM* (Putnam, Conn: Emma Curtis Hopkins Publishing Co., n.d.), 4.

40. Hopkins, *Class Lessons*, 257, 93.

41. Ibid., 172.

42. "Hopkins Metaphysical Association," *Christian Science* I, no. 6 (February 1889): 156, 158; see Hopkins, *Class Lessons*, 80, 196.

43. Hopkins's six-step method was extremely influential. See *Modern Thought* (February 1890): 4–5; Eugene Weeks, "Hints and Helps for Beginners," *Christian Metaphysician*, II no. 3 (May 1888): 81–82; Frances Lord, *Christian Science Healing* (Chicago: Lily Publishing, 1888), 180–209.

44. Hopkins, *Tenth Lesson*, 17, 13–16. Hopkins probably got the term "chemicalization" from Eddy.

45. Hopkins, *Class Lessons*, 281. Descriptions of Hopkins's six stages of healing are scattered through various sections of *Class Lessons*. See 164–67, 205, 243–44, 257–58; see *Tenth Lesson*, 15.

At each of these six steps, the healer was to meditate upon a series of five denials. The healer was to deny:

1. *Heredity* (the belief that one inherited the sins and sicknesses of one's ancestors);
2. *Race Laws* (the belief that humanity was prone to evil; the belief in original sin);
3. *Influence* (the belief that one could be degraded through the evil acts or influence of others. This might have been an allusion to women's fears of seduction, or wives' feelings of degradation resulting from marital rape);
4. *The Law of Cause and Effect* (the belief that specific acts carried irreversible consequences; particularly that secret sins—perhaps women's own sexual desires—brought inevitable retribution);
5. *Healer's Influence* (the belief that the patient could pick up hidden errors in the healer's own character during treatment. This was probably intended as a safeguard against the problem of hypnotic mind control).

The final healing formula consisted of a long series of denials, such as "Dear child, listen to me: you are not suffering the consequences of inheritance. You were not brought forth into the world of flesh, from its lustful passions and sensual appetites. . . . You are not suffering the consequences of the lustful passions and sensual appetites of the race . . . " (through denials of influence, cause and effect, healer's influence). These denials were followed by affirmations, such as "God is your health. You cannot be threatened with disease or sickness, nor fear disease or sickness, nor yield to disease or sickness." "You are alive with the Life of the Spirit, strong with the strength of the Spirit, and your trust is in God. You are ready to acknowledge your perfect health" (Hopkins, *Class Lessons*, 164; *Christian Science* 2 no. 6 [February 1890]: 184).

46. Allusions to feelings of inferiority permeate Hopkins's writings. For example, Hopkins described how the new mental healers were seen as "multitudes of seemingly stupid and inferior people" who have "suddenly sprung into notice as 'teachers of men'" (Hopkins, *Class Lessons*, 242). Hopkins also urged her pupils to stand firm in the face of "surges of fear" caused by the "scorn" of outsiders. *Class Lessons*, 67, see 103.

47. Hopkins, *Class Lessons*, 103; see similar statements on 80, 171.

48. Hopkins recognized these possible confusions. She wrote, "A subtle error the child has made when entering into higher recognition of himself, has been to say, 'I am God.' Not so; one speaker is truer; 'In my highest moment I enter in and know that I do not live—I am lived. I do not think—I am thought. I do not move—I am moved'" (ibid., 55).

49. "Hopkins Metaphysical Association," *Christian Science* 1 no. 1 (September 1888): 17–18 (her italics).

50. Hopkins, *Class Lessons*, 279, see 280.

51. Amy Schrager Lang, *Prophetic Woman: Anne Hutchinson and the Problem of Dissent in the Literature of New England* (Berkeley: University of California Press, 1987), 138, 145–46, 152–53; and Gillian Brown, *Domestic Individualism: Imagining Self in Nineteenth-Century America* (Berkeley: University of California Press, 1990), 1–7.

52. Hopkins's lauding of the "God-Self" seemed to provide women with this man within, or ego. As one of Hopkins's "affirmations" promised the patient, "You are alive with the Life of the Spirit. . . . You are bold and vigorous and hardy and energetic and tough and enduring. You are strong and free and well" (Hopkins, *Class Lessons*, 262–63).

53. Hopkins, *Radiant I AM*, 15, 4.

54. Emma Curtis Hopkins, "C.S. Ordination Address," *Christian Science* 1, no. 7 (March 1889): 174, 175.

55. Emma Curtis Hopkins, "C.S. Ordination Address," *Christian Science* 1, no 10 (June 1889): 272–73.

Hopkins criticized the doctrine of sexual necessity in other sermons as well. She wrote: "The . . . man of the world believes that evil passions and propensities must be pampered by license and indulged by supplies, and he has dragged the lamblings of the mother's flock to sacrifice to his belief in evil.

But the Mother-heart . . . has . . . cried vehemently through the centuries—'It is not right! It is not true! God is not compelling evil. Whatever seems, it is not God who sends it.'" Women's current willingness to speak against "belief in the right of evil" was evidence that "'Woman's hour has come,'" Hopkins explained. Emma Curtis Hopkins, "The Trinity," *Christian Science* 1, no. 5 (January 1889): 112, 110–11.

56. Hopkins, "The Trinity," 112.

57. Hopkins, *Class Lessons*, 72 (her italics); see 78–81.

58. Ibid., 78.

59. "Hopkins Metaphysical Association," *Christian Science* 1, no. 1 (September 1888): 17, her italics; Hopkins, *Tenth Lesson*, 7.

60. "Christian Science Association," *Christian Science* 4 no. 10 (June 1892): 303; see 302. Also see Hopkins, *Bible Interpretations*, 6–7, 13–14.

Hopkins's recommendation that women simply wait for their wishes to be fulfilled was repeated by other mental healers in stories about indigent women finding large sums of money in their purses, or anxious housewives finding a messy room miraculously cleaned. See Ida A. Nichols, "The Money Question According to C.S.," *Christian Science* 2, no. 10 (June 1890): 322; Ida A. Nichols, "God Is Our Support," *Christian Science* 3, no. 5 (January 1891): 144; "Christian Science Association," *Christian Science* 4, no. 5 (January 1892): 146–47; *Harmony* (April 1897): 187.

61. As Hopkins explained, although one might experience a craving for "tobacco, strong drink, [or] other vicious tastes," in fact, "[n]o desire for the undesirable has existence." Such lowly desires were actually "the restless desire for satisfaction seeking a false channel," and were in fact a search not for stimulation, but for "peace." Hopkins, *Class Lessons*, 82. Hopkins also taught that one need not worry about unseemly desires, since one received one's heart's desire only after one became spiritual—at which point one's desires also were spiritual. "Hopkins Metaphysical Association," *Christian Science* 1, no. 1 (September 1888): 18, italics in original.

Hopkins also tried to distinguish between "appetites" and "desires." She told her students to "deny" appetites, while simultaneously telling them *not* to crush their desires. See Hopkins, "Bible Interpretations," *Christian Science* 1, no. 10 (June 1889): 295; Hopkins, "International Bible Lessons," *Christian Science* 2, no. 9 (May 1890): 298.

62. "Christian Science Theological Seminary Notes," *Christian Science* 3, no. 11 (July 1891): 347.

63. "Christian Science Association," *Christian Science* 2, no. 10 (June 1890): 326 (her italics); "Hopkins Metaphysical Association," *Christian Science* 1, no. 1 (September 1888): 17–18 (her ellipses). Also see "Christian Science Association," *Christian Science* 2, no. 8 (April 1890): 258.

64. "Hopkins Metaphysical Association," *Christian Science* 1, no. 4 (December 1888): 93. Also see Hopkins, "The Atonement," 29, 32; Hopkins, *Class Lessons*, 31, 42.

65. In a typical warning to her students against fears that "mesmerism, magnetism, hypnotism, psychology," or "astral bodies" could hurt them, Hopkins said "There is no power of any man or woman or child whereby they may communicate with . . . any other one in or out of the body. *It is pure delusion.* . . . I propose to you to mind your business and keep away from astral bodies, elementals and threats of evil. They are totally unscientific" ("Christian Science Association," *Christian Science* 4, no. 1 [September 1891]: 21 [her italics]).

66. "Editor's Note," *Christian Science* 3, no. 11 (July 1891): 338; "Christian Science Association," *Christian Science* 2, no. 7 (March 1890): 230–31; see "Hopkins Metaphysical Association," *Christian Science* 2, no. 3 (November 1889): 81.

67. "Hopkins Metaphysical Association," *Christian Science* 2, no. 3 (November 1889): 81–82.

68. "Christian Science Association," *Christian Science* 2, no. 9 (May 1890): 295. See "Hopkins Metaphysical Association," *Christian Science* 1, no. 4 (December 1888): 93.

69. "Christian Science: December Review at the Theological Seminary," *Christian Science* 4, no. 5 (January 1892): 131.

70. See notices about Hopkins's activities in *Christian Science,* September 1888 through August 1892.

71. Emma Curtis Hopkins to "My two blessed friends" (Charles and Myrtle Fillmore), October 19, 1894, and November 12, 1894, Archives of the Unity School of Christianity, Unity Village, Missouri. My thanks to Gail Harley for sending me copies of these letters. See Helen Wilmans, "Half Lights," *Mental Science Magazine* 1 (1887): 51–52, for a similar description of infighting among Chicago "metaphysicians."

72. Hopkins to no name (Charles and Myrtle Fillmore), December 4, 1894, 2.

73. Hopkins's later years will be discussed further in chapter 7.

74. Horatio W. Dresser, *A History of the New Thought Movement* (New York: Thomas Y. Crowell Co., 1919), 153–54.

75. M. E. Cramer, "My Spiritual Experience," *Mind* 10, no. 5 (August 1902): 321–26; see Charles Brodie Patterson, "M E. Cramer," *Mind* 10, no. 5 (August 1902): 327–31.

76. Cramer probably chose this new name in order to distinguish her teachings from those of other mental healers in her city. Even at this early date her "college" was but one of many such enterprises in the San Francisco area. Cramer's college, like Hopkins's seminary, offered a series of twelve lessons in spirituality and healing, prepared future teachers and practitioners, sold healing "treatments," and promoted missionary endeavors. See Mrs. M. E. Cramer, *The Unity of Life* (San Francisco: 1888), 10–13. *Harmony* ran from 1887 until 1906, when its operations were damaged by the San Francisco earthquake. Cramer died in 1907. According to J. Gordon Melton, her death was a result of injuries sustained during the earthquake. See Charles S. Braden, *Spirits in Rebellion: The Rise and Development of New Thought* (Dallas: Southern Methodist University Press, 1963), 145, 270; see Patterson, "M. E. Cramer," 328.

77. See *Harmony,* 1888–1906. Cramer's missionary journeys are described in *Harmony* 2, no. 6 (March 1890): 176; no. 7 (April 1890): 205; no. 10 (July 1890): 303; and *Harmony* 9, no. 9 (June 1897): 264; no. 11 (August 1897): 324–329. Also see Cramer, "Confession," *Harmony* 14, no. 7 (April 1902): 222. For locations of Divine Science centers, see *Harmony* 9, no. 6 (March 1897): 173; no. 8 (May 1897): 233; and "Directory of Divine Science Work and Workers," *Harmony* 13, no. 2 (November 1900): opening page.

78. On the relations between Cramer's Divine Science and Hopkins's Chicago group, see *Harmony* 1, no. 8 (May 1889), back-page advertisements; *Har-*

mony 2, no. 10 (July 1890): 318; *Christian Science* 1, no. 4 (December 1888): 104, no. 5 (January 1889): 125, and no. 6 (February 1889): 157; "The Christian Science Association," *Christian Science* 3, no. 12 (August 1891): 370.

79. "Harmony Scientists Directory," *Harmony* 8, no. 11 (August 1896): frontispiece page; "Notes about the Fourth I.D.S.A. Congress," *Harmony* 9, no. 8 (May 1897): 217; see *Universal Truth* (December 1894): 332.

80. See "Report of Home College Monthly Meeting," *Harmony* 2, no. 11 (August 1890): 333, and *Harmony* 3, no. 1 (October 1890): 13; see *Harmony* 2, no. 6 (March 1890) and 11, no. 7 (April 1899). For clergy, see *Harmony* 10, no. 4 (January 1898): 101. Also see directories in *Harmony* 9, no. 4 (January 1897) and 13, no. 2 (November 1900). I am assuming that any person who listed their first name by initial only was male. If some of these were female, the gender ratio was even more skewed toward women.

81. M. E. Cramer, "Religion is One," *Harmony* 15, no. 11 (August 1903): 345–47.

82. Hazel Deane, *Powerful is the Light* (Denver: Divine Science Federation International, 1965), 3–45, see 30, 39.

83. Ibid., 42–53.

84. Ibid., 73, 85, 87, 107; *Harmony* 14, no. 12 (September 1902): 382. It was easy for James to arrange a Divine Science bible study group since she, like her sisters Nona and Alethea, had been a Presbyterian Sunday School teacher. See Louise McNamara Brooks, *Early History of Divine Science* (Denver: First Divine Science Church, 1963), 5–6, 24.

85. Brooks, *Early History*, 5, 24, 33; Deane, *Powerful is the Light*, 97, 107, 111–13; *Harmony* 11, no. 4 (January 1899): 109.

86. Deane, *Powerful is the Light*, 129; Braden, *Spirits in Rebellion*, 275.

87. Deane, *Powerful is the Light*, 125, see 154.

88. Deane, *Powerful is the Light*, 154–56. See Braden, *Spirits in Rebellion*, 170–88, for a history of the International New Thought Alliance.

89. This listing includes only Divine Science churches with ordained ministers. "Student groups" also existed in Colorado, Illinois, Maryland, and California. Deane, *Powerful is the Light*, 151–53; Braden, *Spirits in Rebellion*, 277–78.

90. Deane, *Powerful is the Light*, 174, 191, 196, 201; Braden, *Spirits in Rebellion*, 352–55. For early sales figures of Fox's books, see Louis Schneider and Sanford M. Dornbusch, *Popular Religion: Inspirational Books in America* (Chicago: University of Chicago Press, 1958), 162.

91. Deane, *Powerful is the Light*, 111, 114–16. A 1921 list of students with "advanced degrees" in Divine Science included twenty-nine women and four men. Twenty of the twenty-two Divine Science workers mentioned in early editions of the *Divine Science Weekly* (which ran from 1919 to 1925) were women. Brooks, *Early History*, 76–77, see 42–47.

92. Mary Deering, "Annie Rix Militz: Teacher, Author and Lecturer," *New Thought Bulletin* 28, no. 3 (summer 1945): 5; Charles Brodie Patterson, "Annie Rix Militz," *Mind* 10, no. 1 (April 1902): 9.

93. Patterson, "Annie Rix Militz," 10–11; Julia Winchester, "From San Francisco," *Christian Science* 4, no. 7 (March 1892): 205–6.

94. Patterson, "Annie Rix Militz," 11–13; John Kent Simmons, "The Ascension of Annie Rix Militz and the Home(s) of Truth: Perfection Meets Paradise in Early Twentieth-Century Los Angeles" (Ph.D. dissertation, University of California at Santa Barbara, 1987), 170.

95. Patterson, "Annie Rix Militz," 13–14; Simmons, "Ascension of Annie Rix Militz," 208; see *Universal Truth*, 1894–99; T. R. Slyder, "The Unity Movement: A Search for the Truth to Practical Christianity," 23–24, 33, 35–38, and John K. Simmons, "New Thought, No Thought: The Forgotten History of Annie Rix Militz and Her Contribution to the Unity School of Christianity," both in Institute for the Study of American Religion (ISAR) archives, University of California, Santa Barbara.

96. See Braden, *Spirits in Rebellion*, 514. Rix Militz continued to write, teach, and travel almost until her death in 1924, at the age of sixty-eight. Simmons, "Ascension of Annie Rix Militz," 214, 219–24, 249–57; see *Master Mind* 17, no. 1 (October 1919): 23, and no. 2 (November 1919): 63.

97. Annie Rix Militz, *Primary Lessons in Christian Living and Healing* (New York: Absolute Press, 1904), 16, 19.

98. Rix Militz, *Primary Lessons*, 166, see 173.
Rix Militz offered affirmations for both the "wife who feels herself contaminated by the embrace of her husband" and the woman who "feels herself condemned, because of her desire nature." They were to give themselves "over to thoughts of purity, such as 'I am pure,' 'You are pure.' 'There is nothing in all the world but purity.'" Annie Rix Militz, *Generation and Regeneration: Healing the Organs of Generation* (Lecture 2; n.p., n.d.).

99. Simmons, "Ascension of Annie Rix Militz," 242, see 191–92, 245–49; see Braden, *Spirits in Rebellion*, 314.

100. In Colorado, Fillmore briefly became business partners with Charles Small, the husband of Alethea Small and brother-in-law of Nona Brooks. The two men described their profession as "mining and real-estate speculation." James Dillet Freeman, *The Story of Unity* (Lee's Summit, Mo.: Unity School of Christianity, 1978), 21–38; Charles Brodie Patterson, "Charles Fillmore: A Biographical Sketch," *Mind* 10, no. 2 (May, 1902): 82.

101. See Myrtle Fillmore's healing narrative in Freeman, *Story of Unity*, 47–48, her italics, and 31–45; see Slyder, "The Unity Movement," 1–10.

102. "Emma Hopkins at Kansas City," *Modern Thought* 1, no. 7 (November 1889): 12; Patterson, "Charles Fillmore," 81, 83.

103. The growth of their organization was aided, no doubt, by the accidental fire that destroyed the building housing most of the other New Thought groups in the city. For a short but crucial period, *Modern Thought* was the sole complete New Thought center in Kansas City. Patterson, "Charles Fillmore," 83; Slyder, "The Unity Movement," 6–7, 9–10, 16.

104. See *Modern Thought* 1, no. 10 (February 1890): 4–5, 8; "A Student's

Testimony," "Kansas City College of Christian Science," and Emma Hopkins, "To Young Students," *Christian Science Thought* 2, no. 1 (April 1890): 12–13; Freeman, *Story of Unity*, 101–02; "C.S. Theological Seminary Notes," *Christian Science* 3, no. 9 (May 1891): 282–83; Slyder, "The Unity Movement," 17.

105. Freeman, *Story of Unity*, 81–86.

106. Slyder, "The Unity Movement," 32.

107. *Unity* 3, no 1 (June 1893): 8, cited in Slyder, "The Unity Movement," 19.

108. *Unity* 4, no. 5 (October 1894): 9–10, cited in Slyder, "The Unity Movement," 30–31.

By the early 1960s "Silent Unity" received over 600,000 prayer requests yearly. Oral Roberts began a similar ministry shortly after his followers visited Unity headquarters. See Braden, *Spirits in Rebellion*, 237, 275.

109. Slyder, "The Unity Movement," 26. Myrtle Fillmore continued to work on *Wee Wisdom,* Unity's heavily subsidized children's magazine which is today the longest running children's journal in the nation (see ibid., 23).

110. Freeman, *Story of Unity*, 219; Braden, *Spirits in Rebellion*, 242–43.

111. In 1894 they commissioned H. Emilie Cady, a student of Hopkins, to write a series of twelve lessons for *Unity*. The series, later published as *Lessons in Truth*, became the primary textbook of Unity. (The book has been translated into nine foreign languages, and had sold just under a million copies as of 1963. It is currently available in New Age bookstores.) They hosted visits from Hopkins's Truth Association leaders and closely followed their doings in *Unity*. Braden, *Spirits in Rebellion*, 244–45; Slyder, "The Unity Movement," 35, 38.

112. See "Harmony Scientists Directory" and article by Charles Fillmore in *Harmony* 8, no. 11 (August 1896); see *Harmony* 9, no. 9 (June 1897), 264 and 12, nos. 3–4 (December–January, 1899–1900), 124; Slyder, "The Unity Movement," 20–21.

113. Patterson, "Charles Fillmore," 85; Slyder, "The Unity Movement," 33, 35–38; Simmons, "No Thought, New Thought."

114. Fillmore, cited in Freeman, *Story of Unity*, 250; see Slyder, "The Unity Movement," 26. See Charles Fillmore, *Dynamics for Living*, edited by Warren Meyer (Lee's Summit, Mo.: Unity Books, 1967).

Myrtle Fillmore died in 1931, and Charles in 1948, but Unity continued to thrive. By the late 1970s, there were almost two million subscribers to the three major Unity journals, *Wee Wisdom, Weekly Unity,* and *Daily Word.* Braden, *Spirits in Rebellion* 242–43, 246; Freeman, *Story of Unity*, 215, 219.

115. For others who took this position, see Lord, *Christian Science Healing;* Fanny M. Harley, *Simplified Lessons in the Science of Being* (Chicago: F. M. Harley Publishing Co., 1899); Nellie V. Anderson, *The Right Knock* (Chicago: Nellie V. Anderson, 1889). These women were all students of Hopkins.

116. See Dresser, *History of New Thought*, 192–208; Braden, *Spirits in Rebellion*, 170–88.

117. "Report of the Fourth International Congress of Scientists," *Harmony* 9, no. 9 (June 1897): 250–51; see "Notes About the Fourth I.D.S.A.

Congress," *Harmony* 9 no. 8 (May 1897): 217. Also see Henry Harrison Brown, *New Thought Primer* (San Francisco: "Now" Folk, 1903), 43–45.

CHAPTER 4

1. Ursula Newell Gestefeld, *The Woman Who Dares* (New York: Lovell, Gestefeld and Co., 1892), 299.

2. Ella Wheeler Wilcox, "A Woman's Answer," in "The Restlessness of the Modern Woman," *Cosmopolitan* 31 (July 1901): 314–17, reprinted in *The American Gospel of Success: Individualism and Beyond*, edited by Moses Rischin (Chicago: Quadrangle Books, 1965), 237.

3. Nancy F. Cott, *The Grounding of Modern Feminism* (New Haven, Conn.: Yale University Press, 1987), 16.

Most scholars do not identify the elimination of male desire and the purification of self as the woman movement's unifying theme. Susan Kingsley Kent's *Sex and Suffrage in Britain, 1860–1914* (Princeton: Princeton University Press, 1987) argues that the British suffrage movement was fueled by women's rage over sexual exploitation. No comparable work has been undertaken for the American late-nineteenth-century woman movement.

4. Report is quoted in Anne Firor Scott, *Natural Allies: Women's Associations in American History* (Urbana: University of Illinois Press, 1992), 107.

5. Elizabeth Cady Stanton, "The Moral of the Byron Case," *Independent*, September 9, 1869, cited in William Leach, *True Love and Perfect Union: The Feminist Reform of Sex and Society* (New York: Basic Books, 1980), 121. Also see Stanton, "Home Life" (1875), in Ellen Carol DuBois, ed., *Elizabeth Cady Stanton/Susan B. Anthony: Correspondence, Writings, Speeches* (New York: Schocken Books, 1981), 125–38; Mrs. Helen H. Gardener, "The Moral Responsibility of Women in Heredity," *The Work and Words of the National Congress of Mothers* (New York: D. Appleton and Co., 1897), 133.

6. *Minutes of the National Woman's Christian Temperance Union at Its 11th Meeting* (Chicago, 1884), 50–51, cited in Mari Jo Buhle, *Women and American Socialism, 1870–1920* (Urbana: University of Illinois Press, 1981), 65.

7. Matilda Joslyn Gage, *Woman, Church and State* (1893; reprint, Watertown, Mass: Persephone Press, 1980), 239; Eliza Burt Gamble, "The Influence of Sex on Development," *Mind* 8, no. 2 (May 1901): 98, 97.

As Gage explained, the era of "the Matriarchate or Mother Rule" was characterized by "[c]leanliness, peace, the arts, a just form of government, [and] the recognition of the feminine both in humanity and in the divinity." In contrast, the Patriarchate "materializ[ed] spiritual truths" and promoted "the theory of a male supreme God in the interests of force and authority, wars, family discord [and] the sacrifice of children." Gage, 11, 21; also see W. E. Clark, "Man, Woman and Poverty," *Mind* 10, no. 4 (July 1902): 278–85, for a similar argument.

8. Grover Cleveland, "Woman's Mission and Woman's Clubs," *Ladies Home Journal* 22 (May 1905), in William O'Neill, ed., *The Woman Movement: Feminism in the United States and England*, 163.

9. *New York World,* March 25, 1869: 4, cited in Karen J. Blair, *The Club-woman as Feminist: True Womanhood Redefined, 1868–1914* (New York: Holmes and Meier, 1980), 25.

10. Quotations are from Susan Dye Lee, "Evangelical Domesticity: The Origin of the Woman's National Temperance Union Under Frances E. Willard" (Ph.D. dissertation, Northwestern University, 1980), cited in Scott, *Natural Allies,* 103, and Mary Kavanaugh Oldham Eagle, *The Congress of Women Held in the Women's Building, World's Columbian Exposition* (Chicago, 1894), vol. 1, 175, cited in Scott, 132. Also see Scott, 127.

11. Frances Willard, "The Dawn of Woman's Day," *Our Day: A Record and Review of Current Reform* 2, no. 11 (November 1888), in Nancy F. Cott et al., eds., *Root of Bitterness: Documents of the Social History of American Women,* 2d ed. (Boston: Northeastern University Press, 1996), 400–01; Mrs. Jane Cunningham Croly, *History of the Woman's Club Movement in America* (New York, 1898), 379, cited in Scott, *Natural Allies,* 118; Frances Willard, *Woman and Temperance* (Hartford, Conn., 1883), 43, cited in Buhle, *Women and American Socialism,* 64; see Scott, 111; Blair, *Clubwoman as Feminist,* 49.

12. Gamble, "Influence of Sex," 101.

13. Jane Tompkins, *Sensational Designs: The Cultural Work of American Fiction, 1790–1860* (New York: Oxford University Press, 1985).

14. Horatio W. Dresser claimed that Van-Anderson's two novels were among the most influential books of the 1890s. Van-Anderson's *The Right Knock* went through at least seven editions. Her *Journal of a Live Woman* went through at least three editions; later editions were published under the title *Victoria True, or the Journal of a Live Woman* by the Alice B. Stockham Publishing Company. *Live Woman's* circulation may have been higher than its number of printings would suggest. A woman's claim that her copy had been read by twenty-seven of her friends was cited in an advertisement for *Live Woman.* A 1902 biographical sketch of Van-Anderson described *Journal of a Live Woman* as epitomizing her religious thought.

Horatio W. Dresser, *A History of the New Thought Movement* (New York: Thomas Y. Crowell Co., 1919), 172; Charles Brodie Patterson, "Helen Van-Anderson," *Mind* 10, no. 4 (July 1902): 246; see *Freedom,* June 27, 1900: 1 (advertisement on last page of previous week's issue); back pages of Alice B. Stockham, M.D., *The Lover's World: A Wheel of Life* (Chicago: Stockham Publishing Co., 1903). Dresser states that Henry Wood's *Edward Burton* (1890) was the first New Thought novel. The honor goes to Van-Anderson's 1889 *Right Knock.* See Dresser, 169.

Stockham's *Koradine Letters* was reviewed in both the mainstream and the alternative press. It was warmly praised by prominent woman movement leaders, including Helen M. Gougar, Nellie Blessing Eyster, and Helen E. Starrett. See "Opinions of Koradine Letters," Box 3, Anna Gordon Papers, unmicrofilmed collection, NWCTU Archives, Evanston IL, Folder AA6Correspondence, 1893. My thanks to Carolyn DeSwarte Gifford for sending me these reviews.

I do not have circulation information about Gestefeld's *Woman Who Dares.*

15. New Thought novels also represent a crucial transitional genre in women's fiction. Like sentimental novels, New Thought novels centered around a woman's struggle for mastery over her inner self. Like New Woman novels, many New Thought novels focused on the pain and hypocrisy of married life. New Woman novelists tried to portray a world where women could determine their sexual and emotional lives while knowing that society punished any woman who tried. They dealt with this dilemma either by insisting on the conventional values of their heroines or by realistically portraying the costs of social rebellion. See A. R. Cunningham, "The 'New Woman' Fiction of the 1890s," *Victorian Studies* (December 1973): 177–86. New Thought novels had a unique means of resolving this problem. They insisted that once their heroines learned to rely upon New Thought affirmations, they could pass through all threats unscathed. See Henry Nash Smith, "The Scribbling Women and the Cosmic Success Story," *Critical Inquiry* 1, no. 1 (September 1974): 47–70; Tompkins, *Sensational Designs*, 158, 162.

16. Patterson, "Helen Van-Anderson," 244; see "Christian Science Ordination Services," *Christian Science* 1, no. 6 (February 1889): 165.

17. Patterson, "Helen Van-Anderson," 244, 247; see "Personal Mention," *Christian Science* 1, no. 1 (September 1888): 22; no. 7 (March 1889): 200; no. 9 (May 1889): 255; *Christian Science* 2, no. 8 (April 1890): 272; *Christian Science* 3, no. 2 (October 1890): 52; no. 8 (April 1891): 242.

18. Before moving to Boston, Van-Anderson had offered classes in Chicago. She and her husband L. J. Anderson also engaged in entrepreneurial activities related to their metaphysical beliefs. They sold items such as "Every Day Helps," a calendar with a "choice collection of metaphysical thoughts from the world's great authors," and started the New Era Publishing Company to sell metaphysical tracts.

See advertisement in *Christian Science* 1, no. 4 (December 1888): 105; Nellie V. Anderson, *The Right Knock,* back-page advertisements; *Christian Science* 1, no. 10 (June 1889): 297–98; no. 11 (July 1889): 333; no. 12 (August 1889): 365; *Harmony* 2, no. 10 (July 1890): 304, 318; see Patterson, "Helen Van-Anderson," 247.

19. Patterson, "Helen Van-Anderson," 245; Dresser, *History of New Thought,* 174; see Helen Van-Anderson, "The Church of the Higher Life," *Journal of Practical Metaphysics* 1, no. 3 (December 1896): 76–77.

20. See *Harmony* 9, no. 8 (May 1897): 217, and 12, nos. 3–4 (December–January 1899–1900): 83; Dresser, *History of New Thought,* 196; Braden, *Spirits in Rebellion,* 185.

21. Helen Van-Anderson, "Greenacre Ideals," and Sarah Farmer, "The Purpose of Greenacre," *Mind* 5, no. 1 (October 1899): 28–29, 8–9. See Charles Malloy, "Greenacre," *Mind* 5, no. 1 (October 1899): 3–4. Also see "Metaphysics at Greenacre," *Journal of Practical Metaphysics* 2, no. 2 (November 1897): 56–61, and Ross E. Paulson's biographical entry on Helen Campbell in Edward T. James, Janet Wilson James, and Paul Boyer, eds., *Notable American Women,* 3 vols. (Cambridge, Mass: Belknap Press, 1971), 1, 281; Dresser,

History of New Thought, 176–79; see series, "The Family Circle," edited by Helen Van-Anderson and Florence Peltier Perry, in *Mind,* 1901–1902.

22. Nellie V. Anderson, "A Call on Mrs. Steele," *Christian Science* 1, no. 6 (February 1889): 147–48; *The American Purity Alliance Twentieth Annual Report 1895* (New York: 1896), 11.

23. Van-Anderson, *Right Knock,* 37, 39.

24. Ibid., 77, 301.

I'm assuming "Mrs. Pearl" is Emma Curtis Hopkins because the twelve lessons presented in *The Right Knock* appear to be shorthand notes of the lessons Hopkins taught between 1883 and 1885. The year that *Right Knock* was published Van-Anderson was regularly attending the Hopkins Metaphysical Association. Hopkins endorsed *The Right Knock* as presenting "as sound and reliable Christian Science teachings as have ever been put before the people." Mrs. Pearl's class seems identical to a typical Hopkins class, with about fifty people attending and many healings occuring, and in which backsliding is referred to as "chemicalization." See advertisement in *Christian Science* 1, no. 11 (July 1889): 333. *Christian Science* ran the *Right Knock* in serial form starting in May 1889.

25. Van-Anderson, *Right Knock,* 11, 33.

26. Ibid., 279. The precise meaning of retaining one's "individuality" in marriage is not clear from the text. However, Elizabeth Cady Stanton used the term "individual" or "self-sovereignty" to refer to the right of women to control their sexual lives. See DuBois, ed., *Elizabeth Cady Stanton/Susan B. Anthony,* 95.

27. They describe the Divine mind versus the mortal mind and the need to "cleanse" the latter; the power of thought to control circumstances; "affirmations and denials"; the usefulness of meditation or "the Silence"; and the six steps to healing that were a hallmark of Hopkins's teachings.

28. Van-Anderson, *Right Knock,* 84, 27.

29. Ibid., 51.

30. Ibid., 84; see letters in *Harmony* 2, no. 7 (April 1890): 247, and *Harmony* 8, no. 7 (April 1896): 304.

31. Van-Anderson, *Right Knock,* 297, 218.

Hopkins often used metaphors of high birthright and inherited royalty. See "The Atonement," *Christian Science* 1, no. 2 (October 1888): 29–30; "C.S. Ordination Address," *Christian Science* 1, no. 10 (June 1889): 271. Such metaphors pervaded most early New Thought writings. One woman described her understanding of the doctrine of "birthright" in the following way: "I used to lie awake half the night and cry because I was afraid I should lose my position. . . . I had no . . . understanding that I already lived in my Father's house. 'I, a princess, King-descended,' and therefore no evil could befall me" (from "A Conversation," *Christian Science* 3, no. 2 [October 1890]: 41). Also see Abby Morton Diaz, *Spirit as a Power* (Belmont, Mass.: 1886), 24.

32. Van-Anderson, *Right Knock,* 221.

33. Ibid., 28–9, 81–82, 60.

34. Ibid., 161, 127, see 204–5.

35. Ibid., 234–35, see 166–67.

36. Ibid., 257.

37. Ibid., 300 (italics in text).

38. Van-Anderson, *Live Woman*, 23, 128, 27, 28.

39. Ibid., 15–16, 84–86.

40. Ibid., 163.

41. Ibid., 65–67.

42. Ibid., 65–67, 21–22.

43. Ibid., 64–65, italics in text.

44. Ibid., 65–67.

45. Gillian Brown, *Domestic Individualism* (Berkeley: University of California Press, 1990), 21, 31–32; Martha Banta, *Imaging American Women: Idea and Ideals in Cultural History* (New York: Columbia University Press, 1987), 119, 138, see 164–66, 656–62.

46. Van-Anderson, *Live Woman*, 26, italics in text; see 43.

47. Ibid., 35 (italics in text), 99–100.

48. Jan Lewis, "Mother's Love: The Construction of an Emotion in Nineteenth-Century America," in Andrew E. Barnes and Peter N. Stearns, eds., *Social History and Issues in Human Consciousness: Some Interdisciplinary Connections* (N.Y.: New York University Press, 1989), 209–29; Sheila M. Rothman, *Woman's Proper Place* (New York: Basic Books, 1978), 82; Leach, *True Love and Perfect Union*, 118.

49. Van-Anderson, *Live Woman*, 130–36.

50. Ibid., 132.

51. Judging by Van-Anderson's novels, New Thought appealed to women who had neither the will nor the capability to openly challenge their situations. Even though Victoria's marriage has left her feeling isolated, abused, and helpless, and despite young Violet's observation that her married friends seem "terribly disappointed," the novel lauds married life. Victoria warns Violet about the dangers of marriage, but only by claiming allegiance to a truer, higher form of marriage. See Van-Anderson, *Live Woman*, 31–32.

52. Charles Brodie Patterson, "Ursula N. Gestefeld: A Biographical Sketch," *Mind* 9, no. 4 (January 1902): 250; Charles Braden's biography of Gestefeld in James, James, and Boyer, *Notable American Women*, II, 27–8; Robert Peel, *Mary Baker Eddy: The Years of Trial* (New York: Holt, Rinehart and Winston, 1971), 231–35; see Gestefeld's articles in *The Christian Metaphysician*, January 1887 and July 1887.

53. Peel, *Years of Trial*, 231–35; see Ursula N. Gestefeld, *Jesuitism in Christian Science* (Chicago: Ursula N. Gestefeld, 1888), and the following articles in Eddy's *Christian Science Journal*: "Mrs. Gestefeld's Lectures," 4, no. 7 (October 1888): 345; "Jesuitism in Christian Science," no. 8 (November 1888): 427; "Book Notices" and "Editor's Note Books," no. 11 (February 1889): 575, 583–87. Gestefeld maintained good working relations with Hopkins, Cramer, the Fillmores and other New Thought leaders. After her experiences with Eddy,

however, Gestefeld never joined another teacher's organization. See Louise McNamara Brooks, *Early History of Divine Science* (Denver: First Divine Science Church, 1963), 5; T. R. Slyder, "The Unity Movement: A Search for the Truth of Practical Christianity: A Brief Institutional History" (unpublished paper, Institute for the Study of American Religion (ISAR) Archives, University of California, Santa Barbara), 25, 40–41.

54. Gestefeld's Science of Being differed from standard New Thought teachings primarily in its use of the Bible as an allegorical key to psychic development. Patterson, "Ursula N. Gestefeld," 254; Braden, "Ursula Newell Gestefeld," 27. See Ursula N. Gestefeld, *The Master of the Man* (Chicago: Exodus Publishing Company, 1914) for a typical example of Gestefeld's methods of biblical exegesis.

Gestefeld also published and edited *The Exodus*, a monthly magazine, and created the Exodus Club, a Chicago-based organization devoted to promulgating her faith. By 1902 the Exodus Club had three hundred members.

See copies of *The Exodus* and materials related to the Exodus Club, in archives of the Chicago Historical Society; Slyder, "The Unity Movement," 41; also see *Prominent Women of Illinois, 1885–1932* (Illinois Woman's Press Association, 1932), 15, for description of how Gestefeld's religious meetings "filled our best auditoriums."

55. She spoke frequently at New Thought congresses and served as an officer of the National New Thought Alliance, the east coast-based group that became the dominant national New Thought organization after Malinda Cramer's death in 1906. Brochure, "The Church of 'The New Thought,'" February 22, 1903, at Chicago Historical Society. See "What is Being Done," *Exodus* (October 1903): 264–65; Braden, *Spirits In Rebellion*, 139, 173, 180.

56. Gestefeld contributed one commentary to the *Woman's Bible* in which she briefly summarized Science of Being principles. See *Prominent Women of Illinois;* John William Leonard, ed., *Woman's Who's Who of America, 1914–1915* (New York: American Commonwealth Co., 1914); Mary Wright Sewall, ed., *The World's Congress of Representative Women* (Chicago and New York: Rand, McNally and Co., 1894), 275–79.

57. Gestefeld, *Woman Who Dares*, 22.

58. Ibid., 197–99.

59. Ibid., 212 (italics in text).

60. Ibid., 254, 288.

61. Ibid., 329, 358.

62. The New Thought elements of Gestefeld's *Woman Who Dares* are subtle. Although there is no mention of "going into the Silence," Murva frequently falls into meditative states. Her revelations come from her "indwelling power." Once she begins to listen to her inner voice, she can no longer be hurt by injuries that would incapacitate the average person. See 324, 284.

63. Gestefeld, *Woman Who Dares*, 252, 248.

64. Ibid., 22.

65. Ibid., 9.

66. Ibid., 109, see 126.

67. Ibid., 26, see 75–76.

68. Ibid., 13–14.

69. Ibid., 124, see 102.

70. Ibid., 181, 305, 150, 299, see 187, 217, 212–13. Murva's unhappiness over being "swallowed up" in her husband can be read as a protest against the common depiction of woman as man's internal conscience.

71. Ibid., 315, 317–18. Haddie insists that as a prostitute she has more freedom than married women: "They are bound hand and foot to the men they live with, perfect slaves to their every desire. . . . I am myself and can say, No, when I please. . . . I've got freedom and they've got respectability." Murva is horrified by Haddie's words, but realizes there is "a truth" to them (323, 316).

72. Ibid., 252–53.

73. Ibid., 254.

74. Ibid., 301, see 303.

75. The importance of stillness is depicted in a vision Murva has of a woman bearing a cross. The suffering woman grasps for support and prays for help, but her condition worsens until she stands perfectly still. Only then does a heaven-sent strength enable her to stand erect and throw off the cross. Ibid., 158–59, see 143.

76. Ibid., 262, 284, 350, 247, 292.

77. Ibid., 256–58.

The events leading up to this vision also suggest that women feel sexual desire. Murva had just found one of Harold's ties, which had "escaped" his travel-trunk in order to be "cared for" by her. She is suddenly overcome by a "rush of affection" for Harold. She kisses the tie, which she describes as a "senseless thing," repeatedly. Immediately after kissing her husband's animate yet senseless tie, Murva feels suddenly "weak and trembling"; thus a sexual experience is invoked. See 255. Murva's initial attraction to the naked female body of lust also hints at Murva's lesbian or homoerotic sexual desire.

78. Ibid., see 48–61.

79. Ibid., 136–38.

80. Ibid., 14, my italics; see Linda Gordon, *Woman's Body, Woman's Right: A Social History of Birth Control in America* (New York: Penguin Books, 1976), 99.

81. Gestefeld, *Woman Who Dares*, 326, 357, see 145, 323.

82. Van-Anderson, *Live Woman*, 136.

Similar sentiments were repeated in much early New Thought literature. Emma Curtis Hopkins described how affirmations helped smooth the Holy Mother's "pathway over the needs of mankind," and promised that her students could "rise into the air out of the reach of pain." Emma Curtis Hopkins, "The Ministry of the Holy Mother" (n.p., n.d.), 11, 7–8. Also see Annie Rix Militz's advice that "You live in the spiritual world where nothing can hurt or injure you" and Malinda Cramer's insistence that because truth is "forever above and beyond disturbances," those who follow truth are "protected and shielded by the perfect good at all times." Annie Rix Militz, *Primary Lessons in Christian Living and Healing* (New York: Absolute Press, 1904), 103, see 109; Malinda Cramer, *Lessons in the Science of Infinite Spirit and the Christ Method of Healing* (San Francisco: M. E. Cramer, 1890), 55, 54.

83. Gestefeld's novel *The Leprosy of Miriam* insisted even more stridently that womanly self-assertion was impossible. The plot centers on two sisters. Miriam Hartwell, who is devoted to aiding women rather than men, is described as a "warrior leader." Her sister Sarah is more like Murva; she "appeared to know nothing of strife, to live always in a world of her own which she carried with her as a protecting armor." Only the sheltered and inspiring woman, rather than the active and worldly woman, can aid humanity. As one character explains, "Redemption comes through the woman, but she must be the priestess rather than the warrior, winning her cause first by what she is, afterward by what she does."

The spiritual presence of the book is, again, a man. Paul Masters is a crippled, androgynous figure. His face, "guiltless of beard," combines "a man's strength and dominance with a woman's gentleness and beauty," and his crippled body only makes his "glorious head" stand in sharper relief. Ursula Gestefeld, *The Leprosy of Miriam* (New York: Gestefeld Library and Publishing Co., 1894), 93, 98, 132, 12–13. *Leprosy* implies that because purity requires "strength and dominance," it is available only to men whose bodies have been negated. One can see the usefulness of Hopkins's idea of the "man-child" within. Without him, only men can be whole while women remain half.

84. Augusta Cooper Bristol, "Enlightened Motherhood," *Papers and Letters Presented at the First Woman's Congress of the Association for the Advancement of Women* (New York, 1874), 10–14, cited in Leach, *True Love and Perfect Union*, 93; Matilda Joslyn Gage, "Series of Conventions of the NWSA," *Ballot Box*, June 1881, cited in Leach, 388 n. 71.

85. My thanks to Jacqueline Goldsby for her insights on the ramifications of Stockham's turn from medical tracts to utopian fiction.

86. Entry on Alice Bunker Stockham in Frances Willard and Mary Livermore, *A Woman of the Century* (New York: 1893), 690; Stockham's obituaries in the *Evanston Press*, December 14, 1912, and *New York Times*, December 4, 1912.

87. Alice B. Stockham, *Tokology: A Book for Every Woman* (1883; rev. ed., Chicago: Alice B. Stockham and Co., 1894), ix–xiv, 152 (her italics).

88. Ibid., 156 (her italics), 160.

89. John D'Emilio and Estelle Freedman, *Intimate Matters: A History of Sexuality in America* (New York: Harper and Row, 1988), 67, 176; "A Woman's Hit," *Union Signal*, February 19, 1891, reprinted in back-page advertisements for Alice B. Stockham and Lida Hood Talbot, *Koradine Letters* (Chicago: Alice B. Stockham Co., 1893); Hal D. Sears, *The Sex Radicals: Free Love in High Victorian America* (Lawrence, Kans.: Regents Press, 1977), 262; advertisements in back pages of the 1889 edition of *Tokology*; Alice Bunker Stockham, *Tolstoi: A Man of Peace* (Chicago: Alice B. Stockham & Co., 1900); Robert Edwards,

"Tolstoy and Alice B. Stockham: The Influence of 'Tokology' on *The Kreutzer Sonata*," *Tolstoy Studies Journal* 6 (1993): 87–106, and Leo Tolstoy, "Preface to *Tokology, or the Science of Childbirth By Doctor of Medicine Alice Stockham*," translated by Robert Edwards, in Edwards, 105. My thanks to Terrence Kissak for bringing the Edwards article to my attention.

90. Alice B. Stockham, "What to Read," *The Christian Metaphysician* 1, no. 2 (April 1887): 39–40; see advertisements in back pages of *Tokology*, 1889.

Stockham was smitten with Emma Curtis Hopkins. It was she who suggested that Hopkins's students' organization be called the "Hopkins Metaphysical Association." "We all love our teacher, and her name would be a talisman to lead us to unity and success. Why not name ourselves for her?" Stockham argued. Mary H. Plunkett, "Annual Address," *Truth* 1, no. 1 (November 1887): 5–6; see Hulda B. Loud, "A Skeptic Among the Mental Healers," *Truth* 1, no. 1 (November 1887): 23; "Hopkins Metaphysical Association," *Christian Science* 1, no. 12 (August 1889): 353.

Given Stockham's long involvement with health care it was perhaps inevitable that she would investigate mental healing. But Stockham had more personal reasons to turn to "Christian Science." For years everything Stockham ate had caused her intense pain. Doctors diagnosed her illness as peritonitis, enteritis, colitis, or appendicitis, but could prescribe no cure. Stockham tried to avoid the pain by limiting her diet. But as Stockham described years later, the pain only "recurred so severely as to make life almost intolerable." Stockham apparently believed that the teachings of Hopkins and Evans brought her relief from this condition. See Alice B. Stockham, M.D., "Non-Resistance as a Healing Power," *Nautilus* 12, no. 3 (January 1910): 38.

91. Advertisements in back pages of *Tokology*, 1889; Stockham, "What to Read," 39–40; "Interview in 'The Woman's Penny Paper' (London) with Doctor Alice B. Stockham." In back pages of Stockham and Talbot, *Koradine Letters*, copy located in Frances Willard's personal library, National Woman's Christian Temperance Union Archives, Evanston, Ill.

Less philanthropic in nature were Stockham's real-estate ventures. In 1890 she purchased a block of prime lakefront property in Evanston, Illinois. She advertised the sale of "Stockham Park Lots" and aggressively petitioned Evanston's Board of Trustees for improvements to her property. See *Evanston Index*, April 4 1891; September 6, 1890, 4.

92. Willard and Livermore, *Woman of the Century*, 690; *Prominent Women of Illinois*, 10–12; Rachel Foster Avery, ed., *The Transactions of the National Council of Women of the United States* (Philadelphia: J. B. Lipincott Co., 1891), 354.

93. "Interview in 'The Woman's Penny Paper;'" "Woman Writer on Love Found Guilty," Chicago *Inter-Ocean*, June 6, 1905, 12. See *Evanston Press* obituary, December 14, 1912; Taylor Stoehr, *Free Love in America: A Documentary History* (New York: AMS Press, 1979), 64–65; Sears, *Sex Radicals*, 64, 262; Willard and Livermore, *Woman of the Century*, 690.

Edward Carpenter concluded later editions of his *Love's Coming-of-Age* with excerpts from Stockham's *Karezza*. Stockham returned the favor by publishing his writings and citing him frequently. Beverly Thiele, "Coming-of-Age: Edward Carpenter on Sex and Reproduction," in *Edward Carpenter and Late Victorian Radicalism*, ed. Tony Brown (London: Frank Cass, 1990), 117.

94. Stockham, *Tokology*, 347–49. In both *Karezza* and *Lover's World* Stockham advised readers to meditate upon "high-minded" authors such as Emerson, Carpenter, Evans, Trine, and Gestefeld. Alice B. Stockham, *Karezza: Ethics of Marriage* (1896; rev. ed., Chicago: Stockham Publishing Co., 1903), 24, 131; Alice B. Stockham, M.D., *The Lover's World: A Wheel of Life* (Chicago: Stockham Publishing Co., 1903), 348–54.

On Stockham's career as a mental healer, see Stockham, "Non-Resistance"; Stockham, "What to Read." On Stockham and Cramer, see *Harmony* 9, no. 1 (October 1896): 22–23; 11, no. 12 (September 1899): 371; 14, no. 2 (November 1901): 58; 14, nos. 9–10 (June–July 1902): 159–60; 15, no. 5 (February 1903): 159–60. Stockham participated in Cramer's International Divine Science Association congresses in 1897 and 1899. *Harmony* 9, no. 8 (May 1897): 217, and 12, nos. 3–4 (December–January 1899–1900): 83. On Vrilia Heights, see *Mind* 12, no. 2 (May 1903): 148; entry on Stockham in *Who's Who In America, 1908–1909*. Stockham also participated in the International New Thought Alliance; see *Mind* 13, no. 2 (February 1904): 206 and no. 5 (May 1904): 465.

Stockham brought her New Thought friends into her political circles. In the early 1890s, when she was active in the Illinois Woman's Press Association, practically all of the major players in Emma Curtis Hopkins's Christian Science Theological Seminary joined the organization as well, including Helen Van-Anderson, Ursula Newell Gestefeld, Ida B. Nichols, Fanny Harley, Jane Yarnall, Frances Lord, Sarah Wilder Pratt, and Emma Curtis Hopkins. See Yearbooks, Illinois Woman's Press Association, 1890, 1891, 1892, 1893, 1894–95, at Chicago Historical Society.

95. Stockham, *Lover's World*, 68. Stockham apparently encouraged women to bless marital sexuality in private correspondence as well. As one grateful reader wrote to Stockham, "the new-thought teaching would have caused me to leave my good husband" were it not for Stockham's intervention. "It seemed to me that cohabitation was the lowest act a human could perform. . . . I always felt degraded for days. . . . I do feel so differently now. As you told me, I *blessed the power in him*." Stockham, *Lover's World*, 323 (italics in text).

96. Stockham listed her friend Lida Hood Talbot as a co-author of *Koradine Letters*. My assumption that Talbot contributed ideas to the novel but played only a minor role in its actual writing is based upon a comparison between writing styles of, on one hand, *Koradine Letters* and Stockham's other writings, and on the other, chapters authored by Lida Hood Talbot in Helen Wilmans's *Conquest of Poverty* [1899].

97. Stockham and Talbot, *Koradine Letters*, 90, 139.

98. *Koradine Letters* had many autobiographical echoes, from "Dr. Goodrich," whose experiences as a physician and world traveler paralleled Stockham's own, to Koradine and Edith, who were named after Stockham's nieces,

Cora and Edith Dean. Stockham appears to have attempted to create an "Arcadian Institute" in her Evanston home, where she held girls' club meetings, public addresses by "eminent persons" on "literary and educational topics," and language lessons. See *Evanston Press*, August 15, 1891, February 4, 1893, March 11, 1893, and December 29, 1894; see Willard and Livermore, *Woman of the Century*, 690.

99. Gestefeld, *Woman Who Dares*, 22; Stockham and Talbot, *Koradine Letters*, 231, 237, 347.

100. Stockham and Talbot, *Koradine Letters*, 411, 166, 405, 68–70.

101. Gestefeld, *Leprosy of Miriam*, 12–13.

102. Stockham and Talbot, *Koradine Letters*, 104. Koradine describes a "love palace" that must be "all white,—for of course it would be white if it were built of love" (296). Also see 327, 360, 38; see Tom Lutz, *American Nervousness, 1903: An Anecdotal History* (Ithaca: Cornell University Press, 1991).

103. Stockham and Talbot, *Koradine Letters*, 17–18.

104. Ibid., 18, see 36 for a near-identical episode. Both scenes suggest that white woman's sensual vanity is primitive and unproductive, like a black man's, in contrast to the lustful drives of the white man, that can be channeled to create civilization.

105. Ibid., 244.

106. Ibid., 279–80, see 201, 373, 375.

107. Ibid., 368, 275.

108. Ibid., 46, 70. Tommy's blindness makes him into a near parody of the sheltered and therefore entirely pure woman; see 392. His love for Koradine is likened to the love of a mother, a brother, or a female friend. He reminds Koradine of a "pretty bead bag." This seems to indicate Tommy's sexual impotence; while one might dispute Freud's claim that purses always signify female genitalia, 1890s beaded bags were extraordinarily soft and limp objects.

109. Stockham, *Tokology*, 155; Stockham and Talbot, *Koradine Letters*, 255.

110. Stockham, *Karezza*, 44–45.

111. Stockham and Talbot, *Koradine Letters*, 21.

112. Ibid., 406.

113. Josiah Strong, "Our Country," 1891, excerpted in *Major Problems in American Foreign Policy*, vol. 1: To 1914, edited by Thomas G. Paterson (Lexington, Mass.: D.C. Heath and Co., 1989), 347; Joaquin Miller, *The Building of the City Beautiful* (Cambridge and Chicago: Stone and Kimball, 1893), 10–11; Stockham and Talbot, *Koradine Letters*, 172.

114. Stockham and Talbot, *Koradine Letters*, 122, see 79–80, 415. Stockham also links the sun to whiteness, to love, and to womanhood; see 21, 55, 128, 277, 380, 392, 403. But significantly, "white" female characters are not directly linked to "gold" or "riches." Their relationship to wealth is always mediated. Women are white, and women are like the sun, but women are not like "gold" or "riches." It is only the sun—and Tommy, discussed below—that are linked to both whiteness and riches.

115. Nell Irvin Painter, *Standing at Armageddon: The United States, 1877–*

1919 (New York: W. W. Norton, 1987), 17; see, for example, account of 1905 teamster strike in which headlines announce "State Guard is Ready . . . Gatling Guns in Plenty," *Chicago Record-Herald*, May 24, 1905, 2.

116. The Arcadians insist that blacks and whites are equal since "each alike has access to one source." Militarism is given a negative cast when a lecherous man is identified as a "Colonel." Koradine's father attacks class distinction and private property, vowing that he will not "begrudge, or by any act . . . deprive one of [God's] children . . . of the free use of His sunshine, green trees, fields, fruits and water." Koradine seconds this sentiment. "Helping each other would be much nicer than building fences around our ground and calling things 'mine,'" she muses. Stockham and Talbot, *Koradine Letters*, 217, 84, 135.

117. Ibid., 228–29.

118. Ibid., 247–48.

119. That males can be "little pests" is made clear in Stockham's depiction of Neil Bancroft, an Arcadian student. Neil is a constant source of annoyance to Koradine, as he asks irreverent questions, falls into ponds, or loses himself in the woods. But as the sparrows show, even pests like Neil have their place. The daredevil traits that make Neil so annoying as a boy will serve him well as a man. White male aggression is part of the natural order and ensures both wealth and white racial predominance, a predominance whose benefits are shared by white women.

120. Stockham and Talbot, *Koradine Letters*, 55, 332, 67, 70; see 226, 352. Stockham links Tommy to wealth by likening his face to "new silver" (353, see 56). He defends the wealthy (190). He is compared, as noted above, to a purse that holds money. Koradine's dream also forcefully associates Tommy with whiteness. She dreams of white Tommy lying with a white lion. Then "great, white, tall" men and women leave their "white temple" and encircle the boy and lion, their brightness covering them "like a white robe" (68–70).

121. Stockham and Talbot, *Koradine Letters*, 410, 408.

122. This perhaps explains why Stockham attempted to cast her own money-making ventures as womanly service. In an interview Stockham was quoted as explaining: "'There are two things I want women to work at: Kindergarten study and teaching, in which there is much scope and much need, and' (with a merry [nervous?] laugh) '*book canvassing!*'" Stockham explained that "'Hundreds have maintained themselves, and often families of small children, sometimes an invalid husband, by selling my book TOKOLOGY.'" See "Interview in 'The Woman's Penny Paper'" (italics in text).

123. Edward Carpenter, *Love's Coming-of-Age* (New York and London: Mitchell Kennerly, [1896] 1911), 62. Ellis and Carpenter argued that women should be freed from culture so that they could rediscover their primitive but holy instincts of sex and reproduction. See Havelock Ellis, *The New Spirit*, 4th ed. (Boston: Houghton Mifflin Co., [1890] 1926); Ellis, "The Changing Status of Women," in T. R. Smith, ed., *The Woman Question* (New York: Boni and Liveright, 1918), 220; Thiele, "Coming-of-Age"; Paul Robinson, *The Modernization of Sex: Havelock Ellis, Alfred Kinsey, William Masters and Virginia*

Johnson (New York: Harper and Row, 1976); Margaret Jackson, "Sexual Liberation or Social Control?" *Women's Studies Forum* 6, no. 1 (1983): 1–17; Sheila Rowbotham and Jeffrey Weeks, *Socialism and the New Life: The Personal and Sexual Politics of Edward Carpenter and Havelock Ellis* (London: Pluto Press Limited, 1977).

Stockham published the work of both men, quoted them frequently, and incorporated her own interpretation of their ideas into all of her post-*Koradine Letters* publications, including Alice B. Stockham, *Creative Life: A Special Letter to Young Girls; A Supplement to Koradine Letters* (Chicago: Alice B. Stockham Co., 1893), *Karezza* (1896) and *The Lover's World* (1903).

124. Stockham, *Lover's World*, 63, see 62, 68, 74–75, 98, 105, 318.

125. Stockham, *Karezza*, 113–15; see Stockham, *Creative Life*, 9–10. Stockham hinted that the "true old bachelors and old maids, . . . the really childless" were those who had never conceived thoughts, not children (*Karezza*, 102). She argued that women's "service" to civilization should be the "human and moral" service envisioned by Charlotte Perkins Gilman, rather than the sexual service envisioned by sex radicals and male evolutionary theorists.

126. Stockham, *Karezza*, 29 (Stockham's italics) and 99.

127. Ibid., 98, 109–10, see 71; see Stockham, *Lover's World*, 26.

128. Letter in Stockham, *Tokology*, 156; see Stockham, *Lover's World*, 323 for a similar letter. These letters may not have been authentic, but at the least they reveal Stockham's perspective.

129. Stockham, *Lover's World*, 183–84, 337–38.

130. Ibid., 91, 128.

131. Havelock Ellis believed that wealth would be ensured once paupers, who were feeble-minded racial misfits, were bred out of existence. This put the onus for economic advance not on male competitive energies but on women's reproductive choices (or lack thereof). Stockham's later writings accepted this position. See Havelock Ellis, *The Problem of Race-Regeneration* (New York: Moffat, Yard and Co., 1911).

132. On the discourse of civilization, see Gail Bederman, *Manliness and Civilization* (Chicago: University of Chicago Press, 1995).

CHAPTER 5

1. *The Woman's World*, December 15, 1884, 4.

2. I.[da] A. N[ichols], "God is Our Support," *Christian Science* 3, no. 5 (January 1891):146 (her italics).

3. For typically ambivalent discussions of desire and wealth, see Emma Curtis Hopkins, *Tenth Lesson in Christian Science, from the Lessons of Emma Curtis Hopkins* (Chicago: Christian Science Publishing House, 1891), 7; Frances Lord, *Christian Science Healing* (Chicago: Lily Publishing House, 1888), 380, 335; see preface of London edition (London: George Redway, 1888) for an extended discussion of the ethics of payment for Christian Science treatment.

4. H. Emilie Cady, *Lessons in Truth: A Course of Twelve Lessons in Prac-

tical Christianity (Kansas City: Unity School of Christianity, n.d.) 10, 39–40, 83–84, see 57–58.

5. Nichols, "God is Our Support," 145; I. A. Nichols, "We Make Our Own World," *Christian Science* 3, no. 7 (March 1891): 210; I. A. Nichols, "Be Beautiful, Be Rich, Be Efficient," *Christian Science* 2, no. 11 (July 1890): 354.

6. Elizabeth Towne, *Practical Methods for Self-Development* (Holyoke, Mass.: Elizabeth Towne, 1904), 15; Elizabeth Towne, *How to Grow Success* (Holyoke, Mass.: Elizabeth Towne, 1903), 18, her italics; Karl H. Von Wiegand, "Absent Treatments in Healing," *Mind* 9, no 2 (November 1901): 120–24; William Walker Atkinson, "Doing Things," *New Thought* (August 1902): 9.

7. Helen Wilmans, *A Blossom of the Century* (Florida: Freedom Publishing Co., 1898), 39.

8. This was because Wilmans could not praise wealth and desire as the birthright of woman without redefining both womanhood and the larger conceptual apparatus of spirit or mind over matter that symbolized the hierarchy of male over female. She therefore ultimately rejected the belief in a dead "matter" entirely separate from a spiritual "mind."

9. George Santayana, "The Genteel Tradition in American Philosophy," *Winds of Doctrine: Studies in Contemporary Opinion* (1913; reprint, New York: Harper, 1957), 204, cited in James Livingston, *Pragmatism and the Political Economy of Cultural Revolution, 1850–1940* (Chapel Hill: University of North Carolina Press, 1994), 129–30.

Richard Huber characterized Wilmans as a "forceful, energetic woman who probably saw in the power of the mind a way to even up the score with the physical supremacy of the male." John Cawelti described Wilmans's writings as "debased and perverted" Emersonianism. A. Whitney Griswold called her work a simple "get-rich-quick scheme" that consisted of little more than "esoteric directions for making money." Richard Huber, *The American Idea of Success* (New York: McGraw-Hill Book Co., 1971), 134; John Cawelti, *Apostles of the Self-Made Man* (Chicago: University of Chicago Press, 1965), 97; A. Whitney Griswold, "New Thought: A Cult of Success," *American Journal of Sociology* 40 (November 1934): 314.

10. Helen Wilmans, *A Search for Freedom* (Sea Breeze, Florida: Wilmans Publishing House, [1898] 1903), 68, 47, 76, see 27, 31, 65, 118, 139; see Pleasant Daniel Gold, *History of Volusia County Florida* (Florida: E. O. Painter Printing Co., 1927), 384.

11. Wilmans, *Search for Freedom*, 204–9, 212; Gold, *History of Volusia County*, 384.

12. Helen Wilmans, "A Little Egotism," *The Woman's World*, January 25, 1885, 3; Wilmans, *Search for Freedom*, 276, see 235, 244–45, 252–67; see Gold, *History of Volusia County*, 384.

13. Wilmans, *Search for Freedom*, 276.

14. Ibid., 276, 291.

15. See *The Woman's World*, January 5, 1885, 3; Wilmans, *Search for Freedom*, 277, 282.

16. Wilmans, *Search for Freedom*, 298, 299; *The Woman's World*, January 5, 1885, 3.

17. Wilmans, *Search for Freedom*, 299; Helen Wilmans, "Waste-Paper Basket," *Freedom*, April 24, 1901, 4.

18. Helen Wilmans, *The Conquest of Poverty* (Sea Breeze, Florida: International Scientific Organization, 1899), 18, see 16–24; Wilmans, *Search for Freedom*, 300, see 299–302.

19. Wilmans, *Search for Freedom*, 314; "Life of C. F. Burgman Reads Like Page from Present-Day Fiction," *Daytona Morning Journal*, December 12, 1926, in Eugene Del Mar, ed., "The Life Work (A Testimonial) of Helen Wilmans Post, 1831–1907" (scrapbook, 1931, in manuscript and archives, New York Public Library).

20. Wilmans, *Search for Freedom*, 306, see 342; C. Vann Woodward, *Tom Watson: Agrarian Rebel* (London: Oxford University Press, 1975), 182. *Driven* was a popular success. Wilmans claimed that its plot, the story of a family "driven from one home to another, and finally to desperation and death by the land grabbers and corporationists," was based on stories she told Post about her neighbors in California. See *The Woman's World*, December 15, 1884, 4.

21. Wilmans, *Conquest of Poverty*, 26, 35, 38–42; Wilmans, *Search for Freedom*, 310; *The Woman's World*, December 15, 1884, 3.

22. See *The Woman's World*, January 25, 1885, and March 15, 1886.

23. See Gold, *History of Volusia County*; Wilmans, "Waste-Paper Basket," *Freedom*, August 23, 1899, 5; Wilmans, "Waste-Paper Basket," *Freedom*, October 25, 1899, 11.

24. Wilmans was uneasy about invoking the help of God. "I rather guess I am not working for Him [God] since I come to think about it," she added. "Who knows who he is working for, or what." Letter, Helen Wilmans to "Dear Sir," May 1, 188[5], in archives and manuscript department, Chicago Historical Society. See "Little Helen," *The Woman's World*, April 1, 1885, 4.

25. Helen Wilmans, "A Quiet Home," *The Woman's World*, February 20, 1885, 2; Helen Wilmans, "Money Rules the World," *The Woman's World*, August 15, 1885, 5–6. Wilmans never mentioned Rose or her baby again, but three months later she wrote to thank an anonymous reader who'd mailed her baby dresses for Helen and Jessamine. See "Little Helen," 4.

26. Letter, Wilmans to "Dear Sir"; see *The Woman's World*, January 25, 1885, 3; *The Woman's World*, February 20, 1885; *The Woman's World*, April 15, 1886.

27. *The Woman's World*, September 15, 1885, 2; see *The Woman's World*, June 1, 1885.

28. Wilmans, "Gates are Open," *The Woman's World*, November 25, 1884, 2; Wilmans, *The Woman's World*, April 1, 1885, 1; Wilmans, "Woman's Religion," *The Woman's World*, March 15, 1886, 4.

29. Wilmans, "Gates Are Open," 2.

This "survival of the fittest" perspective literally framed Wilmans's paper. A banner across each issue proclaimed, "The world was made for woman as well as man; but she who fails to pre-empt her own claim need blame no man for it—Helen Wilmans." For example, see *The Woman's World*, January 25, 1885.

30. Wilmans, "Woman in Government," *The Woman's World*, January 5, 1885, 1; *The Woman's World*, January 25, 1885; Wilmans, *The Woman's World*, April 1, 1885, 1.

31. Wilmans, *The Woman's World*, September 15, 1885; Wilmans, *The Woman's World*, January 25, 1885, 1.

32. Wilmans, *The Woman's World*, May 15, 1886, 1.

33. Wilmans, *The Woman's World*, May 1, 1885, 2; Wilmans, "Strike Off Our Fetters," *The Woman's World*, April 15, 1885, 3.

34. Wilmans, "Strike Off Our Fetters," 3.

35. Ibid.

36. Wilmans, "Believe in Yourself," *The Woman's World*, November 25, 1884, 1.

37. Wilmans, "Kick!", *The Woman's World*, May 1, 1885, 2.

38. "Open Letter to My Friends," *The Woman's World*, December 15, 1884, 3; see Helen Wilmans, "Half Lights," *Mental Science Magazine* 1 (1887): 51–55; Wilmans, *Search for Freedom*.

39. Wilmans, *The Woman's World*, November 25, 1884, 4; Wilmans, "In Answer to Many Spiritualists," *The Woman's World*, January 5, 1885, 3; Wilmans, "'The Soul that Sinneth It Shall Die,'" *The Woman's World*, November 25, 1884, 2.

40. Wilmans, "Important Questions Answered," *The Woman's World*, January 5, 1885, 2.

41. J. Gordon Melton, "New Thought's Hidden History: Emma Curtis Hopkins, Forgotten Founder" (unpublished paper, Institute for the Study of American Religion, August 1988), 11–13.

Hopkins's class was not Wilmans's first exposure to Christian Science. In the final edition of *The Woman's World* Wilmans published a notice for Mary Plunkett's journal *Love's Light*, and praised Plunkett as "a beautiful, engaging woman" with whom she felt "a case of love at first sight." See *The Woman's World*, May 15, 1886. Wilmans also claimed to have read and thrown away an early version of Eddy's *Science and Health*. See Wilmans, *Search for Freedom*, 332.

42. Wilmans, "Half-Lights," 52–53; see Helen Wilmans, *Back Numbers: Wilmans Express, Condensed*, with Ada Powers (n.p., n.d.), 7.

43. Wilmans, *Conquest of Poverty*, 91–92.

44. Wilmans, *Search for Freedom*, 345.

Frances Lord transformed Wilmans's *The Woman's World* into a "Christian Science" journal replete with news of Hopkins Metaphysical Association meetings. See *The Woman's World*, June 15, 1887.

45. Wilmans, *Conquest of Poverty*, 93–94; Wilmans, *Search for Freedom*, 351–52.

46. Wilmans, *Search for Freedom*, 352; see Wilmans, "Waste-Paper Basket," *Freedom*, November 8, 1899, 11; Wilmans, "Does It Jar You?" *Freedom*, June 5, 1901, 3.

47. Wilmans, *Back Numbers*, 84–89, 163; Woodward, *Tom Watson*, 228.

48. Wilmans, *Conquest of Poverty*, 96; Wilmans, *Search for Freedom*, 352–53.

49. Woodward, *Tom Watson*, 226, 228, 231; "Gone to Florida," *Atlanta Constitution*, September 16, 1892.

50. Wilmans, *Search for Freedom*, 354–56; *Post v. United States*, 135 Fed. 1 (C.C.A. 5, 1905), 3. Between 1892 and 1897 Wilmans and Post lived in Florida, Atlanta, and Boston.

51. *Freedom*, September 26, 1900; see *Freedom*, August 16, 1899, 8.

52. Advertisement in Wilmans, *Conquest of Poverty* (italics in text).

53. *Freedom*, March 21, 1900, 9; *Freedom*, August 1, 1900, 14. See *Freedom*, April 3, 1901, 11; August 16, 1899, 14; August 23, 1899, 11.

54. Gold, *History of Volusia County*, 383–84; 128 *Federal Reporter*, 951–52; 135 *Federal Reporter*, 3; William Walker Atkinson, "Did Helen Wilmans Renege?" in Del Mar, ed., "The Life Works." Sea Breeze was consolidated into Daytona Beach in 1925. Conversation with Wilmans Baggett, March 30, 1987. On typical middle-class incomes, see Nell Irvin Painter, *Standing At Armageddon: The United States, 1877–1919* (New York: W. W. Norton and Co., 1987), xxiii.

55. Wilmans, *Search for Freedom*, 357–59; Wilmans, *Conquest of Poverty*, 99; see Gold, *History of Volusia County*, 383–84.

56. Letter, Stockham to Wilmans, in *Freedom*, March 14, 1900, 5. When Wilmans announced her plan to open a Mental Science university in Sea Breeze, Flower immediately wrote to Wilmans to express his delight with her idea. He wrote a second time to suggest that Wilmans call her city "City Beautiful." Because of the "influence of names . . . on the human mind," this name would encourage inhabitants to keep their homes beautiful, Flower explained. Letter, Flower to Wilmans, in *Freedom*, April 18, 1900, 11; letter, Flower to Wilmans, in *Freedom*, April 25, 1900, 6. On Talbot and Southworth, see Wilmans, "Waste-Paper Basket," *Freedom*, March 6, 1901, 11; *Freedom*, May 1, 1901, 11; Wilmans, "Thought is Master," *Freedom*, March 28, 1900, 2; "The College Fund," *Freedom*, April 18, 1900, 11; "Sea Breeze Events," *Freedom*, November 7, 1900, 11; "George's Weekly," *Freedom*, April 24, 1901, 12.

57. "Mental Scientists Convene," *Seattle Post-Intelligencer*, July 2, 1900, reprinted in *Freedom*, July 18, 1900, 4–5; see "The Mental Science Association," *Freedom*, February 7, 1900, 5–6; *Freedom*, April 4, 1900, 13; "Defends a New Cult," *Milwaukee Sentinel*, reprinted in *Freedom*, October 3, 1900, 12; "Mental Science Association," *Freedom*, May 9, 1900, 10–12; "Home Again," *Freedom*, October 10, 1900, 5.

58. Letter, Wilmans to Del Mar, October 26, 1901, in Del Mar, ed., "The Life Work," her italics; see C. C. Post, "The Mental Science Association and the International Metaphysical League," *Freedom*, March 28, 1900, 3.

59. Wilmans, *Search for Freedom*, 336, her italics; Wilmans, *Blossom of the Century*, 63, 39; Wilmans, *Back Numbers*, 24; Wilmans, "Waste-Paper Basket," *Freedom*, September 27, 1900, 12.

Wilmans argued that a belief in dead matter countenanced fatalism. "If the substance all about us . . . in . . . the forms of minerals, plants and animals is *dead matter,* infused by living spirit, then our only hope of prolonging our lives will be by some method that will release the spirit from the matter," Wilmans explained. "If I knew this to be the true situation, I would never move my hand to save my own life; I would look forward to the time when my spirit would drop its load of death as the chained . . . prisoner looks forward to the hope of freedom." Wilmans, *Blossom of the Century,* 61 (her italics).

60. Wilmans, *Blossom of the Century,* 31.

61. Ibid., 69; Wilmans, *Back Numbers,* 1 (her italics), see 22, 24.

62. Wilmans, *Blossom of the Century,* 40, 99.

63. Wilmans, *Search for Freedom,* 108–9, 62–63; also see 36, 118–19, 188, 272.

64. Ibid., 91, 64.

65. Ibid., 142, 91.

66. Ibid., 31, 254, 252, 262. Wilmans described this marriage as "the biggest mistake of my life." She added, however, that her marriage "release[d] the brain to its normal action again; and this is the best thing I can say of marriage. It is the death of emotional love." She reserved for herself the right to fall in love again, however. See 265, 255.

67. Wilmans, *Search for Freedom,* 269, 274, see 205; Wilmans, *Back Numbers,* 79; Wilmans, *Conquest of Poverty,* 13. *Conquest of Poverty* included substantial chunks of *Search for Freedom.*

68. Wilmans, *Search for Freedom,* 293–94, 347.

69. She described the rich soil of nature as "the indestructible principle of life itself. . . . it was solid ground and rich in the promise of bearing." She could rely on this natural, material selfhood without eradicating her "surface" self. "The frothy surface me used to go down into the depths of this real me and get courage and consolation from it. . . . I was at home in it, and I was at home nowhere else," she wrote. Wilmans, *Search for Freedom,* 210–11.

70. Wilmans, *Search for Freedom,* 91; Wilmans, "Waste-Paper Basket," *Freedom,* June 5, 1901, 11.

71. Wilmans, *Back Numbers,* 62, 25, 41; see 23, 26, 78, 86.

72. Ellis is quoted in Paul Robinson, *The Modernization of Sex* (New York: Harper and Row, 1976), 27; also see Sheila Rowbotham and Jeffrey Weeks, *Socialism and the New Life: The Personal and Sexual Politics of Edward Carpenter and Havelock Ellis* (London: Pluto Press, 1977). On the turn-of-the-century debate about gendered selfhood, see Livingston, *Pragmatism and the Political Economy of Cultural Revolution,* 65, 69–71, 80–81, 84, 137–47; Elizabeth Lunbeck, *The Psychiatric Persuasion: Knowledge, Gender, and Power in Modern America* (Princeton, N.J.: Princeton University Press, 1994), 209, 264.

Mind magazine printed numerous commentaries on the role of desire in male and female character. For example, see Irene Allen Townsend, "What is

Mental Science?" *Mind* 2, no. 6 (September 1898): 358; Dr. J. R. Phelps, "Love and Desire," *Mind* 10, no. 4 (July 1902): 248–52; Flora Howard, "Dominion," *Mind* 1, no. 2 (November 1897): 96; C. Staniland Wake, "Spiritual Marriage," and Mary Robins Mead, "How to Attain Ideals," *Mind* 4, no. 1 (April 1899): 19–24, 45–49; Dr. G. Sterling Wines, "The Psychology of Mental Healing," *Mind* 4, no. 3 (June 1899): 129; James Garrard Stevenson, "What is Marriage?" *Mind* 6, no. 4 (July 1900): 297; Harriet B. Bradbury, "True Desire," *Mind* 2, no. 2 (May 1898): 97–103; Eliza Burt Gamble, "The Influence of Sex on Development," *Mind* 8, no. 2 (May 1901): 97–100; W. E. Clark, "Man, Woman and Poverty," *Mind* 10, no. 4 (July 1902): 278–85; Anna M. Pennock, "True Womanhood," *Mind* 6, no. 5 (August 1900): 381–85; Alida Chandler Emmet, "Concerning Woman," *Mind* 8, no. 1 (April 1901): 29–32.

73. In addition to the female authors listed in endnote 72, see Nancy McKay Gordon, *Woman Revealed* (Chicago: Nancy McKay Gordon, 1901); Julia Seton Sears, M.D., *The Truth About Woman Suffrage* (New York: New Thought Publishers, 1910); see Joy Dixon, "Sexology and the Occult: Sexuality and Subjectivity in Theosophy's New Age," *Journal of the History of Sexuality* 7, no. 31 (1997): 409–33.

74. Wilmans, *Blossom of the Century*, 101–6 (italics in text).

75. Although Wilmans wrote that her "ordinary animal marriage" had taken her through "all the experiences that make hideous the life of women on the present plane," apparently sex with her husband was not one of those hideous experiences. Wilmans, *Search for Freedom*, 184; Wilmans, "Hope for the Future," *Freedom*, February 14, 1900, 8.

76. Wilmans, *Search for Freedom*, 184. Wilmans called her first husband an "Adonis"; see 203 and 191. Her second marriage to a handsome man fifteen years her junior also involved an apparently nonproblematic sexual relationship. As Wilmans informed her readers, her marriage with Post was based on reason, freedom, and justice, in which sex had its place. Wilmans, "Waste-Paper Basket," *Freedom*, April 24, 1901, 4–5.

77. Wilmans, *Blossom of the Century*, 101; Wilmans, *Search for Freedom*, 183; Wilmans, "Waste-Paper Basket," *Freedom*, May 23, 1900, 11 (her italics).

78. Wilmans, *Search for Freedom*, 168 (her italics), 170, see 184.

79. Helen Wilmans, *The Conquest of Poverty* (Sea Breeze, Florida: Wilmans Publishing House, 1901), 74. The 1901 edition of *Conquest* was repaginated. The chapters by Lida Hood Talbot were omitted, the order of several chapters shifted, and some new material was added. Hereafter references to the revised *Conquest* will include publishing date, to distinguish it from the 1899 version.

80. This animal self was only a problem when repressed (it turns to rend you) or when beaten down by external forces (this forces women to depend upon others for sustenance, like a piece of livestock). Only when woman is repressed or oppressed does she become "matter." She is then forced to suffer, breed, and die in a mindless treadmill of existence. Her inner animal self is her

savior because it "kicks" against ties of slavery. Through its struggles woman becomes not disembodied spirit, nor mindless matter, but fruitful earth and embodied mind.

81. Wilmans, *Conquest of Poverty* (1901), dedication; Wilmans, *Conquest of Poverty*, 99 (her italics).

82. Wilmans, *Conquest of Poverty*, 67–68, 90.

83. Wilmans, *Conquest of Poverty* (1901), 96 (my italics), 140–41.

84. Wilmans, *Conquest of Poverty*, 95.

85. Wilmans, *Conquest of Poverty* (1901), 131; Wilmans, "Marriage," *The Woman's World*, December 15, 1884, 4; *The Woman's World*, September 15, 1885, 3 (her italics); *The Woman's World*, August 15, 1885, 4; Lucinda Chandler, "Woman's Work and Equal Rights," *The Woman's World*, November 25, 1884, 4.

86. Wilmans, *Search for Freedom*, 363; Wilmans, *Conquest of Poverty* (1901), 105.

87. Wilmans, *Conquest of Poverty*, 12; Wilmans, *Conquest of Poverty* (1901), 73.

88. Wilmans, "Waste-Paper Basket," *Freedom*, February 28, 1900, 4–5.

89. Nichols, "God is Our Support," 146 (her italics).

90. Wilmans, *Conquest of Poverty* (1901), 89–90, see 84.

91. Wilmans, *Back Numbers*, 27 (her italics).

92. Helen Wilmans, "Willing Slaves of the Nineteenth Century," *Commonwealth Library* no. 4 (1895): 1–4; Wilmans, *Search for Freedom*, 310.

93. Compare Wilmans, "Willing Slaves," with version in *Search for Freedom*, 307–11.

CHAPTER 6

1. "Statement of Principles," Union for Concerted Moral Effort, Worcester *Evening Gazette*, August 5, 1892, p. 4, col. 3, in Ross E. Paulson, *Radicalism and Reform: The Vrooman Family and American Social Thought, 1837–1937* (Lexington: University of Kentucky Press, 1968), 84.

2. R. Heber Newton, "The New Century's Call," *Mind* 5, no. 3 (December 1899):147.

3. Reform-minded Protestant ministers who embraced New Thought include Hugh Pentecost, J. Stitt Wilson, Benjamin Fay Mills, Henry Frank, and R. Heber Newton. George Herron was sympathetic to New Thought. Minot Savage was fascinated by psychic phenomena. He ordained Helen Van-Anderson. Journalists interested in New Thought include Paul Tyner, Benjamin Flower, Helen Campbell, Ernest Crosby, Bolton Hall, and C. F. Burgman. Populist activists include J. A. Edgarton and C. C. Post. Reform-minded novelists and poets who embraced New Thought include Edwin Markham, Nellie Blessing Eyster, and Ella Wheeler Wilcox. Novelists who were interested in psychic phenomena and Christian Science include Hamlin Garland, Joaquin Miller, William Dean Howells, Edward Bellamy, and Harold Frederic. Socialists interested in

New Thought include Allen Ricker and Josephine Conger. Socialists interested in psychic power or Christian Science include Ernest Untermann, Upton Sinclair, and Eugene Debs. Woman movement leaders interested in New Thought include Abby Morton Diaz, Elizabeth Boynton Harbert, Lucinda Chandler, Louisa Southworth, Clara Colby, Frances Lord, Alice Stockham, Mary Livermore, Frances Willard, and Elizabeth Smith Miller.

4. Charles Brodie Patterson's paraphrase of Trine's words, in Patterson's "Ralph Waldo Trine: A Biographical Sketch," *Mind* 9, no. 5 (February 1902): 327; Ella Wheeler Wilcox, *Every-Day Thoughts in Prose and Verse* (Chicago: W. B. Conkey Co., 1901), 249, 336; see Horatio W. Dresser, *History of the New Thought Movement* (New York: Thomas Y. Crowell, 1919), 179–82.

5. J.[ohn] E.[mery] M.[Clean], "Growth By Absorption," *Mind* 7, no. 6 (March 1901): 464; see J. E. M., "Editorial Department," *Mind* 8, no. 1 (April 1901): 60, and 8 no. 6 (September 1901): 458.

6. For two opposing viewpoints on New Thought and the Progressives, see Donald Meyer, *The Positive Thinkers: Religion as Pop Psychology from Mary Baker Eddy to Oral Roberts* (New York: Pantheon Books, [1965] 1980), 106, 112, and Richard Weiss, *The American Myth of Success: From Horatio Alger to Norman Vincent Peale* (1969; reprinted, Urbana: University of Illinois Press, 1988), 155.

7. Daniel T. Rogers, "In Search of Progressivism," *Reviews in American History* 10, no. 4 (December 1982): 123.

8. Leon Fink, *Workingmen's Democracy: The Knights of Labor and American Politics* (Urbana: University of Illinois Press, 1983), 4–6.

9. Historians generally discuss republicanism as one of the dominant political ideologies of the revolutionary era and early republic whose influence culminated, and ended, with the Civil War. My reading of the sources indicates that the vision of a republican commonwealth did not vanish with the Civil War. Rather, what had been high political philosophy in one generation became the province of reformers and social critics in a later one. See James Livingston, *Pragmatism and the Political Economy of Cultural Revolution, 1850–1940* (Chapel Hill: University of North Carolina Press, 1994), 311.

10. The racialized discourse of civilization is analyzed in Gail Bederman, *Manliness and Civilization: A Cultural History of Gender and Race in the United States, 1880–1917* (Chicago: University of Chicago Press, 1995). See Louise Michele Newman, "Laying Claim to Difference: Ideologies of Race and Gender in the U.S. Woman's Movement, 1870–1920" (Ph.D. dissertation, Brown University, 1992), 7; Linda Gordon, *Woman's Body, Woman's Right: A Social History of Birth Control in America* (New York: Penguin Books, 1976), 142; Elizabeth Lunbeck, *The Psychiatric Persuasion: Knowledge, Gender, and Power in Modern America* (Princeton, N.J.: Princeton University Press, 1994), 123; also see Henry May, *The End of American Innocence* (Chicago: Quadrangle Books, 1959), 26–27, 122–23, 349.

Reformers' talk of "the race" does not mean that they were necessarily racists in the modern sense. First, color was not yet seen as the exclusive marker of race. Racial categories included "Celt," "Gaul," "Anglo-Saxon," and "Teuton," all of whom today would be characterized as European in nationality and "white" in race. Second, then, as now, there was no consistent agreement upon how the boundaries of race should be drawn. Josiah Strong's tract *Our Country*, for example, calculated the numbers of Anglo-Saxons by the numbers of people who spoke English. Finally, unlike modern white supremacists, white Protestants who believed that Anglo-Saxons had reached the pinnacle of human evolution did not necessarily despise "lesser" races. Some believed that the "lower" races were permanently mired in savagery, and eagerly anticipated their eventual extermination. But others believed that all races must eventually "advance." They therefore devoted themselves to these races' "uplift." Both approaches were compatible with a belief in Anglo-Saxon evolutionary superiority.

11. Richard Hofstadter, *Social Darwinism in American Thought* (Boston: Beacon Press, [1944] 1955), 32–66.

12. Historian Paul Boyer describes Flower's writings as the epitome of the "distinctive 1890s blend of political, economic and moral preoccupations." Paul Boyer, *Urban Masses and Moral Order in America* (Cambridge: Harvard University Press, 1978), 170. On Flower's political activities, see B.[enjamin] O.[range] Flower, *Progressive Men, Women and Movements of the Past Twenty-Five Years* (Boston: The New Arena, 1914), 100, 128–29, 153; Henry May, *Protestant Churches and Industrial America* (New York: Harper and Bros., 1949), 227–28; Charles Howard Hopkins, *The Rise of the Social Gospel in American Protestantism* (New Haven: Yale University Press, [1940] 1967), 196; David Pivar, *Purity Crusade: Sexual Morality and Social Control, 1868–1900* (Westport Conn.: Greenwood Press, 1973; Ross E. Paulson, *Radicalism and Reform: the Vrooman Family and American Social Thought, 1837–1937* (University of Kentucky Press, 1968), 92–97.

13. B.[enjamin] O.[range] Flower, "Leprosy of the Soul," *The Arena* 3 (1890–1891): 635; B. O. Flower, "Editorial Notes," *The Arena* 4 (1891): 763–64. Flower describes ideal race characteristics in B. O. Flower, "Edwin Markham: A Prophet-Poet of the Fraternal State," *The Arena* 27, no. 4 (April 1902): 391–414. His critique of monopolists can be found in Flower, *Progressive Men*, 27–58.

Flower usually spoke of "the people" rather than "Anglo-Saxons." He treated the two phrases as synonymous, however. His memoir *Progressive Men, Women and Movements of the Past Twenty-Five Years* surveyed a vast range of reformers and reform movements between the years 1889 and 1914. The book did not mention a single African American leader or reform movement. See Flower, *Progressive Men*, 85; B. O. Flower, "The Proposed Federation of the Anglo-Saxon Nations," *The Arena* 20 (April 1898): 228–29. Flower did publish, and praise, the writings of selected African American leaders whose perspective could be assimilated to an evolutionary framework, including Booker T. Washington and W. H. Councill.

In his later years Flower crusaded against American Catholics. Historians have expressed surprise over such behavior on the part of a major reformer. Flower's anti-Catholic bigotry seems less surprising once one realizes that he had always been concerned with the fate of white Protestants rather than with the fate of "the people" as a whole. See John Higham, *Strangers in the Land: Patterns of American Nativism, 1860–1925* (New York: Atheneum Press, [1955] 1970), 180–84, 369 n. 64. Also see Henry May's discussion of the phrase "the people" in his *End of American Innocence*, 26–27.

14. Flower argued that just as nineteenth-century science had brought material forces under the sway of humanity, so were new breakthroughs in hypnotism and mental healing now bringing invisible spiritual and moral forces under human control. B.[enjamin] O.[range] Flower, "Hypnotism and its Relation to Psychical Research," *The Arena* 5 (1891): 317; see Flower, *Progressive Men*, 81, 83, 97–100, 143–44, 169, 172; see B. O. Flower, "Some of Civilization's Silent Currents," *The Arena* 6 (1892): 772.

15. Flower, "Hypnotism," 331–33, 326, 321–22 (his italics).

16. Flower, *Progressive Men*, 306, see 181, 188–90, 192.

17. B.[enjamin] O.[range] Flower, "A Transitional Period," *The Arena* 3 (1890–91): 124, 125. See B. O. Flower, "Behind the Deed the Thought," *The Arena* 5 (1891–2): 527–28.

18. Flower, *Progressive Men*, 153. Flower's faith in the power of thought to alter the beliefs of others—whether through hypnotism, Christian Science, or spiritualism—informed the content and the structure of his political activism. For example, see B.[enjamin] O.[range] Flower, "Fashion's Slaves," *The Arena* 4 (1891): 419–20; Flower, "Behind the Deed the Thought," 527–28.

19. B.[enjamin] O.[range] Flower, "The Era of Woman," *The Arena* 4 (1891): 382, 384; Flower, "Civilization's Silent Currents," 766; Flower, *Progressive Men*, 143–44, see 145, 150 (where Flower insists that the "clear mental vision, searching logic, and . . . moral courage and enthusiasm" of the "womanly woman" is now "vital to the progress of nations and civilizations").

20. Flower encourages the true man to evolve into a womanly "angel of mercy and love" in "Civilization's Silent Currents," 767.

21. Flower, *Progressive Men*, 131, 129. The Arena Clubs' mode of operation was identical to that of the women's clubs. They presented "a new moral issue" each month for study by the group, publicized their findings, and worked for legislation to right the moral wrong uncovered. See Boyer, *Urban Masses and Moral Order*, 163. The organizations awakening humanity are listed in Flower, "Civilization's Silent Currents," 766; also see Flower, *Progressive Men*, 144; "Symposium on Women's Clubs," *The Arena* 6 (1892): 362–88.

22. Flower, "Era of Woman," 384; Flower, *Progressive Men*, 269–70, see 82, 98–99, 124–25. The phrase "new time" was a favorite with Flower and other like-minded reformers. After Flower left the *The Arena* he edited a journal entitled *The New Time*. He reverently quoted Frances Willard's assertion that the nation was in the "gray light of a coming day, which would be marked by a

moral, social, and economic revolution. . . . perhaps some of us will live to see the full splendor of this new time; for few people realize how deep-rooted, far-reaching and many-sided is the present revolutionary movement" (Flower, *Progressive Men*, 272). New Thought leaders also frequently used the phrase "New Time." See Helen Wilmans, *A Search for Freedom* (Sea Breeze, Florida: Freedom Publishing Co., 1898), 367; Alice B. Stockham and Lida Hood Talbot, *Koradine Letters* (Chicago: Alice B. Stockham Co., 1893), 89; Emma Curtis Hopkins, "C.S. Ordination Address," *Christian Science* 1, no. 7 (March 1889): 174–75; Frances Lord, *Christian Science Healing* (London: George Redway, 1888), 341; Elizabeth Boynton Harbert, "Ordination Address," *Christian Science* 1, no. 6 (February 1889): 141, 143; Elizabeth Boynton Harbert, Ph.D., *Amore* (New York: Lovell, Gestefeld and Co., 1892), 219.

On womanly influence, see Jan Lewis, "The Republican Wife: Virtue and Seduction in the Early Republic," *William and Mary Quarterly* 44, no. 4 (October 1987): 689–721; Jan Lewis, "Mother's Love: The Construction of an Emotion in Nineteenth-Century America," in Andrew E. Barnes and Peter N. Stearns, eds., *Social History and Issues in Human Consciousness: Some Interdisciplinary Connections* (New York: New York University Press, 1989), 209–29; Lori D. Ginzberg, *Women and the Work of Benevolence* (New Haven: Yale University Press, 1990), 15.

23. See biographical entry on Elizabeth Boynton Harbert in Frances E. Willard and Mary A. Livermore, *A Woman of the Century* (New York, 1893), 357; Steven M. Buechler, *The Transformation of the Woman Suffrage Movement: The Case of Illinois, 1850–1920* (New Brunswick, N.J.: Rutgers University Press, 1986), 104–17; Steven M. Buechler, "Elizabeth Boynton Harbert and the Woman Suffrage Movement, 1870–1896," *Signs* 13, no. 1 (autumn 1987): 78–97.

24. Harbert, "Ordination Address," 141, 143; "Hopkins Metaphysical Association" and "Personal Mention," *Christian Science* 1, no. 8 (April 1889): 221, 224, 231; see Kathi L. Kern, *A Secular Faith: Elizabeth Cady Stanton and the Woman's Bible* (Ithaca, N.Y.: Cornell University Press, forthcoming).

25. Harbert, *Amore*, 230.

26. Ibid., 136, 189, 185.

27. Ibid., 148, 244, 276, see 258 for a description of Theodora and Philip's daughter, who prays to her "Heavenly Father and Mother" and is protected by the "God of Love."

28. Ibid., 173, 103, 189, 132.

29. Ibid., 219, 154; see 40, 185, 189, 237, 240 for discussions of New Thought meditation.

30. Ibid., 139, 36, 190, 30.

31. Willard and Livermore, *Woman of the Century*, 357.

32. Harbert, *Amore*, 39 (her italics), 242, 244.

33. Lucinda Chandler, "Motherhood, Its Power Over Human Destiny," quoted in Alice B. Stockham, *Tokology: A Book for Every Woman* (Chicago: Alice B. Stockham Co., 1889), 158.

34. Biographical entry on Lucinda Chandler in Willard and Livermore, *Woman of the Century,* 165; Buechler, *Transformation of Woman Suffrage,* 133; Buechler, "Elizabeth Boynton Harbert," 95; William Leach, *True Love and Perfect Union: The Feminist Reform of Sex and Society* (New York: Basic Books, 1980), 88–91; Kern, *A Secular Faith; The Woman's World,* December 15, 1884: 3; *Illinois Woman's Press Association Yearbook,* 1892, 1894, 1898–1899.

35. Lucinda B. Chandler, "What Should America Do for Womanhood?" *The New Time* (June 1898): 396–99. See reference to Chandler's "Americanism" in Willard and Livermore, *Woman of the Century,* 165.

36. Chandler, "What Should America Do," 398–400.

37. Lucinda B. Chandler, "The Completion of Humanity," *Mind* 10, no. 5 (August 1902): 372, 373, 374.

38. See Jane Johnson Bernardete, "Diaz, Abby Morton," in Edward T. James, Janet Wilson James, and Paul Boyer, eds., *Notable American Women,* 3 vols. (Cambridge, Mass.: Belknap Press, 1971) 1, 471–73; Charles Brodie Patterson, "Abby Morton Diaz: A Biographical Sketch," *Mind* 10, no. 3 (June 1902): 169; *The American Purity Alliance Twentieth Annual Report* (New York, 1896), 11; Willard and Livermore, *Woman of the Century.*

39. Mari Jo Buhle, *Women and American Socialism* (Urbana: University of Illinois Press, 1981), 79; "An Interesting Feature," *Mind* 9, no. 1 (October 1901): 57; see Abby Morton Diaz, *Only a Flock of Women* (Boston: D. Lothrop Co., 1893); Hulda B. Loud, "A Skeptic and the Mental Healers," *Truth,* 1, no. 1 (November 1887): 23; Dresser, *History of New Thought,* 181, 180, 185; "The Metaphysical Club," *The Journal of Practical Metaphysics* 1, no. 2 (November 1896): 57; Patterson, "Abby Morton Diaz," 169; Abby Morton Diaz's four-part series "Hindrances to World-Betterment" in *Mind* 9, nos. 3–6 (December 1901–March 1902).

40. Mrs. Abby Morton Diaz, *Spirit as a Power* (Belmont, Mass: Mrs. Abby Morton Diaz, 1886), 14, 23, 26–29, see 24, 28.

41. Abby Morton Diaz, "The Human Problem According to Law," *The Arena* 6 (1895): 620, 622 (her italics).

42. Diaz, "Human Problem," 622, 624 (her italics).

43. Biographical entry on Helen Campbell in Willard and Livermore, *Woman of the Century,* 148; biographical entry on Campbell in *Notable American Women* 1, 280–81; Boyer, *Urban Masses and Moral Order,* 127; Pivar, *Purity Crusade,* 152; Mary A. Hill, *Charlotte Perkins Gilman: The Making of a Radical Feminist, 1860–1896* (Philadelphia: Temple University Press, 1980), 239; *Bibliography of Settlements,* fourth edition, compiled by Caroline Williamson Montgomery (New York: 1900), 14; Flower, *Progressive Men,* 125.

44. Helen Campbell, "Voice or Echo?" *Journal of Practical Metaphysics* 1, no. 6 (March 1897): 174 (her italics).

See biographical entry on Helen Campbell in *Notable American Women;* Horatio W. Dresser, *The Heart of It,* edited by Helen Campbell and Katharine Westendorf (Boston: Geo. H. Ellis, 1897); Helen Campbell, "Social Settlements and the Civic Sense," *The Arena* 20, no. 5 (November–December 1898): 589–

603; Paul Tyner, "The Metaphysical Movement," *American Monthly Review of Reviews* 25, no. 3 (March 1902): 315; "The New Thought Federation," *Mind* 13, no. 5 (May 1904): 464–65; see Campbell's *Practical Metaphysics* articles: "Some New Statistics," 1, no. 4 (January 1897): 102–3; "The Creed of Joseph Mazzini," 1, no. 8 (May 1897): 233–34; "Outward Bound," 2, no. 2 (November 1897): 45–48. Toward the end of her life Campbell embraced the Baha'i faith, as did her friend Sarah Farmer. By then Farmer's Greenacre had become a Baha'i center. Campbell's remains were buried at Greenacre.

Horatio Dresser, who had studied at Harvard under William James, also served as a link between New Thought and more academic scholars of the "new psychology." See articles in his *Journal of Practical Metaphysics*, 1896–1897, including Chas. M. Barrows, "What is Psychology?" 1, no. 5 (February 1897): 130–33, and "Editorial Department," 1, no. 6 (March 1897): 343; see Gail Thain Parker, *Mind Cure in New England* (New Hampshire: University Press of New England, 1973), 131–49.

45. Campbell, "Social Settlements and the Civic Sense," 593, 590, 595, 596. On Campbell's friend Charlotte Perkins Gilman's relationship to New Thought, see Parker, *Mind Cure in New England*, 89–92.

46. See Norma Kidd Green's biography of Clara Colby in *Notable American Women* 1, 357.

47. See "Personal Mention," *Christian Science* 1, no. 8 (April 1889): 231; advertisement for the *Woman's Tribune* in back pages of *Christian Science* 1, no. 6 (February 1889); advertisement in *Freedom* (August 16, 1899): 16. See Clara Bewick Colby, "Elizabeth Cady Stanton," *The Arena* 29, no. 2 (February 1903): 152, 159; Colby to Elizabeth Morrison Boynton Harbert, 11 October 1912, Harbert Collection Box 3 Folder 34, CSm-H, quoted in Kern, *A Secular Faith*; Green's biography of Clara Colby in *Notable American Women* 1, 357.

48. Frances E. Willard, *How to Win: A Book for Girls* (New York: Funk and Wagnalls, 1886), in *The Ideal of the New Woman According to the Woman's Christian Temperance Union*, ed. and introduced by Caroline DeSwarte Gifford (New York: Garland Press, 1987), 86–90; Frances E. Willard, *Writing Out My Heart: Selections from the Journal of Frances E. Willard, 1855–1896* (Urbana: University of Illinois Press, 1995), 389; advertisement in *Journal of Practical Metaphysics* 2, no. 5 (February 1898): 160; see Frances E. Willard, "The Coming Brotherhood," *The Arena* 6 (1892): 321; *Illinois Woman's Press Association Yearbook*, 1891, 1892, 1893.

49. Frances E. Willard, *Glimpses of Fifty Years* (Chicago: Woman's Christian Temperance Publication Association, 1889), 636. Although Willard was supportive of New Thought, the movement was clearly controversial. She wrote that she was "often asked what [she thought] about the mental method" and that she had been "warned repeatedly against it by excellent and trusted friends" (636).

50. *Bible Year Book*, compiled by Mary F. Haydon (Chicago: The Psychic Research Co., 1903). Harbert, Chandler, Diaz, Campbell, Colby, and Willard were only some of the woman movement leaders who embraced New Thought.

See Indiana suffrage, temperance and Populist activist Helen Gougar's praise of *Koradine Letters*, in "Opinions of Koradine Letters," Box 3, Anna Gordon Papers, unmicrofilmed collection, NWCTU archives, Evanston IL, folder AA6, correspondence 1893. On suffrage and temperance activist Louisa Southworth's New Thought activities, see Louisa Southworth, "The Baccalaureate," *Christian Science* 1, no. 6 (February 1889): 144; "Thought is Master," *Freedom*, March 28, 1900, 2; "Mental Science Association," *Freedom*, April 4, 1900, 13; "The College Fund," *Freedom*, April 18, 1900, 11. On Southworth's suffrage activism, see Susan B. Anthony and Ida Husted Harper, eds., *The History of Woman Suffrage* vol. 4, 1883–1900 (New York: Arno and the New York Times, 1969), 219, 240, 250, 257, 878–79, 879 n. On Elizabeth Cady Stanton's exposure to New Thought, see Elizabeth Cady Stanton, *Eighty Years and More: Reminiscences, 1815–1897* (New York: Schocken Books, 1971), 377, 390–92; Charles S. Braden, *Spirits in Rebellion: The Rise and Development of New Thought* (Dallas: Southern Methodist University Press, 1963), 143, 411, 413. Stanton dismissed mind cure as a "fantasy" and an "epidemic"; see Kern, *Secular Faith*. It was ironic that in an obituary for Stanton, Clara Colby wrote that "Mrs. Stanton was a practical exponent of much that is now taught as the New Thought." Colby, "Elizabeth Cady Stanton," 159.

Perhaps Colby's obituary was not so unjust, however. Although Stanton rejected New Thought, her outlook in her later years contained many of the evolutionary republican elements that informed the views of her New Thought peers. Stanton believed that "woman" could follow the evolutionary laws of heredity, transform the race and save the republic. She simply did not believe that New Thought meditations were helpful means to this end. See Elizabeth Cady Stanton, "Where Must Lasting Progress Begin?" *The Arena* 4 (1891): 295–98.

51. Mary A. Livermore (1820–1905) was also a lifetime member of Diaz's Women's Educational and Industrial Union. Livermore shared the evolutionary republicanism typical of white middle-class reformers of the 1890s. For example, see Mary A. Livermore, "Centuries of Dishonor," *The Arena* 1 (1889–1890): 83–92. She was a friend of Elizabeth Boynton Harbert and an admirer of Alice Stockham's work. She was also friendly with Benjamin Flower, who wrote that Livermore's "clear mental vision, searching logic, and passion for justice . . . made her visits always a source of inspiration, pleasure, and profit." Flower, *Progressive Men*, 145; see Harvey B. Hurd and Robert D. Shippard, eds., *Historical Encyclopedia of Illinois and History of Evanston* 2 (Chicago: Munsell Publishing Co., 1906), 560; see Livermore's warm supporting blurb for Stockham's *Tokology* in the back pages of Stockham, *Tokology*, rev. ed. (1889).

Like Harbert and Flower, Livermore was fascinated by spiritualism, hypnosis, and New Thought. She adored the writings of New Thought author Lilian Whiting. Like Willard, Livermore wrote a supporting blurb for Newcomb's *All's Right With the World*. "Its philosophy is of the divinest character, and I can hardly open its pages anywhere that I do not read a statement which is a veritable spiritual tonic," she wrote. She was close friends with bestselling New

Thought author Ralph Waldo Trine. Trine was married, in 1898, in her home. The ceremony was performed by Livermore's husband, a Universalist minister.

See Elizabeth F. Hoxie's biography of Whiting in James et al., *Notable American Women* 3, 592–93; see *Journal of Practical Metaphysics* 2, no. 5 (February 1898): 160; Patterson, "Ralph Waldo Trine," 327; Robert E. Riegel's biography of Livermore in *Notable American Women* 2, 410–13.

52. Buhle, *Women and American Socialism*, 77, her italics; see Franklin Rosemont, "Bellamy, Edward (1850–1898)," in Mari Jo Buhle, Paul Buhle, and Dan Georgakas, eds., *Encyclopedia of the American Left* (Urbana: University of Illinois Press, 1992), 79–80.

53. Edward Bellamy, *Looking Backwards: 2000–1887* (New York: Modern Library, 1982), quotes on pages 38, 195.

54. Bellamy, *Looking Backwards*, 206.

Bellamy claimed that his 1874 manuscript "The Religion of Solidarity" outlined the philosophical basis of his later writings. The manuscript explained that each person has a dual nature comprising the desirous individual life and the serene, impersonal, "universal life" that recognizes its "solidarity with all things and all existence." Edward Bellamy, *The Religion of Solidarity* (London: Concord Grove Press, 1984), 8, 11, 13; see 25–6. Bellamy viewed "ecstasies, trances and similar suspensions of the sense of personal identity" as glimpses of this higher, universal self. See Rosemont, "Bellamy, Edward (1850–1898)," in Buhle, Buhle, and Georgakas, eds., *Encyclopedia of the American Left*, 80. He was therefore fascinated by telepathy.

Bellamy explained the place of telepathy in "race" evolution in his short story "To Whom This May Come," published in *The Nationalist* in 1889 and reprinted in Bellamy, *Religion*, 44–59. The tale described the inhabitants of a remote island who had practiced a "rigid system of stirpiculture" and thereby developed telepathic powers. Their abilities were the result of "a slight acceleration . . . of the course of universal human evolution, which in time was destined to lead to the disuse of speech and the substitution of direct mental vision on the part of all races." Their eugenic practices had altered their physical form as well. Though of Persian origin, the islanders had become "a white and handsome people" of an obviously "high order of civilization."

55. Buhle, *Women and American Socialism*, 76–77, 79–81; Hill, *Charlotte Perkins Gilman*, 170; Rosemont, "Bellamy Edward (1850–98)," in Buhle, Buhle, and Georgakas, eds., *Encyclopedia of the American Left*.

56. See Robert T. Handy, ed., *The Social Gospel in America, 1870–1920* (New York: Oxford University Press, 1966), 3–14; Hopkins, *Rise of the Social Gospel*; May, *Protestant Churches and Industrial America*.

57. George Herron, *Between Caesar and Jesus*, 1899, cited in Robert M. Crunden, *Ministers of Reform: The Progressive's Achievement in American Civilization, 1889–1920* (Urbana: University of Illinois Press, 1984), 50; George Herron, "The Social Value of Individual Failure," *The Arena* 6 (1895): 641, 638. Herron's radical ideas made him a hero among Populists, socialists, and early Progressives alike (Crunden, *Ministers of Reform*, 47).

58. Hopkins, *Rise of the Social Gospel;* May, *Protestant Churches and Industrial America.*

59. As Josiah Strong explained, the Anglo-Saxons' evolution to spiritual perfection required the full exercise of the race's "peculiarly aggressive traits." Anglo-Saxons must conquer and even exterminate "inferior races," who would then be replaced by "better and finer [human] material." Strong viewed racial violence and spiritual uplift as complementary methods of spiritualizing humanity. Josiah Strong, *Our Country* (1885), in T. H. Breen, ed., *The Power of Words: Documents in American History,* vol. 2, From 1865 (New York: HarperCollins College Publishers, 1996), 88; see Dorothea R. Muller, "The Social Philosophy of Josiah Strong: Social Christianity and American Progressivism," *Church History* 28 (1959): 183–99.

60. Minot Savage, quoted in Benjamin Flower, "Science and Psychical Research," *The Arena* 20 (July 1898): 87; see Muller, "Social Philosophy of Josiah Strong." In contrast to working-class thinkers who opposed capitalism because of exploitative wages and brutal working conditions, most Christian Socialist and Social Gospel theorists opposed unregulated capitalism because it encouraged "selfishness."

61. Charles Brodie Patterson, "R. Heber Newton: A Biographic Sketch," *Mind* 9, no. 1 (October 1901): 7; Hopkins, *Rise of the Social Gospel,* 34, see 33, 107–08, 176; May, *Protestant Churches and Industrial America,* 176–77; see Mary O. Furner, *Advocacy and Objectivity* (Lexington: University Press of Kentucky, 1975), 60, 75; entry on Richard Heber Newton in George Derby and James Terry White, eds., *National Cyclopaedia of American Biography* 3 (New York: J. T. White and Co., 1893), 304.

62. "International Metaphysical League," *Mind* 5, no. 1 (October 1899): 63; see Dresser, *History of New Thought,* 195–96, 199; Patterson, "R. Heber Newton," 8; Tyner, "The Metaphysical Movement"; Braden, *Spirits in Rebellion,* 181–82, 184; "A Word of Congratulations," *Mind* 11, no. 1 (October 1902): 27.

63. Rev. R. Heber Newton, "The New Century's Call," *Mind* 5, no. 3 (December 1899): 131–51. Quotes are from pages 141, 147, 148, 149, 148.

64. Biographical entry on Benjamin Fay Mills in George Derby and James Terry White, *National Cyclopaedia of American Biography* 14 (New York: J. T. White and Co., 1910), 178; see Hopkins, *Rise of the Social Gospel,* 194; entry on Mills in Henry Warner Bowden, ed., *Dictionary of American Religious Biography,* 2d ed (Westport, Conn.: Greenwood Press, 1993), 369–70.

65. Benjamin Fay Mills, "Between the Animals and the Angels," *The Arena* 22, no. 1 (July 1899): 1–14, quotations on pages 5, 6, 7, 11, 8, 13.

66. Mills entry in *National Cyclopedia of American Biography,* vol. 14; Dresser, *History of New Thought,* 240; Frances Bjorkman, "The Literature of the 'New Thoughters,'" *World's Work* (January 1910): 12475; Flower, *Progressive Men,* 132; see Ella Wheeler Wilcox's praise of Mills and his Fellowship movement in *New Thought Common Sense, and What Life Means to Me* (Chicago: W. B. Conkey Co., 1908), 259; see *Power* 4, no. 12 (June 1911): 362.

67. Hugh O. Pentecost began his career as a pro-labor, pro-Single Tax Con-

gregational minister. He eventually embraced anarchism and Helen Wilmans's Mental Science. May, *Protestant Churches and Industrial America,* 237–39; "Mental Science Association," *Freedom,* May 9, 1900, 11; *Freedom,* June 5, 1901, 6.

Henry Frank (1854–1933) had been a Methodist circuit rider and a Congregationalist minister before he rejected all orthodoxy and created the "Rationalist Society of New York." By the turn of the century Frank had allied himself with the New Thought movement. In 1908 he served as the president of the National New Thought Alliance. See biographical entry on Henry Frank in *National Cyclopaedia of American Biography* 23 (New York: J. T. White, 1933), 196; Thomas C. Dyas, "Henry Frank," *Mind* 12, no. 9 (December 1903): 648, 651; Braden, *Spirits in Rebellion,* 328, 184, 185. J. Stitt Wilson was one of the original contributors to the journal *The Social Gospel.* Profoundly influenced by George Herron, Wilson resigned his ministry in 1897 in order to devote himself to the spread of social justice. Wilson went on to become the mayor of Berkeley, California—and one of the honorary vice presidents of the 1904 New Thought Federation. Wilson's outlook had always been congruent with that of most reform-oriented New Thought leaders. See Hopkins, *Rise of the Social Gospel,* 196, 199–200; J. Stitt Wilson, "The 'Social Crusade,'" *The New Time* (April 1898): 235; Braden, *Spirits in Rebellion,* 181.

Wilson's "Isaiah," George Herron, gave the New Thought movement at least passing support as well. Meyer, *Positive Thinkers,* 35; Tyner, "Metaphysical Movement," 316.

Minot Savage (1841–1918), the Congregational-turned-Unitarian preacher who a recent biographer (Henry Warner Bowden) called "one of the greatest preachers of the era," was also a member of the American Psychic Society, a believer in spiritualism, and a friendly ally of the New Thought movement. Bowden, *Dictionary of American Religious Biography,* 470; see Flower, *Progressive Men,* 170–71.

68. These typical quotes are from Wilson, "The 'Social Crusade,'" 235.

69. Boyer, *Urban Masses and Moral Order,* 162–63.

70. Worcester *Evening Gazette,* August 5, 1892, 4, col. 3, cited in Paulson, *Radicalism and Reform,* 84.

71. Paulson, *Radicalism and Reform,* 89, 91. An early supporter of the Unions was clergyman Josiah Strong, who did not agree with the Vroomans' inclusive stance on race. See Paulson, 78, 81, 83–87.

72. *The Kingdom,* 7 (April 27, 1894): 30, cited in Paulson, *Radicalism and Reform,* 93–94; see 92.

73. Flower, *Progressive Men,* 128–29; Paulson, *Radicalism and Reform,* 94 n. 42, 95 n.47, 95–96. The American Institute of Christian Sociology had similar goals. See Hopkins, *Rise of the Social Gospel,* 164–65.

74. See Mrs. Anna Rice Powell, "The American Purity Alliance and Its Work," in Aaron M. Powell, ed., *The National Purity Congress* (New York: American Purity Alliance, 1896), 130–37; Pivar, *Purity Crusade,* 224–25, 238, 242.

75. Pauline Holme, "Address to the National Purity Congress," and Dr. Laura Satterthwaite, "The Great Need of the Moral Crusade," both in Powell, ed., *National Purity Congress*, 189, 63–64; see Aaron M. Powell, "Call for the Congress"; Rev. S. H. Virgin, "The Religious Aspects of the Purity Movement"; Mary Wood-Allen, M.D., "Moral Education of the Young"; Rev. J. B. Welty, "The Need of White Cross Work"; Mrs. J. H. Kellogg, "Purity and Parental Responsibility," in Powell, *National Purity Congress*, xiii, 35, 227, 244, 214.

This was not the only concern discussed at the Congress. Congress speakers approached the issue of purity from a variety of angles. See papers by Rev. Antoinette Brown Blackwell and Drs. Emily and Elizabeth Blackwell, Helen Gardener, Rev. Mary T. Whitney, Frances Harper, Martha Schofield, and Benjamin Flower, in Powell, *National Purity Congress*.

76. J. W. Walton, "Young Men and Morality," and Anthony Comstock, "Demoralizing Literature," in Powell, *National Purity Congress*, 83, 420–21.

77. Mary Travilla, "Our Divine Possibilities," in Powell, *National Purity Congress*, 297 (her italics); see 294, 296, 297–98 for her citation of many of New Thought authors' favorite Bible quotations. "As a man thinketh" can be found in most New Thought tracts. (James Allen's *As A Man Thinketh* [Chicago: Science Press, 1905], is selling widely today.) See citations of the verse in Powell, 84, 295, 314.

78. Participants at the National Congress of Mothers and the National Purity Congress overlapped to some extent, but the National Congress of Mothers represented a more elite group of women. The first mothers' congress culminated in a reception at the White House. See *The Work and Words of the National Congress of Mothers* (New York: D. Appleton and Co., 1897).

79. Mrs. Alice Lee Moque, "Reproduction and Natural Law," in *Work and Words of the National Congress of Mothers*, 128; see Mrs. Mary Lowe Dickinson, "Response to the Address of Welcome," in *Work and Words of the National Congress of Mothers*, 17, and introductory epigrams, 3; see Lewis, "Mother's Love."

80. Miss Amalie Hofer, "What the Kindergarten Means to Mothers," Mrs. Sallie S. Cotten, "National Training School for Women," and Prof. Elmer Gates, "The Art of Rearing Children," in *Work and Words of the National Congress of Mothers*, 57, 211, 248–49. The editors of *Mind* magazine praised Gates's theories. So did Helen Campbell, in "Social Settlements," 590.

81. See Mrs. Mary Lowe Dickinson, "Response to Address of Welcome," and Mrs. Theodore W. Birney, "Address of Welcome," in *Work and Words of the National Congress of Mothers*, 13, 6–7; also see *Through the Years: From the Scrapbook of Mrs. Mears* (Washington, D.C.: National Congress of Parents and Teachers, n.d.), 28.

82. Mrs. Helen R. Wells, "Children's Rights," Mrs. T. W. Birney, "Address of Welcome," Ralph Waldo Trine, "Humane Education in Early Training," and Miss Georgina I. S. Andrews, "The Corner-Stone of the Don't Worry Movement," in *Report of the Proceedings of the Second Annual Convention of the*

National Congress of Mothers (Philadelphia: Geo. F. Lasher, 1898), 14, 15, 115, 130–34. See "A Suggestion by Theodore F. Seward" in back pages of Jeanne G. Pennington, *"Don't Worry" Nuggets* (New York: Fords, Howard and Hulbert, 1898); see Theodore F. Seward, *Don't Worry, or Spiritual Emancipation* (New York: Brotherhood of Christian Unity, 1897).

83. Mrs. H. A. Stimson, "Devotional: Our Responsibility," in *Work and Words of the National Congress of Mothers*, 181; Sarah Farmer, "Our Birthright," *Report of the Proceedings*, 179. Farmer's prayer was in keeping with a resolution passed at the first congress. It asserted that because "law is love and . . . love is the highest expression of God, and . . . its perversion . . . is the sole source of evil, we exhort all mothers to a closer walk with our Father and Mother God, by whose nurture and admonition our children must be brought up if life is ever to be worth living." *Work and Words*, 272.

84. Flower, *Progressive Men*, 100, 153; Jon Bloom and Paul Buhle, "Intercollegiate Socialist Society and Successors," in Buhle, Buhle, and Georgakas, eds., *Encyclopedia of the American Left*, 362; Pivar, *Purity Crusade*, 145–46; see Hopkins, *Rise of the Social Gospel*, 196.

85. See *The New Time*, 1897–98. On Edgerton, see Flower, *Progressive Men*, 180–81; Braden, *Spirits in Rebellion*, 210–17. Also see entry on Benjamin O. Flower in *Who's Who in America, 1899–1900*. See Wilmans's advertisement in final pages of *The New Time*'s August 1898 issue.

Eugene Debs was sympathetic to Christian Science. See Tom Lutz, *American Nervousness, 1903: An Anecdotal History* (Ithaca, N.Y.: Cornell University Press, 1991), 129.

86. "'The Arena' Lives," *The New Time* 3, no. 5 (November 1898): 241–42.

87. Paul Tyner, "Religion in Social Reform," *The New Time* (August 1898): 75–77. Tyner wrote a novel in which a spiritual guide whose "radiant beauty" reflected the "glory of rare womanhood" convinces the narrator that "the real man ever shone in the depths of the better woman's soul, as the real woman lived in the better man." The guide's name was Helena. The book was dedicated to "Helen Campbell, Spiritual Mother Guide Counsellor and Friend." Paul Tyner, *Through the Invisible: A Love Story* (New York: Continental Publishing, 1897), 180, 179, 123.

On Tyner, see Charlotte Perkins Gilman, *The Living of Charlotte Perkins Gilman*, 17, 142; Hill, *Charlotte Perkins Gilman*, 241–42; Paul Tyner, *Cash or Credit? A Solution to the Money Problem* (Madison, Wis.: Impress, 1895); see monthly editorials by Tyner in *The Arena*, October 1898–October 1899.

88. See *Harmony* 9, no. 8 (May 1897): 217, 233; Braden, *Spirits in Rebellion*, 300, 182, 430, 446; see advertisement in back pages of the *Journal of Practical Metaphysics* 2, no. 8 (May 1898).

89. Advertisement in back pages of *The Arena* 20; see *The Arena* 20, no. 5 (November–December 1898): 675–76.

90. W. D. P. Bliss, "Union Reform League Activities," *The Arena* 22 (July–December 1899): 111–13.

91. Paul Tyner, "Under the Rose," *The Arena* 22 (July–December 1899): 290.

92. W. D. P. Bliss, "The Social Reform Union," *The Arena* 22: 272–275; Tyner, "Under the Rose," *The Arena* 22 (July–December 1899): 285–91.

93. "Editorial Announcements," *The Arena* 22 (October 1899): 538.

94. Tyner lavished praise on Wilmans in Tyner, "The Metaphysical Movement," 316. On Tyner's activities, see "International Metaphysical League," *Mind* 4, no. 1 (April 1899): 53–56, and other reports on the League's development in *Mind* 5, no. 1 (October 1899): 63 and 13, no. 5 (May 1904): 460–67; see "Mental Science Association" and "Mr. Tyner Accepts," *Freedom*, May 9, 1900, 10, 12; Rev. Hugh O. Pentecost, "Is Mental Healing Scientific?" *Mind* 4, no. 2 (May 1899): 65–70; and Paul Tyner, "Bodily Immortality and the New Thought," *Mind* 4, no. 6 (September 1899): 351–53; Paul Tyner, "God, Freedom and Immortality," *Mind* 5, no. 3 (December 1899): 191–96; Paul Tyner, "As Broad as It's Long," *Freedom*, June 27, 1900, 1–2; Paul Tyner, "Thought and Feeling," *Freedom*, August 8, 1900, 1–3; *Freedom*, November 14, 1900, 4.

95. "Editorial Announcements," *The Arena* 22 (October 1899) 539–540. Flower again became the editor of *The Arena* in 1904.

96. "Prospectus Condensed," *Mind* 5, no. 3 (December 1899), inside front cover; *Mind* 1, no. 2 (November 1897), see no. 3 (December 1897): 189.

97. "Editorial Department: An Important Announcement," *Mind* 7, no. 2 (November 1900): 143; "The International Metaphysical League" and "Address of Welcome," *Mind* 5, no. 3 (December 1899): 129–33.

McLean promised that the two journals would remain distinct entities. *Mind* would represent "the world of Liberal and Advanced Thought," while *The Arena* would devote itself "to Reform along economic, sociological, political and ethical lines." He also insisted, however, that the two journals shared a "common inspiration." Both believed that "only through the upbuilding of the individual can be brought about the upliftment of the race." "Editorial Department: An Important Announcement," *Mind* 7, no. 2 (November 1900): 142, 143.

98. Entry on B. O. Flower in the *Biographical Encyclopaedia of the United States, 1901*; Braden, *Spirits in Rebellion*, 331.

Benjamin Flower contributed articles to both *Mind* and *The Arena* throughout the existence of both journals (*Mind* ceased publication in 1906). He included a chapter on the New Thought movement in his study *Progressive Men, Women and Movements of the Past Twenty-Five Years*. Flower eventually embraced Mary Baker Eddy's Christian Science. See B. O. Flower, *Christian Science as a Religious and Therapeutic Agent* (Boston: Twentieth Century Company, 1909).

Though largely forgotten today, Edwin Markham was once internationally famous for his 1899 poem "The Man With a Hoe." Markham's writings attacked "self-desire" and survival-of-the-fittest ideas, and praised nature, purity, cooperation, productive labor, and the power of love. He asserted that "the Divine Feminine as well as the Divine Masculine Principle is in God—that he is Father-

Mother, Two-in-One." He became closely affiliated with the New Thought movement. Louis Filler, *The Unknown Edwin Markham* (Yellow Springs, Ohio: Antioch Press, 1966), 63, 107; see B. O. Flower, "Edwin Markham," 391–414, see 409; Edwin Markham, "Poetry and Its Relation to Life," *Mind* 11, no. 1 (October 1902): 40–44; "The Season at Oscawana," *Mind* 12, no. 2 (May 1903): 147; Braden, *Spirits in Rebellion*, 377–78; see Markham's poetry in *Nautilus*, 1912; see Elizabeth Towne, *How to Use New Thought in Home Life* (Holyoke, Mass.: Elizabeth Towne Co., 1915), 133.

99. "Growth By Absorption," *Mind* 7, no. 6 (March 1901): 464–65; "Editorial Department: An Important Announcement," *Mind* 7, no. 2 (November 1900): 143.

100. Sui Sin Far, *Mrs. Spring Fragrance* (Chicago: A. C. McClurg and Co., 1912), 112, cited in Elizabeth Ammond, "The New Woman as Cultural Symbol and Social Reality," in Adele Heller and Lois Rudnick, eds., *1915, The Cultural Moment* (New Brunswick: Rutgers University Press, 1991), 93; see Louise K. Caldwell, "Socialism and Race Improvement," *Nautilus* 11, no. 8 (June 1909): 26–29.

101. A. W. Ricker, "Garnered from the Silence," *Appeal to Reason* no. 372 (January 17, 1903), 4; see his subsequent columns; Josephine Conger, "Hints to the Appeal's Wise Women," *Appeal* no. 382 (March 28, 1903), 5; see *Appeal to Reason* January 3, 1903, 5–7; see John Graham, ed., *"Yours for the Revolution": The Appeal to Reason, 1895–1922* (Lincoln: University of Nebraska Press, 1990), 221.

102. Ernest Untermann, "A Socialist's Confession of Faith," *Appeal* no. 377 (February 21, 1903), 2. On Untermann, see Graham, *Yours for the Revolution*, 7; Buhle, *Women and American Socialism*, 114.

103. Buhle, *Women and American Socialism*, 115, 141 n.16; see editorial by Elizabeth Towne, *Nautilus* 11, no. 5 (March 1909): 11; letter, "From a New Thought Socialist," in *Nautilus* 13, no. 1 (November 1910): 60–61; Caldwell, "Socialism"; Elizabeth Towne, "The Head of the House," *Nautilus* 12, no. 12 (October 1910): 17–18; letters about socialism in *New Thought*, December 1906, 471–73; also Patterson, "Ralph Waldo Trine"; Wilcox, *Every-Day Thoughts*.

Among the devoted fans of the *Appeal to Reason* was Upton Sinclair. He was a life-long socialist as well as a believer in mental telepathy. *Appeal to Reason* commissioned the work for which Sinclair would become famous, *The Jungle*. See Crunden, *Ministers of Reform*, 170, 166, 171.

104. When American Catholics attempted to suppress a virulently anti-Catholic hate-sheet entitled *The Menace* in the early 1910s, Benajmin Flower organized and led a propaganda campaign to "defend" the journal. During these same years Ernest Untermann led an ugly campaign against the "yellow peril" that ultimately convinced the Socialist party to call for immigration restriction. See Higham, *Strangers in the Land*, 173, 180–84, 366 n. 35, 369 n. 64. On the alliance between some purity-oriented female reformers and the 1920s Ku Klux Klan, see Kathleen M. Blee, *Women of the Klan: Racism and Gender in*

the 1920s (Berkeley: University of California Press, 1991), 48–51, 71–72, 103–8, and Nancy MacLean, *Behind the Mask of Chivalry: The Making of the Second Ku Klux Klan* (New York: Oxford University Press, 1994), 116. Also see account of Mary Baker Eddy's former student Augusta Stetson's development from Christian Science leader to Ku Klux Klan supporter in Altman Swinhart, *Since Mrs. Eddy* (New York: Holt Company, 1931).

CHAPTER 7

1. Marie Merrick, "Woman of the Period," *The Arena* 29, no. 2 (February 1903): 161.

2. Elizabeth Towne, *How to Use New Thought in Home Life* (Holyoke, Mass.: Elizabeth Towne Co., 1915), 156 (her italics).

3. See John F. Kasson, *Amusing the Million: Coney Island at the Turn of the Century* (New York: Hill and Wang, 1978); Kathy Peiss, *Cheap Amusements: Working Women and Leisure in Turn-of-the-Century New York* (Philadelphia: Temple University Press, 1986); Lewis A. Erenberg, *Steppin' Out: New York Nightlife and the Transformation of American Culture, 1890–1930* (Chicago: University of Chicago Press, 1981); Paul Boyer, *Urban Masses and Moral Order in America, 1820–1920* (Cambridge, Mass.: Harvard University Press, 1978), 191–202.

4. Lawrence Birken, *Consuming Desire: Sexual Science and the Emergence of a Culture of Abundance, 1871–1914* (Ithaca, N.Y.: Cornell University Press, 1988), 12, 22–37.

5. Birken, *Consuming Desire*, 25–32.

6. Rita Felski, *The Gender of Modernity* (Cambridge: Harvard University Press, 1995), 69, 89–90; William Leach, "Transformations in a Culture of Consumption: Women and Department Stores, 1890–1925," *Journal of American History* 71, no. 2 (September 1984): 319–42.

7. Fred Matthews, "The New Psychology and American Drama," in *1915: The Cultural Moment,* eds. Adele Heller and Lois Rudnick (New Brunswick: Rutgers University Press, 1991), 146; Barbara Sicherman, *The Quest for Mental Health in America* (New York: Arno Press, 1980), 102–10; Gail Bederman, *Manliness and Civilization: A Cultural History of Gender and Race in the United States 1880–1917* (Chicago: University of Chicago Press, 1995).

8. Laboratory studies undertaken by late-nineteenth-century academics helped lay the groundwork for this shift in psychological understanding. These studies prompted a flood of new scholarship on the relationships among consciousness, body, emotion, and environment. Psychologist and philosopher William James argued that the "rationalist consciousness" was but "one kind of consciousness," and posited complex and fluid interactions between layers of consciousness as well as between mind and body. G. Stanley Hall clung to a belief in evolutionary race progress, but posited a human consciousness in which reason was easily disrupted by primitive passions and hereditary impulses. Sociologist Edward Alworth Ross agreed. He argued that the human soul was

not the "highest" part of mind, but rather was a "treacherous compound of strange contradictions" containing echoes of hereditary survivals and long-forgotten deeds. One attained health not by further development of the rational self, he explained, but through embracing the passions and whims Victorians had been taught to repress. James Mark Baldwin, John Dewey, and George Herbert Mead claimed that the mind could only be understood in social context, and that the mind and sensation, and mind and body, were not distinct, but formed through interaction. Prominent neurologists such as James Putnam and Adolph Meyer drew upon the insights of pragmatist philosophers and posited a more fluid interaction of mind and body. Their acceptance of the influence of emotions upon rationality paved the way for their eventual embrace of Sigmund Freud's ideas.

William James, *The Varieties of Religious Experience* (Middlesex, England: Penguin Books, 1982), 423; Ross, quoted in R. Jackson Wilson, *In Quest of Community: Social Philosophy in the United States, 1860–1920* (London: Oxford University Press, 1968), 97–8, see 71–4; see Nathan G. Hale, Jr., *Freud and the Americans: the Beginnings of Psychoanalysis in the United States, 1876–1919* (New York: Oxford University Press, 1971), 104, 110–13, 133–38, 153; Rosalind Rosenberg, *Beyond Separate Spheres: Intellectual Roots of Modern Feminism* (New Haven: Yale University Press, 1982), 58–60, 131; Neil Coughlan, *Young John Dewey* (Chicago: University of Chicago Press, 1973); Sicherman, *Quest for Mental Health*, 208–14.

9. See James B. Gilbert, *Work Without Salvation: America's Intellectuals and Industrial Alienation, 1880–1910* (Baltimore: Johns Hopkins University Press, 1977), vii–ix, 31–43; Hale, Jr., *Freud and the Americans*, 363–65.

The precise model of maturity offered in place of older Victorian paradigms depended upon how one understood the unconscious. Freud viewed the unconscious as the seat of ugly and murderous desires. He argued that unconscious desires would have less power if they were unearthed and acknowledged; the conscious mind could then choose not to act on them with far less expenditure of energy. Freud advised that repression be replaced by sublimation, therefore. In contrast, many of Freud's American popularizers viewed the unconscious as the "true self" that stood free of artificial social convention. These popularizers taught that Victorian repression would best be replaced by the expression of unconscious desires, which were understood as revitalizing and "true" by definition. See Hale, Jr., *Freud and the Americans*, 407; Matthews, "New Psychology," 148.

10. F. H. Matthews, "The Americanization of Sigmund Freud: Adaptations of Psychoanalysis before 1917," *Journal of American Studies* 1, no. 1 (April 1967): 50. Some critics argue that the lauding of subconscious impulses did not free people from conformist pressures. On the contrary, new psychological discourses helped create more insidious methods through which mental-health authorities could "adjust" wayward individuals to community norms. Others point out the fit between new ideals of self-expression and the needs of a consumer capitalist economy. Just as popular psychologists create a view of the self

as requiring self-expression, so does consumer capitalism require a constant craving for new objects. They argue that the very "unconscious inner self" that modern Americans embraced as a source of truth was manipulated by advertisers in order to increase consumption.

See Matthews, "New Psychology," 148–52; Tom Lutz, *American Nervousness, 1903: An Anecdotal History* (Ithaca, N.Y.: Cornell University Press, 1991), 285–88; Hale, Jr., *Freud and the Americans*, 362; Elizabeth Lunbeck, *The Psychiatric Persuasion: Knowledge, Gender and Power in Modern America* (Princeton, N.J.: Princeton University Press, 1994); Philip Rieff, *The Triumph of the Therapeutic* (New York: Harper and Row, 1966); Christopher Lasch, *The Culture of Narcissism* (New York: Warner Books, 1979), see 38–9; T. J. Jackson Lears, "From Salvation to Self-Realization: Advertising and the Therapeutic Roots of Consumer Culture, 1880–1930," in Richard Wightman Fox and T. J. Jackson Lears, eds., *The Culture of Consumption* (New York: Pantheon Books, 1983), 3–38.

11. Sicherman, *Quest for Mental Health*, 343, 356–60; Hale, Jr., *Freud and the Americans*, 53, 76–80; see Gilbert, *Work Without Salvation*, 154–79; George Frederick Drinka, M.D., *The Birth of Neurosis: Myth, Malady and the Victorians* (New York: Touchstone Books, 1984), 162; Robert Thomson, *The Pelican History of Psychology* (Middlesex, England: Penguin Books, 1968), 107; Stephen Jay Gould, *The Mismeasure of Man* (New York: Norton and Co., 1981), 113–233; Louise Michele Newman, ed., *Men's Ideas/Women's Realities: Popular Science, 1870–1915* (New York: Pergamon Press, 1985), 105–55; Daniel Joseph Singal, "Towards a Definition of American Modernism," *American Quarterly* 39, no. 1 (spring 1987): 9.

12. John Chynoweth Burnham, "The New Psychology: From Narcissism to Social Control," in *Change and Continuity in Twentieth-Century America: The 1920s*, eds. John Braeman et al. (Columbus: Ohio State University Press, 1968), 393.

13. Nancy F. Cott, *The Grounding of Modern Feminism* (New Haven: Yale University Press, 1987), 13–50.

14. See E. Anthony Rotundo, *American Manhood: Transformations in Masculinity from the Revolution to the Modern Era* (New York: Basic Books, 1993), 222–83; Bederman, *Manliness and Civilization*; George Chauncey, *Gay New York: Gender, Urban Culture, and the Making of the Gay Male World, 1890–1940* (New York: Basic Books, 1994), 99–127; Kirsten N. Swinth, "Painting Professionals: Women Artists and the Development of American Art, 1870–1920" (Ph.D. dissertation, Yale University, 1995); Felski, *Gender of Modernity*, 79–80.

15. Martha Banta, *Imaging American Women: Idea and Ideals in Cultural History* (New York: Columbia University Press, 1987), 58, 69, 85, 102, 135–38.

16. See David Axeen, "'Heroes of the Engine Room': American 'Civilization' and the War with Spain," *American Quarterly* 36, no. 4 (fall 1984): 481–502; Nina Silbur, *The Romance of Reunion: Northerners and the South, 1865–1900* (Chapel Hill: University of North Carolina Press, 1993), 178; Arnaldo

Testi, "The Gender of Reform Politics: Theodore Roosevelt and the Culture of Masculinity," *Journal of American History* 81, no. 4 (March 1995): 1510–1533; Susan Curtis, *A Consuming Faith: The Social Gospel and Modern American Culture* (Baltimore: Johns Hopkins University Press, 1991), 139; Gail Bederman, "'The Women Have Had Charge of the Church Work Long Enough': The Men and Religion Forward Movement of 1911–1912 and the Masculinization of Middle-Class Protestantism," *American Quarterly* 41 (September 1989): 449–50.

17. Curtis, *Consuming Faith*, 81, 83, 185; Bederman, "'The Women Have Had Charge,'" 438, 440–41, 449–50.

18. Mary O. Furner, *Advocacy and Objectivity* (Lexington: University Press of Kentucky, 1975); see Lunbeck, *Psychiatric Persuasion*, 34.

19. First quote is James Kiernan, in Birken, *Consuming Desire*, 80, see 41; Key is quoted in Jeffrey Weeks, *Sex, Politics and Society: The Regulation of Sexuality Since 1800*, 2d ed. (London: Longman Group, 1981), 126.

20. J. G. Morawski, "The Measurement of Masculinity and Femininity: Engendering Categorical Realities," *Journal of Personality* 53, no. 2 (June 1985): 199–204.

21. Some contemporary feminist theorists believe that Freud's paradigm of sexual development allows for the articulation of female desire. Others believe that Freud presents an accurate picture of the ways in which female sexual development and desire is warped in a patriarchal family context.

22. Joanne Meyerowitz, *Women Adrift: Independent Wage Earners in Chicago, 1880–1930* (Chicago: University of Chicago Press, 1988), 117–39; Carroll Smith-Rosenberg, "The New Woman as Androgyne: Social Disorder and Gender Crisis, 1870–1936," in *Disorderly Conduct: Visions of Gender in Victorian America* (New York: Oxford University Press, 1985), 245–96; Christina Simmons, "Modern Sexuality and the Myth of Victorian Repression," in Kathy Peiss and Christina Simmons, eds., *Passion and Power: Sexuality in History* (Philadelphia: Temple University Press, 1989), 157–77.

23. Pamela S. Haag, "In Search of 'The Real Thing': Ideologies of Love, Modern Romance, and Women's Sexual Subjectivity in the United States, 1920–40," in John C. Fout and Maura Shaw Tantillo, eds., *American Sexual Politics: Sex, Gender and Race since the Civil War* (Chicago: University of Chicago Press, 1993), 161–92.

24. Rotundo, *American Manhood*, 282; Matthews, "New Psychology," 152.

25. Haag, "In Search of 'The Real Thing,'" 164.

26. The I.N.T.A. is still in existence today. See Richard M. Huber, *The American Idea of Success* (New York: McGraw-Hill Book Company, 1971), 124; Frances Maule Bjorkman, "The Literature of the 'New Thoughters,'" *The World's Work* (January 1910): 12472–74; Charles S. Braden, *Spirits in Rebellion: The Rise and Development of New Thought* (Dallas: Southern Methodist University Press, 1963), 184–88.

27. Horatio W. Dresser, "A Talk to Our Policyholders," *Good Housekeeping* 51 (October 1910): 431–35; Ralph Waldo Trine, "A Healthy Mind in a

Healthy Body," *Woman's Home Companion* 40 (April 1913): 13; Bjorkman, "Literature of the 'New Thoughters,'" 12475; advertisement for *Dawn of Tomorrow* in *New Thought*, September 1906; Louise Radford Wells, "Coming Together," *New Thought* (December 1906): 482.

New Thought ideas gripped stage actors as well. Prominent actors and actresses claimed that "New Thought is the salvation of the actor from the beginning of the season to the end." "[A]ffirmations, auto-suggestions—call them what you will," can carry the actor through everything from the "weary besieging of managers' offices" to the "horror of the first night," they explained. "New Thought and the Theatre," *Nautilus* 13, no. 1 (November 1910): 43, see 40–44.

28. Gail Thain Parker, *Mind Cure in New England* (Hanover, N.H.: University Press of New England, 1973), 83. On Marden, see Huber, *American Idea of Success*, 150–55; Braden, *Spirits in Rebellion*, 365. The books of Prentice Mulford, a journalist who first embraced New Thought in the 1880s, were also popular. See Huber, 139–43.

29. Horatio W. Dresser, "The Failure of the New Thought Movement," *Journal of Practical Metaphysics* 2, no. 4 (January 1898): 98; James, *Varieties of Religious Experience*, 94; Woodbridge Riley, "The New Thought," *American Mercury* 1, no. 1 (January 1924): 105.

30. Sydney Flower, "The New Thought in Business," *New Thought* (March 1902): 14.

31. Declarations are quoted in Braden, *Spirits in Rebellion*, 174, 195–96.

32. See Richard Weiss, *The American Myth of Success: From Horatio Alger to Norman Vincent Peale* (Urbana: University of Illinois Press, [1969] 1988); Huber, *American Idea of Success;* Donald Meyer, *The Positive Thinkers: Religion as Psychology from Mary Baker Eddy to Oral Roberts* (New York: Pantheon Books, [1965], 1980); A. Whitney Griswold, "New Thought: A Cult of Success," *American Journal of Sociology* 40 (November 1934): 309–18.

33. John Kent Simmons, "The Ascension of Annie Rix Militz and the Home(s) of Truth: Perfection Meets Paradise in Early Twentieth-Century Los Angeles" (Ph.D. dissertation, University of California-Santa Barbara, July 1987), 214, 219–24, 249–57; see Rix Militz's journal *Master Mind* 17, no. 1 (October 1919): 23, and no. 2 (November 1919): 63.

34. Simmons, "Ascension of Annie Rix Militz," 238–57, 264–67; Riley, "The New Thought," 108; see *Master Mind*, 1913–1916.

After Rix-Militz's death on June 22, 1924, her followers took her body to a local funeral parlor. They were convinced, however, that Rix Militz had simply taken a brief departure from her body in order to learn first-hand about heaven, and that she would soon return to tell them the details. They encamped around her coffin for three days, refusing to allow the undertaker to embalm the body. Finally local health officials forced the followers to inter Rix Militz's corpse. Simmons, 1–3.

35. Braden, *Spirits in Rebellion*, 139, 173, 180; Charles Braden's biographical entry on Ursula Gestefeld, in Edward T. James, Janet Wilson James, and

Paul S. Boyer, eds., *Notable American Women*, 3 vols. (Cambridge, Mass.: Belknap Press, 1971), 2, 27–28.

36. Ursula Newell Gestefeld, *How To Control Circumstances* (Pelham, N.Y.: The Gestefeld Publishing Company, 1901), 68, 40.

37. Helen Van-Anderson, *The Mystic Scroll: A Book of Revelation* (New York: C. E. Ellis Co., 1906), see 193–231.

38. See Margaretta Gray Bothwell, "The Late Convention," *Mind* 13, no. 2 (February 1904): 206; "The New Thought Federation," *Mind* 13, no. 5 (May 1904): 465; "Dr. Alice Bunker Stockham," *New York Times* (obituary), December 4, 1912, 13.

39. "Woman Writer on Love Found Guilty," Chicago *Inter-Ocean*, June 6, 1905; Theodore Schroeder, "Censorship of Sex Literature," *The Medical Council*, Philadelphia, March 1909, 96; see "Dr. Stockham Guilty," *Chicago Record-Herald*, January 6, 1905, 7; "Holds New Woman for Advice on Love," Chicago *Inter-Ocean*, May 21, 1905; "Dr. Alice Stockham," *Evanston Evening Post*, December 4, 1912; Hal D. Sears, *The Sex Radicals: Free Love in High Victorian America* (Lawrence, Kans., 1977), 201, 262.

40. Letter, Helen Wilmans to Eugene Del Mar, October 26, 1901, in Eugene Del Mar, ed., "The Life Work (A Testimonial) of Helen Wilmans Post, 1831–1907" (scrapbook, Manuscript Division, New York Public Library).

41. James Harvey Young, *The Medical Messiahs: A Social History of Health Quackery in Twentieth-Century America* (Princeton, N.J.: Princeton University Press, 1967), 66–67; "A Message from Helen Wilmans" (n.p., n.d.), 4.

42. *United States v. Post*, 113 *Federal Reporter* 852 (D.C.S.D. Fla., 1902); "Message from Helen Wilmans," 5.

43. Letter, Wilmans to Del Mar, May 15, 1902, in Del Mar, ed., "The Life Work."

44. *Post v. United States*, 135 *Federal Reporter*, 1 (C.C.A. 5, 1905), 12; see Young, *Medical Messiahs*, 69–71, for a history of the McAnnulty case.

45. M.[alinda] E. C[ramer], "The Arrest of the Founder of Mental Science," *Harmony* 14, no. 2 (November 1901): 58; Horatio W. Dresser, *A History of the New Thought Movement* (New York: Thomas Y. Crowell Co., 1919), 331–36; see *Freedom*, November 14, 1900, 4.

46. Letters, Wilmans to Del Mar, February 17, 1904 and February 28, 1906, in Del Mar, ed., "The Life Work"; conversation with Wilmans Bagget, March 30, 1987; Pleasant Daniel Gold, *History of Volusia County Florida* (Florida: E. O. Painter Printing Co., 1927), 384.

47. Helen Wilmans, "The Small Doctors," *Freedom*, April 24, 1901, 9; Helen Wilmans, *Blossom of the Century* (Florida: Freedom Publishing Company, 1898), 149–50; letter, Wilmans to Del Mar, June 18, 1903, in Del Mar, ed., "The Life Work;" see *Post v. United States*, 135 *Federal Reporter* 1 (C.C.A. 5, 1905), 2.

Wilmans had been antagonizing the Florida locals for years. The services she held in her Mental Science temple unnerved her Christian neighbors. Letter, Wilmans to Del Mar, June 2, 1900, in Del Mar, "Life's Work." Wilmans refused to conform to public norms of behavior as well. For example, see Helen Wilmans, "Waste-Paper Basket," *Freedom*, August 8, 1900, 10.

48. But Stockham feared the possibility of an animalistic female self, and therefore promoted women's "love and service" as a way to contain it. Believing that wealth was the product of male violence, she could only elevate woman by reconceptualizing wealth as the natural result of a moral character that could be produced through eugenics.

49. Maia Pratt Stanton, "Dominion," *Mind* 7, no. 1 (April 1901): 33. See Helia Shiraz, "Desire," *Freedom*, April 11, 1900, 7; Esther Harlan, "Destiny," in Elizabeth Towne, *How to Grow Success* (Holyoke, Mass.: Elizabeth Towne, 1903), 2.; frontispiece poem on desire in Ella Wheeler Wilcox, *New Thought Common Sense, and What Life Means to Me* (Chicago: W. B. Conkey Co., 1908).

50. William Walker Atkinson, "Stray Thoughts," *New Thought* (July 1906): 249–50; see Flower, "New Thought in Business," 16; William Walker Atkinson, "A Fore Word," *New Thought* (December 1901): 3; Sydney Flower "The Sex Energy," *New Thought* (December 1901): 14; Nancy McKay Gordon, "The Law of Sex," *New Thought* (August 1902): 10; "The Diary of a New Beginner," *New Thought* (July 1906): 240–43.

Atkinson always used gender-inclusive language in his writings. He wrote that "God has no sex. Or perhaps it would be better to say that he combines within himself both the Father-Mother elements." William Walker Atkinson, *Law of the New Thought* (Chicago: Psychic Research Co., 1902), 65. He insisted that men and women would evolve to mental similarity. "[T]he mental powers of woman are also in men, and *vice versa*." Woman must develop her logical capacities and become "an all-around being." Men must cultivate intuition and reject fears of being "womanish," since all truly great men of history have done so. William Walker Atkinson, "The Voice Within," *New Thought* (December 1901): 16–17 (his italics). While Atkinson's popular New Thought writings praised cutthroat competition as natural and beneficial, he also retained remnants of the older New Thought vision that linked the evolution of a new, more androgynous form of humanity to the end of the competitive economic system. See Atkinson, *Law of the New Thought*, 79, 74.

On Atkinson's relationship to Wilmans, see dedication to Wilmans in William Walker Atkinson, *The Secret of Mental Magic* (Chicago: William Walker Atkinson, 1907), 4; William Walker Atkinson, *Thought-Force in Business and Everyday Life*, 10th ed. (Chicago: Psychic Research co., 1901), 63; W. W. Atkinson, "Doing Things," *New Thought* (August 1902): 9; William Walker Atkinson, "Did Helen Wilmans Renege?" in Del Mar, ed., "Life Work." For biographical information, see entry on Atkinson in *Biographical Dictionary of American Cult and Sect Leaders*, ed. J. Gordon Melton (Detroit: Garland Press, 1986), 15.

51. See Florence Morse Kingsley, *The Transfiguration of Miss Philura* (New York and London: Funk and Wagnalls Co., 1901); Florence Morse Kingsley, "Mrs. Follett's Funeral," *Nautilus* 12, no. 8 (June 1910): 25–8; see her column,

"Mother-Thoughts," in *Nautilus*, 1910; see entry on Florence (Morse) Kingsley in George Derby and James Terry White, eds., *National Cyclopaedia of American Biography*, 1903–1909 (New York: J. T. White and Co., 1910).

52. With its circulation of 31,000 it easily overshadowed *New Thought*. The *Nautilus* eventually employed many of *New Thought*'s former writers, including William Walker Atkinson and Ella Wheeler Wilcox. Edwin Markham, Sinclair Lewis, and Florence Morse Kingsley were also regular contributors. Bjorkman, "Literature of the 'New-Thoughters,'" 12472–73; see *The Nautilus*, 1912. At its peak, the circulation of *The Nautilus* was over 90,000 copies per month. See "Mrs. Towne, Religious, Civic Leader, Author, Dead at 95," *Holyoke Daily*, June 1, 1960.

53. Elizabeth Towne (then Elizabeth Struble) began the *Nautilus* soon after she separated from her husband of sixteen years and found herself the sole support of her two "almost grown" children. Her inspiration was Helen Wilmans's *Freedom*. Struble wrote to Wilmans, "So well has FREEDOM taught and so well have I learned and put in practice the principle of success that here the little *Nautilus* bobs up serenely and maybe a bit saucily alongside of FREEDOM, toots her shrill whistle and signals. 'Salute me please,' but if you won't I shall sail along anyhow! Success belongs to us both." Letter reprinted in *Freedom*, December 21, 1898, 8. Others noted the similarity between Towne and Wilmans; see Atkinson, "Doing Things," 9. Towne later claimed Warren Felt Evans as her inspiration; see Braden, *Spirits in Rebellion*, 340.

Soon after starting *The Nautilus*, Struble received her second marriage proposal. Her new suitor was William E. Towne, a New Thought publisher who lived in Holyoke, Massachusetts. Elizabeth divorced Joseph Struble, married William Towne, and relocated *The Nautilus* to Massachusetts in 1900. There Elizabeth Towne started her own publishing company. She wrote numerous popular New Thought tracts. One of them, *How to Wake the Solar Plexus*, sold almost one hundred thousand copies. Meanwhile the *Nautilus*, which now featured Elizabeth Towne as editor and William Towne as associate editor, grew to be the nation's number one New Thought journal. Thomas Dreier, *The Story of Elizabeth Towne and the Nautilus* (Holyoke, Mass.: Elizabeth Towne Co., n.d.) 4, 13.

54. Elizabeth Towne, *Practical Methods for Self-Development* (Holyoke, Mass.: Elizabeth Towne, 1904), 7; see Towne, *How To Grow Success*.

55. Towne, *Practical Methods*, 15, 22; Towne, *How To Grow Success*, 14, see 9.

56. Towne, *Practical Methods*, 26, 41–45; Towne, *New Thought in Home Life*, 174, 46, 71, 167.

57. Towne, *New Thought in Home Life*, 130, 68, 174, 66; Towne, *How to Grow Success*, 16, 18 (her italics).

58. Elizabeth Towne, "Yours to Command," *New Thought* (October 1902): 8 (her italics); see Towne, *How To Grow Success*, 6, 29.

59. Towne, *Practical Methods*, 104–5 (her italics), 122–29, 22, 26.

60. Towne, *How To Grow Success*, 43 (her italics).

61. Towne, *Practical Methods*, 30; Towne, *How To Grow Success*, 61 (her italics), 17.

62. Towne, *How To Grow Success*, 54–56 (her italics).

63. This was of course a myth. Late-nineteenth-century middle-class men did not engage in violent struggle at their workplaces. But the myth of male Darwinian struggle had power. It justified the exclusion of white middle-class women from the sorts of freedoms enjoyed by white middle-class men. Because many late Victorians viewed money-making as the product of struggle, they insisted that it was inappropriate for "refined" women to engage in paid labor. Because these women were barred from paid labor, they could not be independent or "free." Money was believed to be rooted in desire, and desire was a frightening evil in women. Therefore, as Gestefeld's Murva discovered, the pure and womanly woman could not be free. Furthermore, Victorians believed that the forceful will that enabled men to be economic producers also enabled them to conquer their unruly instincts. Thus although white men were identified as lustful, they were also the only ones who could be pure.

See Birken, *Consuming Desire*, 76.

64. Kingsley wrote several New Thought short stories for *The Nautilus*, most of which mocked the hypocrisy of pious women and lavishly praised the modern woman who was willing to spend. These stories, like *Miss Philura*, were then released as separate volumes for a broader audience. Kingsley also kept in the public eye through her membership in the League of Right Living, a group whose goal was to establish centers "for the study and practice of scientific methods in healthful living." The League endorsed a "Course of Reading in Psychotherapy" that was published each month in *Good Housekeeping*. In 1910, the president of the League was Horatio Dresser. Kingsley was one of the League's directors. Other directors included Kingsley's fellow *Nautilus* columnist Edwin Markham and the Rev. Lyman Powell, an eminent Episcopalian rector who had written sympathetically on Christian Science. See *Good Housekeeping*, October 1910, 433.

Syndicated columnist Ella Wheeler Wilcox (1850–1919) was a proponent of New Thought from 1887, when she studied with Emma Curtis Hopkins, through at least 1916, when she was named as an honorary president of the International New Thought Congress. She valued New Thought in part because it provided a useful counter to orthodox Christianity. In her *Heart of the New Thought*, for example, Wilcox contrasted New Thought, or "God's own thought put into practical form," with the "worn out creed" of "orthodox Christianity." "The man who believes that all men are vicious, selfish and immoral is *projecting pernicious mind stuff* into space, which is as dangerous . . . as dynamite. The world has been kept back too long by this false, unholy and blasphemous religion," she wrote. Writing in *Every-Day Thoughts*, which was intended for a mainstream audience, Wilcox was only moderately more restrained. "We do not believe we are poor worms of dust. . . . We believe we are part of a divine system, and that we have a right to happiness, health and suc-

328 / Notes to Pages 239–240

cess," she wrote. As for those who still believed in a God of fire and brimstone, Wilcox planned to make short work of them. "There are only a few old fossils hanging to the cobwebs of these horrible creeds. . . . They are like half-dead flies buzzing in a spider's web. Thank God I have my little broom." Ella Wheeler Wilcox, *Heart of the New Thought* (Chicago: Psychic Research Company, 1902), 33–34, see 74; Ella Wheeler Wilcox, *Every Day Thoughts in Prose and Verse* (Chicago: W. B. Conkey Co., 1901), 202, 103.

On Wilcox and New Thought, see Wilcox, *New Thought Common Sense*, 291; Julian T. Baird, Jr.'s biographical entry on Wilcox in Edward T. James, Janet Wilson James, and Paul S. Boyer, eds., *Notable American Women*, 3 vols. (Cambridge, Mass.: Belknap Press, 1971), 3, 608; Ella Wheeler Wilcox, *The Worlds and I* (New York: George H. Doran Company, 1918); J. Gordon Melton, "New Thought's Hidden History: Emma Curtis Hopkins, Forgotten Founder" (unpublished paper, Institute for the Study of American Religion, August 1988), 13; Sydney Flower, "A Visit to Ella Wheeler Wilcox" and Ella Wheeler Wilcox, "The Sowing of the Seed," in *New Thought* (October 1902): 1–3; Towne, *Practical Methods*, back-page advertisement; Towne, *How to Grow Success*, 10, 75; Towne, *New Thought in Home Life*, 59, 133; "The New Thought Federation," *Mind* 13, no. 5 (May 1904): 465; Braden, *Spirits in Rebellion*, 191–92.

65. H. Emilie Cady, *Lessons In Truth* (n.p., n.d.) 57–8, see 87–8; Malinda Cramer, *Lessons in the Science of Infinite Spirit and the Christ Method of Healing* (n.p.: M. E. Cramer, 1890), 58–65, 230; "Progress of Divine Science," *Harmony* 8, no. 11 (August 1896): 305; Charles Edgar Prather, "Simple Lessons in Psychology," *Power*, June 1911, 369; see *Power*, August 1910 and months following; Hazel Deane, *Powerful is the Light* (Denver: Divine Science College, 1945), 87–88, 109, 118; James Dillet Freeman, *The Story of Unity* (Unity Village, Mo.: Unity Books, 1978), 75–79; T. R. Slyder, "The Unity Movement: A Search for the Truth of Practical Christianity: A Brief Institutional History" (unpublished paper, Institute for the Study of American Religion archives), 11.

66. Richard Ingalese, *The History and Power of Mind* (New York: Occult Book Concern, 1902); see 269 for his discussion of Helen Wilmans; Frank Channing Haddock, *Power of Will* (Meriden, Conn.: Pelton Publishing Company, [1907] 1919), v–vii; see Meyer, *Positive Thinkers*, 164; also see A. A. Lindsay, *New Psychology Complete* (New York: Lindsay Publishing Co., [1907] (13th ed. published 1922).

67. Horatio W. Dresser, Ph.D., "A Talk to Our Policyholders," *Good Housekeeping* 51 (October 1910): 432; see Hale, Jr., *Freud and the Americans*, 232; "Happiness and Health" series in *Good Housekeeping*, 1909–1910.

68. Parker, *Mind Cure in New England*, 151–52; Hale, Jr., *Freud and the Americans*, 225–49; Weiss, *American Myth of Success*, 210–13.

69. See Coughlan, *Young John Dewey*; see Sheldon M. Stern, "William James and the New Psychology," in *Social Sciences at Harvard, 1860–1920*, ed. Paul Buck (Cambridge: Harvard University Press, 1965), 175–222.

70. See Anne Harrington, "Hysteria, hypnosis and the lure of the invisible: The rise of neo-mesmerism in *fin-de-siècle* French psychiatry," in W. F. Bynum, Roy Porter, and Michael Shepherd, eds., *The Anatomy of Madness volume III: The Asylum and Its Psychiatry* (London: Routledge, 1988), 226–46.

71. John Chynoweth Burnham, "Psychiatry, Psychology and the Progressive Movement," *American Quarterly* 12 (1960): 460; John C. Burnham, "Medical Specialists and Movements Towards Social Control in the Progressive Era: Three Examples," in Jery Israel, ed., *Building the Organizational Society: Essays on Association Activities in America* (New York: Free Press, 1972), 26; Hale, Jr., *Freud and the Americans*, 48–53.

72. Frederic W. H. Myers, *Human Personality and Its Survival of Bodily Death* (1903), edited and abridged by Leopold Myers (London: Longmans, Green, 1906), 15, cited in Robert Charles Powell, "The 'Subliminal' Versus the 'Subconscious' in the American Acceptance of Psychoanalysis, 1906–1910," *Journal of the History of the Behavioral Sciences* 15 (April 1979): 156, see 155–65; William James, "The Confidences of a 'Psychical Researcher,'" *American Magazine*, October 1909, cited in Gerald E. Myers, *William James: His Life and Thought* (New Haven: Yale University Press, 1986), 384; see Hale, Jr., *Freud and the Americans*, 241.

73. Myers, *William James*, 374, 30, 373; William James, "The Energies of Men" [1906], in William James, *Essays on Faith and Morals*, Ralph Barton Perry, ed. (New York: New American Library, 1962), 234; see Parker, *Mind Cure in New England*, 151–68 for an illuminating discussion of James's interpretation of New Thought ideas.

74. Elwood Worcester and Samuel McComb, *The Christian Religion as a Healing Power: A Defense and Exposition of the Emmanuel Movement* (New York: Moffat, Yard and Co., 1909), 26–27; see Raymond J. Cunningham, "The Emmanuel Movement: A Variety of American Religious Experience," *American Quarterly* 14, no. 1 (Spring 1962): 50; see Sanford Gifford, "Medical Psychotherapy and the Emmanuel Movement in Boston," in *Psychoanalysis, Psychotherapy and the New England Medical Scene, 1894–1944*, ed. George E. Gifford, Jr. (New York: Science History Publications, 1978), 112.

75. Elwood Worcester, Samuel McComb and Isador H. Coriat, *Religion and Medicine: The Moral Control of Nervous Disorders* (New York: Moffat, Yard and Co., 1908), 134, see 414.

Some of the earliest supporters of the Emmanuel Movement were churchmen who had previously been sympathetic toward New Thought. See Lyman Powell's *Christian Science: The Faith and Its Founder* (New York: G. P. Putnam's Sons, 1907), which attacks Christian Science and praises New Thought, and his *The Emmanuel Movement in a New England Town* (New York: G. P. Putnam's Sons, 1909). The U.S. Surgeon General listed *Religion and Medicine* as among the three or four "great" books on psychiatry. Both *Good Housekeeping* and the *Ladies Home Journal* ran enthusiastic articles about the movement's methods. See Hale, Jr., *Freud and the Americans*, 226, 230, 232–33, 241; Gifford, "Medical Psychotherapy," 115–16.

76. Sicherman, *Quest for Mental Health,* 268; John Duncan Quackenbos, *Hypnotic Therapeutics in Theory and Practice* (New York: Harper and Brothers, 1908), cited in Hale, Jr., *Freud and the Americans,* 245.

New York neurologist George W. Jacoby's *Suggestion and Psychotherapy* (1912), for example, argued that physicians must combat the noxious suggestions of contemporary civilization through psychotherapy, which he defined as suggestion to foster higher cultural aims. Burnham, "Psychiatry, Psychology and the Progressive Movement," 462.

77. Hale, Jr., *Freud and the Americans,* 340, 342.

78. See H. Addington Bruce, *Scientific Mental Healing* (Boston: Little, Brown and Co., 1911); H. Addington Bruce, "New Mind Cure Based on Science," *American Magazine* 70 (October 1910): 773–78; "Masters of the Mind," *American Magazine* 71 (November 1910): 71–81; "Religion and the Larger Self," *Good Housekeeping* 62 (January 1916): 55–61; see Matthews, "Americanization of Sigmund Freud," 45.

See Weiss, *American Myth of Success,* 211–12 for discussion of the apparent New Thought influences on Dr. Isador Coriat and Dr. James Jackson Putnam, two of the earliest American converts to Freud's psychoanalytic theories.

79. Max Eastman, *Enjoyment of Living* (New York: Harper and Brothers, 1948), 259, cited in Sanford Gifford, "The American Reception of Psychoanalysis, 1908–1922," in Heller and Rudnick, eds., *1915,* 138; Max Eastman, "Exploring the Soul and Healing the Body," *Everybody's Magazine* 32 (June 1915): 741, cited in Hale, Jr., *Freud and the Americans,* 400.

80. Gifford, "American Reception of Psychoanalysis," 134–35; see Ellen Kay Trimberger, "The New Woman and the New Sexuality," in Heller and Rudnick, eds., *1915,* 98–115.

81. Mabel Dodge Luhan, *Movers and Shakers,* vol. 3 of *Intimate Memories* (New York: Harcourt, Brace and Co., 1938), 467–73, 319, 511.

82. Hopkins to Mabel Dodge Luhan, September 16, 1919, cited in Gail M. Harley, "Emma Curtis Hopkins: 'Forgotten Founder' of New Thought" (Ph.D. dissertation, Florida State University, 1991), 172, see 154–58, 162, 173; Melton, "Hidden History," 33–34.

83. Harley, "Emma Curtis Hopkins," 150.

84. Emma Curtis Hopkins to Mabel Dodge Luhan, September 16, 1919 (her italics), cited in Harley, "Emma Curtis Hopkins," 171–72.

85. Mabel Dodge Luhan, *Edge of Taos Desert,* Intimate Memories Series (New York: Harcourt, Brace and Company, 1937), 245–46, cited in Harley, "Emma Curtis Hopkins," 198.

Hopkins presented a similar picture of her life as both lonely and elevated in a letter to Luhan dated November 20, 1919. Hopkins wrote, "Things are on the monotonous with my work. You couldn't stand the monotony. It makes you sick. But life breathed on from the Steadfast God makes me buoyantly strong in monotony" (cited in Harley, "Emma Curtis Hopkins," 172).

86. Luhan, *Movers and Shakers,* 467–69, see 470–73. Mabel Dodge Luhan's description casts some light on how New Thought treatment was experienced

by patients. Other first-hand accounts corroborate Luhan's depiction of these sessions as soothing and reassuring. Theodore Robinson, an artist, described his encounters with two New Thought healers in his diaries. On February 20, 1895, Robinson went to see H. Emilie Cady, author of *Lessons in Truth*. "At 12 to see Dr. Cady, a large-featured, homely, good looking woman. She talked very quietly and sensibly and wants me to persevere on the lines of infinite Love, pervading me and 'casting out fear' and apprehension, the cause of my trouble. I like her—she is not too doctrinaire and seems to me to be thoroughly large-minded and sympathetic."

On November 27, 1895, Robinson described his visit with another mental healer: "Again to see Mrs. Montgomery. She dismisses me with a handshake and a God bless you. She has an easy-going, good natured piety (as have many of the faith) that would rather have dismayed my mother, but is *sympathetique* and in earnest—a believer, both in herself and in the God [Good?] outside. She likes Miss Cady's books and gave me one" (Theodore Robinson diary, entries on February 20, 1895, and November 27, 1895, Frick Art Reference Library, New York). My thanks to Kathleen Pyne, of the University of Notre Dame's Department of Art, Art History, and Design, for providing me with her transcription of Robinson's diary entries.

William James published a number of accounts of New Thought healings in *The Varieties of Religious Experience*. For example, see James, *Varieties*, 104.

87. Hopkins to Mabel Dodge Luhan, September 2, 1919, cited in Harley, "Emma Curtis Hopkins," 170–71, see 200–203.

CONCLUSION

1. Woodbridge Riley, "The New Thought," *American Mercury* 1, no. 1 (January 1924): 107; H. L. Mencken, *Prejudices: First Series* (New York: Alfred A. Knopf, 1924), 194, cited in Gail Thain Parker, *Mind Cure in New England* (Hanover, N.H.: University Press of New England, 1973), 57; see Sinclair Lewis, *Elmer Gantry* (New York: Signet Classic [1927] 1980), 222–25.

2. Charles S. Braden, *Spirits in Rebellion: The Rise and Development of New Thought* (Dallas: Southern Methodist University Press, 1963), 285–96, 343; see pamphlet, "The Path of Discovery: The Story of Ernest Holmes" (Los Angeles: United Church of Religious Science, 1987); A. Whitney Griswold, "New Thought: A Cult of Success," *American Journal of Sociology* 40 (November 1934): 315.

3. Emil Coué, *My Method: Including American Impressions* (Garden City: Doubleday, Page and Co., 1923), 7, cited in Richard Weiss, *The American Myth of Success: From Horatio Alger to Norman Vincent Peale* (Urbana: University of Illinois Press, [1969] 1988), 219; John Chynoweth Burnham, "The New Psychology: From Narcissism to Social Control," in John Braeman et al., eds., *Change and Continuity in Twentieth-Century America: The 1920s* (Columbus: Ohio State University Press, 1968), 359; Warren Hilton, *Driving Power of Thought*, vol. 3 of *Psychology and Achievement*, 52–53, cited in Weiss, 220; Weiss, 221.

4. Charles Thomas Hallinan, "My 'New Thought' Boyhood,' *Living Age* 108 (1921): 609, 610. Hallinan described how the arrival of Mr. and Mrs. Van Epps, two "Christ Scientist" missionaries, roiled the small western town of his boyhood. They converted half the town, including Hallinan's entire family. His mother became an enthusiast of Alice Stockham's "Karezza." His sister established a friendship with an "Indian Guide" through her "Ouija board." Hallinan took a course of New Thought study by mail with a Florida healer (most likely Helen Wilmans) who, he reported, was later caught in the "rather cheap and wholly gratuitous prosecutions of the Federal postal authorities." See Hallinan, "My 'New Thought' Boyhood,' 611.

5. Griswold, "New Thought: A Cult of Success"; Parker, *Mind Cure in New England;* see Weiss, *American Myth of Success;* Richard Huber, *The American Idea of Success* (New York: McGraw-Hill Co., 1971); Donald Meyer, *The Positive Thinkers: Religion as Pop Psychology From Mary Baker Eddy to Oral Roberts* (New York: Pantheon Books, [1965], 1980); John Cawelti, *Apostles of the Self-Made Man* (Chicago: University of Chicago Press, 1965).

6. Robert Hill and Barbara Bair, eds., *Marcus Garvey: Life and Lessons* (Berkeley: University of California Press, 1987), xlix–l; "Father Divine Fulfillment of Christian Science," *Spoken Word*, March 30, 1935, 9; Emmet Fox, *The Sermon on the Mount*, 15th ed. (New York: Harper and Brothers, 1938), 112–13; Meridel Le Sueur, *The Girl* (Cambridge, Mass.: West End Press, 1978), 13; see Beryl Satter, "Marcus Garvey, Father Divine, and the Gender Politics of Race Difference and Race Neutrality," *American Quarterly* 48, no. 1 (March 1996): 43–76.

7. Julia Cameron, *Heart Steps; Prayers and Declarations for a Creative Life* (New York: Torcher/Putman Books, 1997), xi–xii; see Norman Vincent Peale, *The Tough-Minded Optimist* (Greenwich, Conn: Fawcett-Crest, 1967) 32; Sarah Schulman, *My American History: Lesbian and Gay Life During the Reagan/ Bush Years* (New York: Routledge, 1994), 158, see 157–59 for an account of Louise Hay's attempt to convince people with AIDS that they could be cured by positive thinking; see Karen De Witt, "Dial 1–800-MY-GURU," *New York Times*, February 5, 1995. Wendy Simonds discusses the New Thought themes in books on the *New York Times Book Review* bestseller list, 1963–91, in her *Women and Self-Help Culture: Reading Between the Lines* (New Brunswick, N.J.: Rutgers University Press, 1992), 135–54.

8. Simonds, *Women and Self-Help Culture*, 2–9, 54–56, 76–77; Wendy Kaminer, *I'm Dysfunctional, You're Dysfunctional: The Recovery Movement and Other Self-Help Fashions* (New York: Vintage Books, 1993), xvi.

9. Wuthnow is quoted in Simonds, *Women and Self-Help Culture*, 77; see Simonds, 46, 48, 174.

10. Simonds, *Women and Self-Help Culture*, 173–212; Gloria Steinem, *Revolution from Within: A Book of Self-Esteem* (Boston: Little, Brown and Co., 1992), 164–65.

11. Michel Foucault, *The History of Sexuality, Volume I: An Introduction*, translated by Robert Hurley (New York: Vintage Books, 1980).

Select Bibliography

I list here first, major works on New Thought and Christian Science, and second, a selection of works on nineteenth- and early twentieth-century U.S. history. This bibliography is intended to guide those who have an interest in further investigation of the early history of New Thought, or those who wish to survey the major primary and secondary sources on U.S. history upon which the arguments in this work were constructed.

I. WRITINGS ON NEW THOUGHT AND CHRISTIAN SCIENCE

New Thought and Christian Science Journals and Newspapers

Christian Metaphysician. Chicago, 1887–88.
Christian Science. Chicago, 1888–92.
Christian Science Journal. Boston, 1885–1889, 1909–10.
Christian Science Thought. Kansas City, Mo., 1890.
Exodus. Chicago, 1897, 1903.
Freedom. Sea Breeze, Fla., 1898–1900.
Harmony. San Francisco, 1896–1903.
Journal of Practical Metaphysics. Boston, 1896–98.
Master Mind. San Francisco, 1911–24.
Mind. New York, 1897–1904.
Mind Cure. Chicago, 1884–87.
Modern Thought. Kansas City, Mo., 1889–90.
The Nautilus. Holyoke, Mass, 1909–10.
New Thought. Chicago, 1901–02, 1906.
Power. Denver, Colo., 1909–11.
Truth. Chicago, 1887.
Universal Truth. Chicago, 1894, 1899.

Primary Sources by New Thought and Christian Science Authors

Allen, James. *As a Man Thinketh*. Chicago: Science Press, 1905.

Atkinson, William Walker. *The Law of the New Thought*. Chicago: Psychic Research Co., 1902.

———. *The New Psychology*. Chicago: Progress Co., 1909.

———. *The Secret of Mental Magic*. Chicago: William Walker Atkinson, 1907.

———. *Thought-Force in Business and Everyday Life*. 10th ed. Chicago: Psychic Research Co., 1901.

———. *Your Mind and How to Use It*. Holyoke, Mass.: Elizabeth Towne Co., 1911.

Barrows, Chas. M. *Facts and Fictions of Mental Healing*. Boston: H. H. Carter and Karrick, 1887.

Bible Year Book. Compiled by Mary F. Haydon. Chicago: Psychic Research Co., 1903.

Brooks, Louise McNamara. *Early History of Divine Science*. Denver, Colo.: First Divine Science Church, 1963.

Brooks, Nona L. *In the Light of Healing: Sermons By Nona L. Brooks*. Compiled by the Rev. Patricia Zarlinger. Denver, Colo.: First Divine Science Church, 1986.

Brown, Henry Harrison. *New Thought Primer*. San Francisco: "NOW" Folk, 1903.

Cady, H. Emilie. *Lessons in Truth: A Course of Twelve Lessons in Practical Christianity*. Kansas City: Unity School of Christianity, n.d.

Clark, William Horatio. "A New Thought Pioneer." *Mind* 9 no. 4 (January 1902): 283–285

Cramer, M. E. *Basic Statements and Health Treatment of Truth*. 2d ed. San Francisco: M. E. Cramer, 1893.

———. *Lessons in the Science of Infinite Spirit and the Christ Method of Healing*. San Francisco: M. E. Cramer, 1890.

———. *The Unity of Life and the Methods of Arriving at Truth*. San Francisco: M. E. Cramer, 1888.

Del Mar, Eugene. *Spiritual and Material Attraction: A Conception of Unity*. Denver, Colo.: Smith-Brooks Printing Co., 1901.

———, ed. "The Life Work (A Testimonial) of Helen Wilmans Post, 1831–1907." Scrapbook, 1931, in manuscripts and archives, New York Public Library.

Diaz, Abby Morton. "The Human Problem According to Law." *The Arena* 6 (1895): 619–24.

———. *The Law of Perfection*. Belmont, Mass.: A. M. Diaz, 1886.

———. *Only a Flock of Women*. Boston: D. Lothrop Co., 1893.

———. *Spirit as a Power*. Belmont, Mass.: Abby Morton Diaz, 1886.

Dresser, Horatio W. "The Failure of the New Thought Movement." *Journal of Practical Metaphysics* 2, no. 4 (January 1898): 98–101.

——. *The Heart of It.* Edited by Helen Campbell and Katharine Westendorf. Boston: Geo. H. Ellis, 1897.

——. *A History of the New Thought Movement.* New York: Thomas Y. Crowell Co., 1919.

——, ed. *The Quimby Manuscripts.* New York: Thomas Y. Crowell Co., 1921.

——, ed. *The Spirit of the New Thought.* New York: Thomas Y. Crowell Co., 1917.

Dyas, Thomas C. "Henry Frank: A Biographical Sketch." *Mind* 12, no. 9 (December 1903): 646–652.

Eddy, Mary Baker. *Christ and Christmas: A Poem.* Boston: Trustees under the Will of Mary Baker Eddy, [1893] 1925.

——. "Mind-Healing History." *Christian Science Journal* 5 no. 3 (June, 1887): 109–118

——. *Miscellaneous Writings: 1883–1896.* Boston: Trustees under the Will of Mary Baker Eddy, 1896.

——. *Science and Health with Key to the Scriptures.* Boston: First Church of Christ, Scientist, [1875] 1971.

Evans, W. F. *Esoteric Christianity and Mental Therapeutics.* Boston: H. H. Carter and Karrick, 1886.

——. *Primitive Mind-Cure.* Boston: H. H. Carter and Co., 1885.

Ewing, William G. "Why Not Be a Christian Scientist?" *The Arena* 25, no. 1 (January 1901): 1–9.

Fillmore, Charles. *Atom-Smashing Power of Mind.* Unity Village, Mo.: Unity School of Christianity, 1949.

——. *Dynamics for Living.* Compiled by Warren Meyer. Lee's Summit, Mo.: Unity Books, 1967.

Fox, Emmet. *Power Through Constructive Thinking.* San Francisco: Harper and Row, [1932] 1989.

——. *The Sermon on the Mount.* New York: Harper and Brothers, 1938.

Gestefeld, Ursula N. *The Builder and the Plan: A Text-Book of the Science of Being.* Pelham, N.Y.: Gestefeld Publishing Company, 1901.

——. *A Chicago Bible Class.* N.p.: United States Book Company, 1891.

——. *How to Control Circumstances.* Pelham, N.Y.: Gestefeld Publishing Company, 1901.

——. *How We Master Our Fate.* 4th ed. Chicago: Coolidge and Waterloo, 1897.

——. *Jesuitism in Christian Science.* Chicago: Ursula N. Gestefeld, 1888.

——. *The Leprosy of Miriam.* New York: Gestefeld Library and Publishing Co., 1894.

——. *The Master of the Man.* 2d ed. Chicago: Exodus Publishing Company, 1914.

——. *The Science of the Christ: An Advanced Statement of Christian Science.* Chicago: Ursula N. Gestefeld, 1889.

―――. *What Is Mental Medicine? A Lecture Delivered Before the Woman's Physiological Institute of Chicago.* Chicago: Magill and McChen Printers, 1887.

―――. *The Woman Who Dares.* New York: Lovell, Gestefeld and Co., 1892.

Gordon, Nancy McKay. *Woman Revealed.* Chicago: Nancy McKay Gordon, 1901.

Haddock, Frank Channing. *Power of Will.* Meriden, Conn.: Pelton Publishing Co., [1907] 1919.

Harbert, Elizabeth Boynton. *Amore.* New York: Lovell, Gestefeld and Co., 1892.

―――. "Ordination Address." *Christian Science* 1, no. 6 (February 1889): 141–43.

Harley, Fanny M. *Simplified Lessons in the Science of Being.* Chicago: F. M. Harley Publishing Co., 1899.

Hopkins, Emma Curtis. *Bible Interpretations.* Pittsfield, Mass.: Sun Printing Co., 1925.

―――. *Class Lessons: 1888.* Compiled by Elizabeth C. Bogart. Marina del Rey, Calif.: DeVorss & Co., 1977.

―――. *Drops of Gold.* Chicago: Emma Curtis Hopkins, 1891.

―――. *High Mysticism.* Santa Monica, Calif.: DeVorss & Co., 1974.

―――. *The Ministry of the Holy Mother.* N.p., n.d.

―――. *The Radiant I AM.* Putnam, Conn.: Emma Curtis Hopkins Publications, n.d.

―――. *Resume: Practice Book for the Twelve Chapters in High Mysticism,* 8th ed. Killingly, Conn.: Mrs. E. C. Darrow, n.d.

―――. *Scientific Christian Mental Practice.* Marina del Rey, Calif.: DeVorss and Co., n.d.

―――. *Tenth Lesson in Christian Science.* Chicago: Christian Science Publishing Co., 1891.

Ingalese, Richard. *The History and Power of Mind.* New York: Occult Book Concern, 1902.

Kingsley, Florence Morse. "Mrs. Follett's Funeral." *The Nautilus* 12, no. 8 (June 1910): 25–8.

―――. *The Transfiguration of Miss Philura.* New York: Funk and Wagnalls Company, 1901.

Lord, Frances. *Christian Science Healing.* Chicago: Lily Publishing House, 1888.

Marden, Orison Swett. *The Miracle of Right Thought.* New York: T. Y. Crowell and Co., 1910.

Militz, Annie Rix. *All the Way.* Los Angeles: Master Mind Publishing Co., 1922.

―――. *Generation and Regeneration: Healing the Organs of Generation.* N.p., n.d.

―――. *Primary Lessons in Christian Living and Healing.* New York: Absolute Press, 1904.

————. *Prosperity Through the Knowledge and Power of Mind.* Los Angeles: De Vorss and Co., 1933.

————. *The Renewal of the Body.* Holyoke, Mass.: Elizabeth Towne Co., 1918.

————. *The Sermon on the Mount.* Rev. ed. New York: Trow Press, 1904.

————. *Spiritual Housekeeping: A Study in Concentration in the Busy Life.* Los Angeles: Master Mind Publishing Co., 1910.

Mulford, Prentice. *The Gift of the Spirit: A Selection from the Essays of Prentice Mulford.* Edited by Arthur Edward Waite. London: William Rider and Sons, 1908.

————. *Thoughts are Things.* London: G. Bell and Sons, [1908] 1935.

Newcomb, Charles. *All's Right with the World.* Boston: Philosophical Co., 1897.

Newton, R. Heber. "The New Century's Call." *Mind* 5, no. 3 (December 1899): 131–51.

Nichols, Ida A. "Be Beautiful, Be Rich, Be Efficient." *Christian Science* 2, no. 11 (July 1890): 353–55.

————. "God is Our Support." *Christian Science* 3, no. 5 (January 1891): 144–47.

————. "The Money Question According to C. S." *Christian Science* 2, no. 10 (June 1890): 321–23.

————. "We Make Our Own World." *Christian Science* 3, no. 7 (March 1891): 208–10.

Patterson, Charles Brodie. "Abby Morton Diaz: A Biographical Sketch." *Mind* 10, no. 3 (June 1902): 167–71.

————. "Annie Rix Militz: A Biographical Sketch." *Mind* 10, no. 1 (April 1902): 9–14.

————. "Charles Fillmore: A Biographical Sketch." *Mind* 10, no. 2 (May 1902): 81–5.

————. *Dominion and Power: or The Science of Life and Living.* 7th ed. New York and London: Funk and Wagnalls Co., 1910.

————. "Helen Van-Anderson: A Biographical Sketch." *Mind* 10, no. 4 (July 1902): 244–47.

————. "M. E. Cramer: A Biographical Sketch." *Mind* 10, no. 5 (August 1902): 327–31.

————. "R. Heber Newton: A Biographical Sketch." *Mind* 9, no. 1 (October 1901): 6–8.

————. "Ralph Waldo Trine: A Biographical Sketch." *Mind* 9, no. 5 (February 1902): 325–29.

————. "Ursula N. Gestefeld: A Biographical Sketch." *Mind* 9, no. 4 (January 1902): 251–54.

————. "What the New Thought Stands For." *The Arena* 25, no. 1 (January 1901): 9–16.

Peale, Norman Vincent. *The Tough-Minded Optimist.* Greenwich, Conn.: Fawcett-Crest, 1967.

Pennington, Jeanne G., ed. *Don't Worry Nuggets*. New York: Fords, Howard and Hulbert, 1898.

Pentecost, Hugh O. "Is Mental Healing Scientific?" *Mind* 4, no. 2 (May 1899): 65–70.

Sears, Julia Seton. *The Truth About Woman Suffrage*. New York: New Thought Publishers, 1910.

Seward, Theodore F. *Don't Worry, or Spiritual Emancipation*. New York: Brotherhood of Christian Unity, 1897.

Shelton, T. J. *I Am Sermons*. Denver: "Christian," 1900.

Southworth, Louisa. "The Baccalaureate." *Christian Science* 1, no. 6 (February 1889): 144–45.

Stockham, Alice B. *Creative Life: A Special Letter to Young Girls; A Supplement to Koradine Letters*. Chicago: Alice B. Stockham Co., 1893.

———. *Karezza: Ethics of Marriage*. Rev. ed. Chicago: Stockham Publishing Co., [1896] 1903.

———. *The Lover's World: A Wheel of Life*. Chicago: Stockham Publishing Co., 1903.

———. "Non-Resistance as a Healing Power." *The Nautilus* 12, no. 3 (January 1910): 37–39.

———. *Tokology: A Book For Every Woman*. Rev. ed. Chicago: Alice B. Stockham and Co., [1883] 1894.

———. *Tolstoi: A Man of Peace*, and Ellis, H. Havelock, *The New Spirit*. Chicago: Alice B. Stockham and Co., 1900.

Stockham, Alice B., and Talbot, Lida Hood. *Koradine Letters*. Chicago: Alice B. Stockham and Co., 1893.

Towne, Elizabeth. *How to Grow Success*. Holyoke, Mass.: Elizabeth Towne Co., 1903.

———. *How to Use New Thought in Home Life*. Holyoke, Mass.: Elizabeth Towne Co., 1921.

———. *Practical Methods for Self-Development*. Holyoke, Mass.: Elizabeth Towne Co., 1904.

Trine, Ralph Waldo. *In Tune with the Infinite*. Indianapolis: Bobbs-Merrill Co., [1897] 1933.

Tyner, Paul. "The Metaphysical Movement." *American Monthly Review of Reviews* 25, no. 3 (March 1902): 312–20.

———. "Religion in Social Reform." *The New Time*, August 1898: 75–77.

———. *Through the Invisible: A Love Story*. New York: Continental Publishing, 1897.

Van-Anderson, Helen. "The Church of the Higher Life." *Journal of Practical Metaphysics* 1, no. 3 (December 1896): 76–77.

———. *The Journal of a Live Woman*. Boston: Geo. H. Wright, 1895.

———. *The Mystic Scroll: A Book of Revelation*. New York: New York Magazine, 1906.

———. *The Right Knock: A Story*. Chicago: Nellie V. Anderson, 1889.

Van Anderson-Gordon, Helen. *The Illumined Life*. Chicago: A. C. McClurg Co., 1912.

Wardlaw, Suzanne E., comp. *The Every Day Book*. Holyoke, Mass.: Elizabeth Towne Co., 1905.

Wilcox, Ella Wheeler. *Every-Day Thoughts in Prose and Verse*. Chicago: W. B. Conkey Co., 1901.

———. *The Heart of the New Thought*. Chicago: New Thought Publishing Co., 1904.

———. *New Thought Common Sense, and What Life Means to Me*. Chicago: W. B. Conkey, 1908.

———. "A Woman's Answer." In "The Restlessness of the Modern Woman" *Cosmopolitan* 31 (July 1901), reprinted in *The American Gospel of Success: Individualism and Beyond*, ed. Moses Rischin. Chicago: Quadrangle Books, 1965: 237

———. *The Worlds and I*. New York: George H. Doran Co., 1918.

Wilmans, Helen. *Back Numbers: Wilmans Express, Condensed*. With Ada Wilmans Powers. N.p., n.d.

———. *A Blossom of the Century*. Sea Breeze, Fla.: Freedom Publishing Co., 1898.

———. *The Conquest of Poverty*. Sea Breeze, Fla.: International Scientific Organization, 1899.

———. *The Conquest of Poverty*. Sea Breeze, Fla.: Wilmans Publishing House, 1901.

———. *A Message From Helen Wilmans*. International New Thought Alliance Archives. (Copy in archives of the Institute for the Study of American Religion, Santa Barbara, California.)

———. *A Search for Freedom*. Sea Breeze, Fla.: Freedom Publishing House, 1898.

———. "Willing Slaves of the Nineteenth Century." *Commonwealth Library* no. 4 (1895): 1–4.

Wood, Henry. *God's Image in Man*. 9th ed. Boston: Lee and Shepard, 1897.

———. *The New Thought Simplified*. 4th ed. Boston: Lothrop, Lee and Shepard, 1903.

Secondary Sources on New Thought and Christian Science

Ahlstrom, Sydney E. *A Religious History of the American People* vol. 2. Garden City, N.Y.: Image Books, 1975.

Anderson, Alan C. "Contrasting Strains of Metaphysical Idealism Contributing to New Thought." Paper presented at the American Academy of Religion Annual Meeting, Boston, December 6, 1987.

———. "Horatio W. Dresser and the Philosophy of New Thought." Ph.D. dissertation, Boston University Graduate School, 1963.

Anderson, Ferne. "Emma Curtis Hopkins: Springboard to New Thought." M.A. thesis, University of Denver, 1981.

Atkins, Gaius Glenn. *Modern Religious Cults and Movements.* New York: Fleming H. Revell Company, 1923.

Beebe, Tom. *Who's Who in New Thought.* Lakemont, Ga.: CSA Press, 1977.

Braden, Charles S. *Christian Science Today: Power, Policy, Practice.* Dallas: Southern Methodist University Press, 1963.

———. *Spirits in Rebellion: The Rise and Development of New Thought.* Dallas: Southern Methodist University Press, 1963.

———. *These Also Believe.* New York: Macmillan, 1949.

Cawelti, John G. *Apostles of the Self-Made Man.* Chicago: University of Chicago Press, 1965.

Dakin, Edwin Franden. *Mrs. Eddy: The Biography of a Virginal Mind.* New York: Charles Scribner's Sons, 1929.

Deane, Hazel. *Powerful is the Light: The Story of Nona Brooks.* Denver: Divine Science College, 1945.

Deering, Mary. "Annie Rix Militz: Teacher, Author and Lecturer." *New Thought Bulletin* 28, no. 3 (Summer 1945): 5–6.

Dreier, Thomas. *The Story of Elizabeth Towne and the Nautilus.* Holyoke, Mass.: Elizabeth Towne Co., n.d.

"Ernest Studies with Emma Curtis Hopkins." Unpublished manuscript, New Thought-High Watch, in archives of Institute for the Study of American Religion, Santa Barbara, California, n.d.

Freeman, James Dillet. *The Story of Unity.* Lee's Summit, Mo: Unity School of Christianity, 1978.

Gottschalk, Stephen. *The Emergence of Christian Science in American Religious Life.* Berkeley: University of California Press, 1978.

Griswold, A. Whitney. "New Thought: A Cult of Success." *American Journal of Sociology,* 40 (November 1934): 309–318.

Hallinan, Charles Thomas. "My 'New Thought' Boyhood: An American Adventure." *The Living Age* 108 (1921): 606–611.

Hanson, Penny. "Woman's Hour: Feminist Implications of Mary Baker Eddy's Christian Science Movement, 1885–1910." Ph.D. dissertation, University of California, Irvine, 1981.

Harley, Gail M. "Emma Curtis Hopkins: 'Forgotten Founder' of New Thought." Ph.D. dissertation, Florida State University, 1991.

Huber, Richard M. *The American Idea of Success.* New York: McGraw-Hill, 1971.

Judah, J. Stillson. *The History of Metaphysical Movements in America.* Philadelphia: Westminster Press, 1967.

Kaminer, Wendy. "Chances Are You're Codependent Too." *New York Times Book Review,* Feb. 11, 1990.

———. *I'm Dysfunctional, You're Dysfunctional: The Recovery Movement and Other Self-Help Fashions.* New York: Vintage Books, 1993.

Kelly, Aidan A. "Twelve-Step Programs and the New Age." In *New Age Encyclopedia,* edited by J. Gordon Melton, Jerome Clark, and Aidan A. Kelly. Detroit: Gale Research, 1990.

Lindley, Susan L. "The Ambiguous Feminism of Mary Baker Eddy." *Journal of Religion*, 64 (July 1984): 318–330.

McDonald, Jean A. "Mary Baker Eddy and the Nineteenth-Century 'Public' Woman: A Feminist Reappraisal." *Journal of Feminist Studies in Religion* 2, no. 1 (spring 1986): 89–111.

Melton, J. Gordon. "Emma Curtis Hopkins: A Twentieth-Century Feminist of the 1880s." Institute for the Study of American Religion (ISAR) archives, University of California, Santa Barbara.

———. "New Thought's Hidden History: Emma Curtis Hopkins, Forgotten Founder." Unpublished paper, Institute for the Study of American Religion (ISAR), August 1988.

Meyer, Donald. *The Positive Thinkers: Religion as Popular Culture from Mary Baker Eddy to Oral Roberts*, New York: Pantheon Books, [1965] 1980.

Milmine, Georgine. *The Life of Mary Baker G. Eddy and the History of Christian Science*. Grand Rapids, Mich.: Baker Book House, [1909] 1971.

Parker, Gail Thain. *Mind Cure in New England*. Hanover, N.H.: University Press of New England. 1973.

"Path of Discovery: The Story of Ernest Holmes." Los Angeles: United Church of Religious Science, 1987.

Peel, Robert. *Mary Baker Eddy: The Years of Authority, 1892–1910*. New York: Holt, Rinehart and Winston, 1977.

———. *Mary Baker Eddy: The Years of Discovery, 1821–1875*. New York: Holt, Rinehart and Winston, 1966.

———. *Mary Baker Eddy: The Years of Trial, 1876–1891*. New York: Holt, Rinehart and Winston, 1971.

Podmore, Frank. *From Mesmer to Christian Science: A Short History of Mental Healing*. New Hyde Park, N.Y.: University Books, 1963.

Powell, Lyman. *Christian Science: The Faith and Its Founder*. New York: G. P. Putnam's Sons, 1907.

———. *The Emmanuel Movement in a New England Town*. New York: G. P. Putnam's Sons, 1909.

Riley, Woodbridge. "The New Thought." *American Mercury* 1, no. 1 (January 1924): 104–08.

Setta, Susan M. "Denial of the Female—Affirmation of the Feminine: The Father-Mother God of Mary Baker Eddy." In *Beyond Androcentrism: New Essays on Women and Religion*, edited by Rita Gross, 289–304. Missoula, Mont.: Scholars Press for the American Academy of Religion, 1977.

Simmons, John Kent. "The Ascension of Annie Rix Militz and the Home(s) of Truth: Perfection Meets Paradise in Early Twentieth-Century Los Angeles." Ph.D. dissertation, University of California, Santa Barbara, 1987.

———. "New Thought, No Thought: The Forgotten History of Annie Rix Militz and Her Contribution to the Unity School of Christianity." Institute for the Study of American Religion (ISAR) archives, University of California, Santa Barbara.

Simonds, Wendy. *Women and Self-Help Culture: Reading Between the Lines.* New Brunswick, N.J.: Rutgers University Press, 1992.

Slyder, T. R. "The Unity Movement: A Search for the Truth of Practical Christianity." Institute for the Study of American Religion (ISAR) archives, University of California, Santa Barbara.

Swinhart, Altman K. *Since Mrs. Eddy.* New York: Holt Company, 1931.

Szasz, Ferenc. "'New Thought' and The American West." *Journal of the West* 23, no. 2 (January 1984): 83–90.

Teahan, John F. "Warren Felt Evans and Mental Healing: Romantic Idealism and Practical Mysticism in Nineteenth-Century America." *Church History* 48 (March 1979): 63–80.

Umansky, Ellen M. *From Christian Science to Jewish Science: Spiritual Healing and American Jews* (Oxford University Press, forthcoming).

Ward, Gary L. "The Feminist Theme of Early New Thought." Institute for the Study of American Religion (ISAR) occasional Paper #1 (1989).

Weiss, Richard. *The American Myth of Success: From Horatio Alger to Norman Vincent Peale.* Urbana: University of Illinois Press, [1969] 1988.

II. SELECTED WRITINGS ON NINETEENTH- AND EARLY-TWENTIETH-CENTURY U.S. HISTORY

Journals and Newspapers

Appeal to Reason. Girard, Kans., 1903.
The Arena. Boston and New York, 1889–1903.
Chicago Daily Inter-Ocean. Chicago, 1889.
Chicago Times. Chicago, 1889.
Evanston Index. Evanston, Ill., 1890–91.
Evanston Press. Evanston, Ill., 1891, 1893, 1894.
The New Time. Chicago, 1897–98.
The Woman's World. Chicago, 1885–88.

SELECTED PRIMARY SOURCES

Allen, Grant. "Plain Words on the Woman Question." *Popular Science Monthly,* December 1889. Reprinted in *Men's Ideas/Women's Realities: Popular Science, 1870–1915,* edited by Louise Michele Newman. New York: Pergamon Press, 1985.

The American Purity Alliance Twentieth Annual Report: 1895. New York: American Purity Alliance, 1896.

Anthony, Susan B., and Ida Husted Harper, eds. *The History of Woman Suffrage,* vol. 4: 1883–1900. New York: Arno and the New York Times, 1969.

Avery, Rachel Foster, ed. *The Transactions of the National Council of Women of the United States.* Philadelphia: J. B. Lipincott Co., 1891.

Bachofen, Johann-Jacob. *Myth, Religion, and Mother-Right,* translated by Ralph Manheim (Princeton, N.J., [1861] 1967). Excerpted in *Women, the Family, and Freedom: The Debate in Documents I, 1750–1880,* edited by Susan Groag Bell and Karen M. Offen, pp. 375–84. Stanford: Stanford University Press, 1983:.

Bellamy, Edward. *Looking Backwards: 2000–1887.* New York: Modern Library, [1888] 1982.

———. *The Religion of Solidarity.* London: Concord Grove Press, 1984.

Bjorkman, Frances Maule. "The Literature of the 'New Thoughters.'" *World's Work* (January 1910): 12471–12475.

Bruce, H. Addington. *Scientific Mental Healing.* Boston: Little, Brown and Co., 1911.

Campbell, Helen. "Social Settlements and the Civic Sense." *The Arena* 20, no. 5 (November–December 1898): 589–603.

———. "Women and the Civic Sense." *New Time,* October 1897: 188–89.

Carpenter, Edward. *Love's Coming-of-Age.* New York and London: Mitchell Kennerley, [1896] 1911.

———. *A Visit to a Gnani: From Adams Peak to Elephanta.* Chicago: Alice B. Stockham and Co., n.d.

Chandler, Lucinda B. "The Completion of Humanity." *Mind* 10, no. 5 (August 1902): 370–73.

———. "What Should America Do For Womanhood?" *The New Time,* June 1898: 396–99.

———. "The Woman Movement." *Arena* 4 (1891): 705–11.

Clark, W. E. "Man, Woman and Poverty." *Mind* 10, no. 4 (July 1902): 278–85.

Clarke, Edward H. *Sex in Education.* Boston and New York, 1873. Excerpted in *Women, the Family, and Freedom: The Debate in Documents I, 1750–1880,* edited by Susan Groag Bell and Karen M. Offen. Stanford: Stanford University Press, 1983: 427–31.

Cleveland, Grover. "Woman's Mission and Woman's Clubs." *Ladies Home Journal* 22 (May 1905). In *The Woman Movement: Feminism in the United States and England,* edited by William O'Neill, 158–163. Chicago: Quadrangle Books, 1971.

Colby, Clara Bewick. "Elizabeth Cady Stanton." *The Arena* 29, no. 2 (February 1903): 152–60.

Comte, Auguste. "The Influence of Positivism upon Women." In *General View of Positivism,* translated by J. H. Bridges. London, 1875; reprint ed., Stanford, Calif., n.d. Excerpted in *Women, the Family, and Freedom: The Debate in Documents I, 1750–1880,* edited by Susan Groag Bell and Karen M. Offen. Stanford: Stanford University Press, 1983: 219–26.

Conger, Josephine. "Hints to the Appeal's Wise Women." *Appeal to Reason* no. 382 (March 28, 1903): 5.

Cooley, Winnifred Harper. "The Future of the Woman's Club." *The Arena* 27, no. 4 (April 1902): 380.

Donnelly, Ignatius. *Caesar's Column: A Story of the Twentieth Century*, edited by Walter B. Rideout. Cambridge, Mass.: Harvard University Press, [1890] 1960.

Eggleston, Edward. *The Faith Doctor: A Story of New York.* Ridgewood, N.J.: Gregg Press, [1892] 1968.

Ellis, Havelock. "The Changing Status of Women." In *The Woman Question*, edited by T. R. Smith, 220–229. New York: Boni and Liverright, 1918.

———. *The New Spirit.* 1890. 4th ed. Boston: Houghton Mifflin Co., 1926.

———. *The Problem of Race-Regeneration.* New York: Moffat, Yard and Co., 1911.

Flower, B.[enjamin] O. "Behind the Deed the Thought." *The Arena* 5 (1891–92): 527–28.

———. *Christian Science As a Religious Belief and a Therapeutic Agent.* Boston: Twentieth Century Company, 1909.

———. "Edwin Markham: A Prophet-Poet of the Fraternal State." *Arena* 27, no. 4 (April 1902): 391–414.

———. "The Era of Woman." *The Arena* 4 (1891): 382–94.

———. "Fashion's Slaves." *The Arena* 4 (1891): 419–23.

———. "Hypnotism and its Relation to Psychical Research." *The Arena* 5 (1891): 316–32.

———. "Leprosy of the Soul." *The Arena* 3 (1890–1891): 637–38.

———. *Progressive Men, Women and Movements of the Past Twenty-Five Years.* Boston: New Arena, 1914.

———. "Proposed Federation of the Anglo-Saxon Nations." *The Arena* 20 (August 1898): 223–37.

———. "Science and Psychical Research." *The Arena* 20 (July 1898): 87.

———. "Some of Civilization's Silent Currents." *The Arena* 6 (1892): 766–68.

———. "A Transitional Period." *The Arena* 3 (1890–91): 124–25.

Froebel, Friedrich. *Mother's Songs, Games and Stories*, translated by Frances and Emily Lord. London: William Rice, 1895.

Gage, Matilda Joslyn. *Woman, Church and State.* Watertown, Mass: Persephone Press, [1893] 1980.

Gamble, Eliza Burt. "The Influence of Sex on Development." *Mind* 8, no. 2 (May 1901): 97–99.

Gardener, Helen H. "The Moral Responsibility of Women in Heredity." In *The Work and Words of the National Congress of Mothers.* New York: D. Appleton and Co., 1897.

Gilman, Charlotte Perkins. *The Living of Charlotte Perkins Gilman.* New York: D. Appleton-Century, 1935.

Herron, George. "Opportunity of the Church." *The Arena* 6 (1895): 42–8.

———. "The Social Value of Failure." *The Arena* 6 (1895): 633–41.

Holmes, Lizzie M. "Woman's Future Position in the World." *The Arena* 20 (September 1898): 33–43.

Illinois Woman's Press Association Yearbook, 1891, 1892, 1893. N.p. Located at Chicago Historical Society.

James, William. *Essays on Faith and Morals,* edited by Ralph Barton Perry. New York: New American Library, 1962.

―――. *The Varieties of Religious Experience.* Middlesex, England: Penguin Books, [1902] 1982.

Jenkins, Therese A. "The Mental Force of Woman." *Popular Science Monthly,* April 1889. Reprinted in *Men's Ideas/Women's Realities: Popular Science, 1870–1915,* edited by Louise Michele Newman. New York: Pergamon Press, 1985.

Livermore, Mary A. "Centuries of Dishonor." *The Arena* 1 (1889–90): 83–92.

Luhan, Mabel Dodge. *Movers and Shakers.* Volume 3 of *Intimate Memories.* New York: Harcourt, Brace and Co., 1936.

Markham, Edwin. "Poetry and its Relation to Life." *Mind* 11, no. 1 (October 1902): 40–44.

Maudsley, Henry. "Sex in Mind and in Education." *Popular Science Monthly,* June 1874. Reprinted in *Men's Ideas/Women's Realities: Popular Science, 1870–1915,* edited by Louise Michele Newman. New York: Pergamon Press, 1985.

Merrick, Marie. "Woman of the Period." *The Arena* 29, no. 2 (February 1903): 161–166.

Miller, Joaquin. *The Building of the City Beautiful.* Cambridge and Chicago: Stone and Kimball, 1893.

Mills, Benjamin Fay. "Between the Animals and the Angels." *The Arena* 22, no. 1 (July 1899): 1–14.

Muzzey, Annie L. "The Hour and the Woman." *The Arena* 22 (August 1899): 263–72.

Powell, Aaron M., ed. *The National Purity Congress, Its Papers, Addresses, Portraits.* New York: American Purity Alliance, 1896.

Report of the International Council of Women. N.W.S.A.: Rufus and Darby, 1888.

Report of the Proceedings of the Second Annual Convention of the National Congress of Mothers. Philadelphia: Geo. F. Lasher, 1899.

Ricker, A. W. "Garnered from the Silence." *Appeal to Reason* no. 372 (January 17, 1903): 4.

Riis, Jacob A. *How the Other Half Lives.* New York: Dover Publications, [1890] 1971.

Sheldon, Charles M. *In His Steps.* New York: Grosset and Dunlap, [1896] 1935.

Smith, A. Lapthorn. "Higher Education of Women and Race Suicide." *Popular Science Monthly,* April 1905. Reprinted in *Men's Ideas/Women's Realities: Popular Science, 1870–1915,* edited by Louise Michele Newman. New York: Pergamon Press, 1985.

Stanton, Elizabeth Cady. *Eighty Years and More: Reminiscences, 1815–1897.* New York: Schocken Books, [1898] 1971.

―――. "Home Life." In *Elizabeth Cady Stanton/Susan B. Anthony: Correspondence, Writings, Speeches,* edited by Ellen Carol DuBois, pp. 125–138 (New York: Schocken Books, 1981).

———. "The Matriarchate." In *Up from the Pedestal: Selected Writings in the History of American Feminism,* edited by Aileen S. Kraditor. Chicago: Quadrangle Books, 1970.

———. "Where Must Lasting Progress Begin?" *The Arena* 4 (1891): 295–98.

Stanton, Elizabeth Cady, and the Revising Committee. *The Woman's Bible.* Seattle: Coalition Task Force on Women and Religion, [1898] 1984.

Stanton, Maia Pratt. "Dominion." *Mind* 7, no. 1 (April 1901).

Strong, Josiah. "Our Country." Excerpted in *Major Problems in American Foreign Policy,* vol. 1: To 1914, edited by Thomas G. Paterson. Lexington, Mass.: D. C. Heath and Co., 1989.

———. "Our Country." Excerpted in *The Power of Words: Documents in American History,* vol. 2: From 1865, edited by T. H. Breen. New York: HarperCollins College Publishers, 1996.

Through the Years: From the Scrapbook of Mrs. Mears. Washington, D.C.: National Congress of Parents and Teachers, n.d.

Tyner, Paul. *Through the Invisible: A Love Story.* New York: Continental Publishing, 1897.

Untermann, Ernest. "A Socialist's Confession of Faith." *Appeal to Reason* no. 377 (February 21, 1903): 2.

Ward, Lester Frank. "Mind as a Social Factor." In *The American Intellectual Tradition,* Vol. 2: 1865 to the Present, 2d ed., edited by David Hollinger and Charles Capper. New York: Oxford University Press, 1993.

Wells, Kate Gannett. "Why More Girls Do Not Marry." *North American Review* 152 (January–June, 1891): 175–81.

Willard, Frances E. "The Coming Brotherhood." *The Arena* 6 (1892):317–323.

———. "The Dawn of Woman's Day," *Our Day: A Record and Review of Current Reform* 2, no. 11 (November 1888). In Nancy F. Cott et al., eds., *Root of Bitterness: Documents of the Social History of American Women,* 2d ed., 399–405. Boston: Northeastern University Press, 1996.

———. *Glimpses of Fifty Years.* Chicago: Woman's Christian Temperance Publication Association, 1889.

———. *How to Win: A Book for Girls.* 1886. In *The Ideal of the 'New Woman' According to the Woman's Christian Temperance Union,* edited and introduced by Caroline DeSwarte Gifford. New York: Garland Press, 1987.

———. "The Woman's Cause is Man's." *The Arena* 5 (1891–92): 712–724.

———. *Writing Out My Heart: Selections from the Journal of Frances E. Willard,* edited by Carolyn DeSwarte Gifford. Urbana: University of Illinois Press, 1995.

Willard, Frances E., and Mary A. Livermore. *A Woman of the Century.* New York: 1893.

Wilson, J. Stitt. "The Social Crusade." *The New Time* (April 1898): 232–36.

Worcester, Elwood, and Samuel McComb. *The Christian Religion as a Healing Power.* New York: Moffat, Yard and Co., 1909.

Worcester, Elwood, Samuel McComb, and Isador H. Coriat. *Religion and Medi-*

cine: The Moral Control of Nervous Disorders. New York: Moffat, Yard and Co., 1908.

Work and Words of the National Congress of Mothers. New York: D. Appleton and Co., 1897.

World's Congress of Representative Women. Chicago and New York: Rand, McNally and Co., 1894.

Youmans, William Jay. "Individuality for Woman." *Popular Science Monthly,* September 1891. Reprinted in *Men's Ideas / Women's Realities: Popular Science, 1870–1915,* edited by Louise Michele Newman. New York: Pergamon Press, 1985.

SELECTED SECONDARY SOURCES

Albanese, Catherine L. *Nature Religion in America: From Algonkian Indians to the New Age.* Chicago: University of Chicago Press, 1990.

———. "Physic and Metaphysic in Nineteenth-Century America: Medical Sectarians and Religious Healing." *Church History* 55 (December 1986): 489–502.

Allen, Ann Taylor. "Spiritual Motherhood: German Feminists and the Kindergarten Movement, 1848–1911." *History of Education Quarterly* 22 (1982): 319–40.

Ammond, Elizabeth. "The New Woman as Cultural Symbol and Social Reality." In *1915: The Cultural Moment,* edited by Adele Heller and Lois Rudnick. New Brunswick: Rutgers University Press, 1991.

Armstrong, Nancy. *Desire and Domestic Fiction.* New York: Oxford University Press, 1987.

Axeen, David. "'Heroes of the Engine Room': American 'Civilization' and the War with Spain." *American Quarterly* 36, no. 4 (Fall 1984): 482–502.

Banta, Martha. *Imaging American Women: Idea and Ideals in Cultural History.* New York: Columbia University Press, 1987.

Barker-Benfield, G. J. *The Horrors of the Half-Known Life.* New York: Harper Colophon Books, 1976.

Bassuk, Ellen L. "The Rest Cure: Repetition or Resolution of Victorian Women's Conflicts?" In *The Female Body in Western Culture,* edited by Susan Rubin Suleiman. Cambridge, Mass.: Harvard University Press, 1986.

Bederman, Gail. *Manliness and Civilization: A Cultural History of Gender and Race in the United States, 1880–1917.* Chicago: University of Chicago Press, 1995.

———. "'The Women Have Had Charge of the Church Work Long Enough': The Men and Religion Forward Movement of 1911–1912 and the Masculinization of Middle-Class Protestantism." *American Quarterly* 41 (September 1989): 432–65.

Birken, Lawrence. *Consuming Desire: Sexual Science and the Emergence of a Culture of Abundance, 1871–1914.* Ithaca: Cornell University Press, 1988.

Blair, Karen J. *The Clubwoman as Feminist: True Womanhood Redefined, 1868–1914.* New York: Holmes and Meier, 1980.

Bledstein, Burton J. *The Culture of Professionalism.* New York: W. W. Norton, 1978.

Blee, Kathleen M. *Women of the Klan: Racism and Gender in the 1920s.* Berkeley: University of California Press, 1991.

Bordin, Ruth. *Woman and Temperance: The Quest for Power and Liberty, 1873–1900.* Philadelphia: Temple University Press, 1981.

Bordo, Susan. "Anorexia Nervosa: Psychopathology as the Crystallization of Culture." In *Feminism and Foucault: Reflections on Resistance,* edited by Irene Diamond and Lee Quinby, 91–109. Boston: Northeastern University Press, 1988.

Boris, Eileen. "Reconstructing the 'Family'": Women, Progressive Reform, and the Problem of Social Control." In *Gender, Class, Race and Reform in the Progressive Era,* edited by Noralee Frankel and Nancy S. Dye, 73–86. Lexington: University Press of Kentucky, 1991.

Boydston, Jeanne. *Home and Work: Housework, Wages, and the Ideology of Labor in the Early Republic.* New York: Oxford University Press, 1990.

Boyer, Paul. *Urban Masses and Moral Order in America.* Cambridge: Harvard University Press, 1978.

Braude, Ann. *Radical Spirits: Spiritualism and Women's Rights in Nineteenth-Century America.* Boston: Beacon Press, 1989.

Brodhead, Richard H. "Sparing the Rod: Discipline and Fiction in Antebellum America." *Representations* 21 (Winter 1988): 68–92.

———. "Veiled Ladies: Toward a History of Antebellum Entertainment." *American Literary History* 1, no. 2 (Summer 1989): 273–288.

Brown, Gillian. *Domestic Individualism: Imagining Self in Nineteenth-Century America.* Berkeley: University of California Press, 1990.

Buechler, Steven M. "Elizabeth Boynton Harbert and the Woman Suffrage Movement, 1870–1896." *Signs* 13, no. 1 (August 1987): 78–97.

———. *The Transformation of the Woman Suffrage Movement: The Case of Illinois, 1850–1920.* New Brunswick, N.J.: Rutgers University Press, 1986.

Buhle, Mari Jo. *Women and American Socialism, 1870–1920.* Urbana: University of Illinois Press, 1981.

Bullough, Vern, and Martha Voght. "Women, Menstruation and Nineteenth-Century American Medicine." In *Women and Health in America,* edited by Judith Walzer Leavitt, 29–36. Madison: University of Wisconsin Press, 1984.

Burnham, John Chynoweth. "Medical Specialists and Movements Towards Social Control in the Progressive Era: Three Examples." In *Building the Organizational Society: Essays on Association Activities in America,* edited by Jery Israel, 19–30. New York: Free Press, 1972.

———. "The New Psychology: From Narcissism to Social Control." In *Change and Continuity in Twentieth-Century America: The 1920s,* edited by John Braeman et al., 351–98. Columbus: Ohio State University Press, 1968.

———. "Psychiatry, Psychology and the Progressive Movement." *American Quarterly* 12 (1960): 457–65.

Carby, Hazel. *Reconstructing Womanhood: The Emergence of the Afro-American Woman Novelist.* New York: Oxford University Press, 1987.

Cayleff, Susan E. "Gender, Ideology and the Water Cure Movement." In *Other Healers: Unorthodox Medicine in America,* edited by Norman Gevitz, 83–97. Baltimore: Johns Hopkins University Press, 1988.

Chauncey, George. *Gay New York: Gender, Urban Culture, and the Making of the Gay Male World, 1890–1940.* New York: Basic Books, 1994.

Cott, Nancy F. *The Bonds of Womanhood: "Woman's Sphere" in New England, 1780–1835.* New Haven, Conn.: Yale University Press, 1977.

———. "Feminist Theory and Feminist Movements: The Past Before Us." In *What Is Feminism?* Eds. Juliet Mitchell and Ann Oakley. New York: Pantheon Books, 1986.

———. *The Grounding of Modern Feminism.* New Haven, Conn.: Yale University Press, 1987.

———. "Passionlessness: An Interpretation of Victorian Sexual Ideology, 1790–1850." In *A Heritage of Her Own,* edited by Nancy F. Cott and Elizabeth H. Pleck. New York: Simon and Schuster, 1979.

———, ed. *Root of Bitterness: Documents of the Social History of American Women.* New York: E. P. Dutton, 1972.

Coughlan, Neil. *Young John Dewey.* Chicago: University of Chicago Press, 1973.

Coward, Rosalind. *Patriarchal Precedents: Sexuality and Social Relations.* London: Routledge and Kegan Paul, 1983.

Crunden, Robert M. *Ministers of Reform: The Progressives' Achievement in American Civilization, 1889–1920.* Urbana: University of Illinois Press, 1984.

Cunningham, A. R. "The 'New Woman' Fiction of the 1890s." *Victorian Studies* (December 1973): 177–186.

Cunningham, Raymond J. "The Emmanuel Movement: A Variety of American Religious Experience." *American Quarterly* 14, no. 1 (Spring 1962): 48–63.

Curtis, Susan. *A Consuming Faith: the Social Gospel and Modern American Culture.* Baltimore: Johns Hopkins University Press, 1991.

———. "The Son of Man and God the Father: The Social Gospel and Victorian Masculinity." In *Meanings for Manhood: Constructions of Masculinity in Victorian America,* edited by Mark C. Carnes and Clyde Griffen. Chicago: University of Chicago Press, 1993.

D'Emilio, John, and Estelle B. Freedman. *Intimate Matters: A History of Sexuality in America.* New York: Harper and Row, 1988.

Douglas, Ann. *The Feminization of American Culture.* New York: Avon Books, 1977.

Drinka, George Frederick. *The Birth of Neurosis: Myth, Malady, and the Victorians.* New York: Touchstone Books, 1984.

DuBois, Ellen Carol, ed. *Elizabeth Cady Stanton/Susan B. Anthony: Correspondence, Writings, Speeches.* New York: Schocken Books, 1981.

————. *Feminism and Suffrage: the Emergence of an Independent Women's Movement in America, 1848–1869.* Ithaca: Cornell University Press, 1978.

DuBois, Ellen Carol, and Linda Gordon. "Seeking Ecstasy on the Battlefield: Danger and Pleasure in Nineteenth-Century Feminist Sexual Thought." In *Pleasure and Danger: Exploring Female Sexuality,* edited by Carol S. Vance. New York: Routledge and Kegan Paul, 1984.

Edwards, Robert. "Tolstoy and Alice B. Stockham: The Influence of 'Tokology' on *The Kreutzer Sonata.*" *Tolstoy Studies Journal* 6 (1993): 87–106.

Ellenberger, Henri F. *The Discovery of the Unconscious.* New York: Basic Books, 1970.

Epstein, Barbara. "Family, Sexual Morality, and Popular Movements in Turn-of-the-Century America." In *Powers of Desire: The Politics of Sexuality,* edited by Ann Snitow, Christine Stansell, and Sharon Thompson. New York: Monthly Review Press, 1983.

————. *The Politics of Domesticity: Women, Evangelism and Temperance in Nineteenth-Century America.* Middletown, Conn.: Wesleyan University Press, 1981.

Erenberg, Lewis A. *Steppin' Out: New York Nightlife and the Transformation of American Culture, 1890–1930.* Chicago: University of Chicago Press, 1981.

Fee, Elizabeth. "The Sexual Politics of Victorian Social Anthropology." In *Clio's Consciousness Raised: New Perspectives on the History of Women,* edited by Mary S. Hartman and Lois Banner. New York: Octagon Books, 1976.

Felski, Rita. *The Gender of Modernity.* Cambridge, Mass.: Harvard University Press, 1995.

Filler, Louis. *The Unknown Edwin Markham.* Yellow Springs, Ohio: Antioch Press, 1966.

Fink, Leon. *Workingman's Democracy: The Knights of Labor and American Politics.* Urbana: University of Illinois Press, 1983.

Foucault, Michel. *The History of Sexuality, Volume 1: An Introduction,* translated by Robert Hurley. New York: Vintage Books, 1980.

Fuller, Robert C. *Alternative Medicine and American Religious Life.* New York: Oxford University Press, 1989.

————. *Mesmerism and the American Cure of Souls.* Philadelphia: University of Pennsylvania Press, 1982.

Furner, Mary O. *Advocacy and Objectivity.* Lexington: University Press of Kentucky, 1975.

Gifford, Sanford. "The American Reception of Psychoanalysis, 1908–1922." In *1915: The Cultural Moment,* edited by Adele Heller and Lois Rudnick, 128–145. New Brunswick: Rutgers University Press, 1991.

————. "Medical Psychotherapy and the Emmanuel Movement in Boston." In *Psychoanalysis, Psychotherapy and the New England Medical Scene, 1894–1944,* edited by George E. Gifford, Jr., 106–118. New York: Science History Publications, 1978.

Gilbert, James B. *Work Without Salvation: America's Intellectuals and Industrial Alienation, 1880–1910*. Baltimore: Johns Hopkins University Press, 1977.

Gilmore, Glenda Elizabeth. *Gender and Jim Crow*. Chapel Hill: University of North Carolina Press, 1996.

Ginzberg, Lori D. *Women and the Work of Benevolence: Morality, Politics, and Class in the Nineteenth-Century United States*. New Haven, Conn.: Yale University Press, 1990.

Gold, Pleasant Daniel. *History of Volusia County Florida*. Florida: E. O. Painter Printing Co., 1927.

Gordon, Linda. *Woman's Body, Woman's Right: A Social History of Birth Control in America*. New York: Penguin Books, 1976.

Gosling, F. G. *Before Freud: Neurasthenia and the American Medical Community, 1870–1910*. Urbana: University of Illinois Press, 1987.

Gould, Stephen Jay. *The Mismeasure of Man*. New York: W. W. Norton, 1981.

Graham, John, ed. *'Yours for the Revolution': The Appeal to Reason, 1895–1922*. Lincoln: University of Nebraska Press, 1990.

Haag, Pamela S. "In Search of 'The Real Thing': Ideologies of Love, Modern Romance, and Women's Sexual Subjectivity in the United States, 1920–40." In *American Sexual Politics: Sex, Gender and Race since the Civil War*, edited by John C. Fout and Maura Shaw Tantillo. Chicago: University of Chicago Press, 1993.

Hale, Nathan G. *Freud and the Americans: The Beginnings of Psychoanalysis in the United States, 1876 – 1917*. New York: Oxford University Press, 1971.

———. *The Rise and Crisis of Psychoanalysis in the United States: Freud and the Americans, 1917–1985*. New York: Oxford University Press, 1995.

Haller, John S., and Robin M. Haller. *The Physician and Sexuality in Victorian America*. New York: W. W. Norton, 1974.

Handy, Robert T., ed. *The Social Gospel in American Life, 1870–1920*. New York: Oxford University Press, 1966.

Harrington, Anne. "Hysteria, hypnosis and the lure of the invisible: The rise of neo-mesmerism in *fin-de-siècle* French psychiatry." In *The Anatomy of Madness, Volume III: The Asylum and its Psychiatry*, edited by W. F. Bynum, Roy Porter, and Michael Shepherd. London: Routledge, 1988: 226–46.

Heller, Adele, and Lois Rudnick, eds. *1915: The Cultural Moment*. New Brunswick, N.J.: Rutgers University Press, 1991.

Henking, Susan E. "Sociological Christianity and Christian Sociology: The Paradox of Early American Sociology." *Religion and American Culture* 3, no. 1 (Winter 1993): 49–68.

Herbert, Christopher. *Culture and Anomie: Ethnographic Imagination in the Nineteenth Century* (Chicago: University of Chicago Press, 1991).

Higginbotham, Evelyn Brooks. *Righteous Discontent: The Women's Movement in the Baptist Church, 1880–1920*. Cambridge: Harvard University Press, 1993.

Higham, John. *Strangers in the Land: Patterns of American Nativism, 1860–1925.* New York: Atheneum Press, [1955] 1970.

Hill, Mary A. *Charlotte Perkins Gilman: The Making of a Radical Feminist.* Philadelphia: Temple University Press, 1980.

Hofstadter, Richard. *Social Darwinism in American Thought.* Boston: Beacon Press, 1958.

Hopkins, Charles Howard. *The Rise of the Social Gospel in American Protestantism.* New Haven, Conn.: Yale University Press, [1940] 1967.

Jackson, Margaret. "Sexual Liberation or Social Control?" *Women's Studies Forum* 6, no. 1 (1983): 1–17.

James, Edward T., Janet Wilson James, and Paul Boyer, eds. *Notable American Women,* 3 vols. Cambridge, Mass: Harvard University Press, 1975.

Kasson, John F. *Amusing the Million: Coney Island at the Turn of the Century.* New York: Hill and Wang, 1978.

Kern, Kathi. *A Secular Faith: Elizabeth Cady Stanton and the Woman's Bible.* Ithaca, N.Y.: Cornell University Press, forthcoming.

Kessler-Harris, Alice. *Out to Work: A History of Wage-Earning Women in the United States.* New York: Oxford University Press, 1982.

Kitch, Sally L. *Chaste Liberation: Celibacy and Female Cultural Status.* Urbana: University of Illinois Press. 1989.

Ladd-Taylor, Mary Madeleine. "Mother-Work: Ideology, Public Policy and the Mothers Movement, 1890–1930." Ph.D. dissertation, Yale University, 1986.

Lang, Amy Schrager. *Prophetic Woman: Anne Hutchinson and the Problem of Dissent in the Literature of New England.* Berkeley: University of California Press, 1987.

Laqueur, Thomas. "Orgasm, Generation and the Politics of Reproductive Biology." In *The Making of the Modern Body: Sexuality and Society in the Nineteenth Century,* edited by Catherine Gallagher and Thomas Laqueur, 1–41. Berkeley: University of California Press, 1987.

Leach, William. "Transformations in a Culture of Consumption: Women and Department Stores." *Journal of American History* 71, no. 2 (September 1984): 319–42.

———. *True Love and Perfect Union: The Feminist Reform of Sex and Society.* New York: Basic Books, 1980.

Lears, T. J. Jackson. "From Salvation to Self-Realization: Advertising and the Therapeutic Roots of Consumer Culture, 1880–1930." In *The Culture of Consumption,* edited by Richard Wightman Fox and T. J. Jackson Lears, 3–38. New York: Pantheon Books, 1983.

———. *No Place of Grace: Antimodernism and the Transformation of American Culture, 1880–1920.* New York: Pantheon Books, 1981.

Lewis, Jan. "Mother's Love: The Construction of an Emotion in Nineteenth-Century America." In *Social History and Issues in Human Consciousness,* edited by Andrew E. Barnes and Peter N. Stearns. New York: New York University Press, 1989.

————. "The Republican Wife: Virtue and Seduction in the Early Republic." *William and Mary Quarterly* XLIV, no. 4 (October 1987): 689–721.

Livingston, James. *Pragmatism and the Political Economy of Cultural Revolution, 1850–1940*. Chapel Hill: University of North Carolina Press, 1994.

Lunbeck, Elizabeth. *The Psychiatric Persuasion: Knowledge, Gender, and Power in Modern America*. Princeton, N.J.: Princeton University Press, 1994.

Lutz, Tom. *American Nervousness, 1903: An Anecdotal History*. Ithaca, N.Y.: Cornell University Press, 1991.

MacLean, Nancy. *Behind the Mask of Chivalry: The Making of the Second Ku Klux Klan*. New York: Oxford University Press, 1994.

Matthews, F. H. "The Americanization of Sigmund Freud: Adaptations of Psychoanalysis before 1917." *Journal of American Studies* 1, no. 1 (April 1967): 39–62.

Matthews, Fred. "The New Psychology and American Drama." In *1915: The Cultural Moment*, edited by Adele Heller and Lois Rudnick, 146–156. New Brunswick, N.J.: Rutgers University Press, 1991.

May, Henry. *The End of American Innocence*. Chicago: Quadrangle Books, 1959.

————. *Protestant Churches and Industrial America*. New York: Harper and Bros., 1949.

Meyerowitz, Joanne. *Women Adrift: Independent Wage Earners in Chicago, 1880–1920*. Chicago: University of Chicago Press, 1988.

Moore, R. Laurence. *In Search of White Crows: Spiritualism, Parapsychology, and American Culture*. New York: Oxford University Press, 1977.

Morantz, Regina. "The Lady and Her Physician." In *Clio's Consciousness Raised: New Perspectives on the History of Women*, edited by Mary S. Hartman and Lois Banner. New York: Octagon Books, 1976.

Morantz-Sanchez, Regina Markell. *Sympathy and Science: Women Physicians in American Medicine*. New York: Oxford University Press, 1985.

Morawksi, J. G. "The Measurement of Masculinity and Femininity: Engendering Categorical Realities." *Journal of Personality* 53, no. 2 (June 1985): 199–204.

Muller, Dorothea R. "The Social Philosophy of Josiah Strong: Social Christianity and American Progressivism." *Church History* 28 (1959): 183–201.

Muncy, Robyn. *Creating a Female Dominion in American Reform, 1890–1935*. New York: Oxford University Press, 1991.

Myers, Gerald E. *William James: His Life and Thought*. New Haven, Conn.: Yale University Press, 1986.

Newman, Louise Michele. "Laying Claim to Difference: Ideologies of Race and Gender in the U.S. Woman's Movement, 1870–1920." Ph.D. dissertation, Brown University, 1992.

Noble, David W. *The Paradox of Progressive Thought*. Minneapolis: University of Minnesota Press, 1958.

Numbers, Ronald L. "The Fall and Rise of the American Medical Profession."

In *Sickness and Health in America,* edited by Judith Walzer Leavitt and Ronald Numbers, 185–196. Madison: University of Wisconsin Press, 1985.

Owen, Alex. *The Darkened Room: Women, Power and Spiritualism in Late Nineteenth-Century England.* London: Virago Press, 1989.

Painter, Nell Irvin. *Standing at Armageddon: The United States, 1877–1919.* New York: W. W. Norton, 1987.

Parsinnen, Terry M. "Professional Deviants and the History of Medicine: Medical Mesmerists in Victorian Britain." In *On the Margins of Science: The Social Construction of Rejected Knowledge,* edited by Roy Wallis. Staffordshire, England: University of Keele, 1979.

Paulson, Ross E. *Radicalism and Reform: The Vrooman Family and American Social Thought, 1837–1937.* Lexington: University of Kentucky Press, 1968.

Peiss, Kathy. *Cheap Amusements: Working Women and Leisure in Turn-of-the-Century New York.* Philadelphia: Temple University Press, 1986.

Pivar, David. *Purity Crusade: Sexual Morality and Social Control, 1868–1900.* Westport, Conn.: Greenwood Press, 1973.

Poovey, Mary. *Uneven Developments: The Ideological Work of Gender in Mid-Victorian England.* Chicago: University of Chicago Press, 1988.

Powell, Robert Charles. "The 'Subliminal' Versus the 'Subconscious' in the American Acceptance of Psychoanalysis, 1906–1910." *Journal of the History of the Behavioral Sciences* 15 (April 1979): 155–65.

Prominent Women of Illinois 1885–1932. Illinois Woman's Press Association, 1932.

Robinson, Paul. *The Modernization of Sex: Havelock Ellis, Alfred Kinsey, William Masters and Virginia Johnson.* New York: Harper and Row, 1976.

Rogers, Daniel T. "In Search of Progressivism." *Reviews in American History* 10, no. 4 (December 1982): 113–32.

Rosenberg, Charles E. *No Other Gods: On Science and American Social Thought.* Baltimore: John Hopkins Press, 1976.

———. "The Therapeutic Revolution: Medicine, Meaning, and Social Change in 19th Century America." In *Sickness and Health in America,* edited by Judith Walzer Leavitt and Ronald Numbers, 39–52. Madison: University of Wisconsin Press, 1985.

Rosenberg, Charles E., and Carroll Smith-Rosenberg. "The Female Animal: Medical and Biological Views of Women and Her Role in Nineteenth-Century America." *Journal of American History* 60 (1973): 332–56.

Rosenberg, Rosalind. *Beyond Separate Spheres: Intellectual Roots of Modern Feminism.* New Haven, Conn.: Yale University Press, 1982.

Ross, Dorothy. "The Development of the Social Sciences." In *The Organization of Knowledge in Modern America, 1860–1920,* edited by Alexandra Oleson and John Voss. Baltimore: Johns Hopkins Press, 1979.

Ross, Elizabeth Dale. *The Kindergarten Crusade: The Establishment of Preschool Education in the United States.* Athens, Ohio: Ohio University Press, 1976.

Rothman, Sheila M. *Woman's Proper Place.* New York: Basic Books, 1978.

Rotundo, E. Anthony. *American Manhood: Transformations in Masculinity from the Revolution to the Modern Era.* New York: Hill and Wang, 1982.

Rowbotham, Sheila, and Jeffrey Weeks. *Socialism and the New Life: The Personal and Sexual Politics of Edward Carpenter and Havelock Ellis.* London: Pluto Press, 1977.

Ruether, Rosemary Radford. "Radical Victorians: The Quest for an Alternative Culture." In *Women and Religion In America, Vol. 3: 1900–1968,* edited by Rosemary Radford Ruether and Rosemary Skinner Keller, 1–10. New York: Harper and Row, 1986.

Russett, Cynthia Eagle. *Sexual Science: The Victorian Construction of Womanhood.* Cambridge, Mass.: Harvard University Press, 1989.

Ryan, Mary P. *The Cradle of the Middle Class.* Cambridge: Cambridge University Press, 1981.

Satter, Beryl. "Marcus Garvey, Father Divine, and the Gender Politics of Race Difference and Race Neutrality." *American Quarterly* 48, no. 1 (March 1996): 43–76.

Schiebinger, Londa. "Skeletons in the Closet: The First Illustrations of the Female Skeleton in Eighteenth-Century Anatomy." In *The Making of the Modern Body: Sexuality and Society in the Nineteenth Century,* edited by Catherine Gallagher and Thomas Laqueur, 42–82. Berkeley: University of California Press, 1987.

Schneider, Louis, and Sanford M. Dornbusch. *Popular Religion: Inspirational Books in America.* Chicago: University of Chicago Press, 1958.

Schrager, Cynthia. "Both Sides of the Veil: Race, Science, and Mysticism in W. E. B. Du Bois." *American Quarterly* 46, no. 4 (December 1996): 551–598.

———. "Pauline Hopkins and William James: The New Psychology and the Politics of Race." In *The Unruly Voice: Rediscovering Pauline Elizabeth Hopkins,* edited by John Cullen Gruesser, 182–209. Urbana: University of Illinois Press, 1996.

Scott, Anne Firor. *Natural Allies: Women's Associations in American History.* Urbana: University of Illinois Press, 1993.

Sears, Hal D. *The Sex Radicals: Free Love in High Victorian America.* Lawrence, Kans.: Regents Press, 1977.

Shuttleworth, Sally. "Female Circulation: Medical Discourses and Popular Advertising in the Mid-Victorian Era." In *Body/Politics: Women and the Discourses of Science,* edited by Mary Jacobus, Evelyn Fox Keller and Sally Shuttleworth, 47–68. New York: Routledge, 1990.

Sicherman, Barbara. *The Quest for Mental Health in America.* New York: Arno Press, 1980.

———. "The Uses of a Diagnosis: Doctors, Patients and Neurasthenia." In *Sickness and Health in America,* edited by Judith Walzer Leavitt and Ronald L. Numbers, 22–38. Madison: University of Wisconsin Press, 1985.

Silbur, Nina. *The Romance of Reunion: Northerners and the South, 1865–1900.* Chapel Hill: University of North Carolina Press,1993.

Simmons, Christina. "Modern Sexuality and the Myth of Victorian Repression." In *Passion and Power: Sexuality in History*, edited by Kathy Peiss and Christina Simmons, 157–177. Philadelphia: Temple University Press, 1989.

Singal, Daniel Joseph. "Towards a Definition of American Modernism." *American Quarterly* 39, no. 1 (Spring 1987): 7–26.

Sklar, Kathryn Kish. "All Hail to Pure Cold Water!" In *Women and Health in America*, edited by Judith Walzer Leavitt, 246–253. Madison: University of Wisconsin Press, 1984.

———. *Catharine Beecher: A Study in American Domesticity*. New York: W. W. Norton, 1973.

Smith, Henry Nash. "The Scribbling Women and the Cosmic Success Story." *Critical Inquiry* I, no. 1 (September 1974): 47–65.

Smith-Rosenberg, Carroll. *Disorderly Conduct: Visions of Gender in Victorian America*. New York: Oxford University Press, 1985.

Stage, Sarah. *Female Complaints: Lydia Pinkham and the Business of Women's Medicine*. New York: W. W. Norton, 1979.

Stallybrass, Peter, and Allon White. *The Politics and Poetics of Transgression*. Ithaca, N.Y.: Cornell University Press, 1986.

Starr, Paul. *The Social Transformation of American Medicine*. New York: Basic Books, 1982.

Stern, Sheldon M. "William James and the New Psychology." In *Social Sciences at Harvard, 1860–1920*, edited by Paul Buck, 175–222. Cambridge: Harvard University Press, 1965.

Stoehr, Taylor. *Free Love in America: A Documentary History*. New York: AMS Press, 1979.

Susman, Warren I. *Culture as History: The Transformation of American Society in the Twentieth Century*. New York: Pantheon Books, 1987.

Swinth, Kirsten N. "Painting Professionals: Women Artists and the Development of American Art, 1870–1920." Ph.D. dissertation, Yale University, 1995.

Tax, Meredith. *The Rising of the Women: Feminist Solidarity and Class Conflict, 1880–1917*. New York: Monthly Review Press, 1980.

Testi, Arnaldo. "The Gender of Reform Politics: Theodore Roosevelt and the Culture of Masculinity." *Journal of American History* 81, no. 4 (March 1995): 1509–33.

Thiele, Beverly. "Coming-of-Age: Edward Carpenter on Sex and Reproduction." In *Edward Carpenter and Late Victorian Radicalism*, edited by Tony Brown, 100–123. London: Frank Cass, 1990.

Tomkins, Jane. *Sensational Designs: The Cultural Work of American Fiction, 1790–1860*. New York: Oxford University Press, 1985.

Trachtenberg, Alan. *The Incorporation of America: Culture and Society in the Gilded Age*. New York: Hill and Wang, 1982.

Trimberger, Ellen Kay. "The New Woman and the New Sexuality." In *1915: The Cultural Moment*, edited by Adele Heller and Lois Rudnick, 98–115. New Brunswick, N.J.: Rutgers University Press, 1991.

Valverde, Mariana. "'When the Mother of the Race is Free': Race, Reproduction and Sexuality in First-Wave Feminism." In *Gender Conflicts: New Essays in Women's History,* edited by Franca Iacovetta and Mariana Valverde. Toronto: University of Toronto Press, 1992.

Weeks, Jeffrey. *Sex, Politics and Society: The Regulation of Sexuality since 1800.* 2d ed. London: Longman, 1981.

Wilson, R. Jackson. *In Quest of Community: Social Philosophy in the United States, 1860–1920.* New York: John Wiley, 1968.

Wood, Ann Douglas. "The Fashionable Diseases: Women's Complaints and their Treatment in Nineteenth-Century America." In *Clio's Consciousness Raised: New Perspectives on the History of Women,* edited by Mary S. Hartman and Lois Banner. New York: Octagon, 1976.

Woodward, C. Vann. *Tom Watson: Agrarian Rebel.* London: Oxford University Press, 1975.

Young, James Harvey. *The Medical Messiahs: A Social History of Health Quackery in Twentieth-Century America.* Princeton, N.J.: Princeton University Press, 1967.

Index

Entries followed by "(ch.)" denote selected fictional characters. Page numbers in *italic type* denote photographs.

Compositor:	G&S Typesetters
Text:	Aldus
Display:	10/13 Aldus
Printer and binder:	Edwards Brothers

MAR 1 0 2000

DATE DUE